An Introduction to Nineteenth Century France

John and Muriel Lough

Longman

Longman Group Limited
London
Associated companies, branches, and representatives
throughout the world

First Published 1978
ISBN 0 582 35118 9 cased edition
ISBN 0 582 35119 7 paperback edition

Printed in Hong Kong by
Sheck Wah Tong Printing Press Ltd

Also by Professor John Lough
An Introduction to Seventeenth Century France
An Introduction to Eighteenth Century France

Contents

Acknowledgements

We are grateful to the following for permission to reproduce copyright material:

Librairie Ernest Flammarion for extracts from *Journal: Mémoires de la vie littéraire*, ed. R. Ricatte, Monaco 1956, 22 vols. by E. & J. de Goncourt and Librairie Plon S.A., for extracts from *Oeuvres complètes*, Paris, 1899–1911 by P. Bourget.

Photographs:

H. Roger-Viollet: pages 18, 32, 33, 70, 71, 90, 92, 97, 99, 156, 183, 185, 191, 311;
Mansell: page 31;
Giraudon: pages 38, 54, 60, 62, 65, 99, 109, 122, 135, 168, 170, 213, 265;
Mary Evans Picture Library: pages 89, 157, 158, 217;
Bibliothèque Nationale: pages 122, 123, 138, 140, 148, 173, 220, 242, 258, 260, 264;
Musée Carnavalet Bulloz: page 214;
Service Technique d'Urbanisme de la Ville de Paris: page 121;
Radio Times Hulton Picture Library: page 199.

Maps:

W. G. Henderson, *The Industrial Revolution on the Continent.* p. 23;
Fontana Economic History Vol. IV, Section 3. p. 87

Graphs:

Annuaire Statistique de la France, 1966, pages 10, 91; *Le Prix du Froment en France 1726–1913*, page 48; A. Prost, *L'Enseignement en France 1800–1967*, pages 215, 216, 219, 221

Preface

This volume has as its aim to bring together the study of the economic, social and political history of the age and that of its literature.

The hundred years from 1814 have been divided into three roughly equal periods, and for each of these a synthesis of economic, social and political history is offered. The introduction provides a general view of the transformation effected in France in the period as a whole, and a briefer conclusion attempts to bring out the changes which have taken place in France between 1914 and the 1970s. These chapters have been illustrated with quotations from contemporary documents, including works of literature.

Two substantial chapters are then devoted to the connections between history and literature. In the first of these the steadily improving position of the writer is related to the spread of education and the growth of the reading public; his dealings with publishers, reviews, newspapers and the theatre are examined in some detail with illustrative texts taken from letters and memoirs of the period. The second of these chapters relates the development of language and literature to the world of nineteenth-century France.

The illustrations form an important part of this book. It is hoped that the combination of extracts from contemporary documents in the original French and the visual aids provided by the reproductions, maps and graphs will all help to bring to life an age which is at once so close to us and yet is rapidly receding into the more distant past.

J.L.   Durham
M.L.   December 1973

A note on French money in the period 1814–1914

Given the constant changes which have taken place since 1914 both in the internal value of money in England and France and in the exchange rate between the pound and the franc, it is obviously impossible to 'translate' into up-to-date English figures sums of money given in French francs in our period. On the other hand throughout these hundred years – unbelievable as it may seem today – the exchange rate between the pound and the franc remained stable at roughly 25 so that it is at least possible to state the value of any given sum of French money in *English money of the time*. The following table may save readers some awkward sums:

(1 franc = 20 sous = 100 centimes)

Francs	£s
25	1
50	2
100	4
250	10
500	20
1,000	40
2,500	100
5,000	200
10,000	400
25,000	1,000

In our period the word *livre* had generally been replaced by *franc*: an *écu* was worth 5 francs and a *louis* or *napoléon* 20 francs.

Illustrations, Maps and Graphs

Maps

Graphs

Introduction

Whether we confine ourselves to events inside France or attempt to view them from a European or even a world angle, French history between the first restoration of the Bourbons in 1814 and the outbreak of the First World War a hundred years later is not lacking in excitement. And although, seen from the 1970s, the rate of change, particularly before the 1850s, appears remarkably slow, the France of President Poincaré on the eve of the catastrophe of 1914 was a very different country from that ruled over by Louis XVIII. Yet even in 1914 many features of French life were still determined by the transformation which the country had undergone in the upheaval of the Revolution and of Napoleon's rule.

If Napoleon's virtual dictatorship temporarily wiped out the political transformation which the Revolution had brought about and took France back to something very close to the absolutism which had been destroyed in 1789, his régime did not represent a complete break with the changes which had taken place in the ten years before his *coup d'état* in 1799. In the social sphere and in that of institutions what he did was to consolidate the achievements of the Revolution. His régime was to rest largely on the support of the two classes which had carried through and profited from that revolution – the middle classes and the peasants.

The lasting effects of the Revolution and Napoleon
Despite some attempts to put the clock back under the Restoration the old society with its division of Frenchmen into the three orders – clergy, nobility and *tiers état* – could not be reinstated; the Revolution had proclaimed that henceforth all men were equal in the eyes of the law and that all were to contribute through taxation to the upkeep of the state according to their means, and no

longer according to their social status. The buying and selling of official posts (*la vénalité des charges*) had also been abolished; henceforth – on paper at least – talent and not wealth was to secure admission to the civil service and the judiciary. The Revolution put an end to the near-monopoly of all high posts in the army, civil service, judiciary and Church which, to the increasing resentment of the middle classes, had been enjoyed by the nobility before 1789.

The Revolution had promoted other changes in harmony with the interests of the middle classes. The guilds, which had long been attacked as reactionary monopolies, were abolished along with the rigid state control over industry which had been denounced in the name of the principle of *laissez-faire*. The obstacles to trade presented before 1789 by a complicated system of internal customs barriers were removed, and the chaos of weights and measures under the *Ancien Régime* was replaced by the metric· system, though several decades were to pass before the new weights and measures were in general use.

A new set of laws, finally embodied in the *Code Napoleon*, gave the new society a legal system which, in contrast to the multiplicity of legal codes which existed in France before 1789, was uniform over the whole country. Its essentially bourgeois attitude to questions of property and the family is notorious. For instance, article 544 stresses the absolute right of the individual to make what use he wishes of his property: 'La propriété est le droit de jouir et disposer des choses de la manière la plus absolue, pourvu qu'on n'en fasse pas un usage prohibé par les lois ou par les règlements.' All the new laws of the Revolutionary and Napoleonic period which regulate relations between masters and men were tilted in favour of the property-owning classes. It was not until the 1860s that article 1781 of the *Code Napoléon*, which deals with the hiring of servants and workmen, was swept away:

> Le maître est cru sur son affirmation,
> Pour la quotité des gages;
> Pour le paiement du salaire de l'année échue;
> Et pour les à-comptes donnés pour l'année courante.

Combinations of workmen to secure higher wages and better conditions were severely discouraged. The English Combination Acts of 1799 and 1800 had their counterpart in the legislation of the Revolutionary and Napoleonic period. In 1791 the *Loi Le Chapelier* forbade under heavy penalties all combinations of workmen. It is true that, like a law of 1803, it also forbade combinations of employers; yet the real aim of these laws is clearly brought out by the much heavier penalties imposed on workmen than on their masters for infractions of the law. It was not until 1864 that work-men were allowed to combine to undertake strike action; and it was twenty years later before trade unions were at last legalized in France, though still not for civil servants.

The peasants too saw some of their aspirations realized by the Revolution. They still formed the overwhelming majority of the population (as recently as 1936 they formed a third of the active population) and they had their own ideas as to what should be done on the land – ideas which from 1789 onwards they gradually translated into reality by bringing pressure to bear on successive revolutionary assemblies. Naturally there were enormous differ-ences among the members of the peasantry, since conditions varied so much from region to region, and moreover there were so many shades of wealth and poverty from the large landowner or tenant-farmer down to the landless labourer, a relatively large class in the often over-populated countryside. It is certain that the Revo-lution did very little for the great mass of landless or nearly landless peasants. Yet the abolition of tithes and feudal dues did benefit many of them as did reforms in the very oppressive system of direct taxes which had existed under the *Ancien Régime*. At first, in 1789, the Constituent Assembly had merely decreed that the peasants were to buy out the holders of feudal dues, but in 1793, in the most radical phase of the Revolution, they were finally abolished without compensation. This measure was undoubtedly of great benefit to the peasants who owned land – and such peas-ants were very numerous before the Revolution – since before 1789 their right of property was incomplete, as they had to make to their lord payments in kind and in money and perhaps also perform certain services. By abolishing the remnants of feudalism the Revolution transformed the peasant's copyhold into freehold, that is, made him absolute proprietor of his land.

What is more, the sales of Church property, the estates of *émigrés* and the royal domain – the so-called *biens nationaux* – gave the peasants an opportunity to acquire more land. It is true that the methods by which this land was sold did not allow the mass of landless or nearly landless peasants to acquire much of it. Some of the land owned by the *émigré* nobles was regained by them, either because it was still unsold at the Restoration or because it was bought back for them by their agents. Again, the amount of land made available for sale varied quite capriciously from region to region; in some parts of France, for instance, the Church owned practically no land, and consequently little or none came on to the market. Above all, it is fairly well established that the principal purchasers of the *biens nationaux* were the more prosperous sections of the peasantry and the wealthy middle classes (see, for instance, the old miser in Balzac's *Eugénie Grandet* whose fortune was based on their acquisition). Yet even so some land probably went to the medium and smaller peasants.

Moreover, if we compare what was happening in France in these years with events in England, we see how the French Revolution strengthened the hold of the peasantry on the land at the very moment when in England the opposite process was in full swing. Here the enclosure movement, combined with the revolution in agricultural techniques, increased productivity, but drove the smaller peasants off the land, reducing them to the status of agricultural labourers or sending them into the towns to seek work in the new factories. In France, although the enclosure movement was given nominal approval by the revolutionary assemblies, it went ahead only very slowly, as did the revolution in agricultural techniques. So far as the land was concerned, the Revolution of 1789 acted, paradoxical as it may sound, as a stabilizing factor in the sense that it tended to preserve the *status quo* and in many ways to preserve it down to our own day. It is wrong to imagine, as is sometimes done, that virtually all the land of France is in the hands of a vast number of small peasant-proprietors; in practice, a considerable proportion of it is in the hands of a relatively small number of owners. That was in fact the position before 1789, a situation which the Revolution, so to speak, froze; by preventing the mass of small peasant landowners from being driven off the land, it maintained the mixture of small, medium and large-scale property which existed before 1789. This has not prevented a gradual move from the countryside to the towns (what the French call 'l'exode rural'), a very gradual process in the nineteenth century, but one which has been enormously speeded up since 1945. Over the last century and a half, from being overpopulated, the French countryside, at least in the less fertile regions, has gradually come to be very sparsely inhabited, as large numbers of the poorer peasants have moved into the towns. There is, however, little doubt that the land policy of the Revolution was one of the factors in the relatively slow industrialization of France in the nineteenth century.

Naturally the French peasants, especially those who had been able to acquire more land, were, like the new bourgeois land-owners, passionately attached to the Revolution. For several generations, well into the second half of the nineteenth century, they were to live in constant fear of an attempt to put the clock back – to revive feudal dues and tithes, and to secure the return of the *biens nationaux*. They supported Napoleon and his régime precisely because he confirmed the land policy of the Revolution.

The Code Civil

Napoleon also endowed France with institutions which consoli-dated the achievements of the Revolution and which in many cases have survived, with modifications, right through the nine-teenth century down to our own day. Just as the Revolution had replaced the chaos of weights and measures which existed in France before 1789, by the simple, clear and uniform metric system, so the revolutionary assemblies sought to provide one code of civil law for the whole of France, to take the place of the chaos of laws before 1789. Under the *Ancien Régime* the southern half of France had been under Roman Law, while the rest of the king-dom had been under customary law (*droit coutumier*) which varied not only from province to province, but even from district to district. The aim of the *Code Napoléon* was to weld into a coherent whole, modifying them where necessary, the large collection of laws produced by the different revolutionary assemblies.

The *Code Napoleon*, more accurately known as the *Code Civil* since Napoleon played only a minor part in its preparation, was promulgated in 1804. It interprets in a fairly conservative sense the principles of the Revolution. While proclaiming such prin-ciples as equality before the law, freedom of conscience and freedom for trade and industry, it confirmed the abolition of feudal dues by making all land freehold. The manner in which the new code regulated the transmission of land by will was also of considerable importance. Before 1789 in most parts of France, while land in the possession of *roturiers* was divided up in equal shares between their children after their death, the estates of the nobility had been held together by the *droit d'aînesse*, which gave the lion's share to the eldest son, and by entail (*substitution*). In its egalitarian attitude to property the Convention had abolished entail and had laid it down that all property should be divided in equal shares between the children of the testator. The *Code Napoleon* went back on this; although it forbade entail save in very exceptional circumstances, it qualified the principle of equal shares among the children of a testator by allowing him to dispose as he wished of a half to a quarter of his estate (half if there was only one child, a third if there were two, a quarter if there were three or more). He could thus, if he liked, give more favourable treatment to his eldest son than to his other children, and help to keep an estate in the family for generations. On the other hand the right conferred upon heirs to insist upon a breaking up of the main part of the estate in equal shares had important consequences; over the last century and a half it has tended to a continuous sub-division of the land, one of the most striking features of the French countryside. The *Code Civil* is often held responsible for the relative decline in the population of France in our period since it encouraged landowners, large and small, to restrict their families so as to be able to pass on their property to their only son.

The *Code Civil* also maintained the Revolutionary principles concerning the family, although it generally interpreted them in a decidedly conservative sense. In 1791 the registration of births, deaths and marriages was taken out of the hands of the Church and entrusted to the municipal authorities. The confirmation of this law by Napoleon has its effects down to our own day on the celebration of marriages in France; while the Roman Catholic Church continues to look upon marriage as a sacrament, the State regards it merely as a civil contract, and it insists that the civil ceremony, which takes place before the mayor with a reading of the relevant articles of the *Code Civil*, must precede any marriage in church. The *Code Civil* also confirmed the institution of divorce, another question on which, then as now, the French Church did not see eye to eye with the State; it is true that the *Code Civil* made divorce far more difficult than it had been during the Revolution, and as in everything concerning the family put women in a very unfavourable position compared with men. In the clerical re-action of the Restoration period divorce was, of course, abolished, and it was not indeed until 1884, after the Third Republic was securely established, that it was re-instituted.

Religion
Napoleon had brought to an end the conflict between Church and State which had arisen during the Revolution over the Civil Constitution imposed upon the French clergy. In 1801 he reached agreement with the Pope over a new Concordat which recognized Catholicism as 'la religion de la grande majorité des Français'.

This formula implied a rejection of the claims of Catholicism to be recognised as the state religion. The Pope had to make other concessions: he had to recognize the French Republic (this was before Napoleon made himself Emperor) as well as the sale of Church property during the Revolution. In return the government undertook to provide the clergy with what was called 'un traitement convenable'. As under the Concordat of 1516, archbishops and bishops were to be chosen by the State, but invested by the Pope as spiritual head of the Church; *curés* were now to be appointed by the bishops, but from among persons acceptable to the government. A similar arrangement was made for French Protestants, both Calvinists and Lutherans, whose pastors were also to be paid by the State. In 1831 this was extended to cover Judaism and its rabbis. Napoleon's religious settlement was to endure for just over a century, until the final separation of Church and State in 1905. For almost the whole of our period the members of the secular clergy were in fact civil servants. The arrangement had two considerable results. Not only did it increase the power of the bishops over the parish clergy; it gradually put an end to Gallicanism, the traditional French seeking for some degree of independence of Rome, and immensely strengthened Ultramontanism, which favoured the absolute authority of the Pope in matters of faith and discipline.

Education
The educational system of France in our period and indeed down to the present day was greatly influenced by the changes brought about by the Revolution and Napoleon. While it is true that the educational projects of the Revolutionary assemblies remained for the most part on paper, those of the Convention, especially before the fall of Robespierre, were particularly far-sighted, and some interesting educational experiments were also carried out during the Directoire. Napoleon's influence on French education was often far from beneficent, and in some spheres, particularly that of primary education, his outlook was much less enlightened than that of the men of the Revolution. It is probable that primary education, especially that of girls, was in a worse position in France in 1815 than it had been in 1789; Napoleon did not wish the education of the masses to go beyond the three R's, and during his reign a good deal of the primary education was provided by religious orders.

It was secondary and higher education, catering for the sons (though not the daughters) of the middle classes, that interested the Emperor. A law of 1806 instituted the *Université*, a body upon which he conferred a monopoly of teaching; in practice it concerned itself with secondary education and with higher education in the Faculties which were set up by a decreee of 1808 to take the place of the universities abolished by the Revolution (it was not until 1896 that a law was passed to recreate universities in France). On paper at least all secondary and higher education was to be given in state establishments, staffed by teachers paid by the state. In practice, even during the Napoleonic period secondary schools outside the state system had nearly as many pupils as the state *lycees*, founded by the Emperor, and the *colleges* run by the towns. With the breaking of this state monopoly of education by the *Loi Falloux* in 1850 the so-called *écoles libres* came to play an important part in French education, particularly the secondary schools. Yet the state system of education, from the primary school to the university, under the control of the Ministry of Education, continues to dominate the French educational scene, partly owing to its monopoly of conferring degrees which include the famous *baccalauréat*, roughly the equivalent of the English General Certificate of Education. Down to our own day all members of the state educational system, including university teachers, remain civil servants (*fonctionnaires*).

Law Courts
In addition to the *Code Civil* which exercised a considerable influence on the legal system of a large number of European and other countries, Napoleon was also responsible for the creation of a complicated system of law-courts, ranging from that of the *juge de paix*, established in every *canton*, to the *Cour de cassation*, the supreme court of appeal, and including the *Conseil d'Etat*, a tribunal which is concerned with the interpretation and execution of laws in so far as they affect government departments or private individuals in their dealings with these departments. To Napoleon France also owes the Banque de France, established in 1800, which gradually developed into France's central bank. But perhaps the most important legacy from the Revolutionary and Napoleonic era was the system of local government and its relations with the central government.

Local government
It was in 1790 that the Constituent Assembly replaced the chaotic

administrative regions of the *Ancien Régime* by a new division of
the country into departments; each department was later divided
into *arrondissements*, beneath them came the *cantons*, and at the base
was the smallest unit of local government, the *commune*. When
Napoleon seized power, he reimposed on France the rigid system
of centralization which goes a long way back into the Ancien
Régime when the agents of the central government in the provinces, the *Intendants*, assisted by their *subdélégués*, exercised strict
control over local government. Using the new framework of
department, *arrondissement* and *commune*, he installed a *Préfet* in
each department, a *sous-préfet* in each *arrondissement* outside the
departmental capital, and a mayor in every *commune*. In the course
of the nineteenth century the system was naturally modified
especially in the direction of making the *conseil général* of the
department and the *conseil municipal* of the commune elective
bodies and conferring on them greater powers. Yet the framework
remains very much the same as that created by Napoleon over a
century and half ago. Although the *maire* is now elected by the
conseil municipal, he is only bound by decisions of that body in
matters of purely communal concern, since he remains what he
was made by Napoleon, a state official charged with carrying out
certain acts on behalf of the central government. Again, although
the *conseils généraux* have been given wider powers, the *préfet*, along
with the *sous-préfets* and other officials under his control, continues
to supervise the working of the offices of the central government
in his department and at the same time exercises very considerable
authority in purely departmental matters. Of course, in the
twentieth century, centralization is not unknown in England, but
to maintain that Whitehall nowadays exercises even greater power
than the corresponding ministries in Paris would seem greatly
exaggerated; certainly in the nineteenth century France was a
much more centralized country than England.

Population
At the beginning of our period (the 1821 census, the first to be held
after Napoleon's downfall, registered 30 million inhabitants)
France was, apart from Russia, the most populous country in
Europe. Germany had considerably less than 30 million inhabit-
ants, Italy only some 20 million, and Great Britain (i.e. England,
Wales and Scotland) 14 millions. However, the population of
France increased only slowly during the next hundred years in
comparison with that of other European countries:

Birth and death rates, 1800–1914.

1821	30,462,000	1872**	36,103,000
1831	32,569,000	1881	37,672,coo
1841	34,230,000	1891	38,343,000
1851	35,783,000	1901	37,962,000
1861*	37,386,000	1911	39,605,000

*   After the annexation of Savoy and Nice (1860).
**   After the loss of Alsace-Lorraine (1871).

By 1911 Great Britain with 41 million inhabitants had practically trebled its population in the space of ninety years; starting
with less than half the population of France in 1821, it had now
overtaken her. In relation to Germany France's position was even
more serious. Instead of facing a disunited country with a population of only some 25 millions at the beginning of the nineteenth
century, by 1871 France was confronted with a united Germany

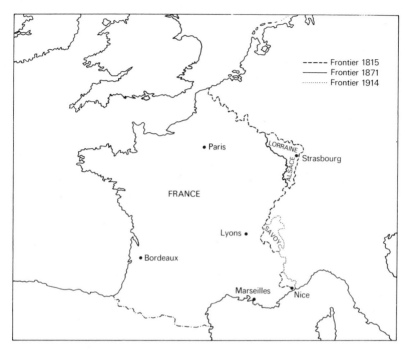

France's Eastern frontiers, 1815–1914.

with 41 million inhabitants against her 36; on the eve of the First World War Germany had nearly 65 million inhabitants against just under 40 in France. By 1911 even Italy (like Germany only fairly recently united) was gradually catching up with France. Two world wars combined with a low birth rate in the inter-war period to keep the population of France more or less stationary at just over 40 millions until about 1950; it is only since that date that in less than a couple of decades it has reached 50 millions. The relative decline in France's position in Europe over the last century and a half is clearly brought out by a simple comparison: in 1801 its inhabitants represented approximately 15 per cent of the population of Europe whereas by 1950 that proportion had fallen to 7·8 per cent.

In the first half of the nineteenth century France's population increased only slightly less rapidly than that of Europe as a whole, but from 1850 onwards the gap between her and her neighbours rapidly widened. After a high birth rate in the latter part of the eighteenth century and the opening decades of the nineteenth came a steady fall from about 1830 onwards. It was, of course, accompanied

by a steady fall in the death rate; infantile mortality in particular was reduced very considerably down to 1914, though less
dramatically than since that date. Yet the decline in the birth rate
prevented the same rapid growth in population as took place in
other European countries from the middle of the nineteenth
century onwards. The explanation of this phenomenon is apparently simple: France was the first country in which married
couples practised birth control on a large scale.

It is perhaps surprising, when one looks back from the second
half of the twentieth century, to discover that in 1801 when the
first census was taken in both countries France had more large
towns and cities than Great Britain. This is illustrated by the
following lists of towns in the two countries with 30,000 or more
inhabitants:

Paris	546,900	London	959,000
Marseilles	111,100	Edinburgh	83,000
Lyons	109,500	Liverpool	82,000
Bordeaux	91,000	Glasgow	77,000
Rouen	87,000	Manchester	75,000
Nantes	73,900	Birmingham	71,000
Lille	54,800	Bristol	61,000
Toulouse	50,200	Leeds	53,000
Strasbourg	49,100	Sheffield	46,000
Amiens	40,300	Plymouth	40,000
Nîmes	38,800	Norwich	36,000
Orleans	36,100	Bath ⎫	
Montpellier	33,900	Newcastle-upon-Tyne ⎬	33,000
Angers	33,000	Portsmouth ⎭	
Metz	32,100	Wolverhampton	31,000
Caen	30,900		
Besançon	30,000		

Though Paris was a much smaller city than London, the four
largest French provincial cities – Marseilles, Lyons, Bordeaux and
Rouen – were considerably larger than any of the cities on this
side of the Channel. But then at that date France had roughly
twice as many inhabitants as Great Britain.

The situation had been almost completely transformed by the
1911 census. By this time the effects of the slower rate of growth of
population in France and the much higher degree of industrialization in this country had had their effect. This is strikingly
revealed by a comparison between the population of the fifteen
largest cities in the two countries:

Paris	2,888,100	London	4,541,000
Marseilles	550,600	Glasgow	1,000,000
Lyons	460,000	Birmingham	880,000
Bordeaux	261,000	Liverpool	753,000
Lille	217,000	Manchester	714,000
Nantes	170,000	Sheffield	455,000
Toulouse	149,600	Leeds	453,000
Saint-Étienne	148,700	Edinburgh	424,000
Nice	142,900	Bristol	357,000
Le Havre	136,200	Bradford	288,000
Rouen	125,000	Hull	278,000
Roubaix	122,700	Newcastle-upon-Tyne	267,000
Nancy	119,900	Nottingham	260,000
Reims	115,200	Stoke-on-Trent	235,000
Toulon	104,600	Portsmouth	234,000

Whereas all the British cities in question had well over 200,000 inhabitants, only Paris and four other cities – Marseilles, Lyons, Bordeaux and Lille – came into that class.

It is not an easy matter to define what is meant by an urban population. When in 1846 the French census began to distinguish the urban from the rural population, the definition adopted took in every *commune* with more than 2,000 inhabitants concentrated at its centre. Nowadays this seems a ridiculously low figure to rank as 'urban', but even on this definition it was not until the 1931 census that the percentage of town dwellers rose above 50 per cent. The figures for the period 1846–1911 show how slowly the balance was shifting from country to town in these years, compared with the much more rapid transformation in Britain:

1846	24·4	1881	34·8
1851	25·5	1886	36·0
1856	27·3	1891	37·3
1861	28·9	1896	39·0
1866	30·5	1901	40·9
1872	31·1	1906	42·1
1876	32·5	1911	44·1

There are unfortunately no satisfactory figures for the different sectors of the active population before the 1851 census; and even after that date the figures are not very reliable. Yet it is possible to estimate the proportion of those engaged in agriculture at something like 52 per cent in the middle of the nineteenth century and 45 per cent in 1900 – extremely high figures when compared with those for Great Britain. As late as 1936 a good third of the active population in France was engaged in agriculture, and it is really only since 1950 that a dramatic fall has occurred, bringing the figure down to 14 per cent in 1970. Even so the corresponding figure for Great Britain is now only 3 per cent.

Industrial development

Naturally the proportion of the active population engaged in industry rose in our period, especially between the 1870s and 1914, but the whole process was a much more gradual one than in this country. This was regarded by many Frenchmen as a very desirable state of affairs. Writing in 1903 of the effects produced by the laws of the 1880s and 1890s imposing protective tariffs on imported agricultural products, a French historian could declare:

> C'est peut-être à ces lois que la France aura dû d'être restée, parmi les grandes nations, celle dont l'agriculture occupe encore plus de la moitié de ses habitants; celle qui se trouve, par conséquent, dans les meilleures conditions économiques, sociales et politiques. Tandis qu'en Allemagne la population industrielle a, depuis un quart de siècle, conquis la suprématie numérique sur les classes rurales; tandis qu'en Angleterre ce phénomène est déjà ancien et que, depuis longtemps, le sol anglais ne produit plus assez pour nourrir ses habitants, la France se suffit à elle-même et jouit de cette richesse agricole qui est, entre toutes les richesses, la plus facile à conserver. (A. Rambaud, *Jules Ferry*, p. 215)

It is well known that in the nineteenth century France never underwent an industrial revolution such as transformed England into 'the workshop of the world'. Although in the early nineteenth century France, along with Belgium, was the most advanced industrial country on the Continent, she had already been left far behind by England in her economic development, and in the second half of the century she was to be rapidly outstripped by Germany and also by the United States.

Down to our own day French industrial development has been hampered by the shortage of coal. In the second half of the twentieth century in which the coal industry is everywhere in rapid decline this has been compensated for by new sources of energy – hydro-electric power (what the French call 'la houille blanche'), natural gas, oil and atomic power – but until quite recent times her relatively small deposits of coal, often of poor quality and relatively very expensive because they were found in places remote from heavy industry, have proved a severe handicap. The gap between the coal production of France and Britain

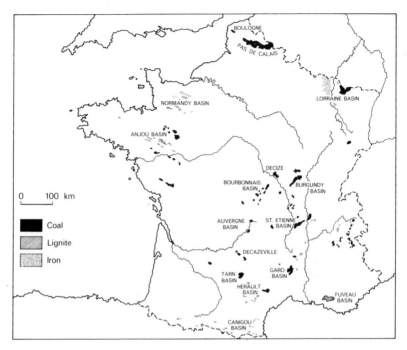

Coal and Iron industries in France.

in our period is clearly brought out by the following figures (in 1000s of metric tons; the first reliable figures for this country date from 1854):

France		Britain
1854	6,827	64,700
1860	8,304	80,000
1870	13,330	110,400
1880	19,362	147,000
1890	26,083	181,600
1900	33,404	225,200
1910	38,350	264,400

Between 1854 and 1910 French coal production multiplied more than fivefold, but although it increased more rapidly in these years than that of Britain, even in 1910 French coal output was only about a seventh of British. Throughout our period France was increasingly dependent on imports of coal which reached nearly 20 million tons in 1910.

There were naturally many other reasons besides the shortage of coal for the slowness of economic development in France in our period. Yet one has constantly to bear in mind that throughout a great part of the nineteenth century, especially down to about 1870, France was the leading economic power on the Continent. However much she lagged behind Britain, however much in the earlier stages she was dependent on our inventions, capital and workmen, she none the less was responsible for a great deal of economic development in many parts of Europe, including even Germany; her capital and engineering skill brought new industries and railways to a great many countries from Spain to Russia.

None the less, after the period of stagnation produced by the Revolutionary and Napoleonic wars, economic development proceeded only very slowly during the Restoration and July Monarchy. It was only after the economic crisis and political instability of the years 1846–1851 that developments speeded up. There is no doubt that the Second Empire coincided with the period of the most rapid economic advance which France had known – the nearest to an industrial revolution which France was to approach down to the second half of the twentieth century. Even so progress between 1870 and 1914 continued at a fairly slow pace, and in that period France fell far behind other industrialized countries.

It is by no means easy to disentangle cause and effect in such matters. Was the slow rise in population a cause of the slow economic development or one of its effects? Was the lack of interest often shown by French entrepreneurs in technical innovations, from the use of coal and the steam-engine onwards, to be explained by the predominance of agriculture and the peasant mentality? Was the imposition of high protective tariffs and even of a complete ban on certain imports throughout the whole of our period, except for the twenty years or so after Louis Napleon's trade agreements with Britain and other countries in the 1860s, a hindrance to economic progress or merely a symptom of the slow economic development of the country? Was the failure to invest in industry a very considerable amount of the capital accumulated in France in our period (most of it went into the land, state loans and very risky foreign investments such as those which vanished for ever in Soviet Russia . . .) due to sheer blindness or the inability to find suitable industrial investments inside France?

Whatever the reasons, there is no question that between 1814 and 1914 national income and industrial production increased more slowly in France than in the other industrialized countries. Yet throughout our period France remained by Continental standards a rich country, a large exporter of capital, and, despite the extremely rapid industrial and commercial progress made by Germany in the period from 1870 or so onwards, even in 1914 it is probable that the income of the average Frenchman was as high as that of the average German. It is true that, as there were over half as many Germans again as Frenchmen, the total national income of France was considerably less than that of her neighbour.

A series of upheavals
From an English point of view, French history since the downfall of Napoleon appears as something of a shambles: a long story of the instability of régimes and governments. The English tend to forget about such far-off events as the Civil War and the Glorious Revolution of 1688 and to stress, not without a certain complacency, how much English history is one of continuous evolution, how the big changes such as the Reform Bill of 1832 or those introduced by the 1945 Labour government were brought about by peaceful, non-revolutionary means.

The contrast with French history since 1815 is certainly striking enough. Even if we leave aside the various phases of the Revolution of 1789 (a succession of different régimes and constitutions) and the Consulate and Empire, and the first restoration of the Bourbons and Napoleon's return from Elba followed by the second Restoration of 1815, we find that French history in the nineteenth century is a constant series of upheavals – in 1830, 1848, 1851, 1870 culminating in the horror of the Paris Commune in 1871. A whole series of different régimes followed one upon another – the Bourbon Monarchy to 1830, the Orléans monarchy to 1848, the Second Republic to 1851, the Second Empire to 1870. It is true that the Third Republic which followed had, judged by French standards, an astonishingly long life; it was to endure for seventy whole years, down to 1940. Yet not only was it followed by a new succession of régimes (Pétain's État Français down to 1944, the Fourth Republic down to 1958, followed by the very different régime of the Fifth Republic); the history of the Third Republic, at least until about 1900, was extremely chequered. It was, as we shall see, almost a decade after its proclamation in 1870 that it was finally established, and after that, not only did it suffer from considerable governmental instability, but the very existence of the Republic continued to be called in question by extremely vociferous opponents.

It is a commonplace that nineteenth-century history after 1815 continued to re-enact the story of the Revolution and Empire. The restored monarchy was assailed by both Republicans and Bonapartists seeking to relive the events of the years from 1789 to 1815. Their chance came in 1848 when Louis Philippe's monarchy collapsed; the second edition of the Republic gave way in 1851 to the second edition of the Empire. This in its turn gave way in 1870 to the third edition of the Republic which was at once threatened by the Commune, in many ways an attempt to live through again the most radical phases of the Revolution of 1789.

The Chambre des Députés.

It is also striking how, since 1848, authoritarian and more democratic régimes have alternated. The Second Republic was followed by the Second Empire, and in due course the Third Republic was followed in 1940 by Pétain's régime, which in its turn was followed by the Fourth Republic which in 1958 was replaced by the much more authoritarian régime of General de Gaulle.

After the downfall of Napoleon France resumed the attempt which had been begun in 1789 to introduce parliamentary government and to make it work. The development of parliamentary institutions was carried a certain distance between 1815 and 1848; at this stage they were, of course, based on a very narrow suffrage. Even though after the Revolution of 1830 the number of voters had been nearly doubled, there were only some 240,000 at the end of the July Monarchy, far fewer in proportion to the size of the population than in this country after the Reform Bill of 1832. The Second Republic then brought about a dramatic change. The enlargement of the franchise in Britain took place by slow stages, by acts of 1867 and 1884 which brought in between them another 3 million or so voters; it was not until the act of 1918 which also gave the vote to a proportion of women over the age of thirty that universal manhood suffrage was instituted in Britain. In contrast in 1848 France plunged at one leap from the very limited franchise of the July Monarchy to universal manhood suffrage; the electorate was raised at a stroke from some 240,000 to over 9 millions. It is true that in 1850 an attempt was made to reduce the number of those entitled to vote by nearly 3 millions, obviously by removing from the register the poorer members of the community; but in practice this electoral law was never applied, and from 1848 onwards all elections in France have been based on universal suffrage (it took, however, nearly a century, until 1945, for women to be given the vote).

The Second Republic produced a constitution instituting a president and a single chamber, but the system did not work and was rapidly brought to an end by Louis Napoleon's *coup d'état* in 1851. In the opening years of his rule parliamentary institutions were reduced, as they had been by his uncle, to a mere façade; it was only gradually in the 1860s, in the period leading up to the so-called 'Empire libéral', that parliamentary institutions were gradually strengthened, but before the process had got very far, the régime collapsed in war.

The Third Republic was the heyday of parliamentary institutions in France and in this period they came closer to the English model. Yet there remained important and significant differences. After the 1848 revolution France never again had a *Chambre des Pairs*; in any case this body had never had either the prestige or the power of our House of Lords. The second chamber set up under the Third Republic was elected indirectly by the deputies and local councillors of each department. More important, under the Third Republic (and under the Fourth) the government was much weaker than under our system: the executive was much more dependent on the legislature, the Senate and *Chambre des Députés*. From the 1870s down to the emergence of the Fifth Republic government instability was a marked feature of French political life. It was rare for governments to last for as long as a whole year; many were defeated after only a few months, weeks, days or even hours.

So not only has France seen a great number of different régimes and constitutions since 1815; inside these régimes (and this was true as early as the 1830s under Louis Philippe) governmental instability has been considerable. It is true that this must not be exaggerated; even in the period from 1870 to 1914 there were a number of prime ministers who remained at the head of the same government for relatively long periods, for instance Ferry from February 1883 to March 1885, Méline from April 1896 to June 1898, Combes from June 1902 to January 1905 and Clemenceau from October 1906 to July 1909. And in France a major cabinet reshuffle such as takes place from time to time in Britain would be counted as a change of government.

These frequent changes of government were due to the fact that no one party ever enjoyed a clear majority over all others; in other words all governments were coalition governments, consisting of members drawn from several parties and depending on the support of the deputies in those parties and possibly in one or two other parties not represented in the government. Inevitably a government consisting of members drawn in almost every case from parties with a wide variety of political views, varying sometimes from Conservative to Socialist or near-Socialist, found it difficult to agree either on long-term policies or on the hundred and one different problems at home and abroad which required a decision. If a few ministers resigned or if one section of the majority withdrew its support and voted against the government in power, down it went.

Political groupings
Moreover, to speak of 'parties' in the years of the Third Republic with which we are concerned is to use a misleading term. In the period 1870–1914 there were strictly speaking no parties, only loose political groupings both in Parliament and in the country. The nearest approach to a closely-knit political party in this period – and that only at the very end, from 1905 onwards – was the

Socialist party, formed out of a union of most of its different groups. The other groups in Parliament were numerous and frequently changed both their labels and their composition; changes of party were frequent, and deputies could move gradually from right to left or (this happened much more frequently) from left to right. It is thus easy to trace back to the multiplicity of political groupings in France the instability of governments under her parliamentary system; but then what, one may ask, is the explanation of this multiplicity? The answer comes back pat: 'French individualism'. But what explains that individualism?

One feature of French political life which goes right back to 1789 is the bitterness of the feelings involved. Unquestionably these things are relative and the situation, in Britain, as in France, changes from period to period. Yet the British have never had the equivalent of the events of the years 1789–1794 to fight all over again in the next century as the French had. The division between Right and Left down even to our own day goes back as far as 1789 and the events of the following years. As we have seen, the Second Republic, at any rate for its founders, re-enacted the Republic of the Girondins and Jacobins, while the Second Empire claimed continuity with the first Napoleon's régime. In our period France saw not only the violent upheavals of the July Revolution of 1830 and the February Revolution of 1848, but also the White Terror of the Restoration, the murderous suppression of the popular rising of June 1848 and the even more murderous repression of the Paris Commune in 1871. Not only was violence in the physical sense an ever-recurring feature of French political life; political controversy was carried on with a passion and a virulence which have seldom been seen in Britain. Throughout the period at least a substantial minority of the nation – whether it was republicans under the monarchy or the empire or monarchists for whom the republic was contemptuously named 'la Gueuse' – rejected the political régime under which they had to live. It was, for instance, typical of the state of passions in the present century that, when the Third Republic collapsed in 1940, one of the first acts of the Vichy régime should have been to replace the ancient republican motto 'Liberté, Égalité, Fraternité' by 'Travail, Famille, Patrie'.

Another complication in French political life arises from the political role played by the Catholic Church in the nineteenth century. On paper at least, France is an overwhelmingly Catholic country – 'la fille aînée de l'Église'. From 1789 onwards France was divided between the Church's supporters and its anticlerical opponents. It has indeed been pointed out that while in the political sphere, the British have had a two-party system and the French are divided into a multiplicity of groups, in the religious sphere the British have a multiplicity of sects and the French have virtually a two-party system.

Under the *Ancien Régime* the Catholic Church, especially in the higher ranks of its clergy, identified itself closely with absolutism and with the existing aristocratic society. In consequence it suffered severely during the Revolution, and although its position was somewhat restored by the Napoleonic Concordat, it had lost most of its wealth and a great deal of its power. Catholicism was no longer the state religion, but merely 'la religion de la grande majorité des Français'. The Restoration meant, of course, a considerable comeback for the Church. Catholicism was once again proclaimed 'la religion de l'État'. and the Church regained a great deal of its control over education and many other spheres of life. Yet by identifying itself with the restored Bourbons it made itself thoroughly unpopular in left wing and centre circles, and suffered another setback with the July Revolution. It was characteristic of its loss of influence that in the revised Charter of 1830 Catholicism is described merely as the religion 'professée par la majorité des Français'. If the clergy had regained a good deal of popularity by the time of the February Revolution, this was quickly lost when advantage was taken of the reaction caused by the insurrection of June 1848 to secure for the Church, through the *Loi Falloux*, increased control over education, and the Church's identification of itself with Louis Napoleon and his empire once again increased its unpopularity in centre and left wing circles. This was further increased by the development of Ultramontanism and the increasing subordination of the French clergy to Rome. In the first decades of the Third Republic the Church continued to favour the monarchist movement and to show itself extremely hostile to the development of the new régime and its institutions. From the 1880s onwards there developed a great battle on the educational front, with the Republican majority supporting 'l'école laïque', which was neutral in the religious sphere, and the Church defending its own schools. Finally the struggle between the Church and the Republic ended in 1905 with the complete separation of Church and State. Though relations between them have improved markedly in recent decades they are still complicated by the rival claims of the state educational system and 'l'école libre'.

Napoleon's Empire at its high point in 1812.

Position in Europe

The decline in France's position in Europe since the downfall of Napoleon scarcely needs to be pointed out. In the age of the Revolution and Napoleon France, 'la grande nation', a large, populous, rich and unified country, possessed the military might which enabled her to conquer vast areas of the Continent. It needed a succession of European coalitions to keep her under control, and for the fifty years after Napoleon's defeat Europe trembled every time France seemed on the verge of overturning the treaties imposed on her in 1815. Yet in 1870 the hollowness of French power was demonstrated in a few weeks by the German armies. From that date down to 1914 France could play only a secondary role in European and world affairs. It is true that she built up for herself a colonial empire second only to that of Britain; but fear of Germany and her alliance with Austria and Italy compelled her to seek the alliance, first, of Russia and then of her old rival, England. From this division of Europe into two armed camps followed inexorably the First World War from which

France was to suffer more heavily than any of her allies as so much of the fighting over four years took place on her territory and her losses in manpower were on a frightening scale.

None the less, despite the decline in her position in Europe between 1814 and 1914, France continued to play a leading cultural role in Europe and in a great part of the world. French continued to serve as an international language in a way which it is not easy to imagine now that Anglo–American is so much more important over the world as a whole. French books of all kinds had a large international market because they could be read by a high proportion of educated people everywhere. The great French writers of the age as well as many who are now forgotten had an international audience which was enlarged, of course, by translations, though many of its members read their works in the original French. French books continued as in the past to be pirated in countries like Belgium and Germany until an international copyright convention came to put a stop to this practice which, of course, depended largely on the existence of a large market for French books outside France. This is not to suggest that the works of writers and scientists from countries like England or Germany did not also possess an international audience, but France continued to play a leading role in this field. The same was true of other arts, painting in particular. Paris, especially with the coming of the railways and steamships and its modernization by Haussmann in the 1850s and 1860s, remained for many people in Europe and other continents the intellectual and artistic capital of the world.

I
Restoration and July Monarchy

If France underwent a drastic transformation in the social and institutional sphere during the Revolutionary and Napoleonic period, she emerged from these years of turmoil very little changed from the economic point of view. It has been said that the France of 1815 was closer to the France of Louis XIV than to the France of Louis Napoleon. Over twenty years of war had stimulated certain industries, but they had had a crippling effect on others and on a great deal of her foreign trade. Forced back inside her 1792 frontiers (and after Waterloo even further back), France had also suffered severe losses of manpower and was burdened with heavy debts. Even though she was, with Belgium, the leading industrial power on the Continent, she continued during the first half of the century to lag behind England, the pioneer of the Industrial Revolution.

Social and economic conditions 1815—1848

The fact is that anything resembling the Industrial Revolution which, between roughly 1750 and 1850, transformed England from a predominantly agricultural country into a predominantly industrial one took place in France – and then on a much more limited scale – only after the Revolution of 1848, during the prosperous years of the Second Empire. There were, of course, all sorts of significant new developments in industry, trade and banking in the period 1815–1848, particularly during the reign of Louis Philippe. For one thing in these years France followed England into the Railway Age. Yet even here, as in industry in general, despite the aid of English engineers, skilled workmen and

capital, France continued to fall behind England. Indeed in many
fields, including railways, she was beginning to lag behind
Germany, which, while in 1815 far behind France in industrial
development, was to far surpass her (and even England) before
the end of the nineteenth century.

A predominantly agricultural country
France remained throughout the period a predominantly agricultural country. A good three-quarters of the population lived in
the country. Down to the middle of the century her population
continued to grow fairly fast (from 27 millions in 1801 to 35
millions in 1846), though already the growth was rather less
rapid than in Europe as a whole. On the other hand her towns
generally grew only slowly. Paris, it is true, grew very fast in these
years – from 547,000 inhabitants in 1801 to 1,053,000 in 1851 –
and this produced serious problems of poverty, disease and crime
in the overcrowded poorer quarters, a situation vividly described
in such novels as Eugène Sue's *Les Mystères de Paris*. Again there
were isolated cases of exceptionally fast growth in a number of
provincial towns such as those connected with the rapidly
developing textile industries; in these fifty years the population of
Mulhouse rose from under 7,000 to close on 30,000 while that of
Roubaix shot up from 8,000 to nearly 35,000. If one takes what
were the ten largest provincial cities in 1801, one finds that in
general their rate of growth was much slower than that of
English cities:

	1801	*1851*
Marseilles	111,100	195,300
Lyons	109,500	177,200
Bordeaux	91,000	130,900
Rouen	87,000	100,300
Nantes	73,900	96,400
Lille	54,800	75,800
Toulouse	50,200	93,400
Strasbourg	49,100	75,600
Amiens	40,300	52,100
Nîmes	38,800	53,600

We may contrast with these figures those for a few English cities
in the same period of fifty years:

	1801	*1851*
Birmingham	71,000	233,000
Leeds	53,000	172,000
Liverpool	83,000	376,000
Manchester	75,000	303,000
Sheffield	46,000	135,000

The 'exode rural' of which, later in the century, French writers were to complain so bitterly was relatively speaking a mere trickle in the period down to 1848; indeed the biggest movement from country to town in France has taken place only since 1945. By the standards of the time France was still a densely populated country and, as so high a proportion of the population lived in the countryside, it follows that this was in many regions distinctly overpopulated. It must be remembered that, as in the eighteenth century, a great many peasants and their families were engaged part-time in domestic or cottage industry, working for the merchants in the nearby towns; again a great part of the iron industry was carried on in the country where both the ore and forests for the supply of wood for smelting were to be found.

If Arthur Young, the agricultural writer, had been able to repeat in 1815 the journeys which he made round France in the years 1787–1789, he would, of course, have found changes. Through the sale of the *biens nationaux* much land had changed hands, though only part of this went to the peasants: a great deal went to wealthy bourgeois who let it out under various forms of tenancy. Feudal dues and tithes had been abolished. Yet he would have found little change in agricultural techniques since 1789. The form of land tenure known as *métayage*, under which the landlord supplied not only the land but also the stock, seed and implements, in return for a share of the crops (generally a half) – 'a detestable system that perpetuates poverty', he had declared – still existed over a considerable part of France.

Even Arthur Young had found progressive farming methods practised in some parts of the country, and these undoubtedly spread in our period, largely through the influence of wealthy landowners. It is said that when, after the July Revolution, many members of the aristocracy left Paris and retired in the sulks to their provincial châteaux, this often had a beneficial influence on their estates. Yet the new methods spread only very slowly, and hardly at all among the medium and poorer peasants. In many parts of France these continued, like their forefathers, to practise subsistence agriculture, working exclusively or almost exclusively to provide for the needs of themselves and their families without seeking to market any of their produce.

Though it is impossible to measure it exactly, there is no doubt that, despite various periods of crisis, French agricultural production did increase fairly substantially during the Restoration and July Monarchy. Yet even if the average peasant was better off in 1848 than he had been in 1815, his standard of living still remained primitive and he was condemned to a life of backbreaking toil. If he could save any money, this normally went not to improving his farming methods, but to the acquisition of a plot of land. As, given the large rural population, there was keen competition for the available land, he often had to pay an exorbitant price for it; this would then involve him in borrowing money which could only be done by paying extortionate rates of interest. At the end of our period the burden of rural indebtedness was a heavy one.

Slow economic development

There were various reasons, apart from the direct effects of the long wars which lasted down to 1815, for the slowness of economic development in France during the first half of the nineteenth century. For over twenty years France had been practically cut off from what had been in the eighteenth century and was now again to be the most important source of technological advances – Britain. Here one must not forget that if British engineers, skilled workmen and capital played an important part in French industrial development in our period, it has also been shown that French engineers, skilled workmen and capital played in their turn quite an important part in the industrial development of other Continental countries – not only, for instance, Italy, Austria and Russia, but even Belgium and Germany. Even so in the sphere of industry France continued to owe a tremendous debt to British technology in this period.

What is more, France was a much bigger country than Britain and she could feed a much larger population from her own resources in years of reasonable harvests and, whereas in Britain the enclosure movement had stimulated migration into the industrial towns and cities, in France the Revolution had strengthened the hold of the peasants on the land. Again, although abundantly supplied with water power, which remained an important source of energy in this period, France was a country with relatively small deposits of coal, and these were situated in awkward places, generally inland and far from the industrial centres; this meant that in an age when transport facilities were still primitive coal was extremely expensive. Moreover the richest coal deposits, those in the Pas-de-Calais, were only discovered right at the end of the July Monarchy. Coal production increased considerably in this period of thirty years or so; by 1847 it had reached 5 million tons and in addition $2\frac{1}{2}$ million tons were imported. Yet this is a tiny figure compared with British coal production, which by this date amounted to some 50 million tons.

Most industry in France continued to be conducted on a small scale. There were abundant iron ore deposits, but these were generally small and scattered in wooded and mountainous districts. For the most part the industry was carried on by very small companies, often family concerns, which drew their labour from the more impoverished local peasantry. Progress in the metallurgical industries was slow. The large supplies of wood which were available in the vast forests of France meant that it was only gradually that such expensive commodities as coal and coke were made use of. In the textile industries, particularly cotton, which were largely dependent on English technical inventions, considerable progress was made in the introduction of machinery for spinning and weaving. One important technical advance was made in France – the invention, by a Lyons engineer, Joseph Marie Jacquard (1752– 1834), of a loom for weaving patterned silks; this was also adapted for the manufacture of other textiles. The introduction of steam-power into the different textile industries went ahead fairly slowly.

The factory system developed steadily in these years, but really large factories were still very much the exception. Domestic or cottage industry still persisted widely and with great tenacity, even though the application of water and steam power made the lot of the worker ever more miserable. Particularly in the textile industries, both for spinning and weaving, the processes were carried on in the worker's own home, sometimes in the towns, but more often in the countryside. As in the previous century, considerable numbers of the poorer peasantry, together with their wives and children, used industrial work to supplement their earnings from agriculture. Indeed quite a number of workers in the towns would return to the farms in the summer. It was no easy task – it certainly proved more difficult than in England – to transform the poorer sections of the peasantry into an industrial proletariat. Yet when one talks about the slow industrial develop-

ment of France in the period between Waterloo and the abdication of Louis Philippe one must make comparisons not only with
'the workshop of the world' but also with France's neighbours on
the Continent. In 1848, for instance, France had more steam
engines in use than all the other Continental countries put together.

The governments of the Restoration period pursued a policy of
high protective tariffs; this was demanded by the landed interest
and by most industrialists, who were afraid of seeing the French
market flooded with foreign (mainly English) goods. This policy
was also pursued, with only minor modifications, by the July
Monarchy. Not only were most of these tariffs high (in 1822, for
instance, the tariff on English iron was raised from 50 to 120 per
cent); there was even a total prohibition on certain imports,
particularly of manufactured goods. While it could be argued that
this high degree of protection encouraged the development of new
industries and the use of new technological processes by shielding
manufacturers from too severe competition, the practical effect
was to keep prices high and to remove the incentive which competition from England would have provided for French industry
to improve its methods of production.

Transport
At the beginning of our period transport was, as everywhere else
in the world, still in a fairly primitive state. Some idea of how slow
and uncomfortable travelling could be is given in the following
description of a journey of some twenty-five miles in the west of
France round about 1820:

> Si l'on voulait se rendre à Angers, capitale de la province, – on n'eût
> pas dit à cette époque, chef-lieu du département, – il fallait mettre
> deux jours à franchir onze lieues. On en faisait six dans une charrette
> à boeufs; on s'arrêtait au Lion–d'Angers, gros bourg que traversait
> l'ancienne route royale de Laval; on soupait à l'unique auberge de
> la *Boule d'or*; on couchait dans l'unique chambre destinée aux hôtes
> privilégiés . . . La nuit ainsi passée, on se remettait en route le
> lendemain de bonne heure, dans une voiture de louage venue
> d'Angers exprès pour vous chercher. Cette voiture à deux roues,
> mais à deux banquettes, avec un cheval porteur,[1] . . . gravissait
> lentement, sur une route pavée, deux côtes escarpées, les *buttes de
> Grilleul*, bien aplanies aujourd'hui, mais qui nous effrayaient alors
> comme des montagnes bordées de précipices. On ne débarquait à
> Angers qu'à l'entrée de la nuit. (Falloux, *Mémoires*, I. 6–7)

[1] Of the pair of horses, the one on which the driver sat.

Considerable improvements were made in the road system during the Restoration and July Monarchy and in consequence the transport of both passengers and goods was speeded up. Rivers like the Seine, Loire and Rhone continued to play an important part, and this was increased by the advent of the steamship, which at first was mainly used on rivers. Characteristically the first iron steamship to make its way up the Seine to Paris in 1822 was an English one. The canal system was considerably developed in these years, but the introduction of railways, which were to revolutionize life in France as everywhere else, took place only very slowly.

The Stockton and Darlington railway, the first public railway with steam traction, was opened in 1825, but it was not until 1832 that the first comparable railway, one covering the 35 miles from Saint-Étienne to Lyons, was opened in France; moreover in the first place it was not built to carry passengers, but to serve a mining and industrial region. For all sorts of reasons right down to 1848 the progress towards a proper railway system covering the whole country and linking Paris with the more important provincial cities and her frontiers was relatively slow. There was considerable opposition to railways. When Parliament granted a concession for Paris's first railway, Louis Philippe's minister, Thiers, is alleged to have declared: 'Il faut donner ça à Paris, comme un joujou; mais ça ne transportera jamais un voyageur ni un colis.' The line in question, that out to Saint-Germain, was not opened until 1837. In 1842 a serious accident – the derailment of a Versailles–Paris train which caused some sixty deaths – led Vigny

Poster advertising the opening of the Paris–Orléans railway in 1843.

Daumier: *Le wagon de troisième classe*.

to insert into 'La Maison du Berger' his famous denunciation of
this horrible new invention:

> Sur ce taureau de fer qui fume, souffle et beugle,
> L'homme a monté trop tôt. Nul ne connaît encor
> Quels orages en lui porte ce rude aveugle,
> Et le gai voyageur lui livre son trésor;
> Son vieux père et ses fils, il les jette en otage
> Dans le ventre brûlant du taureau de Carthage,
> Qui les rejette en cendre aux pieds du Dieu de l'or.

In 1842 France had only 885 kilometres of railway, compared
with 3,600 in Britain and 2,800 in Germany. After the passing of a
railway law in 1842 progress was more rapid and indeed gave rise
to a fever of speculation; even so by 1847 France still had only
some 1,830 kilometres of railway in actual operation, and the
economic crisis of that year, combined with the upset caused by
the 1848 revolution, held up the further development of railways
until the Second Empire. It was only then that France acquired a
national network.

Banking
Although credit facilities improved in our period, the fairly
rudimentary banking system was an obstacle to a more rapid
industrial development. It is true that banking did make considerable progress during the reign of Louis Philippe; at the

View of the Banque de France, rue Croix-des-Petits Champs, Paris, in about 1815.

beginning of his reign he even had two bankers as prime ministers. Yet the Banque de France, founded by Napoleon, was mainly a Paris bank, and credit facilities were difficult to come by in the provinces except from *notaires* and usurers, which meant high rates of interest when money could be borrowed. There were some large merchant bankers in Paris – known collectively as 'la haute banque' – who handled state loans and in the 1830s and 1840s played some part in the financing of railway construction. Attempts were made to set up investment banks, but these foundered in the crisis of 1847. Before the Second Empire banking played only a small positive part in the development of French industry.

The Bourse, Paris (built 1808–1825).

Working and housing conditions

The gradual expansion of industry and the slow drift from the
countryside to the towns eventually produced, particularly in the
reign of Louis Philippe, a small urban proletariat and a degree
of social unrest comparable with the Chartist movement in
England. Both in factories and in domestic industry hours of work
were appallingly long (15 hours was not uncommon) for women
and children as well as men. Wages were generally low and
housing conditions often appalling. The notion that the State
should intervene to secure better working conditions and better
wages for those engaged in industry was unthinkable to the
governments of the day, which accepted implicitly the liberal
principle of *laissez-faire* in the economic field – except, of course,
when it intervened with tariff laws to protect French industry.

Women and children were ruthlessly exploited, particularly in
the cotton industry. In 1840 an observer offered a vivid description
of the women and children who lived in deplorable conditions
in the villages surrounding Mulhouse:

> Il faut les voir arriver chaque matin en ville et en partir chaque soir.
> Il y a, parmi eux, une multitude de femmes pâles, maigres, marchant
> pieds nus au milieu de la boue, et qui, faute de parapluie, portent
> renversé sur la tête, lorsqu'il pleut, leur tablier ou leur jupon de
> dessus, pour se préserver la figure et le cou, et un nombre encore plus
> considérable de jeunes enfants, non moins sales, non moins hâves,
> couverts de haillons tout gras de l'huile des métiers, tombée sur eux
> pendant qu'ils travaillent. Ces derniers, mieux préservés de la pluie
> par l'imperméabilité de leurs vêtements, n'ont pas même au bras,
> comme les femmes dont on vient de parler, un panier où sont les
> provisions pour la journée; mais ils portent à la main ou cachent
> sous leur veste, ou comme ils le peuvent, le morceau de pain qui doit
> les nourrir jusqu'à l'heure de leur rentrée à la maison. (Villermé,
> *Tableau*, I. 26)

Of working conditions and their effect on the children's health
the same observer writes:

> Ils restent seize à dix-sept heures debout chaque jour, dont treize au
> moins dans une pièce fermée, sans presque changer de place ni
> d'attitude. Ce n'est plus là un travail, une tâche, c'est une torture; et
> on l'inflige à des enfants de six à huit ans, mal nourris, mal vêtus,
> obligés de parcourir, dès cinq heures du matin, la longue distance
> qui les sépare de leurs ateliers, et qu'achève d'épuiser, le soir, leur
> retour de ces mêmes ateliers. Comment ces infortunés, qui peuvent à
> peine goûter quelques instants de sommeil, résisteraient-ils à tant de
> misère et de fatigue? (*Tableau*, II. 91)

Finally in 1841, after long debates, a law was passed to limit the employment of children. As it applied only to industrial establishments employing more than twenty people, its effect was bound to be limited. It laid down that no child under eight was to be employed; that children between eight and twelve were not to be employed for more than eight hours a day, and that from twelve to sixteen work should be limited to twelve hours between 5 a.m. and 9 p.m. Under certain conditions, however, children over thirteen could be employed on night work. No child under the age of twelve could be employed unless he also went to school. However, as no government inspectorate was set up to enforce the law (the inspectors were to be chosen by the manufacturers themselves), it remained a dead letter. What is more, this first factory act did nothing to improve the position of workers of either sex over the age of sixteen.

Housing conditions in Paris and in the industrial centres of the provinces were often appallingly bad. Of living conditions in the Mulhouse region Villermé wrote:

> J'ai vu à Mulhouse, à Dornach et dans des maisons voisines, de ces misérables logements, où deux familles couchaient chacune dans un coin, sur de la paille jetée sur le carreau et retenue par deux planches. Des lambeaux de couverture et souvent une espèce de matelas de plumes d'une saleté dégoûtante, voilà tout ce qui recouvrait cette paille. (*Tableau*, I. 27)

Housing conditions in the poorer quarters of Lille were exceptionally bad. Villermé writes:

> Les plus pauvres habitent les caves et les greniers. Ces caves n'ont aucune communication avec l'intérieur des maisons; elles s'ouvrent sur les rues ou sur les cours, et l'on y descend par un escalier, qui en est très souvent à la fois la porte et la fenêtre. Elles sont en pierres ou en briques, voûtées, pavées ou carrelées, et toutes ont une cheminée; ce qui prouve qu'elles ont été construites pour servir d'habitation. Communément leur hauteur est de 6 pieds à 6 pieds et demi prise au milieu de la voûte, et elles ont de 10 à 14 ou 15 pieds de côté. C'est dans ces sombres et tristes demeures que mangent, couchent et même travaillent un grand nombre d'ouvriers. Le jour arrive pour eux une heure plus tard que pour les autres, et la nuit une heure plus tôt. . . .

After describing their miserable furniture, the author goes on to tell how the people lived in such surroundings:

> Je voudrais ne rien ajouter à ce détail des choses hideuses qui

révèlent, au premier coup d'oeil, la profonde misère des malheureux habitants; mais je dois dire que, dans plusieurs des lits dont je viens de parler, j'ai vu reposer ensemble des individus des deux sexes et d'âges très différents, la plupart sans chemise et d'une saleté repoussante. Père, mère, vieillards, enfants, adultes, s'y entassent. Je m'arrête . . . le lecteur achèvera le tableau, mais je le préviens que s'il tient à l'avoir fidèle, son imagination ne doit reculer devant aucun des mystères dégoûtants qui s'accomplissent sur ces couches impures, au sein de l'obscurité et de l'ivresse. (*Tableau*, I. 82–83)

From his exile Hugo was to write of these shocking living conditions which he had earlier observed among the textile workers of Lille:

Un jour je descendis dans les caves de Lille;
   Je vis ce morne enfer.
Des fantômes sont là sous terre dans des chambres,
Blêmes, courbés, ployés; le rachis tord leurs membres
   Dans son poignet de fer.

Sous ces voûtes on souffre, et l'air semble un toxique;
L'aveugle en tâtonnant donne à boire au phtisique;
   L'eau coule à longs ruisseaux;
Presque enfant à vingt ans, déjà vieillard à trente,
Le vivant chaque jour sent la mort pénétrante
   S'infiltrer dans ses os.

Jamais de feu; la pluie inonde la lucarne;
L'oeil en ces souterrains où le malheur s'acharne
   Sur vous, ô travailleurs,
Près du rouet qui tourne et du fil qu'on dévide,
Voit des larves errer dans la lueur livide
   Du soupirail en pleurs. (*Les Châtiments:* 'Joyeuse vie')

To some extent the economic condition of France in these years formed a vicious circle. It is generally agreed that the period from about 1817 down to the early 1850s was one of economic depression and low prices in between two longish periods of economic expansion. The high protective tariffs with which France sought to defend the interests of both her agriculture and her industry led to relatively high costs. The necessity to build up capital in order to finance industry out of profits led to low wages being paid; and these low wages in turn reduced the market for industrial products.

What is more, since even when times were good wages were low, the economic crises of these years bore heavily on industrial workers. These crises struck French agriculture and industry with varying degrees of severity in the periods 1816–1818, 1825–1832, 1836–1839 and 1847–1851. The second and fourth of these obviously played their part in precipitating the revolutions of 1830 and r848. In these periods wages could be drastically reduced or the worker might find himself unemployed; very often bread prices also shot up and, as bread remained the staple diet of the masses, this could lead to severe hardship.

In the 1830s and especially the 1840s there was a considerable development of socialist thought in France, and a good deal of the literature of the reign of Louis Philippe helped to disseminate vaguely socialistic ideas. This is particularly true of certain novels of George Sand and Eugène Sue; the latter enjoyed a phenomenal popularity in the 1840s. Yet in a country still dominated by agriculture the urban working class formed only a very small proportion of the population, and among them factory workers were very much in a minority. There were no trade unions to protect their interests, to fight for higher wages and better working conditions; these were forbidden by law and infractions of that law continued to be punished by imprisonment. Not until the beginning of the twentieth century was there to be a strong political party to espouse their cause.

At the end of our period, in June 1848, there was to be a dramatic clash between the urban working class of Paris – nearly all its members were engaged in quite small-scale industry – and the established order; but the rising was bloodily suppressed. It put the fear of death into the property-owning classes of both town and country; the reaction led straight to the Second Empire.

In French society of this period there were gross inequalities of wealth; appalling poverty existed side by side with the affluence of a small minority, as the novels of the period, particularly those of Eugène Sue, make clear. To conservative thinkers of the time such gross inequalities seemed inevitable; but even to many people who were not blind to the sufferings and narrow lives of the mass of the population in town and country it seemed that there was nothing much to be done about them except through private charity. In the first half of the nineteenth century despite the beginnings of an industrial revolution the national wealth of France, even though it was a relatively rich country by Continental standards, did not appear large enough to permit of better wages, shorter hours and more leisure, or of better housing conditions.

The Restoration

François-Xavier Fabre: Louis XVIII (1755–1824).

Louis XVIII (1814/15–1824)

The epic story of the victories and conquests of the Revolutionary and Napoleonic armies came to a sorry end with the Allied invasion of France and the defeat and abdication of the Emperor. The scene in the streets of Paris in March 1814 is vividly described by an eye-witness:

> C'était un jour d'hiver assez beau, sans froid ni soleil. Tout le boulevard était parcouru par une file lugubre de victimes de la guerre qui, entrées par la barrière de la Villette ou les voisines, se dirigeaient vers les Champs-Élysées et les environs de l'École militaire. Les blessés, les malades, les prisonniers, les paysans fugitifs avec leurs femmes, leurs enfants et leurs meubles, les fourgons

d'ambulance, les charrettes de réquisition défilaient lentement et
pêle-mêle sur la chaussée, au milieu d'une foule curieuse et dés-
oeuvrée. Je crois voir encore des dragons de la garde, couverts de
leur manteau blanc souillé de sang et de boue, montés sur des
chevaux amaigris, le bras en écharpe ou la tête enveloppée de linge.
Un d'eux, entre autres, avait le visage couvert d'un bandage comme
d'un masque sanguinolent. Des grenadiers se traînaient au milieu de
nous, quelques-uns se couchaient par terre, dans les contre-allées,
pour reposer leurs membres blessés, le visage hâve, le regard éteint.
On sortait des boutiques pour leur apporter du pain, du vin, des
secours, quelquefois on leur donnait de l'argent. Qu'on y songe,
c'était une population qui n'avait vu d'armée que fière et brillante,
passée en revue au Carrousel ou au Champ de Mars, par un général
cent fois victorieux! (Rémusat, *Mémoires de ma vie*, I. 137)

Napoleon's abdication left a power vacuum in France and at
first neither the victorious Allies (Austria, England, Prussia and
Russia) nor the defeated French knew quite what to do about
filling it. In 1814, over twenty years after the execution of Louis
XVI and especially after all the changes brought about by the
Revolution and Napoleon, the exiled Bourbons were almost
forgotten in France. Chateaubriand could claim that, when he
published his pamphlet, *De Buonaparte et des Bourbons*, in 1814:

j'appris à la France ce que c'était que l'ancienne famille royale; je
dis combien il existait de membres de cette famille, quels étaient
leurs noms et leur caractère; c'était comme si j'avais fait le dé-
nombrement des enfants de l'empereur de la Chine, tant la République et l'Empire avaient envahi le présent et relégué les Bourbons
dans le passé. (*Mémoires d'Outre-tombe*, II. 501)

None the less the Allies finally decided to restore Louis XVI's
brother, the Comte de Provence, who on the death of the imprisoned Dauphin in 1795 had had himself proclaimed king as
Louis XVIII.

Among opponents of the Restoration it was always a black
mark against it that he and his brother, the Comte d'Artois, the
future Charles X, along with the other members of the royal
family, had been imposed on France by the invaders, that they
had been brought back from exile 'dans les fourgons de l'étranger'.
The memories of the military glories of the revolutionary and
imperial era and of the humiliation of defeat were to linger in
France for decades, and, curiously enough, most stubbornly on the
Left which was always ready for the next half century to have
recourse to military force to follow the example set in the Revolution of bringing liberty to the oppressed peoples of the Continent.

It can well be imagined that financially and economically France was in a poor way after over twenty years of war. To add to the political confusion in which she found herself with the return of the Bourbons and the *émigrés*, many of whom were thirsting to put the clock b'ack and reinstate the Ancien Régime, Napoleon refused to lie down and keep quiet on the island of Elba. Less than a year after his abdication, on 1 March 1815, he landed in the south of France and found enough support to enable him to reinstall himself in Paris without meeting any serious resistance, as the returned Bourbons and the *émigrés* had made themselves thoroughly unpopular. Louis XVIII set off on his travels again and sought refuge on the other side of the frontier in Ghent. Napoleon did his best to exploit this unpopularity by offering a fairly liberal constitution, but nobody trusted him. He succeeded, however, in gathering together a fresh army and set out for the Low Countries to meet the Allies under Wellington and Blücher. On 18 June his reckless adventure came to an end at Waterloo; until his death in 1821 he was to be held on the island of St. Helena in the remote South Atlantic. His captivity and death were not, however, to end his role in French history: 'la légende napoléonienne' had already begun to form around him at St. Helena and it was to weigh heavily on the history of France for another half century.

Ironically one of the writers of the time who played his part in the creation of the legend was Victor Hugo, later to be a bitter opponent of Napoleon's nephew when in 1851 he carried out the *coup d'état* which led the year after to the establishment of the Second Empire. For instance, in the poem 'Souvenir d'enfance', published in the *Feuilles d'Automne* (1831) and dedicated to Napoleon's brother, he recreates the atmosphere of worship which surrounded the emperor at the height of his power in Europe:

> . . . Et ce qui me frappa, dans ma sainte terreur,
> Quand au front du cortège apparut l'empereur,
> Tandis que les enfants demandaient à leurs mères
> Si c'est là ce héros dont on fait cent chimères,
> Ce ne fut pas de voir tout ce peuple à grand bruit
> Le suivre comme on suit un phare dans la nuit,
> Et se montrer de loin sur sa tête suprême
> Ce chapeau tout usé plus beau qu'un diadème,
> Ni pressés sur ses pas, dix vassaux couronnés
> Regarder en tremblant ses pieds éperonnés,
> Ni ses vieux grenadiers, se faisant violence,

Des cris universels s'enivrer en silence;
Non, tandis qu'à genoux la ville tout en feu,
Joyeuse comme on est lorsqu'on n'a qu'un seul voeu,
Qu'on n'est qu'un même peuple et qu'ensemble on respire,
Chantait en coeur: *Veillons au salut de l'empire*!
Ce qui me frappa, dis-je, et me resta gravé,
Même après que le cri sur sa route élevé
Se fut évanoui dans ma jeune mémoire,
Ce fut de voir, parmi ces fanfares de gloire,
Dans le bruit qu'il faisait, cet homme souverain
Passer, muet et grave, ainsi qu'un dieu d'airain . . .

Much more influential were the somewhat sentimental songs of
Béranger, in particular 'Les Souvenirs du Peuple' (1828) in which
an old woman relates how, after seeing Napoleon at the height of
his glory, one day, in the middle of the 1814 débâcle, she found
him knocking at her cottage door asking for food and shelter. She
ends the song by showing her hearers the glass out of which the
emperor had drunk:

– Le voici. Mais à sa perte
Le héros fut entraîné,
Lui qu'un pape a couronné,
Est mort dans une île déserte.
Longtemps aucun ne l'a cru;
On disait: 'Il va paraître;
Par mer il est accouru;
L'étranger va voir son maître.'
Quand d'erreur on nous tira,
Ma douleur fut bien amère!
    Fut bien amère!
– Dieu vous bénira, grand-mère;
    Dieu vous bénira.

Again, ironically, Louis Philippe contributed to the growth of
the legend when in 1840 he negotiated with the British government the transfer of Napoleon's remains from St. Helena and
their solemn reinterment in a tomb under the dome of the
Invalides.

With Napoleon out of the way, Louis XVIII could return from
Ghent for the Second Restoration. The peace treaty of 1815 associated the Bourbons more than ever with the humiliating defeats
of France at the hands of the Allies. In 1814 although she had been
compelled to give up virtually all the territory in Europe over
which she had gained control during the Revolutionary and

Napoleonic wars, she got off relatively lightly; she had been allowed to retain her frontiers of 1792 and thus to keep such territories as Avignon and the surrounding region as well as part of Savoy. She had not been required either to pay a war indemnity or to maintain an army of occupation.

In 1815 the Allies were determined to punish France for the support which had been given to Napoleon after his return from Elba. After Waterloo she was invaded by well over a million Allied troops who swarmed over the greater part of the country, requisitioning and pillaging as they went. By the terms of a new peace treaty France had to give up various fortresses on her eastern frontier as well as the part of Savoy which had been allotted to her in the previous year. The departments on her northern and eastern frontiers were to be occupied by Allied troops for periods varying from three to five years. In addition to meeting the cost of these armies of occupation France had to pay a war indemnity of 700 million francs and to undertake to settle debts owed by previous French governments to individuals in the allied countries. What is more, the four Allies agreed on various means of keeping a close eye on a country which had shown itself so dangerous to peace and the established monarchies, in particular through regular weekly meetings of their ambassadors in Paris.

If it could be said with truth of Louis's younger brother, the future Charles X, and of many of the returning *émigrés* 'Ils n'ont rien appris, ni rien oublié', this was scarcely true of the restored king. He was a man of moderate views, entirely lacking the religious bigotry of his brother and anxious only for as quiet a time as possible on the throne. He was already a man of fifty-nine when he returned to France in 1814. But not only had he to face the opposition of Liberals, Bonapartists and Republicans; he suffered from the excessive fervour of the Royalist party, many of whose members were 'plus royalistes que le roi' in their burning zeal for revenge on the Revolution and in their desire to put the clock back as far as possible. These *Ultra-royalistes* (*Ultras* for short) with their arrogant attitude and their determination to go back to the *Ancien Régime* were mercilessly caricatured in one of the most popular of Béranger's songs:

LE MARQUIS DE CARABAS
   Voyez ce vieux marquis
Nous traiter en peuple conquis;
   Son coursier décharné
De loin chez nous l'a ramené.

Vers son vieux castel
Ce noble mortel
Marche en brandissant
Un sabre innocent.
Chapeau bas! chapeau bas!
Gloire au marquis de Carabas!

Aumôniers, châtelains,
Vassaux, vavassaux et vilains,
C'est moi, dit-il, c'est moi
Qui seul ai rétabli mon roi.
Mais s'il ne me rend
Les droits de mon rang,
Avec moi, corbleu!
Il verra beau jeu.
Chapeau bas! chapeau bas!
Gloire au marquis de Carabas!

Pour me calomnier,
Bien qu'on ait parlé d'un meunier,
Ma famille eut pour chef
Un des fils de Pépin-le-Bref.
D'après mon blason
Je crois ma maison
Plus noble, ma foi,
Que celle du roi.
Chapeau bas! chapeau bas!
Gloire au marquis de Carabas!

Qui me résisterait?
La marquise a le tabouret.
Pour être évêque un jour
Mon dernier fils suivra la cour.
Mon fils le baron,
Quoique un peu poltron,
Veut avoir des croix;
Il en aura trois.
Chapeau bas! chapeau bas!
Gloire au marquis de Carabas!

Vivons donc en repos.
Mais l'on ose me parler d'impôts!
A l'état, pour son bien,
Un gentilhomme ne doit rien.
Grâce à mes créneaux,
A mes arsenaux,
Je puis au préfet

Dire son fait.
Chapeau bas! chapeau bas!
Gloire au marquis de Carabas!

Prêtres que nous vengeons,
Levez la dîme, et partageons;
Et toi, peuple animal,
Porte encor le bât féodal.
Seuls nous chasserons,
Et tous vos tendrons
Subiront l'honneur
Du droit du seigneur.
Chapeau bas! chapeau bas!
Gloire au marquis de Carabas!

Curé, fais ton devoir;
Remplis pour moi ton encensoir.
Vous, pages et varlets,
Guerre aux vilains, et rossez-les.
Que de mes aïeux
Ces droits glorieux
Passent tout entiers
A mes héritiers.
Chapeau bas! chapeau bas!
Gloire au marquis de Carabas.

Such a caricature must not be taken literally, but it does at any rate convey the impression which many of the returning *Ultras* made on their contemporaries.

Moreover Louis XVIII's position was complicated by the fact that, as he had no children, the heir to the throne was his younger brother, the Comte d'Artois. After being a gay spark in his youth, the future Charles X had become a devout and bigotted upholder of the rights of both Throne and Altar and throughout his brother's reign he put himself at the head of the extreme royalist party.

In 1814, on his return from exile in England, Louis XVIII had been graciously pleased to bestow on his subjects, not a constitution but a 'charte constitutionnelle'. 'Nous avons', as the preamble put it, 'volontairement, et par le libre exercice de notre autorité royale, accordé et accordons, fait concession et octroi à nos sujets, tant pour nous que pour nos successeurs, et à toujours, de la Charte constitutionnelle qui suit.' Despite the haughty tone of the preamble the *Charte* represented a compromise between the principles of the *Ancien Régime* and those of the

Revolution. The first four articles, for instance, echo the *Déclaration des droits de l'homme :*

> ARTICLE PREMIER. – Les Français sont égaux devant la loi, quels que soient d'ailleurs leurs titres et leurs rangs.
> ART. 2. – Ils contribuent indistinctement, dans la proportion de leur fortune, aux charges de l'État.
> ART. 3. – Ils sont tous également admissibles aux emplois civils et militaires.
> ART. 4. – Leur liberté individuelle est également garantie, personne ne pouvant être poursuivi ni arrêté que dans les cas prévus par la loi, et dans la forme qu'elle prescrit.

The purchasers of the *biens nationaux* were reassured since their recently acquired property was to be regarded as indistinguishable from all other forms of property and therefore as equally sacred:

> ART. 9. – Toutes les propriétés sont inviolables, sans aucune exception de celles qu'on appelle *nationales*, la loi ne mettant aucune différence entre elles.

While one article guarantees freedom of conscience and freedom of worship, the next insists that Roman Catholicism is the state religion and no longer merely, as defined in the Concordat, 'la religion de la grande majorité des Français':

> ART. 5. – Chacun professe sa religion avec une égale liberté, et obtient pour son culte la même protection.
> ART. 6. – Cependant la religion catholique, apostolique et romaine est la religion de l'État.

As regards political institutions a great deal of power was left in the hands of the king, but the *Charte* did at least permit of the introduction of a parliamentary system more or less on the English model, since his ministers who were alone responsible for the acts of the executive could be members of either of the two chambers. These were a *Chambre des Pairs*, which took over from Napoleon's Senate, and consisted of members of the royal family, the princes of the blood and hereditary or life peers appointed by the king, and a *Chambre des Députés* elected on a very narrow franchise. The method of election of deputies was several times altered during the Restoration, but the franchise was always an extremely restricted one. Under the restored Bourbons and under Louis Philippe to be either an elector or eligible for election to the Chamber one had to pay a stated sum in direct taxes – a *cens*; hence the expression 'monarchie censitaire' which is applied to the form of government in France from 1814 to 1848. The *Charte* laid it down that to be an elector one had to be thirty years of age and pay 300 francs in direct taxes, and to be eligible for election be forty and pay 1,000 francs in direct taxes. This high property qualification meant that only some 90,000 men were entitled to vote and that only some 16,000 in the whole of France were eligible for election to the Chamber.

Louis XVIII soon found himself in difficulties with the *Ultras*. His return from Ghent was followed by the so-called 'Terreur blanche' in considerable areas in the south of France; the government was powerless to prevent the murders of Republicans, Bonapartists and Protestants which took place in towns such as Marseilles, Avignon, Nîmes and Toulouse. The elections which were held in August in this atmosphere (most of the rest of France was occupied by the Allied armies) produced an overwhelmingly royalist majority which at the time led the king to describe it with satisfaction as 'la chambre introuvable'. There was already in the Restoration period some of the government instability for which France is notorious. However, from September 1815 down to the end of 1818 power was in the hands of the Duc de Richelieu, who had emigrated in 1789, entered the Russian army and become governor of Odessa and then of a large area of southern Russia. Despite this background he did his best to pursue a relatively moderate policy at home, while endeavouring to work towards better relations with the Allies and ultimately the freeing of France from the occupying armies.

Paradoxically the *Ultra* majority whose members were 'plus royalistes que le roi' contributed to the development of parliamentary institutions in France by maintaining that the government must be responsible to the majority in the Chamber. As a contemporary observer pointed out, this was the surprising line taken by one of the leading *Ultra* spokesmen, Baron de Vitrolles:

Invoquant à chaque pas les maximes et les exemples de l'Angleterre, M. de Vitrolles établissait que le ministère, qu'il appelait *une institution*, devait avoir dans son sein une rigoureuse unité, avec la majorité des chambres une intime union, et dans la conduite des affaires une responsabilité réelle qui lui assurât, auprès de la Couronne, la mesure nécessaire d'influence et de dignité. A ces trois conditions seulement le gouvernement pouvait être fort. Curieux souvenir à retrouver aujourd'hui! C'est par le plus intime confident de Monsieur le comte d'Artois, et pour faire monter au pouvoir le parti de l'ancien régime que le gouvernement parlementaire a été pour la première fois célébré et réclamé parmi nous, comme conséquence nécessaire du gouvernment représentatif. (Guizot, *Mémoires*, I. 137)

Practically as soon as the Chamber met there was a clash between the ministers and the majority. Things went smoothly when it was a question of voting laws which produced a kind of legal 'Terreur blanche' – laws to imprison without trial persons suspected of plotting against the security of the State, against seditious cries, speeches and writings (punishable by deportation or death) and one setting up 'cours prévôtales' (special courts with a military prosecutor whose sentences were without appeal and were carried out within twenty-four hours) to deal with seditious gatherings and armed rebellion. However, an amnesty law (strictly speaking it was concerned rather with those categories of persons who were to be excluded from the amnesty) did not seem to go far enough for the majority. One *Ultra* deputy who was in favour of the death penalty for whole categories of highly placed persons who had gone over to Napoleon during the Hundred Days expressed himself in favour of the most bloody vengeance:

> Il faut des fers, des bourreaux, des supplices. La mort, la mort seule, peut effrayer leurs complices et mettre fin à leurs complots. . . . Ce ne sera qu'en jetant une salutaire terreur dans l'âme des rebelles que vous préviendrez leurs coupables projets. Ce ne sera qu'en faisant tomber la tête de leurs chefs que vous isolerez les factieux . . . Défenseurs de l'humanité, sachez répandre quelques gouttes de sang pour en épargner des torrents.

Such violent and extreme views were only narrowly rejected by the Chamber. There were further clashes over a new electoral law and the budget until finally, in September 1816, acting under strong pressure from the Allied ambassadors in Paris, Louis XVIII dissolved the Chamber in order to secure a more moderately royalist majority.

On top of the financial difficulties facing the government after Waterloo came an episode which shows how close in the economic sense the France of the Restoration still was to the *Ancien Régime*. The years 1816–1817 saw another grain crisis of the kind which had been only too common in the eighteenth century. This time the crisis was not peculiar to France, as all over Western Europe the grain harvest of 1815 was poor. In 1816 the average price of wheat in France was over 50 per cent higher than it had been in 1814 and in 1817 it was more than double. In June 1817, when

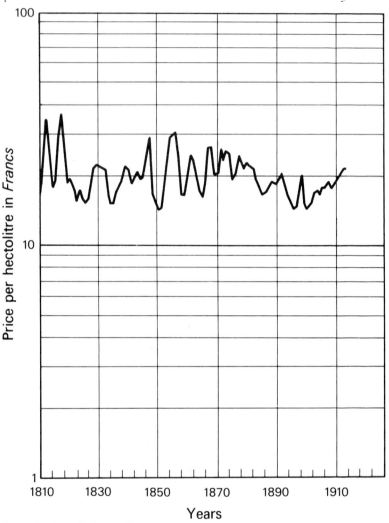

Annual prices of wheat, 1810–1913.

prices reached their peak, they were two and a half times what
they had been in June 1814. The effect on bread prices can be
imagined; the situation was made worse by the shortage of
potatoes, which had begun by now to achieve a certain popularity
in France, thanks partly to the efforts of the agricultural expert,
Antoine Parmentier (1737–1813). The rise in prices produced
riots in many places; attempts were made to impose maximum
prices by force; and, as before the Revolution, the grain shortage
produced unemployment in industry. The government encouraged

imports of grain, but otherwise trusted to the liberal principle of leaving matters to the law of supply and demand. Naturally this did not endear it to the masses, who were the principal sufferers from the crisis, but the political consequences were nothing like as serious as thirty years later when a similar crisis contributed to the downfall of the July Monarchy.

From the dissolution of the *Chambre introuvable* down to 1820 France enjoyed a period of government by moderate royalists which, for all the fury of parliamentary debates, gave it a relative stability. The elections of 1816 had produced a large majority of moderate, constitutional monarchists together with a few 'indé-pendants', i.e. liberals, bonapartists or republicans. Early in 1817 a new electoral law was voted and later that year a fifth of the seats came up for new elections in which the *Ultras* met with a number of defeats at the hands of the moderates and the 'indépendants' increased their numbers to twenty-five. Greater government stability produced a more accommodating attitude among the Allies. In 1818, at one of the periodic congresses which they had agreed to hold among themselves (this one took place at Aix-la-Chapelle), a French representative was invited to take part in the proceedings. France had raised loans to pay off the remainder of the war indemnity and to satisfy the claims of allied nationals, and it was agreed that the army of occupation should evacuate the country on 30 November. France was now well on the way to being restored to her place among the great European powers.

The partial elections of 1818 had led to further defeats of the *Ultras*, but these were counterbalanced by more victories for liberals like La Fayette, who had taken part in the American War of Independence and in the early phase of the Revolution of 1789 and who was to play a decisive role in the July Revolution; they won some twenty seats. It was becoming increasingly difficult for the government to get along by relying entirely on the constitu-tional monarchists in the Chamber; some support was soon to be required either from the *Ultras* or the Left. Throughout the period 1815–1820 one of the main government figures, though he did not become prime minister until shortly before his fall in 1820, was Decazes, a notary's son who despite his bourgeois origins became a great favourite with Louis XVIII. After Richelieu's resig-nation at the end of 1818 a new government sought support from the Left in the Chamber. Resistance from the *Chambre des Pairs* was overcome by the creation of 59 new peers and relatively liberal press laws were passed by both chambers. Yet instead of obtaining favourable results from the elections for the annual renewal of one fifth of the Chamber, Decazes had the mortification of finding that the Left made 25 gains and won 35 out of the 55 seats. What caused a particular sensation was the election at Grenoble of Abbé Grégoire, who had been a member of the Convention and who had only been prevented by absence from voting for the death penalty for Louis XVI. He had been elected at the second ballot with the help of *Ultra* voters, who were out to discredit the relatively liberal policy of the government.

Decazes was thus compelled to seek support from the Right. In November 1819 he became prime minister and formed a new government. In the speech from the throne at the end of November the King announced that a bill for electoral reform would be brought forward; this was clearly intended to block the annual swing towards the Left. However, before it could be tabled, the whole situation was transformed in February 1820 by the assassination of the Duc de Berry, the second son of the Comte d'Artois (more than seven months later his widow gave birth to 'l'enfant du miracle', the Duc de Bordeaux, later known as the Comte de Chambord, who after his grandfather's abdication in 1830 was to remain the pretender to the French crown as 'Henri V' until his death in 1883). Both the death of the Duc de Berry and the birth of his posthumous child were duly celebrated in odes of the young Victor Hugo, then in his most acutely royalist phase.

The assassination was the signal for the Right to launch a violent campaign against Decazes who was absurdly accused of complicity in the crime. Despite continued support from the King he was compelled to resign and to accept the post of ambassador in London and the title of duke. His place was taken by the Duc de Richelieu whose second government lasted until nearly the end of 1821. He hoped that a moderately right wing policy would enable him to govern with the support of the Right in parliament, but before two years were out he had to make way for a new government further to the right.

Two laws were rapidly passed instituting a press censorship and giving the government the right to detain for three months any person accused of plotting against the security of the State. Richelieu also brought in a new electoral law, called 'la loi du double vote' because, in addition to the 258 deputies chosen in the *arrondissements* by electors paying 300 francs in direct taxes, another 172 were to be elected by that quarter of the electorate in each department who paid the largest amount in direct taxes. The purpose of giving the wealthiest electors two votes was naturally to increase the strength of the Right. The government had prepared the way for the elections which followed in November 1820 by reducing the taxes of thousands of politically unreliable electors who were thus deprived of the vote. The censorship was also a help. There were 224 seats to be filled – the 172 which had been newly created and 52 seats representing the usual fifth of the existing Chamber. Of the 450 deputies of the new chamber only 80 belonged to the Left as against 160 *Ultras*, nearly half of whom had been members of 'la Chambre introuvable'. Some of these were admitted to the government, among them the Comte de Villèle, a minor nobleman who was soon to succeed Richelieu at the head of the government, while Chateaubriand, another of the *Ultra* leaders, was sent as ambassador to Berlin.

Various reactionary measures were taken by the government, particularly in favour of the Catholic clergy and of Church schools. A royal ordinance placed the secondary schools in the official State system, the *Université*, under the supervision of the bishops. The preamble of the ordinance is very revealing for the atmosphere of this period of clerical-monarchist reaction:

> Les bases de l'éducation des collèges sont la religion, la monarchie, la légitimité et la Charte. – L'évêque diocésain aura, pour ce qui concerne la religion, le droit de surveillance sur tous les collèges de son diocèse. Il les visitera lui-même ou les fera visiter par un de ses vicaires généraux et provoquera auprès du Conseil royal de l'instruction publique les mesures qu'il aura jugées nécessaires. Il sera distribué des médailles d'or aux professeurs des collèges qui se seront distingués par leur conduite religieuse et morale et par leur succès dans l'enseignement.

Church secondary schools, which were outside the State system, could also be granted equivalent status with those inside it. However, in a variety of different fields Richelieu did not give satisfaction to the *Ultras*, and he finally threw in his hand in disgust in December 1821.

Then began a period of full-blooded reaction under right wing royalists which was to last until the beginning of 1828. Although he was not at first prime minister, the most important figure in the government was Villèle, who had withdrawn from Richelieu's government shortly before his resignation. One consequence of the formation of an openly *Ultra* government was to drive the Left into revolutionary conspiracies. An elaborate system of secret conspiratorial groups with its headquarters in Paris was set up all over

France on the model of the secret society known as the *Carbonaria*, which flourished in Italy at a time when under Metternich and the Holy Alliance repression of all liberal movements on the Continent was in full swing. The *Charbonnerie* was liberal and republican in aims, but it also won a good deal of support among Bonapartists. While most of its original founders were obscure young men, some of the parliamentary leaders of the Left, including La Fayette, were members of the select group at its head in Paris. Plans for insurrections amongst garrisons at various points in the provinces to take place simultaneously at the end of December 1821 misfired completely, and further attempts in the following February led to nothing but the arrest and execution of a general and of various other officers and non-commissioned officers. La Fayette and the other leaders who were involved in these conspiracies could not be implicated for lack of proof, but their failure meant the end of the *Charbonnerie*, and the leaders of the Left reverted to purely legal forms of opposition.

Meanwhile Villèle's government was going ahead with its counter-revolutionary programme. In addition to purging the administration of high officials with liberal or bonapartist leanings, it introduced two new laws on the press which had the effect of ruining most of the newspapers of the Left. A variety of measures were taken to strengthen the position of the Church. The Panthéon was cleared of the remains of Voltaire and Rousseau and became once again a church. A bishop was placed at the head of the *Université*, a post which carried with it the appointment of teachers in secondary schools. His first circular reveals the spirit in which he proposed to set about this side of his functions:

> Je sais que mon administration doit être paternelle; mais je sais aussi que la rigueur est mon premier devoir, et que la modération sans force n'est que de la pusillanimité. Celui qui aurait le malheur de vivre sans religion ou de ne pas être dévoué à la famille régnante devrait bien sentir qu'il lui manque quelque chose pour être instituteur de la jeunesse. Il est à plaindre; même il est coupable.

Institutions of university rank were not spared either. The École Normale Supérieure was closed; the lectures of various professors at the Sorbonne, including those of Guizot, the future prime minister of Louis Philippe, were suspended; the Faculties of Law and Medicine, which drew the overwhelming majority of students in Paris until near the end of the century, were reorganized and professors of liberal views eliminated. Nineteen archbishops and bishops were given peerages, which admitted them to the *Chambre des Pairs*, and the laws concerning Sunday observance were rigorously enforced.

Another characteristic episode of this period of reaction was in the field of foreign policy where France, with the approval of the other Continental powers but in the face of violent hostility from England, resorted to armed intervention to restore the absolute power of another Bourbon monarch, Frederick VII of Spain. In 1823 a French expeditionary force crossed the frontier and easily overcame the armies of the liberal government. The king was reinstated in his full power and enabled to carry through the most furious reaction. The government decided to cash in on the success of the expedition. At the end of the year the Chamber was dissolved, and in the elections which took place in February and March 1824 the liberal opposition suffered a crushing defeat. As against 110 seats in the old Chamber it now held only 19; many of its leaders, including La Fayette, failed to secure re-election. This result had been achieved largely by means of intense government pressure on the tiny electorate. One of the first acts of the new Chamber was to pass a new electoral law which abolished the principle of an annual election for one fifth of the seats in the assembly; in future elections were to be held only every seven years.

In September 1824 Louis XVIII died. In the closing years of his reign he had had little power or influence. He had warned his successor of the dangers of following a completely reactionary policy, but these warnings were of no avail. Only six years after his death the last Bourbon was to be driven from the throne.

Charles X (*1824–1830*)

The Comte d'Artois was already a man of sixty-seven when he ascended the throne. Since the beginning of the Restoration he had been the leader of the *Ultra* party. Although he began his reign with various conciliatory gestures such as the abolition of the censorship, he also insisted on reviving the solemn religious ceremony of coronation (*le sacre*) which was held in Rheims cathedral in May 1825, and after it in the best traditions of the monarchy of the *Ancien Régime* he touched 121 persons suffering from the king's evil. This ceremony aroused very different emotions among contemporaries. The young Victor Hugo, still filled with Catholic-Royalist fervour, produced a fulsome ode, *Le Sacre de Charles X*, which concludes with this prayer:

Jean-Auguste Dominique Ingres: Charles X (1757–1836).

O Dieu! garde à jamais ce roi qu'un peuple adore!
Romps de ses ennemis les flèches et les dards,
Qu'ils viennent du couchant, qu'ils viennent de l'aurore,
    Sur des coursiers ou sur des chars!
Charles, comme au Sina, t'a pu voir face à face!
    Du moins qu'un long bonheur efface
    Ses bien longues adversités.
Qu'ici-bas des élus il ait l'habit de fête.
Prête à son front royal deux rayons de ta tête;
    Mets deux anges à ses côtés!

The poet was rewarded for this effort by a grateful king. A very different note was struck by Béranger in his highly satirical *Le Sacre de Charles le Simple* as can be seen from the opening verse:

Français, que Reims a réunis,
Criez: Montjoie et Saint-Denis!
On a refait la sainte ampoule,
Et comme au temps de nos aïeux,
Des passereaux lâchés en foule
Dans l'église volent joyeux.
D'un joug brisé ces vains présages
Font sourire sa majesté,
Le peuple s'écrie: Oiseaux, plus que nous soyez sages;
Gardez bien, gardez bien votre liberté. (*bis*)

However, by the end of 1827 divisions in the ranks of the *Ultras* were to bring down the right wing government of Villèle, which had been kept in office by Charles X.

The trouble had begun shortly before the death of Louis XVIII when Chateaubriand, who, as minister for foreign affairs, had been largely responsible for the French intervention in Spain, fell foul of both the old king and Villèle and as a result was ignominiously dismissed from office. The chief government newspaper, the *Journal des Débats*, transferred its support to the outraged Chateaubriand and began to criticize Villèle's administration in unmeasured terms. The result was that in addition to the weak Left opposition he now had to face opposition on the Right. Although the combined votes of the two oppositions in the Chamber could not seriously threaten the Government, they tended to combine in the same attacks on it. Chateaubriand was inevitably driven to use the arguments of the liberal opposition as one can see from his first contribution to the *Journal des Débats*:

Une administration timide, sans éclat, pleine de ruse, avide de pouvoir; un système politique antipathique au génie de la France et contraire à l'esprit de la Charte; – un despotisme obscur, prenant l'effronterie pour de la force; – la corruption érigée en système; – les hôtels des ministres devenus des espèces de bazars où les consciences étaient mises à l'encan; – la liberté des élections violée par de déplorables circulaires; – la France, enfin, livrée à des baladins politiques.

What is more, Chateaubriand could count on a good deal of support among his colleagues in the *Chambre des Pairs*, which often successfully resisted measures brought forward by Villèle.

The first of these was a law offering compensation to those *émigrés* whose land had been sold as *biens nationaux*. Although this bill aroused fierce controversy at the time ('le milliard des émigrés' offered a fine rallying cry for the Left opposition), from a long term point of view its effect was to strengthen the hold on their property of those who had bought or inherited the *biens nationaux*, since those who had received compensation could scarcely continue to demand the return of their land. 'Depuis le milliard de M. de Villèle', wrote Stendhal a decade or so later, 'les paysans n'ont plus peur de la restitution des biens nationaux.' (*Mémoires d'un Touriste*,XXI.151)

In the following year the government laid before the *Chambre des Pairs* a bill which aimed at restoring, in a modified form, the law of primogeniture. While the *Code civil* allowed a father a certain freedom to favour one of his children in his will, the bill meant that, unless an equal division of the estate was expressly laid down, the so-called 'quotité disponible' would automatically go to the eldest son. Although the bill only affected some 80,000 of the wealthiest families in France, it was widely felt that this was only a first step towards restoring in full the law of primogeniture and thus of strengthening the position of the landed aristocracy by preventing their estates from being broken up. After heated debates the *Chambre des Pairs* threw out the main clauses of the bill and sent it on to the *Chambre des Députés* in a mutilated form which was passed by the lower house. The peers' rejection of the main part of the bill made them extremely popular in Paris.

Urged on by the king and the *Ultra* majority, the government introduced various bills to strengthen the position of the Catholic Church. In 1825, for instance, a bill against sacrilege was introduced. In the case of such a crime being committed on the consecrated host, 'volontairement, publiquement et par haine ou mépris de la religion', the penalty laid down was death. In the debate on this bill in the Chambre des Pairs some extraordinary views were put forward. The Vicomte de Bonald, one of the main counter-revolutionary theorists, particularly distinguished himself in his defence of the death penalty for such a crime:

> On se recrie sur la peine de mort appliquée au sacrilège. Osons proclamer ici des vérités fortes. Si les bons doivent leur vie à la société comme service, les méchants la lui doivent comme exemple. Oui, la religion ordonne à l'homme de pardonner, mais en prescrivant au pouvoir de punir . . . Et d'ailleurs en punissant le sacrilège, que fait-on si ce n'est de le renvoyer devant son juge naturel?

Despite strong opposition the bill was passed by both chambers. In practice it was never applied, but those who supported it were anxious to make a strong gesture in favour of Catholicism.

The alliance of the Throne and the Altar naturally encountered fierce opposition among liberal-minded people. Much was heard of the occult influence of a mysterious Catholic body known as 'la Congrégation'. Such a body did exist (it had been founded in 1801 by an ex-Jesuit) and it flourished in many provincial towns as well as in Paris. But much more important from a political point of view was the secret society known as the 'Chevaliers de la Foi', founded in 1810 by Ferdinand de Bertier; this had played a considerable role in the events of 1814 and 1815 and several of its leaders became ministers during the Restoration. Quite a number of members of this secret society were also members of the Congrégation. The nefarious influence of this occult power is vividly described by Stendhal in *Le Rouge et le Noir* and by Balzac in *Le Curé de Tours*.

A particular butt of anti-clerical writers in these years was the Society of Jesus which, despite its suppression in the 1760s, had quietly established itself in France and was beginning to play a part again in secondary education. Its reappearance on the scene was the subject of a song by Béranger, 'Les Révérends Pères', which expressed the antipathy which the Jesuits inspired in many Frenchmen:

> Hommes noirs, d'où sortez-vous?
> Nous sortons de dessous terre,
> Moitié renards, moitié loups,
> Notre règle est un mystère.
> Nous sommes fils de Loyola;
> Vous savez pourquoi l'on nous exila.
> Nous rentrons; songez à vous taire!
> Et que vos enfants suivent nos leçons.
> C'est nous qui fessons,
> Et qui refessons
> Les jolis petits, les jolis garçons.

The pro-Catholic policy of the government undoubtedly did much to strengthen the Left in these years when it was recovering from its defeat at the last election in 1824.

In face of the attacks of the two oppositions Villèle's government could count on little support from the press, as the newspapers with the largest circulations were hostile to it. At the end of 1826 it laid before the *Chambre des Députés* a bill intended to curb both the newspaper and periodical press and also the production of books and pamphlets. What the minister in charge of the measure described as 'une loi de justice et d'amour' was violently attacked

by both Left and Right; even the *Académie Française* lodged an
official protest against the bill. When after long debates the chamber voted in March 1827, the opposition managed to muster
the surprising number of 134 votes and, as the *Chambre des Pairs*
showed itself hostile, the government finally withdrew the measure.

In the following month, when Charles X was persuaded to
review for the first time in his reign the largely bourgeois *Garde
Nationale* of Paris, a minority among these civilians in uniform
showed their hostility by such cries as 'Vive la liberté de la presse!
Vive la Charte! A bas les ministres! A bas les jésuites!' That very
evening a royal ordinance suppressed the Paris *Garde Nationale*;
this meant an open breach between Charles and the middle
classes of the capital.

The government also proceeded in the summer to reimpose the
censorship which had been abolished at Charles's accession. Its
unpopularity had been manifested in recent by-elections which
had been won by one or the other opposition. As the law passed
in 1824 for seven-year parliaments could not apply to the chamber
which had voted it, in November the king decided that sooner
than wait for the next general election in 1829, the best course
was to try and take the two oppositions by surprise by dissolving
the Chamber. The two oppositions of Left and Right succeeded
in making electoral agreements and the supporters of Villèle
were in a minority of some 150–180 in the new chamber against
as many liberals and some 60–80 members on the right. In Paris
the liberals had won an overwhelming victory.

In these years great interest was aroused in France by the
Greek struggle for independence from the Turks. The death of
Byron at Missolonghi in 1824 had its repercussions in France, and
the general enthusiasm for the Greek cause is reflected in some
of the poems of Hugo's *Les Orientales* (1829), for instance in the
poem entitled 'Enthousiasme':

> En Grèce! en Grèce! adieu, vous tous! il faut partir!
> Qu'enfin, après le sang de ce peuple martyr,
>   Le sang vil des bourreaux ruisselle!
> En Grèce, ô mes amis! vengeance! liberté!
> Ce turban sur mon front! ce sabre à mon côté!
>   Allons! ce cheval, qu'on le selle!
> Quand partons-nous? Ce soir! demain serait trop long.
> Des armes! des chevaux! un navire à Toulon!
>   Un navire, ou plutôt des ailes!
> Menons quelques débris de nos vieux régiments,

Et nos verrons soudain ces tigres ottomans
   Fuir avec des pieds de gazelles!

Although a number of French volunteers went out to fight on the Greek side and large subscriptions were raised inside France to aid the Greek cause, the French government was far from anxious to get involved in the conflict of interest between England and Russia over the future of the Turkish empire. However, in 1827, by the Treaty of London the three powers agreed to impose their mediation and later in that year in the battle of Navarino squadrons of the three allied navies utterly destroyed the Egyptian fleet which was supporting Turkey against the Greek rebels. This event was purely accidental, being caused by some rash firing on the part of the Egyptians. In the following year a French expeditionary force of 15,000 men was landed in Morea and persuaded the Egyptian army to withdraw from the fight. By 1829 Greece had secured virtual independence of Turkey.

Given the parliamentary situation, it was no easy task to find a successor to Villèle who remained in office until the beginning of January 1828. The most prominent figure in the new government, the most liberal of the whole Restoration period, was the Minister of the Interior, Martignac. His task was an impossible one. The concessions which he could make to the Left in such matters as milder press laws and a reduction in the Church's influence on education did not go far enough to satisfy it; nor did they have the support of Charles X, who was determined to have a government after his own heart. 'Nous faisons ce que nous pouvons', Martignac is alleged to have said in private, 'mais ce que nous pouvons, c'est de reconduire la monarchie jusqu'au bas de l'escalier, tandis qu'on la jetterait par les fenêtres'. He and the other ministers had warned the king in a memorandum that, given the situation in the *Chambre des Députés*, it was essential to seek support on the left, and that if the king was unwilling to permit this, he would have to dissolve the Chamber, but would then find that an election would simply make the Left stronger:

> Alors il ne resterait plus à votre Majesté que cette double alternative, ou de baisser son front auguste devant la Chambre, ou de recourir au pouvoir constituant à jamais aliéné par la Charte, et qu'on n'invoquerait follement une fois que pour plonger la France dans de nouvelles révolutions, au milieu desquelles disparaîtrait la couronne de saint Louis.

The king refused to listen to this warning. In August 1829

Adolphe Thiers (1797–1877).

Martignac and his colleagues were dismissed. The chief figure in the new government, although he was not immediately given the title of prime minister, was the Prince de Polignac, the son of Marie Antoinette's favourite and an out-and-out reactionary. The choice of the other ministers did nothing to remove the impression that the aim of the king and his new government was to bring about a counter-revolution by means of a *coup d'état* since it was obvious that it could never obtain a majority in the Chamber.

The new government was greeted with angry attacks in the liberal press. The young historian and journalist, Adolphe Thiers, who was to play a prominent part in French political life for the next fifty years, summed up the tactics which were to be followed by his party in the coming months: 'Enfermons les Bourbons dans la Charte, fermons exactement les portes; ils sauteront immanquablement par la fenêtre.' Indeed the solution to the problem presented by the obstinacy of Charles X – his replacement by the Duc d'Orléans – was already clearly foreshadowed in the comparison which Thiers made between the situation in France and the Glorious Revolution of 1688, which replaced James II by William of Orange:

Tout s'est opéré alors dans le plus grand calme. Il y eut une famille remplacée par une autre famille. Une dynastie ne savait pas régner sur une société nouvellement constituée, et l'on choisit une famille qui le sût mieux. Jacques II a été détrôné parce qu'il a . . . aimé ce que son peuple détestait, voulu ce qu'il repoussait, fait ce qu'il condamnait.

The months passed without the government taking any particularly significant action until the next session of Parliament opened, at an inordinately late date, in March 1830. The king's speech was aggressive in tone. In it he declared:

Si de coupables manoeuvres suscitaient à mon gouvernement des obstacles que je ne veux pas prévoir, je trouverais la force de les surmonter dans ma résolution de maintenir la paix publique, dans la juste confiance des Français et dans l'amour qu'ils ont toujours montré pour leurs rois.

In reply the Chamber voted an address which, in polite and respectful language, clearly maintained the principle that a government must be based on the support of the majority of the elected representatives of the nation:

La Charte . . . consacre comme un droit l'intervention du pays dans la délibération des intérêts publics. Elle fait du concours permanent des vues politiques de notre gouvernement avec les voeux de notre peuple la condition indispensable de la marche régulière des affaires publiques. Sire, notre loyauté, notre dévouement, nous condamnent à vous dire que ce concours n'existe pas.

This address was voted by 221 votes to 181.

In a constitutional monarchy the government's duty would have been to resign; but that was not at all how the king saw things. Instead the Chamber was dissolved and new elections held from the end of June into July. From these the opposition emerged victorious; the supporters of the address increased in numbers from 221 to 274. Still the government did not resign; instead it was preparing a *coup d'état*.

At the end of May a large expeditionary force had left Toulon for North Africa; its aim was to capture Algiers, nominally in order to put an end to the piratical activities of the Algerians and to the slavery of Christians which followed from them, in practice to increase French power in the Mediterranean. That was why the move aroused such hostility from Wellington and his government. The capture of Algiers on 5 July marked the beginning of France's gradual penetration into Algeria and conquest of the whole country. Until quite recently French historians used to chalk it up to the credit of the Restoration that it founded 'l'Algérie française', but since 1962, when after a bitter struggle between the French and the Arabs Algeria became an independent state, this no longer seems a particularly useful achievement. In the short run, instead of helping to prop up Charles X's régime, it merely

E. Delacroix: *La Liberté gardant le peuple* (le 28 juillet 1830).

helped to precipitate its fall as the troops sent to Algeria were not available to support the government's attempt at a *coup d'état*.

On 26 July, acting under powers which he claimed were conferred upon him by Article 14 of the *Charte* ('Le roi . . . fait les règlements et ordonnances nécessaires pour l'exécution des lois et la sûreté de l'Etat') Charles X issued the famous *quatre ordonnances*. The first of these imposed even more serious restrictions on freedom of the press; the second, allegedly because in the recent elections manoeuvres had been employed 'pour tromper et égarer les électeurs', dissolved the new Chamber; the third further restricted the number of persons eligible to vote, and the fourth fixed the date of the new elections for September.

Obviously the intention of these royal ordinances was to put the clock back and to reinforce the royal power; yet the government took no serious steps to put down any trouble in Paris. The reaction was prompt and violent. In three days – 27, 28 and 29 July, ('les trois Glorieuses') – the Bourbons were finally driven from the throne. On 27 July barricades were set up in the streets of Paris; the insurgents seized various public buildings and hoisted the *tricolore* flag; by 29 July it flew over the royal palaces of the Louvre and Tuileries. Charles and the Dauphin abdicated in favour of the Comte de Chambord, a boy of nine, but the whole of the royal family eventually made its way across the Channel to England, finding a temporary home in Holyrood Palace. Like his grandson after him, Charles X ended his days in exile in Austria.

The victory of the 'trois Glorieuses' had been won by the republican masses of Paris, but the result was not to be a republic. A second attempt at setting up a constitutional monarchy was made by the liberal politicians who manoeuvred behind the scenes and cheated the republicans of their victory. On 30 July, when the situation was still far from clear, a candidate for the vacant throne was suddenly produced in the person of the Duc d'Orléans, a descendant of the younger brother of Louis XIV; his father, Philippe Égalité, after voting for the death sentence on Louis XVI, had been guillotined in his turn during the Terror. The duke had fought in the revolutionary armies and had taken part in the two battles at Valmy and Jemappes which had saved the republic. It is true that he had then emigrated and that he was an immensely wealthy man who had also done very well out of the 'milliard des émigrés'; but during the Restoration he had been looked upon in some opposition circles as a possible alternative to the members of the older branch of the royal family. In a flamboyant proclamation he was now presented by his backers as the man of the hour:

> Charles X ne peut plus rentrer dans Paris: il a fait couler le sang du peuple.
> La république nous exposerait à d'affreuses divisions; elle nous brouillerait avec l'Europe.
> Le duc d'Orléans est un prince dévoué à la cause de la Révolution.
> Le duc d'Orléans ne s'est jamais battu contre nous.
> Le duc d'Orléans était à Jemappes.
> Le duc d'Orléans a porté au feu les couleurs tricolores, le duc d'Orléans peut seul les porter encore; nous n'en voulons pas d'autres.
> Le duc d'Orléans s'est prononcé; il accepte la Charte comme nous

l'avons toujours voulue et entendue.

C'est du peuple français qu'il tiendra sa couronne.

On the following day the duke made his appearance at the Hôtel de Ville, the headquarters of the republicans; there La Fayette, a venerable figure of seventy-five who had been given command of the Garde Nationale and who at this moment had it in his power to have himself proclaimed president of the republic, appeared at a window with the duke. The crowd, up till then fairly hostile, was won over to the duke's side:

> . . . Il saisit un drapeau tricolore qui était à sa portée et, prenant le bras du général La Fayette, se dirigea vivement vers une des fenêtres de l'Hôtel de Ville donnant sur la place de Grève qui était à ce moment encombrée d'une immense multitude de laquelle s'échappaient surtout les cris de; 'Plus de Bourbons!'
>
> A l'apparition du duc d'Orléans et de La Fayette enveloppés tous deux, pour ainsi dire, dans les plis du drapeau national, un cri s'élança des entrailles de cette multitude, et ce cri, cette fois unanime, fut celui de: 'Vive le duc d'Orléans! Vive La Fayette!' . . . la révolution était terminée. (Odilon Barrot, *Mémoires*, I. 125)

For the next eighteen years France was to be ruled by Louis Philippe Ier, who, instead of the traditional title of 'roi de France', bore that of 'roi des Français'.

The July Monarchy

In 1814 the *Charte* had been graciously bestowed on the French people by Louis XVIII; this time the Chamber of Deputies first revised the *Charte* and then asked the Duc d'Orléans whether he would accept these conditions and thus become 'Roi des Français'. On 9 August at a solemn ceremony at the Palais Bourbon in the presence of members of both houses of Parliament the new king swore to observe the revised *Charte*.

The amended constitution was in practice a compromise between the views of the constitutional monarchists and those of the republicans. It goes without saying that the preamble of the 1814 *Charte* in which the king had graciously bestowed these constitutional laws on the French people was scrapped. Catholicism ceased to be the state religion; it was now merely the religion 'professée par la majorité des Français'. The article dealing with the press was modified to include the clear statement: 'La censure ne pourra jamais être rétablie', though, as we shall see, this did

Horace Vernet: Louis-Philippe (1773–1850) with the Dukes of Orléans and Nemours.

not prevent the new régime from imposing severe restrictions on the freedom of the press. It can well be imagined that Article 14, the one invoked by Charles X in promulgating the four ordinances which had brought about his downfall, was drastically amended. The original wording, 'Le roi . . . fait les règlements et ordonnances nécessaires pour l'exécution des lois et la sûreté de l'État', was modified by cutting out the words 'et la sûreté de l'État' and by putting in their place 'sans pouvoir jamais ni suspendre les lois elles-mêmes ni dispenser de leur exécution'. Henceforward the king was to share the initiative in the making of laws with the two chambers. The age of eligibility for election to the Chamber of Deputies was lowered from forty to thirty, and it was now possible to have a vote at twenty-five instead of thirty. Article 67 laid it down that France's flag should once again be the tricolour and not the white flag of the Restoration: 'La France reprend ses couleurs. A l'avenir, il ne sera plus porté d'autre cocarde que la cocarde tricolore.' Trivial as the question of the flag may appear, it was to have its importance in French history into the early days of the Third Republic.

Louis Philippe was already a man of fifty-seven when he ascended the throne; after eighteen years as king he had become an obstinate old man and this undoubtedly contributed to his downfall in 1848. Although he had accepted the conditions laid down by Parliament, throughout his reign he was determined not to be a mere figurehead. Behind a façade of parliamentary government his aim was to govern as well as reign. This led to a great deal of government instability; in eighteen years France had seventeen different governments. It is true that a great many ministers figured in half a dozen or more governments. While it was partly rivalry among this very limited political personnel which produced such instability, it was also the result of the king's determination to play the leading part in the conduct of both home and foreign affairs. During the 1830s there were very frequent changes of government and sometimes long periods passed before a new one could be formed; however in 1840 Louis Philippe at last found a government after his own heart, one in which Guizot was in effect prime minister though he bore the title only in the last few months before his fall in the crisis of February 1848.

The Legitimists, those who remained loyal to the Comte de Chambord, Charles X's grandson, in whose favour he had abdicated, still remained a force to be reckoned with, at any rate in the opening years of the reign. Many members of the aristocracy, including Chateaubriand, refused to recognize the usurper and withdrew from public life. In 1832 the Duchesse de Berry, the widowed mother of the Comte de Chambord, made a romantic and futile attempt to stir up armed resistance by secretly entering France and making for the centre of true blue royalism, the Vendée. The expedition proved a complete fiasco; the duchess (the niece of Louis Philippe's queen) was arrested and imprisoned in a fortress; the discovery that the widowed princess, who was secretly married to an Italian count, was pregnant caused some embarrassment to her loyal supporters, many of whom (Chateaubriand among them) had a poor opinion of the whole enterprise.

However, the main political division of these eighteen years is summed up in the expressions 'parti de la résistance' and 'parti du mouvement'. The first consisted of those who were convinced that, with a bourgeois king like Louis Philippe on the throne, the revolution begun in 1789 had been carried far enough. Their opponents, those with more radical, democratic views, were bitterly disappointed with the outcome of the July Revolution which, instead of giving them a republic, had fobbed them off with Louis Philippe.

The bourgeois nature of the July Monarchy is underlined in a striking passage in Tocqueville:

En 1830, le triomphe de la classe moyenne avait été définitif et si complet que tous les pouvoirs politiques, toutes les franchises, toutes les prérogatives, le gouvernement tout entier se trouvèrent renfermés et comme entassés dans les limites étroites de cette bourgeoisie, à l'exclusion, en droit, de tout ce qui était au-dessous d'elle et, en fait, de tout ce qui avait été au-dessus. Non seulement elle fut ainsi la directrice unique de la société, mais on peut dire qu'elle en devint la fermière. Elle se logea dans toutes les places, augmenta prodigieuse-ment le nombre de celles-ci et s'habitua à vivre autant du Trésor public que de sa propre industrie, (*Souvenirs*, p. 30)

The social character of the new regime is clearly brought out by the terms of the electoral law of 1831 which can usefully be com-pared with the Reform Bill passed in this country in the following year. The suffrage was somewhat enlarged, but France was still a 'monarchie censitaire'. To have a vote a citizen had to pay 200 francs in direct taxes, and to be eligible for election as a deputy 500 francs. The number of electors was nearly doubled, compared with what it had been under the Restoration. Even so it was now only 167,000 for the whole of France, and if the figure was to rise to some 240,000 at the end of the reign as more people paid the necessary amount in taxes, the changes in the franchise brought about by the July Revolution did not extend it nearly as far as our own fairly modest Reform Bill. This gave the vote to some 500,000 persons, which meant that whereas in this country with its much smaller population 32 out of every 1,000 inhabitants had a vote, the corresponding figure for France was only 5.

The *Chambre des Pairs* had been retained in the revised *Charte* as 'une portion essentielle de la puissance législative'. Although the king had the power to appoint to peerages, whether hereditary or for life, in practice Louis Philippe created only life peers. Victor Hugo was to be among those created in the 1840's. According to *Victor Hugo raconté par un témoin de sa vie* (i.e. by Hugo himself writing in the third person) he did not pay sufficient in taxes to be able to stand for parliament and his only chance of taking part in politics was to get himself elected to the Academy which made him eligible for a peerage:

Il y avait deux tribunes, celle des députés et celle des pairs. Député, il ne pouvait l'être; la loi électorale d'alors était faite pour de plus riches que lui; *Notre Dame de Paris* et *Les Feuilles d'Automne* n'équi-valaient pas à une terre ou à une maison. Il y avait bien un moyen de tricher la loi, assez usité, si l'on avait un ami propriétaire; il vous prêtait sa maison. Mais, quand M. Victor Hugo eût emprunté la maison d'un ami, les électeurs du cens étaient peu sympathiques aux littérateurs; les écrivains étaient pour eux des rêveurs bons à les amuser dans les intervalles de leurs affaires sérieuses, mais, du moment qu'il était un penseur, et surtout un poète, on devenait radicalement incapable de bon sens et de rien entendre aux choses pratiques. Je ne sais par quelle erreur M. de Lamartine avait pu être élu[1]; c'était déjà trop d'un poète, on n'en aurait certainement pas admis deux.

Restait la chambre des pairs. Mais pour pouvoir être nommé, il fallait être d'une des catégories où le roi devait choisir. Une seule était accessible à M. Victor Hugo, l'académie. (II. 467–468)

After unsuccessful attempts in 1836, 1839 and 1840, he was finally elected in 1841 and a peerage followed in 1845. However, the assembly to which he finally secured entry was never under Louis Philippe an impressive or influential body.

Another characteristic institution of the régime was the *Garde Nationale* which had a double function – to maintain order at home and to play its part in the defence of the country. In practice its main purpose was to protect the new régime, a function which along with the regular army it performed fairly efficiently in the very unsettled opening years of the reign. On the other hand its defection in 1848 was greatly to influence Louis Philippe's decision to abdicate so that in the long run it contributed to the downfall of the July monarchy. It was essentially a bourgeois institution, and while it appealed to many bourgeois, particularly those who reached the rank of officer in it and might even be invited to royal receptions at the Tuileries, it was anathema to writers of the time such as Balzac who even served short prison sentences sooner than do their guard duty in it.

Down to 1835, in addition to the escapade of the Duchesse de Berry, the régime continued to face serious opposition from the Left. Indeed in the first months of its existence it had a very shaky start. When Charles X's ministers were put on trial for their part in the events leading up to the July Revolution, popular opinion, including that of the *Garde Nationale*, was strongly in favour of the death penalty. When they were sentenced to life imprisonment by the *Chambre des Pairs*, it was only by a subterfuge that the authorities got them to Vincennes, away from the crowds shouting for vengeance for the blood shed in July. In February 1831 when the

---

[1] Lamartine, on paper a wealthy landowner, had finally been elected to the Chamber in 1833. It is typical of the tiny electorates of the reign of Louis Philippe that in his first attempt to secure election he had been defeated by 198 votes to 181.

Legitimists held a service in the Église Saint Germain l'Auxerrois in the heart of Paris, for the anniversary of the assassination of the Duc de Berry, this demonstration led the hostile crowd to wreck the inside of the church; later the archbishop's palace, next to Notre Dame, was invaded, its contents thrown out and the building partly demolished.

On top of these disorders in Paris came a formidable insurrection in Lyons in November. The silk industry there normally employed some 50,000 workers, not in factories but in domestic industry. At this moment the industry was going through a crisis and wages were extremely low. After negotiations the employers agreed to pay rather better, but then went back on the agreement. As a result barricades were set up in the streets of Lyons, the Hôtel de Ville was occupied by the insurgents and the troops were driven out of the city. In November 1831 Lamartine, who was serving in the *Garde Nationale* some forty miles away at Mâcon, wrote:

> Je vous écris au milieu du corps de garde, mon cheval sellé à côté de moi, botté et armé depuis quarante-huit heures. Lyon, comme vous le savez déjà, a été *conquis* sur la garde nationale et la ligne par 30 à 40,000 ouvriers qui y règnent maintenant au milieu des excès du désordre inséparable d'une pareille domination. Nous avons été sur le point ce matin de marcher en masse au secours des citoyens lorsqu'on nous a appris la fatale reddition de la ville. Il y faudra autre chose que quelques centaines d'hommes de garde nationale. C'est le *27 juillet* du commerce et de la propriété. La garde nationale de Lyon, si belle et si nombreuse, a manqué à ses devoirs et à sa propre conservation; elle ne s'est pas présentée ou mal présentée, et retirée sur le champ chez elle à l'heure du feu. Elle est maintenant victime de sa faute, rançonnée, pillée et menacée de tous les désastres. On dit cependant que, parmi ce peuple d'ouvriers vainqueurs, on tâche de rétablir un certain ordre provisoire, mais le moment où il faudra leur arracher des dents leur conquête et une ville de cent quatre-vingt mille habitants fait trembler. (*Correspondance générale de 1830 à 1848*, I. 218–219)

Large numbers of fresh regular troops had to be sent into the city before the government could restore order. Characteristically the new wage agreement was cancelled.

There was further trouble in Paris in the following year. In June Republicans, Legitimists and Bonapartists joined in an armed insurrection which was put down on the second day by the army and *Garde Nationale* (the last stand of the insurgents at a barricade in the Cloître Saint-Merri forms a famous episode in

Hugo's *Les Misérables*). Martial law was declared in Paris and the republican opposition driven underground. However, it reorganized itself in a variety of societies and began to combine social aims with the purely political. The government brought in a number of laws to interfere with their activities; the result was a series of insurrections in April 1834. The trouble began with a second insurrection in Lyons in which both republicans and silk workers joined; this lasted for four days and ended with a bloody repression. There were disturbances in many provincial towns, but the chief repercussions were naturally felt in Paris where barricades were set up in the east end of the city. A merciless repression followed; there was the appalling massacre in the Rue Transnonain: thousands of suspects were arrested and a large number of insurgents from Paris and the provinces were put on trial before the *Chambre des Pairs*. The heavy sentences imposed broke the republican party as a political force for the next decade

Daumier: *La rue Transnonain* (1834).

or so, especially as in the following year the notorious 'lois de Septembre' were passed which were directed against all subversive movements. Under these laws severe penalties were imposed for attacks on the principles of the gove nment in the press (this put an end among other things to the caricatures of Louis

Lat.

LES POIRES,

Faites à la cour d'assises de Paris par le Directeur de la CARICATURE.

Vendues pour payer les 6,000 fr. d'amende du journal le *Charivari*.

" Si, pour reconnaître le monarque dans une caricature, vous n'attendez pas qu'il soit désigné autrement que par la ressemblance, vous tomberez dans l'absurde. Voyez ces croquis informes, auxquels j'aurais peut-être dû borner ma défense :

Ce croquis ressemble à Louis-Philippe, vous condamnerez donc ?

Alors il faudra condamner celui-ci, qui ressemble au premier.

Puis condamner cet autre, qui ressemble au second.

Et enfin, si vous êtes conséquens, vous ne sauriez absoudre cette poire, qui ressemble aux croquis précédens.

Ainsi, pour une poire, pour une brioche, et pour toutes les têtes grotesques dans lesquelles le hasard ou la malice aura placé cette triste ressemblance, vous pourrez infliger à l'auteur cinq ans de prison et cinq mille francs d'amende!! Avouez, Messieurs, que c'est là une singulière liberté de la presse!!

Charles Philipon, *Les Poires*: cartoon of Louis-Philippe which appeared in *Le Charivari*, a satirical journal of the time.

Philippe), and the theatre censorship was also stiffened. It is true that in 1839 another armed insurrection was organized in Paris by a secret society, *la Société des Saisons*, but it was quickly put down. Trade unions were, of course, still illegal, but there was none the less a widespread strike movement in Paris and some provincial towns in 1839 and 1840. These may be said to have heralded the naked class war which raged in Paris between February and June 1848.

Socialist theories had already begun to emerge during the Restoration with the writings of Claude Henri de Saint-Simon (1760–1825) and Charles Fourier (1772–1837). Both these men exercised a considerable influence in certain restricted circles, particularly Saint-Simon, whose followers achieved considerable notoriety at the beginning of the new reign. They were succeeded by a whole group of socialist thinkers from the next generation, the most prominent of whom were Pierre-Joseph Proudhon (1809–1865) whose first work of note, *Qu'est-ce que la propriété?* (1840) contains on the opening page the famous answer, 'La propriété, c'est le vol', and Louis Blanc (1811–1882), who in his *De l'Organisation du travail* (1839) urged that the State should assist in the setting up of producers' cooperatives so as gradually to replace the capitalist system. These and other theorists had a considerable influence on the writers of the period, especially George Sand and Eugène Sue. Even proletarian poets emerged in these years. A good deal of the socialist thought of the time, especially when it had filtered down into works of literature, was of a singularly vague and naïve kind. Writers were convinced that all sorts of wonderful reforms could be achieved without violence, simply by the spread of brotherly love and by collaboration between the different social classes. The events of the years 1848–1851 were to produce a shattering disillusionment from which many of them never recovered.

One of the most prominent political figures of the first half of the reign was Adolphe Thiers (1797–1877) who was to live long enough to suppress the Paris Commune, make peace with Bismarck and be the virtual founder of the Third Republic. From very modest beginnings (he was an illegitimate child), he worked himself up through journalism and his *Histoire de la Révolution française* to a political career. As a journalist he had played a prominent part in replacing Charles X by Louis Philippe and was quickly rewarded with various posts in the governments of the reign. He became prime minister in 1834, but resigned two years later when he clashed with the king who was determined to keep the reins of power in his own hands. Thiers argued that, as he was backed by a majority in Parliament, Louis Philippe must accept his policy as prime minister. He had a second spell in this office in 1840, but once again clashed with the king, this time over foreign policy. In the grave international crisis of that year over Egypt (France was isolated diplomatically) the king acted as a restraining influence on the bellicose Thiers and negotiated behind his prime minister's back. Thiers once again resigned and returned to the writing of his *Histoire du Consulat et de l'Empire*, re-emerging in 1848 to take once more a prominent part in affairs.

1840 marks the arrival in power as virtual prime minister of François Guizot (1787–1874). Although he had played some part in politics before 1830 (he was one of the 221 deputies who voted the address criticizing the policy pursued by Charles X) he was by profession a historian. He held a chair at the Sorbonne and was responsible for many publications. Among other posts which he held in the 1830s was that of Minister of Education which he occupied in successive governments from 1832 to 1837. It was he who was responsible in 1833 for a new law on primary education. By a coincidence it was in this same year that in England the government began to make grants to voluntary societies running primary schools, but here it was not until 1870 that the State assumed the obligation to provide primary education. Guizot's act did not make primary education either compulsory or (except for the poorest pupils) free. As one of the leaders of the 'parti de la résistance' he considered that the revolution of 1830 had gone far enough and he naturally had very narrow views as to what either the pupils in the state schools or the teachers in training should be taught. On the other hand he did effect considerable improvements in the salaries and housing of teachers, who in the past had often been part-time only and had been miserably paid. By the end of the reign considerable progress had been made in the field of primary education; in his memoirs Guizot could summarize the results of his 1833 law thus:

> En 1832, avant la loi du 28 juin 1833, il y avait en France 42,092 écoles primaires, communales ou privées, et dans ces écoles 1,935,624 élèves, garçons ou filles. Au 1er janvier 1848, sous l'influence de la loi du 28 juin 1833, le nombre des écoles primaires s'était élevé à 63,028, et celui des élèves à 3,530,135. Ainsi, dans l'espace de quatorze années, l'instruction primaire avait acquis 20,936 écoles et 1,594,511 élèves de plus. (*Mémoires*, VIII. 163)

Impressive as these figures are, they mask a great many deficiencies, in particular in the field of the education of girls which, compared with that of boys, made relatively slow progress until after the middle of the century. Guizot still left plenty of educational reforms for the Third Republic to carry out.

In the period from 1840 to 1848 in which Guizot, first as foreign minister and then as prime minister, was in power, he was content to govern the country with a majority in a Chamber elected by a tiny minority of the population. He was interested only in maintaining the position of the wealthier middle classes and was increasingly out of touch with feeling in the country. In his memoirs he not only sets forth the accusation that this was the case, but even admits that it contains a certain element of truth:

> Je m'arrête ici un moment pour dire quelques mots d'un reproche qu'on m'a souvent adressé, et qui n'est pas dénué de vérité, quoiqu'il manque complètement de justice. Je ne me préoccupais, m'a-t-on dit, que des questions et des luttes parlementaires, point des intérêts et des aspirations populaires; mes pensées et mes efforts se renfermaient dans les Chambres et me faisaient oublier le pays; je faisais tout pour les désirs et la préponderance des classes moyennes, rien pour la satisfaction et le progrès du peuple. Je repousse ces mots, *tout* d'une part et *rien* de l'autre . . . . (*Mémoires*, VIII. 539)

The notion of political equality was one which he would not accept as he made clear in a speech in the Chamber in 1837:

> Il y a dans notre Charte des droits qui ont été conquis pour tout le monde, qui sont le prix du sang de tout le monde. Ces droits, c'est l'égalité des charges publiques, c'est l'égale admissibilité à tous les emplois publics, c'est la liberté du travail, la liberté des cultes, la liberté de la presse, la liberté individuelle! Ces droits, parmi nous, sont ceux de tout le monde; ils appartiennent à tous les Français; ils valaient bien la peine d'être conquis par les batailles que nous avons livrées et par les victoires que nous avons remportées. . . . Serait-il donc nécessaire, après cela, d'établir cette absurde égalité politique, cette aveugle universalité des droits politiques qui se cache au fond de toutes les théories qu'on vient apporter à cette tribune? (*Mémoires*, IV. 270–271)

In the 1840s Guizot obstinately refused to give in to the agitation from the Left for electoral reform. Even quite a modest reform such as giving the vote to all jurors (this would have meant adding some 18,000 names to the electoral roll) was obstinately resisted. One of the abuses of parliamentary government under the July Monarchy (it had also existed under the Restoration) was the considerable number of deputies who were civil servants and therefore bound to support the government in power; here too Guizot dug his heels in and resisted all attempts at reform. In his memoirs in speaking of a bill brought forward in 1842 by a deputy named Ganneron he even argues that this was quite a trivial matter:

> En fait, au 1er janvier 1842, sur les 459 membres dont la Chambre des députés était composée, il y avait 149 fonctionnaires salariés. Dans ce nombre, 16 étaient des ministres ou de grands fonctionnaires politiques que la proposition de M. Ganneron pour l'extension des incompatibilités parlementaires laissait toujours éligibles. Sur les 133 députés restants, 53 étaient des magistrats inamovibles. La Chambre ne contenait donc que 80 députés amovibles et placés, à ce titre, dans la dépendance du pouvoir. (*Mémoires*, VI. 370)

But these eighty deputies, who already formed a substantial bloc, could also be added to by the government if it chose to appoint other members to offices of profit under the Crown; and this device was certainly made use of under the July Monarchy. The charge of parliamentary corruption can scarcely be rebutted.

Tocqueville who was a deputy from 1839 onwards has a famous passage on the situation in France under the Guizot régime with the predominance of the wealthy middle classes:

> Maîtresse de tout comme ne l'avait été et ne le sera peut-être jamais aucune aristocratie, la classe moyenne qu'il faut appeler la classe gouvernementale, s'étant cantonnée dans son pouvoir et, bientôt après, dans son égoïsme, prit un air d'industrie privée, chacun de ses membres ne songeant guère aux affaires publiques que pour les faire tourner au profit de ses affaires privées et oubliant aisément dans son petit bien-être les gens du peuple.
>
> La postérité, qui ne voit que les crimes éclatants et à laquelle, d'ordinaire, les vices échappent, ne saura peut-être jamais à quel degré le gouvernement d'alors avait pris, sur la fin, les allures d'une compagnie industrielle, où toutes les opérations se font en vue du bénéfice que les sociétaires peuvent retirer. Ces vices tenaient aux instincts naturels de la classe dominante, à son absolu pouvoir, à l'énervation et à la corruption même du temps. (*Souvenirs*, p. 31)

If the July Monarchy is often described as a 'régime juste-milieu' – the phrase derives from the king's speech from the throne in January 1831 when he declared: 'Nous cherchons à nous tenir dans un juste milieu également éloigné des excès du pouvoir populaire et des abus du pouvoir royal' – the spirit of Guizot's period of office is summed up in the words he himself used in a speech delivered in the Chamber: 'Enrichissez-vous.' The attitude of complacent conservatism and resistance to change adopted by successive governments was several times denounced by Lamartine. In 1839, for instance, he came out with the famous words,

'La France s'ennuie', or to quote him more accurately and in context, he attacked the régime in the following terms:

Vous avez laissé manquer le pays d'action. Il ne faut pas se figurer, Messieurs, que, parce que nous sommes fatigués des grands mouvements qui ont remué le siècle et nous, tout le monde est fatigué comme nous et craint le moindre mouvement. Les générations qui grandissent derrière nous ne sont pas lasses, elles; elles veulent agir et se fatiguer à leur tour. Quelle action leur avez-vous donnée? La France est une nation qui s'ennuie. (Chambre des Députés, 10 Jan. 1839)

In 1842, attacking a speech by Guizot, he denounced him and his supporters as 'immobiles, inertes, implacables. Oui, implacables à toute amélioration.' He went on to coin another famous phrase:

Et si c'était là en effet tout le génie de l'homme d'État chargé de diriger un gouvernement, mais il n'y aurait pas besoin d'un homme d'État, une borne y suffirait. (Chambre des Députés, 15 Feb. 1842)

Such attacks did not make the slightest impression on Guizot.

The elections of 1846 raised the government's majority in the Chamber to over 100, but this result, given the limited suffrage, was quite unrepresentative of feeling in the country. Further modest proposals for electoral reform were once again turned down, but by now France was in the grip of an economic crisis which undoubtedly contributed to the sudden collapse of the whole régime in February 1848.

In 1845 began another food crisis, outwardly less severe than in 1817, but much more serious in its consequences. This time other Western European countries were affected by a similar crisis, most tragically in Ireland where the potato famine of 1845–1849 caused nearly a million deaths. In France the 1845 harvest, both of grain and potatoes, was a poor one, and the same thing happened again in 1846; this meant that bread prices rose sharply in 1846 and still further again in 1847.

Writing from her country house at Nohant in central France in July 1846 George Sand declares: 'Le bled est cher et la misère grande!' (*Correspondance*, VII, 416) and in December, after another poor harvest, she insists on immediate payment for her latest novel because of the general distress all around her:

Je compte mes derniers écus de cent sous; je puis bien vivre à crédit, mais les pauvres n'en trouvent pas sur le marché au blé; et le pain est plus cher ici qu'à Paris. Pour le moment j'ai *soixante* bouches *d'extra* sur mon budget. Des gens qui se sont sauvés jusqu'à présent de

la détresse, sont forcés de mendier. Ils ne peuvent s'y résoudre, ils
envoient leurs petits enfants encore propres et bien habillés comme
on l'est dans la Vallée Noire; mais ces petits fichus blancs et ces
petites vestes bien brossées cachent de pauvres estomacs qui ne vivent
que de châtaignes, et qui souvent n'en ont pas depuis deux jours.
(ibid., p. 546)

When one reads these and similar passages in her letters, including
an account of riots in her neighbourhood at the beginning of 1847,
one sees how close to the *Ancien Régime* the age of Louis Philippe
still was from the economic point of view.

As was usual in the pre-industrial age (and France was still a
predominantly agricultural country) the food crisis produced a
general economic crisis. This was the last time in French history
that a depression originated in the agricultural sector and then
spread to trade and industry; it was also the last occasion in time
of peace when food shortages caused serious hardship over wide
areas of the country. Peace-time shortages were gradually ended
in the second half of the century by the revolution in transport
brought about by the coming of railways and steamships.

This economic crisis led to a considerable amount of unemployment in many, though not all, regions of France, especially in
the textile industries. Partly under the influence of a similar
English crisis, it also called a halt to the development of railways
which had been proceeding at a fairly rapid pace in the 1840s;
the reduced demand for rails had obvious effects on the metal
industries. The distress caused by this economic crisis was to have
serious consequences for the régime.

Another source of discontent was the foreign policy pursued by
Louis Philippe. At this period of the century it was the Left in
France that favoured an aggressive foreign policy. The memory of
French might in the Revolutionary and Napoleonic period, the
humiliation of the defeats of 1814 and 1815, the severe terms
imposed by the Allies after Waterloo, the desire, in a reactionary
Europe dominated by Metternich, to come to the aid of the
oppressed peoples in countries like Italy and Poland, all these
combined to make the cautious foreign policy pursued by Louis
Philippe appear inglorious and humiliating in the eyes of the
opposition.

His position was a difficult one. He had been put on the throne
by a revolution, and in the eyes of the autocrats who ruled Austria,
Prussia and Russia 'le roi des barricades' was inevitably an object
of suspicion. It was natural for him to look to begin with for

support from England, the most liberal of all the European powers, but the traditional Anglo-French rivalry which was to persist until the beginning of the twentieth century and the *Entente Cordiale*, kept on coming to the surface throughout the reign though at times there was something approaching an *Entente*. At the very beginning of his reign Louis Philippe had to face serious problems; the July Revolution had sparked off similar liberal and nationalist movements over a considerable part of Europe. The most difficult problem of all was presented by Belgium which under the 1815 settlement had been united with the Kingdom of the Netherlands. In 1830 the Belgians revolted and demanded their independence. Many Frenchmen (and some Belgians) hoped that this would lead to the country's union with France, but annexation would undoubtedly have led to trouble with England which would never have tolerated such a step. Instead Louis Philippe sent Talleyrand to London to negotiate the setting up of an independent state in Belgium and contented himself with marrying off one of his daughters to the new king of that country.

Despite relatively good relations with England in the opening years of his reign, as soon as by the mid-1830s the king had securely established himself on his throne, he sought a rapprochement with the continental powers. Though the attempt to marry his eldest son, the Duc d'Orléans, to a Habsburg archduchess was a failure, he did succeed in forming closer contacts with these autocratic régimes. In 1840, however, when Europe was for months on the brink of war, France found herself completely isolated. The trouble arose over the powerful Pasha of Egypt, Mehemet Ali, whom France supported in his war against his overlord, the Sultan of Turkey. The news that England, Austria, Prussia and Russia had signed an agreement to intervene on the side of Turkey caused fury in France where Thiers, a very bellicose figure, was then in power. This in turn aroused intense nationalist feeling in Germany and inspired 'Die Wacht am Rhein'. Alfred de Musset's retort, 'Le Rhin allemand', opens with an aggressive reminder of French military exploits in that area:

Nous l'avons eu, votre Rhin allemand,
    Il a tenu dans notre verre.
    Un couplet qu'on s'en va chantant
    Efface-t-il la trace altière
Du pied de nos chevaux marqué dans votre sang?

While Thiers was all for pursuing an aggressive policy, Louis Philippe came down as usual on the side of caution. In face of this attitude Thiers resigned and a peaceful solution followed. Once again the king's policy was denounced as weak by the opposition.

Despite continued clashes of interest between the two countries the new foreign minister, Guizot, gradually succeeded in bringing about a better understanding between England and France. This was symbolized in 1843 by the short stay which Queen Victoria made in Louis Philippe's country house, a visit which he returned at Windsor in the following year. However, differences between the two countries which extended as far away as Tahiti came to a head in 1846 over the question of the Spanish marriages. The Queen of Spain and her younger sister were both looking for husbands. Against the opposition of Queen Victoria and Palmerston who did not wish to see an increase of French influence in Spain Louis Philippe managed to get the younger girl married to one of his sons. This infuriated English opinion and marked the end of the *Entente*.

Louis Philippe and Guizot now swung back again to a rapprochement with the Continental autocracies, a policy which was even more unpopular with the opposition. Both were convinced that France must play the role of guardian of the established order in Europe at a time when there were clear signs of the revolts which were to erupt in 1848. This final twist to the foreign policy pursued since the beginning of the reign aroused anger and a feeling of humiliation in France.

The immediate cause of the revolution of 1848 was the political agitation for electoral reform. Guizot as prime minister continued to pursue the same policy of resistance to all change. The campaign for electoral reform began in 1847 with monster banquets in provincial centres, seasoned by inflammatory speeches by the opposition spokesmen amongst whom Lamartine figured prominently. There is a highly ironical account of one of these occasions in a letter of Flaubert written from Rouen in December 1847:

> J'ai pourtant vu dernièrement quelque chose de beau et je suis encore dominé par l'impression grotesque et lamentable que ce spectacle m'a laissée. J'ai assisté à un banquet réformiste! Quel goût! quelle cuisine! quels vins! et quels discours! Rien ne m'a plus donné un absolu mépris du succès, à considérer à quel prix on l'obtient. Je restais froid et avec des nausées de dégoût au milieu de l'enthousiasme patriotique qu'excitaient 'le timon de l'état, l'abîme

où nous courons, l'honneur de notre pavillon, l'ombre de nos étendards, la fraternité des peuples' et autres galettes de cette farine. Jamais les plus belles oeuvres des maîtres n'auront le quart de ces applaudissements-là. Jamais le *Frank* de Musset[1] ne fera pousser les cris d'admiration qui partaient de tous les côtés de la salle aux hurlements vertueux de M. Odilon Barrot[2] et aux éplorements de Mc Crémieux[3] sur l'état de nos finances. Et après cette séance de 9 heures passées devant du dindon froid, du cochon de lait et dans la compagnie de mon serrurier qui me tapait sur l'épaule aux beaux endroits, je m'en suis revenu gelé jusque dans les entrailles. Quelque triste opinion que l'on ait des hommes, l'amertume vous vient au coeur quand s'étalent devant vous des bêtises aussi délirantes, des stupidités aussi échevelées. (*Correspondance*, II. 78–79)

Such a dillusioned account should not, however, leave the impression that provincial centres shared the non-political cynicism of the young Flaubert.

The old king and Guizot apparently began the year 1848 in a quite complacent mood. It is true that behind the scenes there was considerable anxiety among some members of the royal family. The original heir to the throne, the Duc d'Orléans, having been killed in a road accident in 1842, the next in succession to the seventy-four-year old king was his grandson, the Comte de Paris, a boy of nine. One of the boy's uncles wrote in November 1847 a letter full of foreboding:

Il me paraît difficile que, cette année, à la Chambre, le débat ne vienne pas sur cette situation anormale qui a effacé la fiction constitutionnelle et a mis le Roi en cause sur toutes les questions. Il n'y a plus de ministres, leur responsabilité est nulle; tout remonte au Roi. Le Roi est arrivé à cet âge où l'on n'accepte plus les observations. Il est habitué à gouverner, et il aime à montrer que c'est lui qui gouverne. Son immense expérience, son courage et ses grandes qualités font qu'il affronte le danger audacieusement, mais le danger n'existe pas moins. . . . Le pis est que je ne vois pas de remède.

In a speech delivered in the Chamber on 27 January 1848, exactly four weeks before the collapse of the whole régime, Tocqueville predicted the coming upheaval:

Regardez ce qui se passe au sein de ces classes ouvrières, qui aujourd'hui, je le reconnais, sont tranquilles. Il est vrai qu'elles ne

---

1 The hero of *La Coupe et les lèvres, poème dramatique.*
2 Odilon Barrot (1791–1873) was the leader of the left wing royalist opposition.
3 Adolphe Crémieux (1796–1880), a politician considerably further to the left.

sont pas tourmentées par les passions politiques proprement dites au
même degré où elles en ont été tourmentées jadis[1]; mais ne voyez-
vous pas que leurs passions, de politiques, sont devenues sociales? Ne
voyez-vous pas qu'il se répand peu à peu dans leur sein des opinions,
des idées, qui ne vont point seulement à renverser telles lois, tel
ministère, tel gouvernement, mais la société, à l'ébranler sur les
bases sur lesquelles elle repose aujourd'hui? N'écoutez-vous pas ce
qui se dit tous les jours dans leur sein? N'entendez-vous pas qu'on y
répète sans cesse que tout ce qui se trouve au-dessus d'elles est
incapable et indigne de les gouverner; que la division des biens faite
jusqu'à présent dans le monde est injuste; que la propriété repose
sur des bases qui ne sont pas des bases équitables? Et ne croyez-vous
pas que, quand de telles opinions prennent racine, quand elles se
répandent d'une manière presque générale, quand elles descendent
profondément dans les masses, elles doivent amener tôt ou tard, je
ne sais pas quand, je ne sais comment, mais elles doivent amener tôt
ou tard les révolutions les plus redoutables?

Telle est, messieurs, ma conviction profonde; je crois que nous
nous endormons à l'heure qu'il est sur un volcan (*Réclamations.*), j'en
suis profondément convaincu (*Mouvements divers.*) (*Oeuvres complètes,*
I. ii. p. 372)

Despite the scepticism which these predictions aroused, they were
twice to be fully realized in Paris, first in 1848 and then again in
the Commune of 1871.

As the crowning effort in the campaign for electoral reform a
monster banquet was arranged for 22 February in Paris. After
long negotiations both the government and the opposition – the
latter being afraid of things going too far – agreed to it being called
off. However, its place was taken by a mass demonstration which
was banned by the government. On the 23rd barricades appeared
once again in the streets of Paris. Louis Philippe then dismissed
Guizot and tried to get a more liberal government formed; but
it was too late. What finally precipitated the revolution was that
on the evening of that day, owing to a misunderstanding, troops
opened fire on the crowds outside the Foreign Ministry and caused
many casualties, several of them fatal. On the next day (24
February) Paris was covered with barricades. At this critical stage
the *Garde Nationale* suddenly abandoned the king and went over
to the insurgents. 'Le roi Louis-Philippe,' as a contemporary put
it, 'ne comptait pas sur l'armée. Il ne s'appuyait que sur la
bourgeoisie, sur la classe moyenne; il croyait à la garde nationale,
le malheureux, et c'est par là que tout a croulé.' (Prosper Ménière,

[1] In the 1830s.

Mémoires, p. 276.) At this point Louis Philippe lost his nerve and abdicated in favour of his grandson. His daughter-in-law, a German princess, tried vainly to persuade the Chamber to proclaim her son, the Comte de Paris, king. Instead a provisional government was set up at the Hôtel de Ville and the Republic proclaimed.

Louis Philippe and his family made their way, not without difficulty, to the Channel coast and found refuge once again in England. He died two years later at Claremont in Surrey. A restoration of the monarchy in France was to remain a serious possibility for several decades, but though there is still in the 1970s an Orleanist claimant to the throne in the person of another Comte de Paris, after a century of republican institutions his prospects do not appear bright.

2
Second Republic, Second Empire and the Beginnings of the Third Republic (1848-1879)

The three decades between the Revolution of 1848 and the final establishment of the Third Republic, which was to last until Hitler's invasion of France in 1940, were a period of considerable political instability. The Second Republic, proclaimed in Paris in February 1848, lasted on paper until December 1852 when Louis Napoleon assumed the title of Emperor; but it had really died a year earlier when he carried out his successful *coup d'état* which had been foreshadowed from the moment of his election as President in December 1848. Indeed as a progressive force bringing with it promise of radical reforms the Republic may be said to have died in the bloodbath of 'les journées de Juin', only four months after its proclamation.

The Second Empire, it is true, was to last for nearly eighteen years, for as long as the July Monarchy; but though for a considerable period of its existence opposition to it was driven underground, its enemies emerged with increasing strength in the 1860s and not a finger was raised in defence of the régime when it collapsed ignominiously after the Emperor's surrender at Sedan. The proclamation of the Third Republic on 4 September 1870 was immediately followed by the siege of Paris, military defeat and the appalling civil war of the Commune. The new régime led a very shaky existence during most of the seventies. During all these years France lived on the very verge of a monarchist restoration; even when in 1875 constitutional laws were passed containing the words 'le Président de la République', what the majority in the National Assembly intended was a monarchist constitution. In these years the candidate for the throne supported by the Legitimists and Orleanists, the Comte de Chambord ('Henri V'), had a rival in the Bonapartist claimant, the Prince Imperial, until he lost his life in 1879 while serving in the British

83

army in a war against the Zulus. Even after the Republicans had won a clear majority in the elections to the *Chambre des Députés* in 1876, they still had to face a monarchist President and a Senate with a monarchist majority; a determined attempt was made by their opponents to cancel out their electoral victory. It was not indeed until 1879 that the Republicans secured a majority in the Senate and were able to elect a republican President; only then did 'la République des Ducs' give way to the 'la République des Républicains'.

Social and economic conditions (1848-1879)

These three decades, at any rate from the early 1850s onwards, saw a rapid transformation in the economic field. All over Western Europe, down to the Great Depression which began in 1873, but which affected France more slowly than England and Germany, a period of rapid expansion followed on the period of low prices and relative stagnation of the previous decades. In these years France moved forward in the economic field more rapidly than in any period before the transformation which began in the 1950s. It is true that there were crises and setbacks in these years; there were periods of recession starting in 1857 and 1867, and inevitably the war with Prussia and the Commune which followed played havoc with the French economy; but she recovered from these disasters with a speed which astonished the world. It is also the case that as early as the mid-1870s her agriculture began to suffer from a fall in prices and other troubles, but other sectors of the economy continued to prosper until 1882. It was only after this date that France entered upon a period of economic stagnation which was to last until nearly the end of the century.

Population
These years of economic expansion were accompanied by a decided slackening in the rate of increase of her population. Comparisons between the different censuses from 1846 to 1881 are made rather difficult by the annexation of Savoy and Nice in 1860 and the loss of Alsace-Lorraine in 1871, but the following figures show how very slowly her population was increasing:

	Total	*Increase*
1846	35,402,000	
1851	35,783,000	381,000

	Total	Increase
1856	36,039,000	256,000
1861	37,386,000	1,347,000
1866	38,067,000	681,000
1872	36,103,000	–
1876	36,906,000	803,000
1881	37,672,000	766,000

Compared with the increase of 1,170,000 in the period 1841–1846, the slow growth of the periods 1846–1851 and 1851–1856 marks a turning point in the demographic history of France, the beginning of a phase of slow increase in population or even stagnation which was to last right into the 1940s. In contrast, between 1851 and 1881 the population of Great Britain was rising very rapidly, from roughly 20 to 29 millions – an increase of 9 millions against only two in France.

By the 1860s alarm was beginning to be expressed at this slackening in the rate of increase of the population especially given a comparatively small amount of emigration – an alarm which arose out of its inevitable political and military consequences. For instance, one commentator wrote gloomily on the eve of the Franco–Prussian War:

> ... C'est à la nation la plus nombreuse qu'appartient inévitablement l'ascendant militaire et politique avec tous les avantages matériels et moraux qui en découlent. Il faut donc considérer comme *absolument chimérique* tout projet et toute espérance de conserver à la France son rang relatif dans le monde, si ces espérances, ces projets, ne prennent pas pour point de départ cette maxime: *le nombre des Français doit s'augmenter assez rapidement pour maintenir un certain équilibre entre notre puissance et celle des autres grandes nations de la terre.*
>
> Or, quarante millions de Français, concentrés sur notre territoire, ne sont guère suffisants pour faire équilibre aux cinquante et un millions d'Allemands que la Prusse réunira peut-être sur notre frontière, et à la population croissante de la Russie dans un avenir un peu plus éloigné; mais combien ce chiffre de quarante millions devient insignifiant, si nous faisons le compte des individus de langue anglaise qui couvriront le globe, quand les États-Unis auront atteint leur complet développement, et quand les États anglais de l'Océanie seront en pleine prospérité! (Prévost-Paradol, *La France nouvelle*, pp. 413–414)

The cry was repeated by various newspapers and even in a speech by Louis Napoleon, but no action was taken to deal with the problem.

As might be expected in a period of considerable economic expansion a number of French cities increased their population fairly rapidly. A greatly enlarged Paris (from 1860 onwards it had twenty *arrondissements* instead of twelve) saw its population more than double in these years. It rose from 1,053,000 in 1851 to 2,269,000 in 1881. Some of the provincial cities which had been relatively large at the beginning of the century were now expanding rapidly:

	1851	1881
Marseilles	195,300	360,100
Lyons	177,200	376,600
Bordeaux	130,900	221,300
Lille	75,800	178,100
Toulouse	93,400	140,300

Again some smaller towns were also growing very fast:

Saint-Etienne	56,000	123,800
Le Havre	29,000	105,900
Reims	45,800	93,800
Roubaix	34,700	91,800

On the other hand the growth of the larger French towns was very varied; it was sometimes relatively slow:

Rouen	100,300	105,900
Nantes	96,400	124,300
Amiens	52,100	74,200
Nîmes	53,600	63,600

Moreover one must make the inevitable comparison with what was happening in Britain. Between 1851 and 1881 the population of Birmingham shot up from 233,000 to 401,000 and that of Liverpool from 376,000 to 553,000, while Sheffield more than doubled its population, which rose from 135,000 to 285,000. In 1881 not only Birmingham and Liverpool, but Glasgow and Manchester were larger than either Lyons or Marseilles.

A national railway system

Perhaps the most important step forward in France in these years was the creation of a national railway system. This undoubtedly gave the impetus for the boom of the 1850s, stimulated the iron and steel industry and opened up the country to further economic progress, not only in trade and industry, but also in the long run in agriculture, which still remained of the highest importance

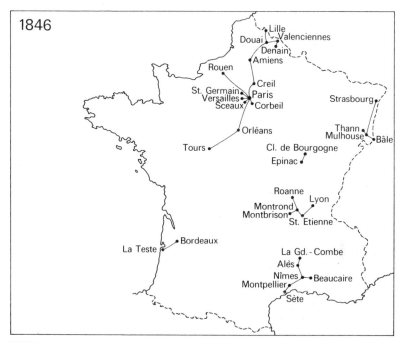

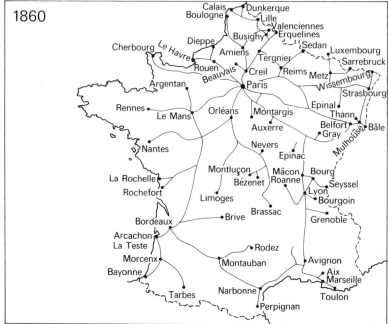

The spread of railways in France 1846–1860.

since roughly half the male active population was employed in it. While the railway network continued to expand under the Third Republic, it was during the Second Empire that the main lines were completed and put into operation and that a second network to serve the smaller towns was started. In the twenty years down to 1870 France multiplied the lines open to traffic by nearly six and more or less made up for her slow start under Louis Philippe. She now had some 17,500 km of railways in operation against 19,500 in Germany and 24,500 in the United Kingdom. By 1880 this figure had been raised to some 24,000 km. What is more, French engineers and capital made a big contribution to railway construction in other countries on the Continent, from Spain to as far away as Russia.

In France the State played a large part in the construction and running of the railways even though in the 1840s Parliament had turned down proposals for nationalization (one of these was eloquently supported by Lamartine). Other public works were undertaken during the Second Empire; roads were improved – not only the main roads, but also local roads which were important for getting agricultural produce to the railways. The most famous public works of the period were carried out in the cities – not only in Paris, though the schemes pushed through there by Baron Haussmann are the best known, but also in many provincial centres. This modernization involved not merely the construction of new streets and the buildings that went with them, but also the provision of a proper water supply and an efficient system of sewage disposal to meet the growing needs of the expanding towns and cities.

Banking and investment

These years also saw the establishment of a modern banking system. In them were founded the joint stock banks (nationalized in 1945) in whose branches we change our travellers' cheques: the *Comptoir National d'Escompte de Paris*, incorporated in 1854, the *Crédit Lyonnais* established in 1863 and the *Société Générale*, which dates from 1864. Another well-known institution, the investment bank known as the *Banque de Paris et des Pays-Bas*, was founded by amalgamation in 1872. Down to 1867 there were all sorts of legal restrictions on the formation of joint stock companies (*sociétés anonymes*); when these were removed, a large increase in their number quickly followed. Although in the economic field France was rapidly being overhauled by Germany, she still remained in

The Crédit Lyonnais, Paris.

many ways a leader on the Continent, and her innovations in the sphere of banking, particularly those introduced during the Second Empire, served in many ways as a model for the rest of Europe.

In this period France's wealth enabled her to rival England in the field of foreign investments. Her capital exports – whether in the form of investments in government loans or in such public works as railways – rose rapidly from 1851 onwards; perhaps as much as a third of French savings went abroad in the period 1851–1880. Although after 1866 French imports exceeded exports, her income from her foreign investments helped to finance the unfavourable balance of trade as did the growth of the tourist industry, which had been fostered by the coming of railways and steamships.

Indeed henceforth the income from foreign investments generally equalled or even exceeded the total of new investments made abroad. Although this rush to invest money in foreign countries was to slacken off in the last two decades of the nineteenth century, down to 1914 France continued to pour money into this form of investment. It has often been argued that the money would have been much better invested at home; apart from the fact that a great deal of it was never seen again, the relatively slow economic development of France down to 1914 could well be attributed to too much capital going abroad. Industry, so the argument runs, was starved of capital while banks and the private investor preferred to seek abroad a higher rate of interest than was available at home. It can be said on the other side that industry made little use of the generally low rates of interest which obtained in France.

Industry

Though there were considerable developments in French industry in these three decades, the great bulk of French workers continued to be employed in small establishments. Most of the Paris workers who fought in the Commune were not factory workers. While domestic industry was slowly dying out in most of the textile industries, large-scale industry was chiefly confined to a relatively small number of centres in the provinces.

The production of coal, the basis of industrial power in the nineteenth century, continued to increase rapidly; some $4\frac{1}{2}$ million tons in 1851, it had doubled by 1861 and doubled again by 1881. Yet France had to import half as much again as she produced in order to meet the demand, and her own output of just

Horse-drawn coal truck and miners at work.

under 20 million tons in 1881 has to be compared with the British output of 160 million. Moreover the dearness of coal continued to be a serious handicap for French industry. 'Mon ami, l'ingénieur,' Taine noted on a visit to Manchester, 'me dit que mille kilos de houille coûtent ici de 5 à 8 shillings; à Paris, 23 francs; à Roubaix, de 15 à 18; dans les Vosges, de 34 à 40.' (*Notes sur l'Angleterre*, p. 298) In contrast France is rich in iron ore deposits. Despite the loss of part of the Lorraine field in 1871, French output was roughly doubled in the period 1851–1881, though it was only

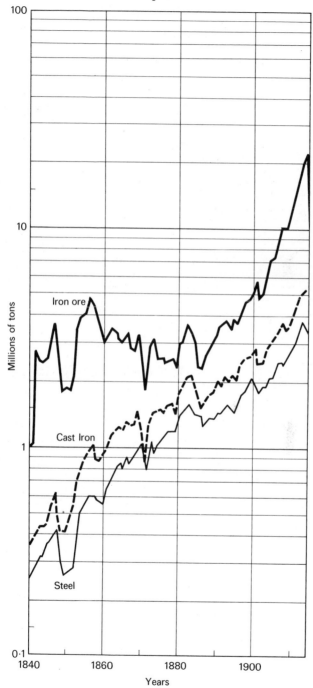

Production of iron ore, cast iron and steel, 1840–1914.

after 1900 that she became one of the largest producers of iron ore in the world.

The number of steam engines employed in industry was multiplied eight times between 1850 and 1880. Coke gradually replaced

La Forge (engraving).

charcoal in the smelting of iron and blast-furnaces became much larger. In the 1860s the Bessemer converter was introduced from England and this led to a rapid growth in the production of steel, which was now increasingly used to replace iron in the manufacture of rails. Further progress followed from the invention of the alternative open-hearth method of making steel by a Frenchman, Pierre Martin (1824–1915), and the German, Werner von Siemens. The increasing concentration of the iron and steel industry led to the founding in 1864 of the *Comité des Forges*, which remained a powerful employers' association down to 1940. It was characteristic of the new importance of heavy industry that Eugène Schneider, the owner of the famous works at Le Creusot, which by the late 1860s employed some 10,000 men, and also the first president of this employers' federation, should have been president of the *Corps Législatif* in the closing years of the Second Empire.

At this stage in the century France's cotton industry was the largest on the Continent. While it suffered severely from the shortage of its raw material during the American Civil War, it employed in normal times some 400,000 workers. It was mainly concentrated in three centres – Mulhouse, Normandy and the Département du Nord. Mulhouse, the most progressive of these, was lost along with Alsace in 1871, but some of the industry moved over the frontier into the Département des Vosges, and by the middle of the 1870s France's consumption of raw cotton had reached a higher figure than during the Second Empire, though after 1876 this figure was not to be exceeded until the 1890s. In the woollen industry small workshops continued to function alongside large factories with modern machinery; if the French cotton industry was smaller than the English, in this period the French woollen and worsted industry was about the same size as in England. The silk industry, mainly centred in Lyons, did not go over to power-driven machinery because of the nature of its raw material. Supplies of this proved increasingly difficult to secure because the number of silkworms raised in the Rhone valley in this period was much reduced by epidemics, and an increasing amount of raw silk had to be imported from the Far East. The Lyons industry produced mainly luxury goods and tended to be

The Pont Neuf in 1860.

undercut by foreign manufacturers who produced cheaper wares. However, it exported a considerable proportion of its products, England being its best customer.

Working conditions

Factory workers still remained a small minority in these years. If domestic industry was in rapid decline, it was still important in a number of regions, and a great many industrial workers continued to be employed in small workshops where a great variety of luxury goods were produced. This was true of Paris as well as of provincial towns. A working class movement was still in an embryonic state. In the 1850s, after Louis Napoleon's *coup d'état*, the workers were very much held down; trade unions were illegal and so were strikes. In the 1860s, it is true, the Emperor relaxed some of these laws; the result was a considerable amount of social unrest and some large-scale strikes, particularly in the last days of the declining Empire. For instance, in 1870 there was a big strike at Le Creusot. Then came the Paris Commune and its bloody repression. The movement lost many of its leaders, either through death or exile.

In 1872, in the reaction which followed the Commune, a law aimed at the First International was passed punishing with imprisonment members of any international organization having as its aim to 'provoquer à la suspension du travail, à l'abolition du droit de propriété, de la famille, de la patrie, de la religion ou du libre exercice des cultes'. Although some small trade unions did exist, it was not until 1884 that they were finally legalized, and the political movement for Socialism did not begin to secure a wide following until the 1880s.

Very long hours continued to be worked in industry. In March 1848 a decree of the provisional government reduced the working day to ten hours in Paris and eleven in the provinces. In September, after the crushing of the June insurrection, the Constituent Assembly voted a somewhat vague law which laid down a higher maximum of twelve hours. In practice there was a slight trend during the Second Empire towards a ten-hour working day, but conditions varied enormously and hours of work, for women and children as well as men, were generally very long. In the notes which he took during a visit to Lancashire in the early 1860s Taine makes a comparison between French and English factory workers which takes us right back into the industrial atmosphere of the period:

Des manufacturiers français me disent que chez nous l'ouvrier travaille parfaitement bien pendant la première heure, moins bien la seconde, encore moins bien la troisième, et ainsi de suite en diminuant, en sorte que, pendant la dernière heure, il ne fait plus rien de bon. Sa force musculaire fléchit, et surtout son attention se relâche. – Ici, au contraire, l'ouvrier travaille aussi bien pendant la dernière heure que pendant la première. D'ailleurs sa journée n'est que de dix heures et non de douze, comme celle de l'ouvrier français. – Par suite de cette attention plus soutenue, l'Anglais peut mener plus d'ouvrage. Chez Shaw, pour conduire 2,400 broches, il suffit d'un homme et de deux enfants; en France, il faut deux hommes et trois, quatre enfants, quelquefois davantage. En revanche, en certaines qualités, l'ouvrier français est plus adroit; par exemple, dans les Vosges, les tisserands font les étoffes beaucoup plus correctes et jolies. (*Notes sur l' Angleterre*, p. 305)

The only factory act passed during this period, in 1874, while it set up an inspectorate to see that it was enforced, did not represent a big step forward, as can be seen from its main provisions:

ART. 2. – Les enfants ne pourront être employés par des patrons ni être admis dans les manufactures, usines, ateliers ou chantiers avant l'âge de douze ans révolus.

Ils pourront être toutefois employés à l'âge de dix ans révolus dans les industries spécialement déterminées par un règlement d'administration publique rendu sur l'avis conforme de la commission supérieure ci-dessous instituée.

ART. 3. – Les enfants, jusqu'à l'âge de douze ans révolus, ne pourront être assujettis à une durée de travail de plus de six heures par jour, divisée par un repos.

A partir de douze ans, ils ne pourront être employés plus de douze heures par jour, divisées par des repos.

ART. 4. – Les enfants ne pourront être employés à aucun travail de nuit jusqu'à l'âge de seize ans révolus.

La même interdiction est appliquée à l'emploi des filles mineures de seize à vingt-et-un ans, mais seulement dans les usines et manufactures.

ART. 7. – Aucun enfant ne peut être admis dans les travaux souterrains des mines, minières et carrières avant l'âge de douze ans révolus. Les filles et les femmes ne peuvent être admises dans ces travaux.

Although it was not published until 1885, Zola's *Germinal* portrays events during the Second Empire when women still worked down the pit. It is clear from this factory act that an enormous amount still remained to be done to ensure safe and healthy working conditions for those employed in industry.

Trade

Trade with foreign countries played a relatively small part in the French economy during the nineteenth century. We have seen how in most years from 1867 onwards France had an unfavourable trade balance, which was covered by her income from foreign investments, from tourism and from various invisible earnings. Shipbuilding was handicapped by the distance from the ports to the deposits of coal and iron. Although the total of exports and imports rose by more than four times between 1851 and 1879, France had only a relatively small overseas trade and no bulky exports like coal, so that she had no need of a large merchant navy. Throughout the period steamships were coming slowly into use, and regular passenger services were established between France and North America and other parts of the world. Among French ports Marseilles grew in striking fashion. Taine was quite staggered by its growth when he revisited it in 1863, though it should be said that the forecast of half a million inhabitants was not realized until after 1900:

> Marseille est une grande, une énorme ville; deux cent cinquante mille habitants; on dit qu'elle en aura cinq cent mille lorsque le canal de Suez sera achevé. Elle croît tous les jours, on bâtit, on perce partout, on abat des pans de collines, on fait de nouveaux ports; je l'ai vue, il y a quatre ans, c'est à ne pas la reconnaître. Même changement qu'à Paris: maisons monumentales, sculptées, toutes neuves et splendides, à sept étages, beaucoup plus vastes et magnifiques qu'à Paris; je n'en ai vu de pareilles qu'à Londres.
> (*Carnets de voyage 1863–1865*, pp. 110–111)

Even so, throughout these years the great majority of ships entering French ports were foreign – mainly, of course, British. The total tonnage of the British merchant navy was roughly six times as large as that of the French.

There are no statistics to show how internal trade developed in these years, but the advent of a railway network as well as better roads and canals, the introduction of the electric telegraph which came into use in Europe in the 1850s and in intercontinental communications in the 1860s, and the growth of towns and cities – all these factors helped to create a national, indeed an international market in place of the purely local or regional market. As wholesale and retail trade expanded, more and more people came to be employed in this sector of the economy, from the big merchant down to the corner shopkeeper. One significant development in this period was the emergence of department

The main staircase in the *Bon Marché*.

stores (*grands magasins*) in Paris. These were based on new sales
methods; they gradually offered a wider and wider variety of
goods, with marked prices to replace the traditional haggling
between tradesman and customer. Thanks to their large turnover,
increased by advertising, they could undercut their smaller rivals
in the retail trade, as they were able to survive with smaller profit
margins. The shops we know today were mostly in existence by
1870. The *Bon Marché*, for instance, was founded in 1852 and the
Louvre three years later; the *Printemps* followed in 1865 and the
Samaritaine in 1869 (the *Galeries Lafayette* came much later, in
1895). The struggle between the department store and the smaller
retailers is vividly described in one of Zola's novels in the *Rougon-
Macquart* series – *Au Bonheur des Dames*, published in 1883. The
novel which is set in the period of the Second Empire relates the
story of a *vendeuse* who ends by marrying her boss, the founder of
Au Bonheur des Dames. He explains to a sceptical financier how in
running a successful department store everything turns on a rapid
renewal of the capital through ever-increasing sales:

> Vous entendez, monsieur le baron, toute la mécanique est là. C'est
> bien simple, mais il fallait le trouver. Nous n'avons pas besoin d'un
> gros roulement de fonds. Notre effort unique est de nous débarrasser

très vite de la marchandise achetée, pour la remplacer par d'autre, ce qui fait rendre au capital autant de fois son intérêt. De cette manière, nous pouvons nous contenter d'un petit bénéfice, comme nos frais généraux s'élèvent au chiffre énorme de seize pour cent et que nous ne prélevons guère sur les objets que vingt pour cent de gain, c'est donc un bénéfice de quatre pour cent au plus ; seulement, cela finira par faire des millions, lorsqu'on opérera sur des quantités de marchandises considérables et sans cesse renouvelées. . . .

The rest of his explanation of the workings of the system is given in indirect speech:

Ce fut d'abord la puissance décuplée de l'entassement, toutes les marchandises accumulées sur un point, se soutenant et se poussant ; jamais de chômage ; toujours l'article de la saison était là, et, de comptoir en comptoir, la cliente se trouvait prise, achetait ici l'étoffe, plus loin le fil, ailleurs le manteau, s'habillait, puis tombait dans des rencontres imprévues, cédait au besoin de l'inutile et du joli. Ensuite, il célébra la marque en chiffres connus. La grande révolution des nouveautés partait de cette trouvaille. Si l'ancien commerce, le petit commerce agonisait, c'était qu'il ne pouvait soutenir la lutte des bas prix, engagée par la marque. Maintenant, la concurrence avait lieu sous les yeux mêmes du public, une promenade aux étalages établissait les prix, chaque magasin baissait, se contentait du plus léger bénéfice possible ; aucune tricherie, pas de coup de fortune longtemps médité sur un tissu vendu le double de sa valeur, mais des opérations courantes, un tant pour cent régulier prélevé sur tous les articles, la fortune mise dans le bon fonctionnement d'une vente, d'autant plus large qu'elle se faisait au grand jour. N'était-ce pas une création étonnante ? (*Oeuvres complètes*, IV. 765–766)

In the novel all the small tradesmen of the neighbourhood are ruined by the department store; in real life its spread from Paris to the provinces and the creation of the chain-store, although they have made life increasingly difficult for the *petits commerçants*, have not yet by any means driven them out of business.

Agriculture

It was, however, agriculture which in our period continued to be by far the most important sector of the French economy. Here too various changes were at work. If in these years towns were expanding, some of them fairly rapidly, while the total population was increasing only slowly, there must have been a steady drift from the country into the towns. Such agricultural statistics as are available for nineteenth-century France are full of defects, which

J. F. Millet: *La Fenaison* ('The Hay Harvest').

make them very difficult to interpret correctly, but it would seem that the main movement off the land in this period was less among the smaller peasant landowners than among the farm servants and day labourers. Rural industry, once so important, was now in rapid decline. In some regions indeed a labour shortage began to develop; this encouraged the use of machinery in agriculture and also led to the immigration, mainly for seasonal work, of Belgians, Spaniards and Italians. The increased use of machinery and of artificial fertilizers led to some increase in output.

French agriculture had its problems in these years. The phylloxera, an insect accidentally imported from America, began to attack French vines in the 1860s and from 1879 to 1890 threatened to put paid to production of wine in France; it is estimated that between 1875 and 1879 the production of wine fell by over two-thirds. Prices of agricultural products fluctuated fairly sharply in these years. After the grain shortages and high prices of 1846 and 1847 wheat prices (France was the largest producer in Europe after Russia) fell for several years and, owing to further shortages which

Gustave Courbet: *L'enterrement à Ornans*.

caused considerable embarrassment to Louis Napoleon and his government, they rose steeply in the mid-1850s. After falling again, they tended to rise fairly steadily until 1874. In 1875 came a sharp fall, and although prices recovered down to 1882, there then set in a period of low prices, which lasted until they began to pick up again in 1896. Meat prices, after rising steeply from 1852 onwards, fell sharply in 1875. One can conclude then that round about 1880 French agriculture moved into a period of depression which was to last until 1896. The basic cause would seem to have been the competition from the exports of foreign countries, particularly North America, which was the result of the advent of railways and steamships. This was to lead to demands for protective tariffs on agricultural products.

As before, agriculture continued to be carried on in a relatively small minority of large farms, a larger number of medium ones and, as small peasant landowners continued to be very numerous, in a very large number of small undertakings, run by the peasant and his family without hired labour. In many regions *metayage* was gradually being replaced by tenancies for which a money rent was paid. Better local roads and, above all, the railways had brought great numbers of peasants out of the traditional subsistence agriculture in which they marketed little or none of their produce. Now they exchanged a great part of their products for those of industry. The general standard of living on the land was slowly rising, though, as we have seen, agriculture met with decided setbacks in this period and worse was to follow down to nearly the end of the century.

Second Republic

Although in 1848 the Chartist movement fizzled out in England, this year saw a series of revolutions over a considerable area of Europe. The proclamation of the Republic in Paris increased the fears of autocratic rulers that the French would imitate the example of the First Republic and seek to liberate the oppressed peoples of Europe from their oppressors. Despite considerable pressure from the extremists to pursue such a policy one of the first acts of Lamartine who occupied the post of foreign minister in the provisional government was to seek to reassure the other European powers that France had no intention of exporting its revolution.

The early phases of the revolution in France, down to June 1848, were dominated, at any rate in Paris, by the politically active working classes, complete with red flag. To the upper classes of society red revolution seemed to have arrived. Tocqueville offers a vivid picture of the situation on 25 February:

> Je passai tout l'après-midi à me promener dans Paris. Deux choses me frappèrent surtout ce jour-là: la première, ce fut le caractère, je ne dirai pas principalement, mais uniquement et exclusivement populaire de la révolution qui venait de s'accomplir; la toute-puissance qu'elle avait donnée au peuple proprement dit, c'est-à-dire aux classes qui travaillent de leurs mains, sur toutes les autres. La seconde, ce fut le peu de passion haineuse et même, à dire vrai, de passions vives quelconques que faisait voir dans ce premier moment ce bas peuple devenu tout à coup seul maître du pouvoir.
>
> Quoique les classes ouvrières eussent souvent joué le principal rôle dans les événements de la première République, elles n'avaient jamais été les conductrices et les seules maîtresses de l'État, ni en fait, ni en droit; la Convention ne contenait peut-être pas un seul homme du peuple; elle était remplie de bourgeois et de lettrés. La guerre entre la Montagne et la Gironde fut conduite, de part et d'autre, par des membres de la bourgeoisie, et le triomphe de la première ne fit jamais descendre la puissance dans les seules mains du peuple. La révolution de Juillet avait été faite par le peuple, mais la classe moyenne qui l'avait suscitée et conduite, en avait recueilli les principaux fruits. La révolution de Février, au contraire, semblait faite entièrement en dehors de la bourgeoisie et contre elle. (*Souvenirs*, pp. 91–92)

This situation was not, however, to last more than a bare four months.

The Left was naturally filled with enthusiasm at the dramatic change which had taken place. Writing on 8 March from Nohant to which she had returned from Paris to help her friends to 'révolutionner le Berry qui est bien engourdi', George Sand speaks in lyrical terms of the coming of the Republic:

> Vive la république! Quel rêve, quel enthousiasme et en même temps quelle tenue, quel ordre à Paris! J'en arrive, j'y ai couru, j'ai vu s'ouvrir les dernières barricades sous mes pieds. J'ai vu le peuple grand, sublime, naïf, généreux, le peuple français réuni au coeur de la France, au coeur du monde, le plus admirable peuple de l'univers. J'ai passé bien des nuits sans dormir, bien des jours sans m'asseoir. On est fou, on est ivre, on est heureux de s'être endormi dans la fange et de se réveiller dans les cieux. Que tout ce qui vous entoure ait courage et confiance. La république est conquise, elle est assurée, nous y périrons tous plutôt que de la lâcher. (*Correspondance*, VIII. 329–331)

The first result of the revolution was naturally to intensify the economic depression from which France was suffering. Trade was brought almost to a standstill; unemployment rose. On the Bourse stocks and shares fell, and there was a run on the banks. On the other hand to enthusiastic supporters of the revolution the millennium seemed just around the corner, not only in France itself, but all over Europe, wherever the peoples had risen against their oppressors. Memories of the first Revolution played a considerable part in the Paris of these early weeks of the new régime; clubs on the model of those of 1789 and the following years proliferated, and even women attempted for the first time to play a political role. The stamp duty on newspapers was abolished, and with complete freedom of the press a flood of new papers and of pamphlets were published.

The provisional government proclaimed at the Hôtel de Ville represented a compromise between moderates and radicals, between those who, like Lamartine, were supporters of a democratic republic and those who, like Louis Blanc, saw in the revolution the means of transforming the economic and social life of France on more or less socialist lines.

From the very beginning there was a clash on the question of the flag of the Republic. On 25 February at the Hôtel de Ville the extremists demanded the adoption of the red flag, but by one of his dazzling rhetorical improvisations Lamartine, who at this period was the outstanding figure in the government, persuaded the crowd to retain the *tricolore* flag. Although the majority of the members of the government were very far from being socialists, they were compelled by the pressure of the Paris masses to introduce certain social reforms. The chief of these were decrees limiting the working day in Paris to 10 hours and 11 in the provinces, and to recognize the right to work. The serious unemployment problem led to the setting up of the so-called *Ateliers nationaux*. This certainly represented a considerable change in government attitudes to the problem of unemployment since under the July Monarchy the State, in accordance with the principle of *laissez-faire*, had refused to intervene in such matters. However, the *Ateliers nationaux* were a mere travesty of the producers' co-operatives advocated by Louis Blanc in *De l'organisation du travail*. The unemployed, many of whom were skilled artisans from the luxury trades for which Paris had an international reputation, were set to work on completely unproductive tasks such as levelling the Champ de Mars.

Faced with all manner of financial problems, the provisional government took a step which was unlikely to endear it to French taxpayers; it raised direct taxes by 45 per cent. In the meantime it had decreed elections to a Constituent Assembly for 9 April, elections to be based for the first time on universal manhood suffrage. At one stroke the number of electors was suddenly raised from some 240,000 to over 9 million. The extreme radicals were not at all anxious for immediate elections as they guessed only too correctly what the outcome would be in a country which was still overwhelmingly agricultural and where a large part of the electorate was still illiterate. There was obviously a yawning gap between the revolutionary sentiments of the more radical section of the population of Paris and the outlook of the provinces. It was consciousness of this which caused George Sand to pen (anonymously) the startling opening paragraph of the official *Bulletin de la République* for 15 April:

> Citoyens,
> Nous n'avons pu passer du régime de la corruption au régime du droit dans un jour, dans une heure. Une heure d'inspiration et d'héroïsme a suffi au peuple pour consacrer le principe de la vérité. Mais dix-huit ans de mensonge opposent au régime de la vérité des obstacles qu'un souffle ne renverse pas; les élections, si elles ne font pas triompher la vérité sociale, si elles sont l'expression des intérêts d'une caste, arrachée à la confiante loyauté du peuple, les élections, qui devraient être le salut de la République, seront sa perte, il n'en faut pas douter. Il n'y aurait alors qu'une voie de salut pour le

peuple qui a fait les barricades, ce serait de manifester une seconde fois sa volonté, et d'ajourner les decisions d'une fausse représentation nationale.

The hint of a second revolution if the elections turned out badly for the radicals created something of a stir.

Finally sufficient pressure was brought to bear on the government to make it postpone the elections for a fortnight, though this was unlikely to make any real difference to the result. In the meantime all sorts of socialist demands were being put forward in the Paris clubs, for the nationalization of the *Banque de France*, insurance companies, the mines, railways and canals.

When the elections finally took place on 23 April, they produced a crushing defeat for the extreme Left. It won only about 100 seats out of the 876 in the Constituent Assembly which consisted overwhelmingly of moderate Republicans, Orleanists and Legitimists. When it met on 4 May, the provisional government resigned and was replaced by a 'commission exécutive' of five members of whom Lamartine, then at the height of his popularity, was one. Characteristically Louis Blanc and the only manual worker in the provisional government, Albert, were not elected to this body.

Inevitably the extremists in Paris were scarcely satisfied with this situation. On 15 May, on the pretext of presenting a petition in favour of the independence of Poland, a large-scale demonstration finished up by invading the assembly and declaring its dissolution. An attempt was then made to set up a new provisional government at the Hôtel de Ville, but this was foiled and the leaders arrested. A vivid description of the atmosphere in Paris at the moment when he returned from his electoral campaign in Normandy is furnished by Tocqueville:

Je trouvai dans cette ville cent mille ouvriers armés, enrégimentés, sans ouvrage, mourant de faim, mais l'esprit repu de théories vaines et d'espérances chimériques. J'y vis la société coupée en deux: ceux qui ne possédaient rien, unis dans une convoitise commune; ceux qui possédaient quelque chose, dans une commune angoisse. Plus de liens, plus de sympathies entre ces deux grandes classes, partout l'idée d'une lutte inévitable et voisine. Déjà les bourgeois et le peuple, car ces anciens noms de guerre avaient été repris, en étaient venus aux mains avec des fortunes contraires, à Rouen et à Limoges. A Paris il ne se passait guère de jours sans que les propriétaires ne fussent atteints ou menacés soit dans leur capital, soit dans leurs revenus; tantôt on voulait qu'ils fissent travailler sans vendre, tantôt qu'ils déchargeassent leurs locataires du prix des loyers, sans avoir eux-mêmes d'autres revenus pour vivre. . . .

Cependant un sombre désespoir s'était emparé de cette bourgeoisie ainsi opprimée et menacée, et ce désespoir se tournait insensiblement en courage. J'avais toujours cru qu'il ne fallait pas espérer de régler par degrés et en paix le mouvement de la révolution de Février, et qu'il ne serait arrêté que tout à coup par une grande bataille livrée dans Paris. Je l'avais dit dès le lendemain du 24 février; ce que je vis alors me persuada que non seulement cette bataille était en effet inévitable, mais que le moment en était proche, et qu'il était à désirer qu'on saisît la première occasion de la livrer. (*Souvenirs*, pp. 117–118)

The immediate cause of the clash was the closing of the *Ateliers nationaux*.

Swollen by an influx of unemployed provincials, the total number of men on their pay-roll exceeded in the end 100,000 which represented a heavy drain on the Treasury. In June the Assembly voted to abolish them. On 22 June a decree was issued whereby bachelors between the ages of 18 and 25 were offered a choice between dismissal or joining the army; the rest, if they could not find work privately in Paris, were to be employed on public works in the provinces.

The result was the *Journées de Juin*. On 23 June, the day after the issue of the decree, barricades were once again set up in the streets of Paris and fierce fighting continued until the 26th. The insurrection was quite unplanned; it is clear that it was a completely spontaneous rising. In view of the serious situation the Assembly gave full powers to the Minister of War, General Cavaignac, who proceeded to suppress the insurrection in the most ruthless manner, aided by troops and *gardes nationaux* brought in from the provinces, thanks to the newly built railways. Thousands were killed in the street fighting; some 15,000 were arrested of whom over 4,000 were deported, mostly to Algeria. Renan, then a student in Paris, offers in a letter to his sister a vivid account of the scene in the streets of Paris just after the fighting had ended:

Dans la rue Saint-Martin, dans la rue Saint-Antoine et dans la partie de la rue Saint-Jacques qui s'étend du Panthéon jusqu'aux quais, pas une maison qui ne fut labourée de boulets. Quelques-unes en étaient à la lettre percées à jour. Toutes les devantures, toutes les fenêtres étaient criblées de balles; de larges traces de sang, des armes brisées ou abandonnées marquaient encore les lieux où le combat avait été le plus acharné. Les barricades construites avec un art merveilleux, non plus de pavés, mais avec les pierres des trottoirs,

présentaient l'aspect de forteresses à angles rentrants et saillants, et se
succédaient tous les cinquante pas. La place de la Bastille surtout
offrait l'image la plus effrayante du chaos. Tous les arbres en étaient
coupés, ou tordus par le boulet; ici, des maisons abattues et dévorées
par les flammes; là, de vraies tours construites de madriers, de
voitures renversées et de pierres entassées; au milieu de tout cela un
peuple étourdi et se possédant à peine au milieu de ces scènes qui
dépassent l'imagination, des soldats endormis de fatigue sur le pavé
presque sous les pieds du peuple, la rage des vaincus se trahissant
sous une tranquillité affectée, le désordre des vainqueurs se frayant
un chemin sur les barricades renversées, ailleurs la pitié publique
réclamant l'aumône pour les blessés, et recueillant le linge qui
convient à leurs blessures, tout se réunissait pour offrir un de ces
spectacles d'une sublime originalité, où tous les tons de l'humanité se
font entendre à la fois dans un admirable désordre . . . (*Oeuvres
complètes*, IX. 1088–1089)

The brutal repression which followed the defeat of the insurrection
sickened Renan, even though at bottom he was on the side of the
forces of order. His horror is expressed in his outburst in another
letter written a fortnight later:

Je suis toujours pour ceux qu'on massacre, lors même qu'ils sont
coupables. Ivres de sang, les gardes mobiles ont commis dans ce
quartier des indignités, qu'on hésite à raconter. Postés sur la terrasse
de l'École des Mines, après la bataille finie, ils s'amusaient à tirer à
loisir et par forme de délassement sur les personnes qui se présentaient dans toute la longueur des rues adjacentes où la circulation
n'était pas encore interdite. Encore était-ce là un reste des fureurs du
combat. Mais ce qu'il y a d'affreux, d'épouvantable, ce sont les
hétacombes de prisonniers qui ont été immolés deux et trois jours
après. Durant des après-midi entiers, j'ai entendu d'incessantes
fusillades dans le jardin du Luxembourg, et pourtant on n'y com-
battait pas. . . . Cela m'exaspérait à tel point que je voulus m'en
éclaircir; j'allai voir une de mes connaissances dont les fenêtres
donnent sur le jardin. Hélas! c'était trop vrai, et si je ne le vis pas de
mes yeux, j'y vis quelque chose de plus affreux encore, quelque chose
qui ne s'effacera jamais de ma mémoire, et qui, si je ne m'élevais à
un point de vue plus général, laisserait dans mon âme une haine
éternelle. Des malheureux entassés dans les combles, sous les plombs,
étouffant, manquant d'air, mettaient la tête à une étroite lucarne
pour respirer. Eh bien! chaque tête qui paraissait servait de point de
mire aux gardes nationaux placés en bas, et était accueillie par une
balle. Je dis après cela que la bourgeoisie est capable des massacres
de septembre,[1] et encore . . . les septembriseurs tuaient ceux qu'ils

[1] In 1792.

croyaient les ennemis de la France; les épiciers tueront ceux qu'ils
croient les ennemis de leur boutique. (ibid. p. 1097)

The triumph of the forces of property was symbolized by a new
law passed by the Assembly which re-introduced the 12-hour
working day.

The *Journées de Juin*, like the Paris Commune of 1871, left behind bitter memories among the working-class inhabitants of
Paris. They also marked the virtual end of the Republic, at any
rate in any progressive sense, though on paper it lingered on until
the proclamation of the Empire in December 1852. On 11 July *Le
Peuple constituant*, founded after the February Revolution by the
Christian democrat Lamennais (1782–1854), had to close down
because, as under the monarchy, newspapers were compelled
once more to put up a large sum of money as security to meet
possible fines levied on them. The situation as seen from the extreme Left is well summed up in his famous farewell to his readers:

> *Le Peuple constituant* a commencé avec la République, il finit avec la
> République; car ce que nous voyons, ce n'est pas, certes, la Répub-
> lique. Ce n'est même rien qui ait un nom. Paris en état de siège,
> livré au pouvoir militaire, livré lui-même à une faction qui en fait
> son instrument; les cachots et les forts de Louis-Philippe encombrés
> de quatorze mille prisonniers, à la suite d'une affreuse boucherie
> organisée par des conspirateurs dynastiques devenus, le lendemain,
> tout-puissants; des proscriptions, telles que 1793 n'en fournit pas
> d'exemple; des lois attentatoires au droit de réunion, détruit de fait;
> l'esclavage et la ruine de la presse, par l'application monstrueuse de
> la législation monarchique remise en vigueur; la garde nationale
> désarmée en partie; le peuple décimé et refoulé dans sa misère, plus
> profonde qu'elle ne le fut jamais; non, encore une fois, non! ce n'est
> pas la république, mais, autour de sa tombe sanglante, les saturnales
> de la réaction!
>
> . . . On voulait à tout prix nous réduire au silence. On y a réussi
> par le cautionnement. Il faut aujourd'hui de l'or, beaucoup d'or
> pour jouir du droit de parler; nous ne sommes pas assez riches.
> Silence aux pauvres!

Not only the Socialists and the Radicals (*Montagnards*, so-called
after their ancestors in the first Revolution), but also the moderate
Republicans, as Tocqueville points out, had suffered a severe
setback:

> Telles furent les journées de Juin, journées nécessaires et funestes;
> elles n'éteignirent pas en France le feu révolutionnaire, mais elles
> mirent fin, du moins pour un temps, à ce qu'on peut appeler le
> travail propre à la révolution de Février. Elles délivrèrent la nation

de l'oppression des ouvriers de Paris et la remirent en possession d'elle-même.

Les théories socialistes continuèrent à pénétrer dans l'esprit du peuple sous la forme de passions cupides et envieuses et à y déposer la semence de révolutions futures; mais le parti socialiste lui-même demeura vaincu et impuissant. Les Montagnards, qui ne lui appartenaient pas, sentirent bientôt qu'ils étaient irrévocablement atteints par le même coup qui l'avait frappé. Les républicains modérés ne tardèrent pas à voir eux-mêmes que cette victoire qui les avait sauvés, les plaçait sur une pente qui pouvait les conduire hors de la république, et ils firent aussitôt effort pour se retenir, mais en vain. (*Souvenirs*, p. 178)

The events which followed down to December were to make this new situation very clear.

Work on a new constitution for France, which had been interrupted by the *Journées de Juin*, was resumed in the following months and the task was completed by 4 November. As a two-chamber system was considered to be more suited to a monarchy than a republic, only one Legislative Assembly, elected by universal suffrage, was established. Although some members proposed that the President of the Republic should on the first occasion be elected by the Assembly or that members of the Bonaparte family should not be eligible, it was finally decided that the election should take place by universal suffrage. The president was to hold office for four years and to enjoy very wide executive powers, but nothing was laid down as to what was to happen in the case of a conflict between the executive and the legislative powers.

In the presidential election which took place on 10 December there were five candidates. On paper the man with the best chance was General Cavaignac, the head of the government since June and the victor in the civil war which had raged in Paris. There were three other Republican candidates – Lamartine, whose popularity had undergone a rapid decline since the earlier part of the year, Ledru-Rollin, a *Montagnard*, and the Socialist Raspail, who had been in prison since the abortive attempt to overthrow the government on 15 May. There was also one dark horse, the nephew of the first Emperor, Louis-Napoléon Bonaparte, who had entered the Assembly in June at a by-election and had made a poor impression there. In Paris he had the support of many conservative politicians like Thiers who thought that they could do what they liked with such an obvious cretin, and a

Hippolyte Flandrin: Napoléon III.

tremendous propaganda campaign in his favour was carried on both in the capital and the provinces. In Paris he undoubtedly found support among many workers who were disillusioned with the republic, while in the provinces many illiterates voted for the name. It is even said that some naïve electors thought that the great Napoleon in person was the man they were voting for. Some idea of the atmosphere in which the election took place in the provinces is conveyed in the childhood memories of the historian, Ernest Lavisse:

> Mais l'élection présidentielle se prépare. Sur le marché, des colporteurs vendent de grandes images au bas desquelles s'alignent les couplets de chansons à la gloire de l'Empire. La marmaille chante à tue-tête:
>> *Dis-moi, soldat; dis-moi, t'en souviens-tu?*
> Tout le pays achète un almanach plein d'anecdotes glorieuses. Le portrait de Louis-Napoléon, orné de sa signature orthographiée, est affiché dans les cabarets. Je monte sur un haut tambour pour voir de près la signature de Napoléon. Dans les rues, Jupin et Huchon, les vétérans impériaux, se redressent et se rengorgent . . . – Le Nouvion donna une énorme majorité à Louis Napoléon, le 10 décembre 1848. (*Souvenirs*, pp. 80–81)

This tiny *bourg* in Picardy followed the general trend of voting in the presidential election. Louis Napoleon won a sweeping victory as details of the voting show:

Louis Napoleon	5,534,520 votes
General Cavaignac	1,448,302
Ledru-Rollin	371,431
Raspail	36,964
Lamartine	17,914

With nearly 75 per cent of the votes cast Louis Napoleon had run away with the contest.

Officially he was the son of the great Napoleon's younger brother, Louis, whom he had put on the throne of Holland. After the collapse of the first Empire he continued to live abroad, in Germany and Switzerland, where he was brought up by his mother, who was separated from her husband. He had taken part in the *Carbonari* conspiracies in Italy and had also served in the Swiss Army. After the death of the first Napoleon's heir, nominally Napoleon II ('L'Aiglon'), in 1832, he became the Bonapartist pretender to the throne of France.

Unlike later claimants to that throne, he was not content to remain inactive in exile abroad. In 1836 he staged an abortive rising in Strasbourg with the aim of overthrowing Louis Philippe; when this failed, he was arrested and deported to the United States by the French government. He quickly returned to Europe and from London he published in 1839 his *Des Idées napoléoniennes*, in which he attributed to his uncle the aim of founding a federal Europe and establishing liberty in France. In the next year, at Boulogne, he made a second and peculiarly burlesque attempt to drive out Louis Philippe. This time, after his arrest, he was sentenced to life imprisonment and confined in the gloomy fortress of Ham in north-eastern France. It was only after spending six years in captivity that he managed to escape, disguised as a work-man named Badinguet (a nickname which his enemies were ever afterwards to fix on him). After his escape he took refuge in London and did not return to France until after the February revolution.

On 20 December the newly elected President made his appear-ance in the Constituent Assembly and in accordance with Article 48 of the constitution swore the following oath:

> En présence de Dieu et devant le Peuple français, représenté par l'Assemblée nationale, je jure de rester fidèle à la République démocratique, une et indivisible, et de remplir tous les devoirs que m'impose la Constitution.

Less than three years later he was to violate this solemn oath, but at first he moved fairly cautiously in the direction of exercising personal power. The first ministry which he appointed consisted of Royalist parliamentarians who were, of course, only too willing to carry out various anti-republican measures which suited the President. The life of the Constituent Assembly came to an end in May 1849 when the elections to the Legislative Assembly set up by the new constitution took place. The results proved a disaster for the moderate Republicans (Lamartine and other members of the provisional government were defeated). The 'parti de l'Ordre', in which Orleanists, Legitimists, Bonapartists and Catholic poli-ticians formed a loose union, was the principal victor with some 450 seats out of 715 against only some 70 moderate Republicans. The whole of northern and most of western France down to the Pyrenees voted solidly for the Right. On the other hand the Left, *la Montagne*, came out of the elections in a much stronger position with something like 200 seats and over a third of the votes cast; not only did it achieve a slight majority in Paris itself, but what was more impressive was its success in a whole bloc of rural departments running from central France to the Alps. Part of this success was undoubtedly due to the effect of the economic de-pression on the medium and poorer peasants. Right-wing opinion was much put out by the results of these elections; if the Paris workers had been crushed in the *Journées de Juin*, democratic semi-socialist views had triumphed over a considerable area of the French countryside.

It is true that when the Legislative Assembly met at the end of May, the left-wing leaders played into the hands of the conservative majority by organizing an abortive insurrection in Paris. The French troops which had been sent to Italy were now being used to destroy the Roman Republic and to restore the temporal power of the Pope in defiance of Article V of the preamble to the constitution:

> [La République française] respecte les nationalités étrangères, comme elle entend faire respecter la sienne; n'entreprend aucune guerre dans des vues de conquête, et n'emploie jamais ses forces contre la liberté d'aucun peuple.

When the *Montagne*'s motion to impeach the President and his ministers for this breach of the constitution was defeated in the Assembly, its leaders called upon the French people to rise and defend the constitution. Although the movement in Paris proved a complete fiasco, it is significant that this time the provinces, including Lyons, did respond to the call and demonstrated their anger. However, the main leaders of the *Montagne* had to flee abroad to avoid arrest and thus weakened their party in the Assembly, while the government intensified its anti-republican measures.

In October 1849 the President began to assert his position more strongly by dismissing the existing government and forming a new one drawn entirely from outside the Assembly. To consolidate his position he sought the support of Catholics; after restoring the temporal power of the Pope, he gave considerable power over education to the Church. The *Loi Falloux*, passed in 1850, officially broke the somewhat nominal state monopoly of secondary education; it was made much easier to open *écoles libres* (Catholic schools) which were now recognized officially as much as the state *lycées* and the municipal *collèges*. During the next fifty years the religious orders came to play an increasingly important part in education, both primary and secondary, often with minimal academic qualifications. What is more, clerical representatives were also given a considerable degree of control over the state primary and secondary schools. Terrified by the social upheaval which France had just gone through, even the free-thinking conservatives in the Assembly welcomed this clerical control over education, particularly in primary schools. As Thiers, one of their leaders, brutally put it:

> Je veux encore là rendre toute-puissante l'influence du clergé; je demande que l'action du curé soit forte, beaucoup plus forte qu'elle ne l'est, parce que je compte beaucoup sur lui pour propager cette bonne philosophie qui apprend que l'homme est ici pour souffrir, et non cette autre philosophie qui dit au contraire à l'homme: *jouis.*

At the same time the government gave its *préfets* the power to suspend or dismiss elementary schoolteachers (*instituteurs*) who were regarded as dangerous supporters of the republic.

Yet although the government used all sorts of methods to crush it, the republican movement still remained strong. In March 1850 when thirty by-elections had to be held to replace the deputies who had lost their seats as a result of the Paris demonstration of the previous June, twenty-one seats went to the *Montagne*. A month later the anger of conservatives was further increased by the election in Paris of Eugène Sue, the popular novelist famed for his anti-clerical and vaguely socialistic views. The conservatives in the Assembly hastily passed a new electoral law (31 May) directed against what Thiers described in a famous phrase as 'la vile multitude'. By insisting on a three years' residence qualification they reduced the number of electors by nearly a third.

Louis Napoleon expressly dissociated himself from this law since he was using every means to retain wide popular support. According to Article 45 of the constitution his term of office was strictly limited to four years which expired in May 1852:

> Le président de la République est élu pour quatre ans, et n'est rééligible qu'après un intervalle de quatre années.

Obviously this was not good enough for a Bonaparte. 1852 was a year to which both President and Assembly looked forward with anxious anticipation; the Assembly which was elected for a three year term was also due for renewal in that same year, indeed the same month. The majority of the Republicans, conscious of their growing strength, decided to lie low in the interval and concentrate on securing an electoral victory in 1852. In 1850 their faith in the coming of 'la République démocratique et sociale' two years later was vividly expressed in the following lines from a song composed by the poet, Pierre Dupont (1821–1870), a writer for whom, somewhat surprisingly, Baudelaire professed a great admiration:

C'est dans deux ans, deux ans à peine,
Que le coq gaulois chantera;
Tendez l'oreille vers la plaine,
Entendez ce qu'il vous dira.
Il dit aux enfants de la terre
Qui sont couchés sous leur fardeau:
Voici la fin de la misère,
Mangeurs de pain noir, buveurs d'eau.

Des monts sacrés où la lumière
Forge ses éclairs et ses feux,
Viens, en déployant la bannière,
    Dix-huit cent cinquante-deux (*bis*).
        (*Muse populaire*, pp. 232–233)

The monarchist majority in the Assembly would obviously have preferred to secure a restoration. Although the death of Louis Philippe in 1850 seemed to facilitate a fusion of Orleanists and Legitimists since the Comte de Chambord was childless and could have been succeeded on the throne in due course by Louis Philippe's grandson, the Comte de Paris, all negotiations between the two monarchist parties broke down, largely because of the intransigeance of Chambord who, twenty years later, was once again to wreck the possibility of a restoration after the collapse of the Second Empire.

The clash between this royalist majority in the Assembly and the President filled the whole of the year 1851. A campaign was organized throughout France to secure a revision of the constitution and in particular of Article 45. Under this pressure the Assembly discussed the question of revision in June and July. Finally by a considerable majority (446–270) the Assembly voted in favour of revision; but this was not enough. The Republicans had been joined in their opposition by conservatives like Thiers, and the constitution required that the motion be passed 'aux trois quarts des suffrages exprimés'.

The deadlock between President and Assembly was finally broken by the *coup d'état* carried out after long preparation by Louis Napoleon on 2 December, the anniversary of his uncle's victory at Austerlitz in 1805. On the morning of that day the people of Paris woke to find placarded on the walls a proclamation by the President in which he called upon the French people to decide between him and the Assembly. With it was the following decree:

AU NOM DU PEUPLE FRANÇAIS
LE PRÉSIDENT DE LA RÉPUBLIQUE
DÉCRETE

ART. 1.

L'Assemblée nationale est dissoute.

ART. 2.

Le Suffrage universel est rétabli. La loi du 31 mai est abrogée.

ART. 3.

Le peuple français est convoqué dans ses comices à partir du 14 décembre jusqu'au 21 décembre suivant.

ART. 4.

L'état de siège est décrété dans l'étendue de la 1re division militaire.

ART. 5.

Le Conseil d'État est dissous.

ART. 6.

Le Ministre de l'intérieur est chargé de l'exécution du précédent décret.

Fait au Palais de l'Élysée, le 2 décembre, 1851.

LOUIS-NAPOLÉON BONAPARTE.
Le Ministre de l'intérieur.
De Morny

This was patently a violation of the oath which Louis Napoleon had sworn three years earlier. On paper such a situation was dealt with by Article 68 of the Constitution:

Toute mesure par laquelle le président de la République dissout l'Assemblée nationale, la proroge ou met obstacle à l'exercice de son mandat, est un crime de haute trahison. – Par ce seul fait, le président est déchu de ses fonctions; les citoyens sont tenus de lui refuser obéissance; le pouvoir exécutif passe de plein droit à l'Assemblée nationale. Les juges de la Haute Cour se réunissent immédiatement à peine de forfaiture.

The President, however, had taken care to have the army on his side and to direct his propaganda in the first place against the monarchist majority in the Assembly. Its most prominent leaders had been arrested during the night, and during the day those of its members who assembled outside the Palais Bourbon which had been seized by the army simply passed resolutions of protest. It was from the Left that the only attempt at armed resistance came. On the evening of 2 December a group of Republican deputies, among them Victor Hugo, issued a call to arms and on the following morning several of them attempted to rouse to action the workers of the east end of Paris. Because of the bitter memories of June 1848 they met, however, with general indifference. The fact that deputies were actually paid – if only a modest 25 francs a day – also rankled; when one of their number, a doctor from Nantes named Baudin, was taunted with this, his answer was to leap on to a barricade shouting, so the story goes, 'Vous allez voir comment on meurt pour 25 francs'; he was promptly shot by the facing troops. It is true that a small number of barricades were set up in the traditional places in the east end, but these were thinly manned and were easily disposed of on the following day. Finally on the afternoon of that day (4 December) the unarmed crowds on the *Grands Boulevards* were fired on by the troops. There were several hundred casualties and Paris was terrorized into submission.

It is significant that the *coup d'état* encountered more serious opposition in certain parts of the provinces – especially the centre and south. Here, surprisingly enough, opposition came mainly in rural areas, and was particularly strong in the south-east, in the Basses-Alpes, for instance. The main group of the Republican forces was formed by the peasants, but artisans (not factory workers) also played an important part, and leadership at local level was often provided by professional men such as doctors and lawyers. They were intent on defending the republic, but not the republic of the 1848 constitution; their war-cry was 'Vive la République démocratique et sociale!'. This was the new republic which they hoped would emerge from the elections of May 1852.

However, these local uprisings could not resist the armed might of the President, and their defeat was followed by mass arrests all over France, even in regions which had not reacted to the *coup d'état*. 'Le socialisme,' wrote Comte de Viel-Castel on 14 December, 'est un crime qui doit être poursuivi comme le serait le parricide.' (*Mémoires*, I. 235)

Altogether some 25,000 to 30,000 Republicans were arrested. Former deputies got off relatively lightly; expulsion from France was the fate of Victor Hugo, for instance, who used his exile to produce a blistering pamphlet, *Napoléon le Petit*, and the violent invective of his next collection of verse, *Les Châtiments*. The prisons of those regions which had offered resistance to the President were crammed with Republicans. Some 15,000 persons were sentenced to various terms of imprisonment in the following months and over 9,000 were deported to Algeria.

In the meantime the plebiscite announced by the decree of 2

December had taken place on 21–22 December. In the government propaganda which led up to it great play was made with the 'red menace' ('le spectre rouge'). The provincial risings in defence of the republic were exploited to try to prove that Louis Napoleon had saved the country by forestalling the red terror which would have taken place in 1852. In the plebiscite the electors were asked to pronounce on the following proposition:

> Le peuple français veut le maintien de l'autorité de Louis Napoléon Bonaparte et lui délègue les pouvoirs nécessaires pour établir une constitution sur les bases proposées dans la proclamation.

Although about a million and a half voters abstained, Louis Napoleon won a resounding victory with 7,436,216 *oui* against only 646,737 *non*. It is clear that the President had behind him all the conservative forces of France, including the Catholic Church.

The new constitution was rapidly put together in January 1852; it was largely based on the one promulgated by the first Napoleon after he seized power in 1799. It conferred enormous power on Louis Napoleon who was to continue as President for ten years; not only was executive power entrusted to him, but also the initiative in proposing laws. There was no question of having ministers responsible to Parliament; the President alone was responsible to the nation. In the proclamation which preceded the constitution Louis Napoleon made clear his conception of his position as President,

> Étant responsable, il faut que son action soit libre et sans entraves. De là l'obligation d'avoir des ministres qui soient les auxiliaires honorés et puissants de sa pensée, mais qui ne forment plus un Conseil responsable, composé de membres solidaires, obstacle journalier à l'impulsion particulière du chef de l'État, expression d'une politique émanée des Chambres, et par là même exposée à des changements fréquents, qui empêchent tout esprit de suite, toute application d'un système régulier.

An extremely important role was given to the *Conseil d'État*, whose forty to fifty members were appointed and dismissed by the President. This body on which the ministers sat with the right to speak and vote was given two functions by the constitution:

> ART. 50. – Le Conseil d'État est chargé, sous la direction du président de la République, de rédiger les projets de loi et les règlements d'administration publique, et de résoudre les difficultés qui s'élèvent en matière d'administration.

ART. 51. Il soutient au nom du gouvernement la discussion des projets de loi devant le Sénat et le Corps législatif.

The successor body to the *Assemblée Législative* – the *Corps Législatif* – continued to be elected by universal suffrage, but it had virtually no power. It met for only three months in the year and while its debates were public, the only version of them to be published was a summary of its proceedings drawn up by its president. As in the Fifth Republic ministers could not be members of this body. It had no power to propose laws, and all bills, even the budget, were submitted to the *Conseil d'État* before coming to it. Any amendments which it proposed had to go back to the *Conseil d'État* for it to decide whether they could be discussed by the *Corps Législatif*.

The Senate, composed of notabilities such as cardinals, marshals and admirals as well as of persons appointed by the President, was not a second chamber sharing legislative power with the *Corps Législatif*. Its functions were to safeguard the constitution by annulling laws voted by the lower chamber which it considered unconstitutional and to amend or interpret the constitution by what were called *sénatus-consultes*. Its sittings were secret.

This authoritarian régime was obviously only a prelude to the restoration of the Empire. On 7 November 1852 was published a *sénatus-consulte*, the first article of which read: 'La dignité impériale est rétablie. *Louis-Napoléon Bonaparte* est Empereur des Français, sous le nom de *Napoléon III*.' The following proposal was to be submitted to the French people for its approval:

> Le Peuple français veut le rétablissement de la dignité impériale dans la personne de *Louis Napoléon Bonaparte*, avec hérédité dans sa descendance directe, légitime ou adoptive, et lui donne le droit de régler l'ordre de succession au trône dans la famille *Bonaparte*, ainsi qu'il est prévu par le sénatus-consulte du 7 novembre 1852.

The plebiscite, held a fortnight later, produced an even larger majority than the one held in December of the previous year – 7,824,189 *oui* against 253,145 *non*. On 2 December, the anniversary of the *coup d'état*, Louis Napoleon entered Paris as Emperor.

To this same year belongs one of the most famous poems of Hugo's *Châtiments* in which the exiled poet flays the new dictator. An official newspaper had related how, when Louis Napoleon was shown a copy of Hugo's pamphlet, *Napoléon le Petit*, he had looked at it for a moment 'avec le sourire du mépris sur les lèvres'. Hugo retorted:

L'HOMME A RI
Ah! tu finiras bien par hurler, misérable!
Encor tout haletant de ton crime exécrable,
Dans ton triomphe abject, si lugubre et si prompt,
Je t'ai saisi. J'ai mis l'écriteau sur ton front;
Et maintenant la foule accourt, et te bafoue.
Toi, tandis qu'au poteau le châtiment te cloue,
Que le carcan te force à lever le menton,
Tandis que, de ta veste arrachant le bouton,
L'histoire à mes côtés met à nu ton épaule,
Tu dis: je ne sens rien! et tu nous railles, drôle!
Ton rire sur mon nom gaîment vient écumer:
Mais je tiens le fer rouge et vois ta chair fumer.

Second Empire

In contrast to his immediate predecessors on the throne of France, Louis Napoleon was a relatively young man when he came to power; at the time of his election as President he was only forty. He was undoubtedly an extremely complex character who baffled even those contemporaries who knew him well. After his downfall in 1870 he had a bad reputation in France and with historians generally. He was looked upon as an adventurer who failed. For the greater part of his reign France was subjected to a repressive form of government which denied to its people such essential liberties as freedom of the press and freedom of assembly; the country became a police state and parliamentary democracy was reduced to an empty sham. In recent years a good deal of whitewash has been applied to the Second Empire. It is true that, compared with the totalitarian régimes of the twentieth century, Louis Napoleon's system of government with its repression of political opponents appears relatively mild; and, as we shall see, he was far from being an out-and-out reactionary. Above all, from the strictly economic point of view the Second Empire marks a most important stage in French history; these twenty years or so were a period of rapid expansion. France made a sudden leap forward, the nearest equivalent to our Industrial Revolution, comparable in many ways with the vast changes which have taken place in France since 1945. Even so it is difficult to see how the severe verdict passed by many earlier historians on 'l'homme de Sedan' can be reversed.

In a famous speech which he delivered in Bordeaux in October 1852, shortly before he made himself Emperor, he had not only uttered the famous words, soon to be belied by events, 'L'Empire, c'est la paix'; he had also sketched out a programme for the economic development of France:

> Nous avons d'immenses territoires incultes à défricher, des routes à ouvrir, des ports à creuser, des rivières à rendre navigables, des canaux à terminer, notre réseau de chemins de fer à compléter. Nous avons, en face de Marseille, un vaste royaume à assimiler à la France. Nous avons tous nos grands ports de l'Ouest à rapprocher du continent américain par la rapidité de ces communications qui nous manquent encore.

During the years which he spent in England he had seen at first hand the vast increase in national wealth brought about by the Industrial Revolution, and he wanted to see a similar development in France. He had a stroke of good fortune in that, while he first came to power in 1848 in the midst of an economic depression, the early part of his reign as Emperor happened to coincide with a general upward movement in prices, brought about by a massive influx of gold from California and Australia. In France as elsewhere this led to an industrial boom which he did his best to encourage by means of public works (including the reconstruction of Paris), the setting up of credit banks to foster industrial and agricultural progress and pushing ahead with the construction of a national railway network. The railway boom stimulated in its turn the iron and steel industry.

This feverish industrial activity was temporarily halted by an economic crisis which began in 1857; but the Emperor strove to overcome this by giving more help to the railway companies, by making loans to industry and by pushing on with the programme of public works. His policy of reducing tariffs by signing commercial treaties with England and other countries was also aimed at stimulating the development of French industry. Louis Napoleon did see clearly how far France lagged behind England in industrial development and he followed a deliberate policy of economic expansion. Unquestionably the pace of industrialization was greatly speeded up during the Second Empire, and French capital also played its part in the development of foreign countries, both in Europe and further afield, as, for instance, in the construction of the Suez Canal.

Among the public works carried out during the Second Empire was the rebuilding of Paris, a task carried out by Baron Haussmann who occupied the post of Préfet de la Seine from 1853 to

Roads planned and executed under Haussmann, 1853–1870.

1869. The Paris we know today is a very different place from the Paris of Balzac. The great interest which Louis Napoleon showed in the planning and execution of the modernization of the city arose out of a variety of motives. One was to reduce the large amount of unemployment which existed at the beginning of his reign; another was to try to remove some of the worst slums, peculiarly dangerous in times of cholera epidemics which were only too frequent in the nineteenth century. His main object, however, was to cut broad avenues and boulevards through the jungle of narrow streets in which barricades could easily be set up.

A new network of highways was constructed, beginning with the extension eastwards of the Rue de Rivoli and the construction of the Boulevard de Sébastopol and the Boulevard Saint-Michel, running across the city on a north–south line. A good example of Haussmann's work is the Avenue de l'Opéra, a wide street, cutting across the narrow old streets of the neighbourhood and with an imposing public building at one end – the Opera house, begun in 1862 in the heyday of the Empire, but not opened until 1875. All manner of new buildings belong to this period – the extensions to the Louvre and to the Bibliothèque Nationale, the Hôtel-Dieu and the famous iron buildings of the Halles, the removal of which has

The Opéra (built 1862–1875).

Interior of the *pavillon à la volaille*, les Halles, in 1864.

caused such an uproar in the 1970s. Nor were open spaces forgotten; both the Bois de Boulogne and the Bois de Vincennes were laid out during the Second Empire. This period saw an enormous transformation on which Paris has lived for a hundred years. It is only now, under the pressure of serious traffic problems, that a new transformation of the capital is under way with, for instance, the removal of the Halles to the *banlieue*.

Engraving of the rue Soufflot and the Panthéon, about 1860.

The changes carried out by Haussmann were far from meeting with universal approval. For one thing, the financing of the operation had its shady side, which was exposed in a famous pamphlet with a punning title, *Les Comptes fantastiques d'Haussmann*, by Jules Ferry (1832–1893), soon to be one of the founders of the Third Republic. One result of the changes wrought by Haussmann was to drive a great many of the poorer inhabitants of the capital out into the *banlieue*. Often they had lived in the upper parts of houses where less impecunious members of society had their flats; their exodus from the capital in the face of rents which they could no longer afford meant a widening of the gulf between the different social classes. Again, many people disliked the new Paris, because they no longer felt at home in it; Proudhon denounced what he called

> la ville neuve, monotone et fatigante de M. Haussmann, avec ses boulevards rectilignes, avec ses hôtels gigantesques, avec ses quais magnifiques, mais déserts; avec son fleuve attristé, qui ne porte plus que des pierres et du sable; avec ses gares de chemin de fer qui, remplaçant les ports de l'antique cité, ont détruit sa raison d'être; avec ses *squares*, ses théâtres neufs, ses casernes neuves, son macadam, ses légions de balayeurs et son affreuse poussière; ville peuplée d'Anglais, d'Allemands, de Bataves, d'Américains, de Russes, d'Arabes; ville cosmopolite où ne se reconnaît plus l'indigène. (*De la Capacité politique des classes ouvrières*, pp. 1–2)

On the other hand, whatever its practical and aesthetic drawbacks, the reconstruction of Paris undoubtedly stimulated employment there throughout the Second Empire.

These years saw a considerable development in the banking system with the formation not only of such establishments as the *Société Générale* and the *Crédit Lyonnais*, but also of new banks concerned with the development of agriculture and industry. The provision of mortgages on agricultural land (hitherto these had been inordinately expensive) was the aim of the *Crédit Foncier*, set up with government authorization in 1852. In practice, agriculture received little assistance from it as most of its money went into the development of urban property and into the financing of public works in the towns. In contrast to this solidly established and unspectacular bank the *Crédit Mobilier* had a very chequered career. This bank, authorized by the government a few weeks after the *Crédit Foncier* and given at first much official support, aimed to further the industrial development of the country by mobilizing the money of savers, large and small. After paying large dividends and seeing its shares quadruple in value, the bank was already in difficulties by 1856, and although its founders, the brothers Émile and Isaac Péreire, managed to keep going until 1867, when they were forced to resign, the bank was finally wound up in 1871. However, it had done a great deal, especially in the boom years of the 1850s, to promote the industrial development of France. It assisted in the formation of various French railway companies and also participated in the development of railways in other countries as far afield as Russia; it helped to finance such diverse activities as shipping, coal-mining and insurance and also took a considerable part in property development in Paris and Marseilles.

The most spectacular achievement of French capital and engineering abroad during the Second Empire was the construction of the Suez Canal. While in Egypt, Louis Napoleon's uncle had had the idea of a canal to link the Mediterranean and the Red Sea, but nothing came of the project. In 1854 the French engineer, Ferdinand de Lesseps (1805–1894), was granted a concession by Egypt, but this had to be ratified by the Sultan of Turkey. Opposition from England led to delays until finally De Lesseps went ahead without having the concession confirmed by the Sultan. In 1859 he floated the *Compagnie de Suez* and ten years later the canal was opened in the presence of the Empress Eugénie.

One economic field in which the Emperor intervened directly was that of commercial relations with foreign countries. Here he made use of the right to make commercial treaties which was reserved to him by the constitution of 1852. From the beginning he was determined to reverse the traditional policy of high protective tariffs and to negotiate lower rates of duty with other countries. In 1860 he secured a commercial treaty with the England of Gladstone and Cobden; in return for a reduction in duties on such French products as silk, wines and spirits, France agreed to remove entirely her existing ban on the importing of a wide range of English goods and to reduce tariffs on others. This was followed by similar agreements with such Continental countries as Belgium and the German *Zollverein*. Many French industrialists were bitterly opposed to this policy of lower tariffs and maintained that they would be ruined by their English competitors; but the Emperor argued that if France wanted to sell more of her goods abroad, she would have to be prepared to buy more from other countries. It is probable that this reduction in French tariffs compelled some industries to introduce more efficient methods of production and thus contributed to the great surge forward in economic development which France made during the Second Empire.

During the economic boom of the 1850s the unemployment which had been one of the many troubles of the Second Republic virtually vanished, but if money wages rose, prices rose faster, and in the expanding towns housing conditions were often deplorable. In the 1860s there were periods of considerable unemployment (the cotton industry was badly hit by the American civil war), but real wages seem to have risen slightly. Strikes were still forbidden and trade unions were still illegal, but although, as we shall see, in the last years of his reign Louis Napoleon began to flirt with the workers and to relax the laws against collective action, the Second Empire ended with bitter discontent among large sections of the French workers.

The reign of Louis Napoleon falls roughly into two halves – the period down to about 1860 when he was unrestricted master of France and also enjoyed considerable success, and a second period in which he was compelled to make more and more concessions to the opposition at home and pursued abroad a policy which led to the inglorious end of the régime at Sedan.

During the first half of his reign he followed policies inspired by an outlook which had much in common with a more recent authoritarian régime in France, the Fifth Republic. Like General de Gaulle, Louis Napoleon thought of himself as being above party; he considered himself to be entrusted with a national mission in contrast with the parties, their faction fights and the resultant anarchy. His aim was to reduce to impotence the Legitimist, Orleanist and Republican opposition parties and to carry out a policy which he held to be in the national interest. From the time of his marriage in 1853 to a Spanish Countess, Eugénie Marie de Montijo, and the birth of an heir, the Prince Imperial, three years later, he was naturally concerned with the future of his dynasty.

Again there is a striking analogy between the Second Empire and the Fifth Republic in the deadness of political life in the opening years of both régimes, though this result was achieved by much more brutal means under Louis Napoleon. On paper there was still a legislative assembly (the *Corps Législatif*) elected by universal suffrage, but its powers were extremely limited. The elections of 1852 were managed quite openly by the government.

On top of the brutal repression of all opposition to the *coup d'état* came the gagging of the press and a ban on all public meetings. The elections were simply turned into another plebiscite. 'En votant pour les amis de Louis-Napoléon,' declared his half-brother, the Duc de Morny, 'on aura une seconde fois l'occasion de voter pour le prince lui-même.' All sorts of official pressure were exercised by the *préfets* in favour of the candidates who supported the new régime. The result was that these secured practically all of the 261 seats; only three outright opponents were elected, two in Paris and one in Lyons, and these refused to take the oath, so that the opposition was not represented at all. The elections of 1857 did not produce a very different result, except that this time the five Republicans who were elected did take their seats. In other words in the first part of the reign political life was almost dead; the real activity was in the economic sphere and in foreign affairs.

The long term aim of Louis Napoleon's foreign policy was to upset the territorial settlement of Europe imposed by the Congress of Vienna in 1815 after his uncle's final downfall. The conduct of foreign affairs he kept in his own hands with results which in the end proved highly unfortunate for France.

'L'Empire, c'est la paix,' Louis Napoleon had maintained in a famous speech shortly before he made himself emperor. 'Malheur,' he had declared, 'à celui qui, le premier, donnerait en Europe le signal d'une collision, dont les conséquences seraient incalculables!' Yet within eighteen months France was involved in the Crimean War with Russia, and this was followed by a war with Austria in 1859, the Mexican adventure of the 1860s and the final clash with Prussia in 1870.

The Crimean War, which lasted from 1854 to 1856 and saw the unusual spectacle of the traditional enemies, England and France, fighting together in alliance against Russia, brought the new regime a certain amount of prestige when it was at last brought to a victorious conclusion. However, the Italian question was much more important since it was to haunt the Emperor to the end of the reign. Louis Napoleon had been personally involved in Italian affairs as a young man and he sympathized with the Italian aspiration for unity. In the 1850s, under the leadership of its prime minister, Cavour, the kingdom of Sardinia was striving to unify the country; this was bound to involve a conflict with Austria which held the provinces of Lombardy and Venetia as well as with the Pope whose temporal power extended over a considerable area of central Italy and was a formidable obstacle to unification.

In 1858 another of the numerous attempts made on the Emperor's life took place while the Empress and he were on their way to the Opéra. Three bombs, made in Birmingham, were thrown at the carriage by Italian patriots led by a man called Orsini, causing some 150 casualties among the guards and by-standers. Before his execution Orsini wrote a letter to the Emperor in which he called upon him to reverse the settlement of 1815 and to bring about the unity and independence of Italy. This letter was duly published in the official newspaper, *Le Moniteur*. What is more, later in the year Louis Napoleon had a secret meeting on French soil with Cavour; together they agreed on plans for redrawing the map of Italy, an Italy from which Austria was to be excluded.

War with Austria followed in 1859. The French army was quite unprepared for a campaign on this scale, but the Emperor led his forces into Northern Italy and succeeded in defeating the Austrians in bloody battles at Magenta and Solferino. Then, in face of the hostility of England and other European powers, who were alarmed at France breaking out of the frontiers assigned to her in 1815, Louis Napoleon hastened to make peace with Austria, leaving his Sardinian ally in the lurch.

Out of this war France made considerable territorial gains. In 1860 she annexed, after plebiscites, Savoy along with Nice and the surrounding province; but Louis Napoleon's intervention in Italian affairs alienated both Italian patriots and the majority of French Catholics, whose support had hitherto been one of the main pillars of the imperial régime. Although, thanks to Louis Napoleon's intervention, the King of Sardinia had secured Lombardy from Austria, the French troops which had been sent to Rome to restore the Pope's temporal power, were kept there until 1870, thus preventing the new kingdom of Italy from having its natural capital. On the other hand Catholics in France were furious because the progress made towards Italian unity in 1860 had meant the loss of the greater part of the papal territory, which was now practically reduced to Rome itself. The Empress was a strong supporter of the temporal power of the Pope and events in Italy produced a very strong reaction from the French clergy, who protested violently at what had been allowed to happen there. During the rest of the reign this breach between Church and State widened. One sign of this was seen in the activities of Victor

Duruy (1811–1894) as minister of education between 1863 and 1869; among the many reforms which he endeavoured to push through was the creation of a state system of secondary education for girls. Even this modest attempt – public lectures given by the masters of the *lycées* – encountered furious hostility from the Catholic Church.

The trade agreement with England in 1860 (partly entered into to assuage resentment in this country at French intervention in Italian affairs) was also highly unpopular with many industrialists, an influential body. In order to gain fresh support for the regime the Emperor was forced, step by step, to abandon the constitution of 1852 and to make one concession after another in the direction of a less autocratic form of government. From 1860 onwards the so-called 'Empire liberal' began to emerge with the gradual reinforcement of parliamentary institutions. A decree published towards the end of that year granted to the Senate and *Corps Legislatif* the right to discuss and vote annually an address in reply to the speech from the throne. Whereas under the 1852 constitution there had been no contact between ministers and the two chambers, now ministers without portfolio were to be appointed to ensure such contact, and the proceedings of both houses were to be published.

The 1860s saw a gradual revival of political parties and of the opposition – Legitimists, Orleanists, Catholics and Republicans. The 1863 elections to the *Corps Législatif* produced a great increase in political activity. The opposition was by no means united; some parties wished merely to reform the Empire and others to destroy the whole régime. Together they obtained just under two million votes against rather more than five million for the government candidates; this meant that they had trebled their number of votes since 1857 and now held 32 seats, 17 of which went to Republicans. Though this result could be held to be a fair success for the government, it was far from satisfied with it. Its candidates were generally in a minority in the larger towns and there was one sore spot in particular: Paris elected nothing but opposition deputies (Thiers and eight republicans) and it did so by a crushing majority, by 153,000 votes to 22,000. Moreover, some of the government candidates owed their election to Catholic votes and were on occasion capable of combining with the opposition and voting against the government.

Mounting difficulties abroad combined with growing opposition at home to compel further concessions. In July 1866 a

sénatus-consulte gave the *Corps Législatif* the right to discuss amendments to laws even when these had been rejected by the *Conseil
d'État*; it also abolished the constitutional provision which limited
its sessions to three months in a year. Further changes were
heralded by a letter of Louis Napoleon published in January 1867
in *Le Moniteur*. Suffering increasingly from ill-health, 'l'homme de
Décembre' now declared: 'Aujourd'hui je crois qu'il est possible
de donner aux institutions de l'Empire tout le développement
dont elles sont susceptibles, et aux libertés publiques, une extension nouvelle, sans compromettre le pouvoir que la nation
m'a confié.' Decrees followed which, while they abolished the
voting of an address, restored to the deputies what remains an
important feature of French parliamentary assemblies, the so-
called *droit d'interpellation*, the right to put down a request to a
minister for an explanation of his actions. Although ministers
continued to be chosen outside the assembly and remained responsible to the Emperor alone, henceforward they would appear
in either assembly in person, where necessary, to take part in
debates. Then came another *sénatus-consulte* which greatly enlarged the powers of the Senate, making it a real second chamber,
examining laws voted upon by the *Corps Législatif*. In addition
new and more liberal laws on the press and freedom of assembly
were promulgated.

   The opposition continued to grow in strength. It came from
many quarters, including conservative ones. 'L'Empereur a contre
lui les classes dirigeantes,' wrote the *préfet de police* of Paris in 1867.
In addition to Legitimists, Orleanists and the Catholic opposition
there was now a powerful Republican movement. There was also
a revival of political interest among the working classes, both in
Paris and in various provincial centres. It is clear that in the
1860s the Emperor made a deliberate effort to secure support
among the workers. In 1862, for instance, the government paid
the travelling expenses of two hundred Paris workers who went to
visit the international exhibition being held in London. There
they made contact with the English labour movement (they were
much impressed with the shorter hours, higher wages and the
trade unions in England) and this eventually led to the formation
of a French section of the First International when it was founded
in London in 1864. Although trade unions were not made legal
until 1884, in 1864 a law was passed to allow workers to combine
to take strike action, and four years later they were given *de facto*
permission to combine on a more permanent footing. The last

years of the Second Empire saw a considerable number of strikes, in various provincial centres as well as in Paris.

When the next elections to the *Corps Législatif* took place in 1869, the growth of the opposition was clearly revealed. This time the government candidates, despite the usual official backing and the jerrymandering of constituencies, secured just under 60 per cent of the votes cast against rather over 40 per cent for the opposition – 4,600,000 votes against some 3,300,000. This was a very different state of affairs from what had happened in the 1852 elections when only three opposition deputies secured election; this time 30 Republicans were elected and the Orleanists secured over 40 seats. Once again all the Paris deputies belonged to the opposition. Though the republican party – strong in Paris and certain provincial cities – was numerically weak over the country as a whole, the supporters of an authoritarian empire to whom the changes made since 1860 were anathema now found themselves in a minority in the *Corps Législatif*. The majority of its members, although they formed a very miscellaneous group, which included Orleanists, government-supported candidates, Catholics and independents, were in favour of further reforms to strengthen the parliamentary régime and to make the executive responsible to the elected representatives of the nation.

If the Emperor's power was being gradually eroded, what finally undermined the whole régime was the failure of his foreign policy. In the 1860s France encountered difficulties both in Europe and overseas, but it was the German question which proved the chief cause of Louis Napoleon's downfall. For centuries one of the main aims of French foreign policy had been to keep Germany weak and divided. Now under the leadership of Prussia and its prime minister, Bismarck, the unification of Germany was carried through, ending with the proclamation of the Reich in the Galerie des Glaces at Versailles in 1871. At each of the decisive steps taken by Bismarck towards unification, Louis Napoleon found himself outmanoeuvred.

He failed to support England in preventing Schleswig-Holstein from being taken from Denmark in 1864. In that year and again in 1865 he had meetings with Bismarck at Biarritz, a resort which the Empress and he helped to put on the map. In the course of these interviews Bismarck established that France would remain neutral in a war between Prussia and Austria, which was the next step in his plans for the unification of Germany.

France did indeed do nothing while Prussia crushed the

Austrian army at Sadowa in 1866. After considering armed intervention in Germany, Louis Napoleon finally offered only to
mediate between the two countries. He allowed Prussia to establish
domination over the other North German states by setting up the
North German Confederation, believing that Germany would
remain divided into three parts – the North German Federation,
the South German states and Austria. Above all, he imagined that
Bismarck would offer him some substantial compensation in
return for his neutrality during the war with Austria. What he
demanded kept on changing – first Luxemburg and part of the
territory on the left bank of the Rhine to the north of Alsace, then
Belgium. He got no change out of Bismarck; indeed Bismarck
humiliated him by getting a conference meeting in London to
neutralize the grand duchy of Luxemburg.

The result of the disastrous foreign policy pursued by the
Emperor was that, when the Franco–Prussian war broke out in
1870, France was completely isolated.

Things were not improved by the policy which he pursued outside Europe. It is true that the Second Empire saw a doubling of
France's colonial possessions, but it must be remembered that in
1848 these were relatively small. In the century-long struggle
between England and France which ended in 1815 France had
lost most of her colonies. All she was left with after Waterloo was a
few scattered territories – the little islands of Saint-Pierre and
Miquelon off Newfoundland; Martinique and Guadeloupe in the
West Indies; in South America French Guiana; the island of La
Réunion in the Indian Ocean; and a few trading posts in India,
the most important of which was Pondicherry. Charles X had
begun the conquest of Algeria just before his downfall, and this
was completed during the reign of Louis Philippe, which also saw
the annexation of Gabon and nearby trading posts in West Africa
as well as that of the island of Tahiti and the Marquesas in the
Pacific.

During the Second Empire France consolidated her hold over
Algeria; the number of European settlers was almost doubled.
Penal colonies were established both in French Guiana and in the
Pacific island of New Caledonia. There was considerable French
activity in West Africa where Senegal was added to her colonial
empire. In the Far East France began to intervene in Indo-China;
she conquered Cochin-China, the region in the south of which
Saigon is the capital, and followed that up by establishing a
protectorate over Cambodia.

The so-called Mexican adventure, however, proved disastrous. Louis Napoleon took advantage of the American Civil War, as a result of which the Monroe doctrine was temporarily in suspense, to intervene in Mexican affairs. In 1862 a French expeditionary force was sent out to set up a new empire. Louis Napoleon persuaded the Archduke Maximilian, the brother of the Emperor of Austria, to go out to Mexico and be proclaimed emperor there. Maximilian was duly installed as emperor in 1864, but guerilla warfare with the legitimate government continued. It was soon clear that the expedition was a failure, but Louis Napoleon did not dare abandon Maximilian. As soon as the American Civil War ended in 1865, the United States government reminded France of the Monroe doctrine and told Louis Napoleon to get out. However, Maximilian refused to give up his throne; when French troops were finally withdrawn at the beginning of 1867, he stayed behind, was captured by the Mexican troops and shot. The whole expedition proved a calamitous failure. It weakened the French army in the critical year 1866 in which Prussia defeated Austria, and its disastrous end was a considerable blow to Louis Napoleon's prestige at home and abroad.

The end of the Second Empire came about in a curiously confused and abrupt manner. The strengthening of the opposition parties in the elections of May 1869 led to fresh concessions in the direction of parliamentary government. In September a *sénatus-consulte* increased the powers of both the *Corps Législatif* and the Senate; what is more, ministers could now be chosen among the members of both houses and were in future to form a council presided over by the Emperor, although they were still responsible to him alone and not to Parliament. Finally in December Louis Napoleon charged Émile Ollivier (1825–1913), one of the more moderate opposition leaders, with the formation of a government, though one without a prime minister. In April 1870 yet another *sénatus-consulte* was issued, a long document which offered virtually a new constitution in place of that of 1852. It further increased the power of the two houses of Parliament, even though ministers were still not made clearly and unambiguously responsible to them. Approval for the constitutional changes introduced since 1860 was sought in a plebiscite held in May. It is a curious fact that, only four months before the ignominious collapse of the whole régime, Louis Napoleon won a resounding vote of confidence except in Paris and some of the larger provincial cities. The new constitution was ratified by 7,358,000 *oui* against

1,572,000 *non*; although the *non* had more than doubled since the plebiscite of December 1851, the number of *oui* was almost as great as it had been after the *coup d'état*.

It is possible that but for the Franco–Prussian war the Second Empire might have survived down to the death of Louis Napoleon in 1873 and that his heir, the Prince Imperial, who was born in 1856, would simply have succeeded him. In practice things turned out very differently; on 4 September the Republic was proclaimed in Paris. Louis Napoleon was finally outmanoeuvred by Bismarck. At this moment the Spaniards were looking for a king; the throne was offered to a Hohenzollern prince who was a cousin of the King of Prussia. When his acceptance was made known in July, the French were furious. However, the King of Prussia agreed to his cousin withdrawing his candidature, and the prince withdrew. That seemed the end of the matter, but the French government refused to leave well alone. It demanded from the King of Prussia a promise never to support the prince's candidature again. This gave Bismarck his opportunity; by manufacturing the famous Ems telegram he turned the King's refusal into almost insulting terms.

The fury of the French government made them lose all self-control and ignore such obvious facts as that France was diplomatically isolated and could expect no help from any of the European powers, and that the French army was in no way prepared to take on single-handed the Prussian and other German armies. On 19 July France declared war on Prussia. The complacency of the government in face of this conflict has become proverbial. The Minister for War is alleged to have said 'Nous sommes archiprêts; il ne manque pas un bouton de guêtre', while in the deba e in the *Corps Législatif* on the voting of war credits Émile Ollivier uttered the famous words: 'De ce jour commence pour les ministres, mes collègues et pour moi, une grande responsabilité. Nous l'acceptons le coeur léger.'

The opening weeks of the war proved disastrous for France and the régime. Three German armies quickly invaded Alsace and Lorraine. Alsace soon had to be abandoned and by the end of August one French army under Marshal Bazaine was bottled up in Metz and on 1 September another under Marshal Mac-Mahon was defeated at Sedan. The next day Louis Napoleon gave himself up to the Prussians and went off to captivity in Germany until the end of the war when he retired into exile in England. Two days later the Republic was proclaimed in Paris.

The Beginnings of the Third Republic

The new régime had a grim start. It began with military defeat and the invasion of France. In Paris the Republicans formed a 'Gouvernement de la Défense Nationale'. On 15 September the Foreign Minister, who had declared: 'Nous ne céderons ni un pouce de notre territoire, ni une pierre de nos forteresses', had a fruitless interview with Bismarck outside Paris. The war continued. On the 18th two German armies arrived outside the capital and soon cut it off from the rest of France. The Minister of the Interior,

Léon-Joseph Bonnat: Léon Gambetta (1838–1882).

the young Republican leader, Léon Gambetta (1838–1882), escaped by balloon to Tours and tried from there to organize resistance to the invaders. Fresh armies were formed in the provinces, but the attempt to come to the assistance of the be-sieged capital by forcing a way northwards from Orleans ended in failure as did some half-hearted attempts to break out of Paris. The whole of eastern and northern France was gradually occupied by the German armies. Paris was first starved and then bom-barded. Gambetta and the other ministers who were with him were forced to abandon Tours and to withdraw to Bordeaux. Finally, after the failures of Thiers's visits to the capitals of England, Austria and Russia in an attempt to persuade the other powers to intervene, at the end of January 1871 – ten days after the King of Prussia had been proclaimed Emperor of Germany at Versailles – Paris capitulated. An armistice was signed so that elections to a National Assembly could be held. Gambetta whose motto was still 'guerre à outrance' was compelled to resign.

The elections, which took place in great haste in February when half the country was occupied by German armies, were domin-ated by the question as to whether France should continue to fight on or, whatever the cost, seek an immediate peace. The electorate clearly showed itself in favour of peace; it also returned a strongly conservative majority, reminiscent of those in the assemblies of 1848 and 1849. Against some two hundred Re-publicans of various shades were ranged some four hundred mon-archists, mainly Orleanists with a fair number of Legitimists and some thirty Bonapartists. Four days after the election the National Assembly met in the theatre at Bordeaux and proceeded to elect Thiers, the former Prime Minister of Louis Philippe and a severe critic of Louis Napoleon, 'chef du pouvoir exécutif de la Répub-lique française'. The royalist majority, while quite willing to leave to the Republic the odium of the peace treaty with Germany, stressed the provisional nature of the new régime.

In the negotiations with Bismarck which followed France was compelled to cede to Germany the whole of Alsace and part of Lorraine; in addition she had to pay a war indemnity of 5,000 million francs, a colossal sum in the money of that time, and to submit to the occupation of twenty-one of her eastern departments until the money was paid.

The outcome of the war was a shattering blow to French national pride. The days in which France had been the leading military power on the Continent were clearly over. The impression made by the disasters of 1870 is vividly summed up in the words of a contemporary who, like so many others, had expected a rapid and complete French victory:

> L'État français, ébranlé jusqu'au fond de ses entrailles, vit ce qu'il n'avait encore jamais vu, souffrit ce qu'il n'avait jamais cru possible. Ni les malheurs de la guerre de Cent Ans, ni les deux invasions déterminées par le Premier Empire ne se trouvaient être comparables en rien à la profondeur de la chute ou la France se trouva plongée: le chef de la nation se rendant prisonnier, et avec lui l'élite des chefs militaires, une armée immense prise au collet et ne pouvant plus s'en défendre! Quand avait-on jamais rien vu, rien rêvé de pareil? (Gobineau, *Ce qui est arrivé à la France en 1870*, p. 158)

A writer like Flaubert was plunged into a kind of frantic despair. After the capitulation of Paris he wrote to his niece who had taken refuge in England:

> La capitulation de Paris, à laquelle on devait s'attendre pourtant, nous a plongés dans un état indescriptible! C'est à se pendre de rage! Je suis fâché que Paris n'ait pas brûlé jusqu'à la dernière maison, pour qu'il n'y ait plus qu'une grande place noire. La France est si bas, si déshonorée, si avilie, que je voudrais sa disparition complète. (*Correspondance*, VI. 197)

The loss of the two eastern provinces to Germany was to rankle until their return in 1918; until then 'la ligne bleue des Vosges', to use Jules Ferry's phrase, was never to be forgotten. But the troubles of 'l'année terrible' were not yet over. Next came the Paris Commune. The Assembly decided to move from Bordeaux, but considering Paris to be in too radical a mood, it installed itself in the palace of Versailles on 20 March, though the government returned to Paris.

Two days earlier a *Commune* (meaning simply a city council) had been set up by the Paris national guards on the model of the *Commune* which had played so important a part in the events of the Revolution of 1789. The mass of the population of the capital, after being starved and bombarded into submission, was in a feverish state of ultra-patriotism; it regarded as a betrayal of the capital the weak resistance offered to the Germans by the military authorities and the shameful peace which the reactionary Assembly had voted.

As soon as the insurrection broke out, Thiers decided, in the light of the experience of the street fighting of 1830 and 1848, to withdraw both government and regular troops from Paris to

The proclamation of the Commune from the Hôtel de Ville.

Versailles and to undertake from there the siege of the capital.
The elections to the Commune, held on 26 March, saw a turn-out
of rather less than 50 per cent of the voters, but under the circumstances this was quite a high figure; they produced a clear
majority of revolutionaries though these rapidly split into a
majority and `a minority. Though the English press of the period
speaks of them as 'communists' the *communards*' leaders were men
of widely differing left-wing views, ranging from Republicans
whose eyes were still fixed on the events of the first French

revolution to men of more or less clearly defined socialist views, some of whom were members of the International. They were very far from being united on the policy to be pursued now that they were for the moment masters of Paris. Some idea of the general leftward tendency of the Commune can be gathered from such measures as the attempt to reorganize primary education and make it both free and completely secular, to bring about the separation of Church and State (many priests, including the Archbishop, were arrested) and to effect some minor improvements in the position of workers and artisans.

On 19 April the Commune published a 'Déclaration au Peuple Français' in which it set forth its aims and appealed for support from the provinces:

> Il faut que Paris et le Pays tout entier sachent quelle est la nature, la raison, le but de la Révolution qui s'accomplit; il faut, enfin, que la responsabilité des deuils, des souffrances et des malheurs dont nous sommes les victimes, retombe sur ceux qui, après avoir trahi la France et livré Paris à l'étranger, poursuivent avec une aveugle et cruelle obstination la ruine de la Capitale, afin d'enterrer, dans le désastre de la République et de la Liberté, le double témoignage de leur trahison et de leur crime.
>
> La Commune a le devoir d'affirmer et de déterminer les aspirations et les voeux de la population de Paris; de préciser le caractère du mouvement du 18 Mars, incompris, inconnu et calomnié par les hommes politiques qui siègent à Versailles.
>
> Cette fois encore Paris travaille et souffre pour la France entière, dont il prépare, par ses combats et ses sacrifices, la régénération intellectuelle, morale, administrative et économique, la gloire et la prospérité.
>
> Que demande-t-il?
>
> La reconnaissance et la consolidation de la République, seule forme de gouvernement compatible avec les droits du Peuple et le développement régulier et libre de la société.
>
> L'autonomie absolue de la Commune étendue à toutes les localités de la France et assurant à chacune l'intégralité de ses droits, et à tout Français le plein exercice de ses facultés et de ses aptitudes, comme homme, citoyen et travailleur.
>
> L'autonomie de la Commune n'aura pour limites que le droit d'autonomie égal pour toutes les autres communes adhérentes au contrat, dont l'association doit assurer l'Unité française.

The Commune was to mark the beginning of a completely new era in French history:

> C'est la fin du vieux monde gouvernemental et clérical, du mili-

Leon y Escosura: The Rue de Rivoli in May 1871.

tarisme, du fonctionnarisme, de l'exploitation, de l'agiotage, des monopoles, des privileges, auxquels le proletariat doit son servage, la Patrie ses malheurs et ses desastres.

However, almost from the beginning of its existence the Commune was engaged in armed conflict with the government at Versailles, under the eyes of the German troops established to the north and east of the capital.

The struggle raged from 2 April until 28 May, at first in the *banlieue* and finally in the streets of Paris. On Sunday, 21 May, the Versailles troops managed to make their way into the capital. 'La semaine sanglante' which followed saw ghastly street battles in which all sorts of public buildings, including the Palais des Tuileries and the Hôtel de Ville, went up in smoke. Many hostages, among them the Archbishop, were shot by the *communards*, while the army carried out both individual and mass executions as it gradually gained control over the capital. No exact figures are available for the number of its victims, but the appalling figure of at least 20,000 is generally accepted. On the evening of 28 May the commander of the Versailles forces issued a proclamation in which he declared:

L'armée de la France est venue vous sauver. Paris est libéré. Aujourd'hui la lutte est terminée: l'ordre, le travail et la sécurité vont renaître.

A very different reaction came from the young Rimbaud who had followed events in Paris closely from Charleville; his poem, 'L'Orgie Parisienne ou Paris se repeuple', ends with the lines:

– Société, tout est rétabli: – les orgies
Pleurent leur ancien râle aux anciens lupanars:
Et les gaz en délire, aux murailles rougies,
Flambent sinistrement vers les azurs blafards!

In the repression which followed the collapse of the Commune some 38,000 people were arrested; 13,000 of these were sentenced to terms of imprisonment, thousands of them being deported to the penal colony of New Caledonia in the Pacific. Until 1876 Paris and the larger provincial cities remained under martial law with the restrictions on freedom of the press and of assembly which that implies. Many *communards*, including some of its leaders, managed to escape from Paris and to take refuge in England and other countries, but this bloodbath in the capital – the second in less than twenty-five years – was to make the extreme Left in France powerless for a whole decade. What is more, the merciless repression of the Commune during 'la semaine sanglante' has left bitter memories down to our own day.

Not only did the Third Republic have tragic beginnings – invasion, defeat and the two sieges of Paris; despite the fact that in the end it was to prove the longest lived of all political régimes in France since 1789, it also had a very shaky start. The years down to 1879 were filled with a long and complicated struggle to decide what sort of a régime France was to live under.

The National Assembly elected in February 1871 continued to sit until the end of 1875. It was inevitable that the monarchist and clerical majority should accept the Republic merely as a transitional régime between the fallen Empire and a restored monarchy. However, despite its clear victory over the Republicans, a restoration was not a simple matter. There were two claimants to the throne – the Comte de Chambord, the grandson of Charles X, supported by the Legitimist members of the Assembly, and the Comte de Paris, the grandson of Louis Philippe, who was backed by the much larger number of Orleanist members. As the Comte de Chambord was childless, on paper it was an easy matter for the two groups to reach an agreement that 'Henri V' should now ascend the throne and be succeeded in due course by his younger rival, the Comte de Paris. The way seemed open in the summer of 1871 for an immediate restoration of the monarchy. However, in July the Comte de Chambord issued a manifesto raising one final difficulty which for the moment caused the abandonment of all such plans; he refused to give up the white flag of the Bourbons for the *tricolore*. Thiers, a conservative if ever there was one, but more and more convinced of the necessity for a republic as 'le gouvernement qui nous divise le moins', jokingly declared that the Comte de Chambord was 'le Washington français'; he had founded the Republic.

Thus the monarchist majority in the Assembly found itself completely blocked and was compelled to leave power in the hands of Thiers for another couple of years. In that period he succeeded in raising the necessary loans to pay off the war indemnity and thus secured the end of the German occupation of eastern France; hence the statues to 'le libérateur du territoire' which one finds in towns in that region. However, on 24 May 1873 ('le 24 Mai') he was driven from power by the monarchist majority.

Once again the restoration of the monarchy appeared imminent. To take the place of Thiers the Assembly immediately elected as President a conservative and Legitimist soldier, Marshal Mac-Mahon (1808–1893), a descendant of an Irish Jacobite family who had distinguished himself not ·only in the Crimean War and the battle of Magenta, but also at the catastrophe of Sedan and in the repression of the Commune. A new government was installed under the Duc Albert de Broglie (1821–1901); its avowed aim was to 'rétablir l'ordre moral', to check the radical tendencies in the country revealed in recent by-elections. Massive pilgrimages were organized by the Catholic Church in which prayers were offered for the restoration of the monarchy and of the temporal power of the Pope who since 1870 had been confined to the Vatican city.

Though 'la République des Ducs' was intended to serve as a transition to the restoration of the monarchy, months of laborious negotiations between the different royalist groups in the Assembly and the Comte de Chambord ended in yet another fiasco. When everything, down to carriages and flags, was ready for the triumphant return of 'Henri V', in the autumn of 1873 he once again rejected the condition laid down by the monarchist majority, that he should accept the *tricolore* flag.

The majority in the Assembly was thus driven back on the expedient of appointing Marshal Mac-Mahon president for a seven-year term in the hope that in the course of that time he would succeed in bringing about a restoration; but inevitably this served in practice to strengthen the still shaky Republic. A 'commission des lois constitutionnelles' was set up by the Assembly, but the monarchist majority tried to drag out the proceedings as long as possible in the hope that 'something would turn up'. It was not until January 1875, when the constitutional laws at last came up for discussion before the Assembly, that an amendment (named after its mover 'l'amendement Wallon') introduced into them the first mention of a President of the Republic:

> Le Président de la République est élu à la majorité absolue des suffrages par le Sénat et par la Chambre des Députés réunis en Assemblée Nationale. Il est nommé pour sept ans. Il est rééligible.

This amendment was carried by the tiniest of all possible majorities, by 353 votes to 352. By this narrow margin and in this roundabout way the Third Republic at last began to acquire, if not a constitution (it never had one), at least a set of constitutional laws.

One explanation of the paradox of a monarchist assembly ending up by establishing a republic is that there had been considerable changes in its composition since the freak election of February 1871. At subsequent by-elections, starting from the summer of that year, the Republicans under their leader Gambetta had gradually won more and more seats. Yet it is clear that the constitutional laws finally voted in the course of 1875 were thoroughly conservative in intention and could perfectly well have been adapted to a monarchy. The wide powers given to the President would have been very acceptable to a constitutional monarch. If the Chamber of Deputies was to be elected by universal male suffrage (women were not given the vote until 1945), a second chamber, the Senate, was set up as a conservative counterbalance to it. Three-quarters of the members of the Senate were to be elected for a nine-year term, but only by an indirect method. In each department the electors were to consist of the deputies, members of the *Conseils généraux* and the *Conseils d'arrondissement* and one delegate from every *commune*; this would ensure an enormous preponderance for rural France. The remaining seventy-five members were to be elected for life, in the first place by the National Assembly and then, as vacancies occurred, by the Senate. Membership of the Senate was to be restricted to men of forty or over. The powers given to the President included the right to dissolve the Chamber of Deputies provided that he had the approval of the Senate.

The majority in the National Assembly had anticipated that the presence of seventy-five life-members in the Senate would not only give the monarchists in it a permanent majority, but would also enable the President to hold the threat of dissolution over the Chamber of Deputies. However, in the elections which took place just before the Assembly ended its labours the Legitimists ganged up with the Republicans to defeat most of the Orleanist candidates, including the Duc de Broglie. Over two-thirds of the life-Senators were republicans. As a result, when the elections to the Senate took place early in 1876, the monarchists found themselves with only a tiny majority – 151 seats against 149. In the newly elected Chamber of Deputies they were outnumbered by at least two to one by the Republicans. In contrast to the state of affairs in 1848 the Republicans had spread their influence beyond the cities and towns of France to the countryside, as a prominent politician of the later years of the Third Republic was to point out:

> Paris, les grandes villes, les centres industriels et ouvriers déclenchent les mouvements; si la province ne suit pas, et si dans la province les campagnes ne suivent pas, tôt ou tard le mouvement avorte. C'est ce que comprirent si bien Gambetta et ses amis; grâce à eux la République, qui par deux fois avait échoué chez nous, s'implanta, quand elle eut conquis les campagnes et les petites villes, où les campagnes viennent au jour de marché ou de réunions, prendre leurs mots d'ordre. (Paul-Boncour, *Entre deux Guerres*, I. 35)

In the 1876 elections the Bonapartists made a surprising comeback with as many seats as the Legitimists and Orleanists put together.

The triumph of the Republic was still not assured in face of a narrow monarchist majority in the Senate and a monarchist President with wide powers. The inevitable clash came on 16 May 1877 ('le Seize Mai') when Marshal Mac-Mahon dismissed a Republican ministry with a large majority in the Chamber of Deputies and called on the Duc de Broglie to form a government. He got together a very right-wing collection of ministers, similar to that of May 1873 after the downfall of Thiers. It was quite clear that the government was hopelessly in a minority in the Chamber, so in June Mac-Mahon asked the Senate to approve its dissolution. On 19 June the Chamber passed by 363 votes to 158 a motion of no confidence in De Broglie's government:

La Chambre des Députés,

Considérant que le ministère formé le 17 mai par le Président de la République et dont M. le duc de Broglie est le chef, a été appelé aux affaires contrairement à la loi des majorités, qui est le principe du gouvernement parlementaire, qu'il s'est dérobé le jour même de sa formation à toutes explications devant les représentants du pays, qu'il a bouleversé l'administration intérieure afin de peser sur les décisions du suffrage universel par tous les moyens dont il pourra disposer;

Qu'à raison de son origine et de sa composition, il ne représente que la coalition des partis hostiles à la République; coalition conduite par les inspirateurs des manifestations cléricales déjà condamnées par la Chambre;

Que c'est ainsi que, depuis le 17 mai, il a laissé impunies les attaques dirigées contre la représentation nationale et les provocations directes à la violation des lois;

Qu'à tous ces titres il est un danger pour l'ordre et pour la paix, en même temps qu'une cause de trouble pour les affaires et pour les intérêts;

Déclare que le ministère n'a pas la confiance des représentants de la nation, et passe à l'ordre du jour.

Three days later the Senate voted its approval of the dissolution of the Chamber.

Four months elapsed before the elections took place. In this period Mac-Mahon and the government brought every conceivable form of pressure to bear on the electorate in order to defeat the Republican majority. In a manifesto to the French people the President declared:

La lutte est entre l'ordre et le désordre . . .

Vous voterez pour les candidats que je recommande à vos libres suffrages.

Français,

l'heure est venue.

Allez sans crainte au scrutin.

Rendez-vous à mon appel et moi, placé par la Constitution à un poste que le devoir m'interdit d'abandonner, je réponds de l'ordre et de la paix.

The Republicans on their side carried on massive propaganda throughout France. Their leader, Gambetta, was particularly active. It was he who in a famous speech at Lille called on the President either to submit to the decision of the electors or to resign:

Ne croyez pas que quand ces millions de Français, paysans, ouvriers, bourgeois, électeurs de la libre terre française, auront fait leur choix, et précisément dans les termes où la question est posée; ne croyez pas que quand ils auront indiqué leur préférence et fait connaître leur volonté, ne croyez pas que lorsque tant de millions de Français auront parlé, il y ait personne à quelque degré de l'échelle politique ou administrative qu'il soit placé, qui puisse résister.

Quand la France aura fait entendre sa voix souveraine, croyez-le, bien, Messieurs, il faudra se soumettre ou se démettre. (*Discours*, VII. 230)

Although the elections did not turn out as well as Gambetta and other Republican leaders had hoped (they lost more seats than they gained), they still had a clear majority in the new Chamber – 323 seats against just over 200.

After the elections the Duc de Broglie resigned. At first Mac-Mahon tried to set up another government acceptable to him, but it was promptly defeated in the Chamber. There were rumours of a *coup d'état*, but at the end of 1877 the President at last gave way and appointed a ministry acceptable to the Republican majority. The ascendancy of Parliament over the President had been clearly established; never again in the long history of the Third Republic did a President venture to dissolve the Chamber of Deputies.

Mac-Mahon hung on to his office for just over another year, long enough to preside over the Paris exhibition of 1878 which aimed to show how quickly France had recovered from the disasters of the Franco-Prussian War and the Commune. At the beginning of the following year the renewal of a third of the membership of the Senate gave the Republicans a clear majority in the upper house. Mac-Mahon's term of office did not expire until 1880, but on 30 January 1879, as a result of a disagreement with the government over army appointments, he suddenly resigned. That same day the Chamber of Deputies and Senate met together in one national assembly and elected in his place one of the Republican leaders, Jules Grévy (1807–1891), who in 1848 had opposed the creation of the office of President and who could therefore be relied upon not to make full use of the powers conferred on him by the constitution. This marked the end of the equivocal situation in which the Republic was established and run by men who were utterly opposed to this form of government.

3
The Heyday of the
Third Republic (1879-1914)

Despite alarms and excursions which at the time seemed to threaten the very existence of the régime – the Boulanger crisis in 1887–1889, the Panama scandal in 1892–1893 and the Dreyfus Affair ('L'Affaire') from 1897 onwards – the Republic survived, indeed grew stronger as the decades passed, and in fact was to live on through one world war and only finally to collapse in the disaster of 1940, a full seventy years after its proclamation. It thus set up a record for any régime in France since 1789. No doubt there was a considerable amount of government instability in the period down to 1914, but, despite the fury of its more extreme opponents to whom it was simply 'la Gueuse' (in the rudest sense of the term), the Republic stood up to all attacks.

Social and economic conditions

There is an almost uncanny agreement among historians as to the general trend of the French economy in this period. The depression which had begun in agriculture in the 1870s and which affected the other branches of economic activity in the 1880s, was to last down to about 1896. Then in the closing years of the century came a fresh period of economic expansion which continued until the outbreak of the first world war. This was 'la belle époque' on which after 1918 those who had lived through it were to look back with nostalgia. As far as industrial development was concerned France might continue to lag behind Britain and Germany, not to mention the U.S.A., but she was still a rich country and in the early part of the twentieth century times were good, at least for those who had the money to enjoy them. These years were also, as in England, a period of considerable social unrest and numerous strikes.

Cafés in the boulevard Montmartre.

Population

It is scarcely necessary to labour further the fact that the population of France was by now growing very slowly indeed; it increased by just under two millions between 1881 and 1911. By 1911 Germany had nearly 65 million inhabitants against just under 40 in France. With 41 million inhabitants Great Britain had practically trebled its population since 1821; not only London, but all the leading British cities had expanded to a size quite unparalleled in France. On the eve of the First World War France continued to have a much larger rural population than this country; in 1911 55·9 per cent of the population lived in *communes* with less than 2,000 inhabitants. It is true that the population of the towns increased by more than 4 millions between 1881 and 1911, thus enlarging substantially the home market for agricultural products. Yet this decline in the proportion of the population living in rural areas was a very gradual one compared with the much more rapid fall between 1945 and the 1970s. In 1914 a good 40 per cent of the male active population was still engaged in agriculture, a proportion which by 1970 had fallen to a mere 14 per cent.

Agriculture

Progress in agriculture, though considerable, was decidedly uneven. After a long period of depression prices began to rise again from 1896, partly owing to the protective tariffs which the farmer, like the industrialists, succeeded in obtaining in the 1880s and 1890s. The share of cereals in total agricultural production fell, although, despite the steady decline in the acreage given up to them, this tended to be made up for by increased yields, particularly in Northern France. Increased demand for meat, milk, butter and cheese led to a great extension of grassland and livestock and dairy farming. There was increasing specialization in agriculture as improved communications made it possible both to find a market for the particular product of a region and to buy in from outside those things which the region did not itself produce. There was, for instance, a greatly increased production of vegetables, fruit and flowers, a good deal of it for export.

The increasing labour shortage in certain regions led both to the immigration of more foreign labour and to the increased use of machinery. There do not seem to have been any noteworthy changes either in the ownership of land or in the proportion of farmers owning their own land as against those who rented it from a landlord. The situation is clearly described in the introduction to the *Statistique agricole* for 1882:

> Les moyens et gros cultivateurs détiennent ensemble les trois quarts du territoire agricole, tandis que les millions de nos paysans en ont à peine le quart. On est donc dans l'erreur quand on croit que le sol de la France est entre les mains de la petite culture. Il serait plus exact de dire qu'il appartient pour une très large part à la propriété moyenne, si on considère comme appartenant à la moyenne culture les exploitations de 10 à 50 hectares.[1] La très grande culture est fort rare.

This meant that the overwhelming majority of farms were very small, though, as before, medium-sized farms were fairly numerous and, particularly in certain regions of Northern France, there were some very large establishments employing a good deal of hired labour. In 1906 France had nearly 250 farms employing over 50 workers. This was altogether exceptional; but there were none the less over 45,000 farms employing between 6 and 50 workers and another 1,300,000 with one to five workers. Farms employing paid labour probably accounted for a good third of the

[1] Roughly 25 to 125 acres.

A *moissonneuse-lieuse* (reaper-binder)

total number of agricultural holdings, but the overwhelming
majority of these continued to be worked by the peasant, be he
owner, tenant farmer or *metayer*, without any labour except that of
his own family. Use could obviously not be made of machines on
these smaller holdings, which often consisted of scattered plots of
land, but there is evidence that on the medium and larger farms
machinery began to come into its own in this period especially
in the form of mowing machines and reapers and binders.

One very important sector of French agriculture – wine-grow-
ing – went through a serious crisis in these years. By 1890 the
ravages of the phylloxera had almost completely destroyed the
established vineyards; the situation was only gradually restored
by importing American stocks and grafting French vines on to
them. The total area given over to vineyards fell sharply; in 1914
it was less than two-thirds of what it had been in 1871. In the
meantime the industry had to face the competition of Algerian
and foreign wines, and as soon as production had recovered
around 1900, there began a long crisis which lasted until 1910
over-production, especially in the South, led to a drastic fall in
prices and to a corresponding fall in land values. In some regions
vineyards could not even find a purchaser. In 1907 the sorry
situation of this branch of agriculture gave rise to serious disorders
in the South of France.

If by the end of the nineteenth century agricultural methods
had, broadly speaking, been considerably modernized, particu-

larly in the reduction of the amount of land left fallow, the yield
of French agriculture in a given area was still lower than in this
country; the yield of wheat per acre, for instance, was nearly 50
per cent higher in Britain than in France, and that of potatoes
more than 50 per cent. While small-scale farming in wine-
growing or horticulture can be extremely efficient, the fact that
France continued to give a living of sorts to so many peasants with
tiny holdings meant that crop yields were often low and that these
peasants enjoyed only a very modest standard of living. Naturally
there were wealthy farmers making a very comfortable living from
the land, but, despite the progress made in the hundred years
with which we are concerned, the housing, work conditions and
outlook on the world of many French peasants still remained
extremely primitive. Yet their very numbers continued to make
them a powerful force in a land of universal manhood suffrage.

Transport and communications
Although the Republic did not devote as much attention to public
works as Louis Napoleon had done, successive governments did a
considerable amount to extend the railway system and to improve
both canals and port facilities. In 1878 the plan put forward by
Charles Freycinet (1828–1923), one of Gambetta's lieutenants
during the Franco-Prussian War and later several times prime
minister, concerned first of all the construction of a third railway
network. This scheme eventually ran into difficulties as the State
found itself burdened with thousands of miles of unprofitable new
lines (no doubt by the 1970s they have long since been closed!),
mixed up with the main lines run by private companies. An
obvious solution would have been to nationalize the entire network, but this was unlikely to appeal to a Parliament in which an
overwhelming majority was convinced of the virtues of private
enterprise. By an agreement reached in 1883 the private companies took over the new lines constructed or to be constructed
under the Freycinet plan, though the State kept a network of
some 3,000 km in the triangle Tours–Nantes–Bordeaux and
secured running rights to Paris over the lines of the private companies. The State still continued to subsidize the private companies until these eventually became more or less self-supporting
except for the *Chemin de Fer de l'Ouest* which was finally nationalized
in 1909. The establishment of a national system in the SNCF
(*Société Nationale des Chemins de Fer Français*) had to wait until 1938.
Between 1881 and 1913 the length of lines in operation was

increased from 24,000 km to 39,000. In the same period considerable progress was also made with improving the secondary
roads.

The Freycinet plan also covered canals. During the Second
Empire enthusiasm for railways had somewhat cooled interest in
this form of transport, but a bill for a new canal – the *Canal de
l'Est* linking the rivers Saône and Meuse – had been passed by the
National Assembly in 1874. In the new plan what proved more
important than the construction of new canals was the standard-
ization of existing ones so as to permit of through communication
without transshipment. Between 1886 and 1913 the tonnage of
goods carried on French canals and rivers nearly doubled. Even
so the railways remained far and away the chief carriers of goods.

Considerable improvements to port facilities were also effected
under the Freycinet plan; but France's merchant navy continued
to play a very modest part in international trade. In the period
1904–1913 only a small proportion of the tonnage entering and
leaving her ports was French. Despite state subsidies for shipbuilding her merchant navy remained small, not only in comparison with that of Britain (in 1914 its total tonnage was nearly
ten times that of the French merchant fleet), but also compared
with that of Germany or even Norway. Moreover in the period
just prior to 1914, while the overwhelming proportion of the
British and German merchant navies consisted of steamships,
nearly half of the French ships were sailing vessels. In 1892 the
French government actually gave a subsidy for the building of
sailing ships; while such vessels were useful for the Mediterranean
coastal trade, this measure scarcely assisted in the modernization of
the merchant navy. As earlier, shipbuilding in France was handicapped by the distance between her ports and the centres of the
coal and metallurgical industries. As a result a great many French
ships continued to be built in British yards.

Trade and finance

Overseas trade, indeed trade with all foreign countries, continued
to play a relatively small part in France's economy. Her imports
tended to sag between 1880 and 1898; then began a slow rise,
followed by fairly rapid growth in the years from 1906 to 1913 by
which time they were roughly double their value thirty years
earlier. Exports continued to fall well below imports, following
roughly the same course which reflected the increased prosperity
of France from the end of the nineteenth century down to 1913.

In this period a very high proportion of French savings continued to be invested abroad. In 1914, when her foreign investments were worth some 50,000 million francs, France was still,
after Britain, the leading creditor nation, and these investments
were spread over a very wide area of the world, including her
colonial empire. However, a large part of the money (by 1914
over a quarter of it) went to Russia, a process which successive
governments undoubtedly encouraged in their desire to secure and
then keep up the alliance with Russia. Needless to say, a great deal
of this money – and not only what was lost when the Soviet
Union repudiated Tsarist debts – was never seen again by French
investors. It has often been argued, as we have seen, that the huge
amounts of French capital invested abroad from the middle of the
nineteenth century onwards might have been more safely as well
as more usefully invested in France. What is more, these foreign
investments did not contribute as they did in Britain to a comparable growth in exports.

Banking also developed in these years. Though local banks
continued to exist, a network of branches was gradually set up over
the whole country by the big national organizations, starting with
the *Banque de France*. This bank, for instance, increased the
number of its branches five-fold between 1881 and 1913. This
meant that the big banks were able to attract the deposits from a
mass of small and medium savers scattered over the whole country.
In dealing with these deposits the French banks came more and
more to pursue a cautious line. The crash of the *Union Générale*,
the bank of the Catholic and Legitimist aristocracy and middle
classes, which took place in 1882 after its investments, mainly in
Central Europe, had proved disastrous, encouraged them even
more strongly to follow this policy. If in this period the deposit
banks did not invest in French industry, it should be said that the
well established industrial firms did not turn to them for finance,
and from the point of view of the banks there was everything to be
said for seeking assured profits in such activities as placing foreign
loans with their customers, collecting a handsome commission
and leaving it to them to bear the risks of such investments.

Industry and resources
Industry continued to develop, expanding at a faster rate than in
Britain during the period between 1900 and 1913, but with every
year that passed falling further behind German industry. In this
period industry as well as agriculture sought and finally obtained

increased tariff protection against foreign competition. Louis Napoleon's policy of reducing tariffs by agreement with England and other countries was highly unpopular with French industrialists. After his disappearance from the scene an attempt was at once made to reverse this policy, but various complications prevented this reaction from being carried very far.

In the 1880s a renewed demand for increased protection arose out of the depression from which French industry was suffering and this was finally secured for both industry and agriculture by a law of 1892 which is associated with the name of Jules Méline (1838–1925). The hands of future governments were tied in their negotiations with other countries as the law laid down two tariffs for every article on which there was a duty – a maximum where there was no trade agreement with the country concerned, and a minimum which could be offered to another government with which an agreement was being concluded. Imported industrial goods, particularly in engineering and textiles, were now subject to a very heavy duty. The aim of such tariffs was obviously to give both French industry and agriculture a virtual monopoly in the home market. This policy was undoubtedly harmful to foreign trade; it invited reprisals from other countries although it should be said that if England was long to remain devoted to free trade, both Germany and the U.S.A. were also pursuing a policy of protection in these years. While these tariffs undoubtedly stimulated industrial activity in France down to 1914, they also had obvious disadvantages, among them that it made many products which had to be imported very expensive and that it removed the stimulus of foreign competition.

France continued to suffer from her inadequate supplies of coal. Production climbed only slowly during the 1880s; by 1890 it had reached 26 million tons, by 1900 33 million and by 1914 nearly 41 million tons. Home production continued to be insufficient to meet demand and a great deal of coal had to be imported. Coal imports kept pace with home production, rising from some 10 million tons in 1880 to 25 millions in 1913, by far the highest figure down to that date. To keep these figures in perspective one has to remember that in 1913 British coal output reached 287 million tons, 73 million of which were exported.

France's position with regard to iron ore was very different; she produced considerably more than she needed and exported on a large scale. The output rose from 8 million tons in 1880 to the record figure of nearly 22 million in 1913; almost half of this was exported, mainly to Germany. The German annexation of part of Lorraine had meant the loss to France, not only of important iron and steel works, but also of part of the great field of iron deposits which is to be found there. This ore – the so-called *minette* – contains a high proportion of phosphorus which hitherto had made it useless for steel-making. However, in 1877 a young English chemist, Sidney Gilchrist Thomas (1850–1885), took out a patent for a method of eliminating phosphorus from molten pig iron as found in the Bessemer converter. This process quickly spread to the Continent and was of particular importance to France because of her large deposits of iron. Of the 22 million tons of iron ore produced in 1913 almost all came from one small corner of what remained to France of the province of Lorraine; but, as we have seen, this did not lead to a proportionate increase in her production of iron and steel as so much of the ore went to Germany.

None the less the output of this industry did rise substantially, from the nineties onwards. Production of pig-iron and ferro-alloys – this was mainly concentrated in Lorraine – trebled between 1880 and 1913. Again the total amount of steel cast in France on the eve of the first world war had risen to nearly 5 million tons. In this industry expansion had undoubtedly been rapid, but French output needs to be compared with that of Britain and Germany; their output of steel came to $7\frac{1}{2}$ million tons and 17 million respectively. What is more, as iron and steel were protected by tariffs, French prices remained high and were uncompetitive in foreign markets.

It is obvious that the use of steam power must have greatly increased in the period with which we are concerned. Between 1880 and 1913 the amount used in industry was multiplied nearly seven times. Moreover from roughly the beginning of the present century a new source of energy – electricity generated in hydro-electric installations (what the French call 'la houille blanche') – was tapped and this was eventually to compensate to some degree for France's poor coal resources.

Though they no longer held the dominant place in the economy which had once been theirs, the textile industries continued to be important, employing nearly a million people, more than half of them women. In the cotton industry power looms had by this time replaced handlooms; the Rouen area was now less important than the Département du Nord and the Département des Vosges (the latter had made remarkable progress since the loss of the cotton industry of Alsace). A good deal of the cloth produced in

France, particularly dress materials, went abroad, but exports of woollens as a whole declined in the opening decade of the twentieth century. The silk industry was also very dependent on exports. The French output of raw silk had fallen to insignificant proportions and most of the raw material now had to be imported from the Far East. In many countries high tariffs were an obstacle to exports, but England still remained an important customer; it is said that more French silk was sold here than in France itself.

In two new fields France was to be a pioneer in the period just

Early bicycle (1861).

before 1914 – the motor car and the aeroplane. In one of his autobiographical works Georges Duhamel (1884–1966) records his childish memory of the coming of the motor car and the new noun *automobile* round about 1890:

> Au soir d'un de ces jeux, comme nous revenions au bourg, nous vîmes passer sur la route une merveille surprenante: la première automobile qu'il m'ait été donné d'apercevoir. Tous les gens étaient sur leur porte et commentaient le phénomène sans mesurer l'étendue de la révolution qu'il annonçait. Le mot d'*automobile* n'était pas encore inventé. Les curieux disaient, comme dans les journaux: 'C'est une voiture-sans-chevaux.' (*Inventaire de l'abîme*, p. 97)

In the motor industry France led the way in Europe, though, compared with what happened in the United States, this new form of transport was taken up only slowly. By 1914 such well-known French firms as Renault, Citroën and Peugeot were already in existence. In 1913 France's output of motor vehicles was twice that of Britain; half of it was exported, a considerable number of the vehicles coming to this country. Yet while growth was rapid – from a production of 2,000 vehicles in 1900 to 45,000 in 1913 – the numbers employed in the industry were still small and it was very

Early car: a Daimler of 1892.

scattered. The aeroplane, which had originated in the U.S.A. with the Wright brothers in 1903, was further developed in France and in 1909 Louis Blériot made his famous flight across the Channel from Calais to Dover. However, it needed the stimulus of the 1914–1918 war to give rise to an aircraft industry and to make the aeroplane a convenient means of transport.

Another new invention, the telephone, was slowly coming in from the U.S.A.; the number of subscribers in France rose gradually from 12,000 in 1889 to 310,000 in 1913. Something of the impact of this mysterious new instrument is conveyed in a famous passage in Proust's *Le Côté de Guermantes*:

Un matin, Saint-Loup m'avoua qu'il avait écrit à ma grand-mère pour lui donner de mes nouvelles et lui suggérer l'idée, puisqu'un service téléphonique fonctionnait entre Doncières et Paris, de causer avec moi. Bref, le même jour, elle devait me faire appeler à l'appareil et il me conseilla d'être vers quatre heures moins un quart à la poste. Le téléphone n'était pas encore à cette époque d'un usage aussi courant qu'aujourd'hui. Et pourtant l'habitude met si peu de temps à dépouiller de leur mystère les forces sacrées avec lesquelles nous sommes en contact que, n'ayant pas eu ma communication immédiatement, la seule pensée que j'eus, ce fut que c'était bien long, bien incommode, et presque l'intention d'adresser une plainte; comme

Blériot landing at Dover – July 25th, 1909.

nous tous maintenant, je ne trouvais pas assez rapide à mon gré, dans ses brusques changements, l'admirable féerie à laquelle quelques instants suffisent pour qu'apparaisse près de nous, invisible mais présent, l'être à qui nous voulions parler et qui, restant à sa table, dans la ville qu'il habite (pour ma grand-mère c'était Paris), sous un ciel différent du nôtre, par un temps qui n'est pas forcément le même, au milieu de circonstances et de préoccupations que nous ignorons et que cet être va nous dire, se trouve tout à coup transporté à des centaines de lieues (lui et toute l'ambiance où il reste plongé) près de notre oreille, au moment où notre caprice l'a ordonné. (II. 132–133)

Radio was invented at the end of the nineteenth century, but, like the aeroplane, it did not begin to come into its own until after 1914.

In two fields, however – the chemical and electrical industries – France lagged behind other advanced countries. Notoriously it was the Germans who, from the latter part of the nineteenth century, were the leaders in the chemical industry. While French production of some chemicals was comparatively high, the handicap of not having cheap coal and consequently cheap coal-tar products was a formidable one and France remained a large importer of chemicals. Again despite the development of hydro-electric power from about 1900 onwards the French electrical industries remained relatively backward. Yet in one field – the aluminium industry – France played a leading role; in 1887 an American and a Frenchman – Louis Toussaint Héroult (1863–1914) – took out simultaneously a patent for preparing the metal by electrolysis from bauxite, an ore of which France happens to have large deposits.

The limited horizons of French economic life down to 1914 and indeed well beyond are admirably described in a striking passage by a Frenchman who had lived through this period:

La France d'avant 1914, et même celle d'avant 1939, offrait cette caractéristique, après tout enviable, d'avoir peu besoin de l'extérieur, soit comme fournisseur, soit comme client: nous réglions plus qu'aisément une balance commerciale déficitaire, soit par le revenu de nos capitaux investis au dehors, soit par de multiples exportations invisibles. Cette traditionnelle aisance, parée d'autonomie, avait développé chez nous, par contraste avec l'insécurité militaire d'une frontière toujours menacée, un sentiment épanoui de sécurité économique, inconnu par exemple de l'Angleterre. C'était un peu comme un bonheur domestique, ingénument affiché, mais offensant pour les voisins. Le régime Méline, né d'une alliance entre l'industrie et l'agriculture, avait aggravé cette conscience de sécurité et favorisé je ne sais quelle paresse des industriels à l'égard des exportations: le producteur français songeait moins à la conquête de nouveaux marchés qu'à la défense par privilège du sien. (André Siegfried in *L'Année Politique*, 1957, p. xviii)

If for the most part industry was still conducted on a small scale, large undertakings, both in the Paris region and in various parts of the provinces, marked the trend towards greater concentration. A visit to the famous Schneider works at Le Creusot in 1892 inspired a journalist to write the following lines to describe the impression made on him on the night of his arrival by this establishment which employed 12,000 men (plus some 4,000 in the company's mines):

A petits pas, je m'achemine avec mon compagnon à travers les rues désertes. Je regarde autour de moi; c'est toute une ville éblouissante, fantastique, aux pignons et aux murs de verre, illuminés de la lumière bleue des lampes électriques.

– Les ateliers n'arrêtent pas, me dit mon contremaître; il y a une équipe de jour et une équipe de nuit.

Autour de nous, tout près et très loin, comme une armée de géants, la foule des cheminées crache des tourbillons de fumée vers le ciel où les étoiles clignaient plus faiblement. Nous gravissons une pente assez abrupte, bordée de maisons aux façades sinistres. Tout à coup, à mi-côte, devant une rampe en fer qui commence à la dernière maison, éclate à nos yeux un spectacle terrifiant, formidable, grandiose.

Un gouffre immense est sous nos pieds, borné, au fond, par une rangée de feux sombres; au centre, dans le trou, un flamboiement extraordinaire illumine les façades vitrées de halls gigantesques, les spectres prodigieux de tourelles de fer, les pignons des hangars, les bras rigides des grues, des amoncellements de métaux; sur le ciel bleu profond sali de tourbillons de fumée, toutes les choses prennent des développements surhumains; c'est un chaos inouï de formes in-attendues, heurtées, rudes, disproportionnées, sur lesquelles se projettent, démesurées, les ombres d'hommes gesticulant follement devant la gueule des fours, enjambant des ruisseaux de feu liquide qui serpentent dans la terre noire; de temps en temps, des guichets de brasiers s'ouvrent sur des constructions basses d'où s'échappent, par vingtaines, des flammes ardentes, et c'est, par ces portes d'enfer, une dégringolade continue de gros blocs rouges qu'un plancher roulant entraîne sous des jets d'eau. (J. Huret, *Enquête sur la question sociale*, pp. 13–15)

Unfortunately this trend towards concentration cannot be

accurately measured as there is no series of industrial censuses for the period as a whole. The 1906 census showed that more than half the industrial labour force was still employed in establishments with from one to five workers. Those with over 500 workers employed only a tenth of the total number of industrial workers. However, the acceleration in the process of concentration is shown by the enormous increase in the total horsepower of steam used in the average industrial establishment between 1882 and 1912; this rose from 16·3 h.p. to 51.3, and this does not count in gas-engines, which were much used in small establishments, nor electric power, which was increasingly employed.

Employment and trade unions

It is no easy task to try to picture the lot of the average industrial worker in these years of growing national prosperity. The exact course of both nominal and real wages is not easily plotted, and inevitably conditions varied enormously from industry to industry and from region to region. In 1884 an act was passed which legalized trade unions (*syndicats*). Although trade unionists were suspicious of the new law (it also legalized such things as producers' and consumers' co-operatives), it was followed by a considerable expansion of the existing unions and the foundation of new ones. The CGT (*Confédération Générale du Travail*), the equivalent of our TUC, was founded in 1895. By 1914 there were about a million trade unionists in France, though only a minority of these were affiliated to the CGT. This body was nothing like as representative of French workers as the TUC, founded in 1868 and with over two million trade unionists affiliated to it by 1913. The relative smallness of trade union membership in France obviously reflects the smaller place occupied by industry in the economic life of the country. In the 1880s a variety of Socialist parties sprang up to defend the interests of the workers; it is true that they did not attain a precarious unity until 1905 with the formation of the SFIO (*Section Française de l'Internationale Ouvrière*).

At the beginning of this period the worker lacked any state system of social security to cover sickness, unemployment and old age. No laws existed which effectively limited the hours of work of adults, or secured safe working conditions or ensured compensation for industrial injuries. Some idea of the conditions under which an industrial worker lived is conveyed in the dialogue between the journalist who visited the works at Le Creusot in 1892 and the foreman who showed him round:

– Combien d'heures travaillent-ils?

– La journée est de douze heures; mais, en réalité, ils ne travaillent que dix heures, parce qu'ils se reposent un peu et qu'ils mangent.

– Et ils gagnent?

– Oh! ça varie beaucoup! Les manoeuvres gagnent de 2 fr.55 à 3 francs par jour, les bons ouvriers, les ajusteurs, les chauffeurs, les contremaîtres comme moi peuvent aller de cent sous à dix francs; mais, bien sûr, ajouta-t-il en riant, qu'il y en a plus à trois francs qu'à dix! C'est même la très grande majorité.

Je ne pus m'empêcher de m'écrier:

– En voilà un métier! En voilà un métier!

– Oh! allez! répliqua mon guide d'un ton dégagé, ils ne sont pas plus malheureux que d'autres! Ils ne se plaignent pas d'ailleurs; ils y sont tellement habitués! Pensez donc: on vient ici en sortant de l'école et on ne s'en va que quand on n'est vraiment plus bon à rien.

– Y a t-il souvent des grèves, ici?

– Jamais. La dernière remonte à 1871. Oh! ils savent bien que ça ne servirait à rien d'abord; et puis ceux qu'on pincerait pourraient être sûrs de leur affaire . . .

After a eulogy of the methods by which school-leavers were taken on and trained, the foreman continued:

Tenez, c'est comme pour les accidents: il y a une infirmerie gratuite, un chirurgien, gratuit aussi, pour les opérations, parce que vous savez, ici, les accidents ne sont pas rares, il y en a même tous les jours, plus ou moins; pensez donc! sur des milliers d'ouvriers, il y en a toujours qui ne font pas attention . . .

– Ils sont payés, les ouvriers, quand ils sont blessés?

– Oh! je crois bien; on leur donne un tiers de leur journée, et 'les pharmacies' pour rien. Vous comprenez bien que si on payait davantage, il y en aurait qui se feraient blesser exprès, histoire de pouvoir se reposer tranquillement chez eux!

– Et quand ils meurent?

– Eh bien! leurs femmes, s'ils sont mariés, ont une pension.

– De combien?

– Ça dépend encore du nombre des enfants; ça peut être vingt, trente et même quarante francs par mois! Je vous dis, ici, il n'y a pas à se plaindre; M. Schneider fait bien les choses, c'est un brave homme qui a le coeur sur la main; il est député d'ailleurs, conseiller général et maire du Creusot, ce qui prouve bien qu'on connaît son bon coeur.

– Il doit y avoir encore d'autres avantages? demandai-je à ce contremaître modèle.

Il réfléchit un moment et ajouta en souriant d'un air malin, très content de sa trouvaille:

– Ah! et puis, ici, les ouvriers peuvent devenir propriétaires!
– Comment cela?
– Mais oui! La Compagnie nous avance l'argent qu'il nous faut
pour faire bâtir une maison; on rembourse tant par mois, et, au bout
d'un certain temps, on a sa petite maison et son petit jardin à soi. . . .
Alors, quand vient la retraite, on peut faire le rentier!
– On a une retraite aussi?
– Et c'est la Compagnie qui paie, s'il vous plaît! On ne nous retient
pas un sou sur nos journées, comme on fait dans presque toutes les
usines.
– Une retraite de combien?
– Eh! mais, ça va de dix ou quinze francs par mois, à trente et
quarante francs, ça dépend des salaires, car la Compagnie verse tous
les ans à la caisse en proportion de ce que l'ouvrier gagne. C'est bien
généreux de la part de la Compagnie, il n'y a pas à dire.

Une odeur épouvantable de houille, de soufre, de suie, de pous-
sière sortait du gouffre; on se sentait comme enveloppé, pénétré par
la fumée.

– Alors, dis-je, pour résumer, voilà des gens nés ici, entrés à l'école
de M. Schneider, qui ont passé toute leur vie, douze heures par jour,
été comme hiver, dans ce grand trou-là, à respirer ça, à s'éreinter, et
qui finissent leurs jours, s'ils sont bien sages et s'ils ont fait des
économies, dans des maisonnettes avec 20 francs par mois de
pension? (J. Huret, *Enquête sur la question sociale*, pp. 16–19)

It need hardly be said that M. Schneider, the son of the original
founder of the firm, was not in favour either of the restrictions on
the employment of women and children imposed by the law of
1874 or of a shorter working day for adult males:

– La journée de huit heures?
– Oh! je veux bien! dit M. Schneider, affectant un grand dés-
intéressement, si tout le monde est d'accord, je serai le premier à en
profiter, car je travaille souvent moi-même plus de dix heures par
jour . . . Seulement, les salaires diminueront ou le prix des produits
augmentera, c'est tout comme!

Au fond, voyez-vous, la journée de huit heures, c'est encore un
dada, un boulangisme. Dans cinq ou six ans, on n'y pensera plus, on
aura inventé autre chose. Pour moi, la vérité, c'est qu'un ouvrier
bien portant peut très bien faire ses dix heures par jour et qu'on doit
le laisser libre de travailler davantage si ça lui fait plaisir. (ibid.
p. 34)

Even more downright were the comments of Baron Alphonse de
Rothschild on what workers would do if they were given an
eight-hour day: 'Savez-vous ce qu'ils feront, la majorité? Eh

bien! ils iront boire! Ils iront davantage au cabaret, voilà tout!
Que voulez-vous qu'ils fassent?' (ibid., p. 64)

That same year 1892 did see the passage of a new factory act,
but it can be imagined that the restrictions which it imposed on
hours of work appear nowadays grotesquely inadequate. Young
persons under sixteen could not be employed for more than ten
hours a day, women and young persons between sixteen and eighteen for more than eleven hours and men for more than twelve. . .
A law passed in 1900 reduced the working day of adult males as
well as women and young persons by stages to ten hours, a goal
to be achieved in 1904, but the agitation amongst trade unionists
for an eight-hour day did not get anywhere except for miners, in
whose favour a law was passed in 1905. In the following year a
weekly day of rest was made compulsory in all industrial and
commercial undertakings.

It is notorious that, compared with England and especially
Germany, France was extremely slow in introducing legislation
on social security. In 1928 when a comprehensive social security
law covering sickness, disablement, and old age was about to be
voted by the Chamber of Deputies one speaker underlined the
slowness with which such matters were dealt with by the French
Parliament in the following terms:

> C'est ici en 1880 que s'est produite la première manifestation
> parlementaire en faveur des Assurances sociales obligatoires, par le
> dépôt de la proposition de loi Martin Nadaud qui est du 29 mars
> 1880 sur les accidents du travail. Cette proposition, discutée longue-
> ment dans son principe et dans ses modalités, ne devient une réalité
> que dans la loi du 9 avril 1898 sur les accidents du travail. On a mis
> dix-huit ans à faire ce premier pas. Puis en 1890, on dépose une
> proposition de loi; c'est la propostion Laisant du 18 juillet 1890 sur
> les retraites ouvrières et paysannes obligatoires. Cette proposition ne
> devient une réalité que dans la loi du 5 avril 1910. Cette fois on a mis
> vingt ans pour faire ce second pas. Un projet de loi sur les Assurances
> sociales est déposé en mars 1921. Nous sommes en 1928 et nous ne
> l'avons pas encore voté. Ainsi donc depuis 1880, quarante-huit
> années ont passé et nous n'avons pas encore parachevé l'oeuvre que
> nous commencions alors. (E. Antonelli, *Trente-trois ans de la sécurité
> sociale en France*, p. 16)

Greater controversy was aroused by the law on retirement
pensions than by the law which made the employer responsible for
compensation for industrial injury or death. Under the pension
scheme the employer and employee were to pay the same contri-

bution, and the rest was to be made up by the State. The pension, available at sixty-five, amounted to the princely sum of 60 francs a year. The opposition to the law came not only from the Right, but also from the trade unions, who were opposed to their members paying a contribution and to what they regarded as the late age for receiving the pension. The resistance encountered by the law is vividly described by the first minister who had to try to apply it:

> Parce que l'âge de la retraite était un peu tardif, ce fut *la retraite pour les morts*.
>
> Parce que le chiffre de la pension avait été fixé un peu bas, en attendant que le mécanisme financier eût fait ses preuves, ce fut *la retraite dérisoire*.
>
> Enfin, la loi . . . était fondée sur la capitalisation, non sur la répartition . . . Il était dès lors facile de faire apparaître une disproportion entre l'argent amassé dans la caisse et la retraite attribuée. Et ce fut *l'escroquerie des retraites*.
>
> Et l'étrange était que sur ces points, pour une fois, adversaires de droite et gauche du socialisme, intransigeants du patronat et extrémistes du syndicalisme fussent d'accord. (Paul-Boncour, *Entre deux Guerres*, I. 204)

In practice three-quarters of all wage-earners did not bother to take out cards under the scheme, and it was not until the 1928 act was brought into operation that retirement pensions became a reality. Insurance against unemployment (it was argued that this was less necessary than in more heavily industrialized countries like England) was not brought in until as late as 1958, whereas it had been introduced in this country in 1911.

By this period certain changes in the distribution of the active population were becoming increasingly more marked. If we divide the active population into three sectors – *primary* (agriculture, forestry and fishing), *secondary* (industry, building, public works, water, gas and electricity) and *tertiary* (distribution, public services, etc.), we have seen how the proportion engaged in the first of these groups was gradually falling, a process which has been enormously speeded up since 1945; the second group continued to expand slowly down to 1914, while the third group which, as in all advanced countries, was to become the largest of all by the 1960s, was already growing steadily in our period.

Thus the number of persons employed on the railways rose from 223,000 in 1881 to 321,000 in 1906. The distributive trades were expanding rapidly: in 1906, 1,183,000 persons were employed in commerce, hotels and cafés. The proportion of women employed was growing, not only in the textile industries, but in commerce, offices and the public service. Civil servants (*fonction-naires*) increased rapidly in the half century down to 1914; by then their numbers had reached nearly half a million. A considerable part of this rise was due to the expansion in education since all teachers in the state system – primary, secondary and university – are *fonctionnaires*. From 1866 to 1914 the numbers employed in the education service rose from 65,000 to 150,000, the only comparable figure being that for the Post Office which in 1914 employed 123,000. Domestic service reached its peak in our period; in 1881 there were well over a million domestic servants, 70 per cent of whom were women. Thereafter a decline set in, which has enormously speeded up since 1914 with the gradual substitution of the 'help' for the maid living in.

Distribution of wealth

It can well be imagined that, despite the country's democratic institutions, French society at the beginning of the present century was very far from being egalitarian. As income tax (established permanently in England in 1842) was not introduced in France until the passing of laws in the period 1914–1917, if one wishes to form some idea of the distribution of wealth down to 1914, all one can do is to make use of information concerning inheritance. If we take the figures for 1910, covering only those estates which had a net credit balance (it must be remembered that tens of thousands of adults died leaving no assets at all), we find that there were 298,900 estates of between one and 10,000 francs; 45,500 of between 10,001 and 50,000 francs; 7,700 of between 50,001 and 100,000 francs; 7,100 of between 100,001 and one million; and 600 of over one million. In other words, some five-sixths of these estates were under 10,000 francs. On the other hand, while the total value of the property bequeathed came to 5,320 million francs, well over 3,000 millions of this – considerably more than half – belonged to the 7,700 estates of over 100,000 francs. It is clear that there was still widespread poverty at the base of this society, and at the top a marked concentration of the wealth of the country in a relatively small number of hands. In between these two extremes came none the less a considerable number of very comfortable fortunes which reflected the collective wealth of a fairly prosperous middle class. The society of 'la belle époque' contained a rich variety of shades of poverty and wealth.

Political History (1879-1914)

With the installation of 'la République des Républicains' in 1879 came a new political atmosphere. Though the elections of 1881 aroused nothing like the same excitement as those of 1877, they further strengthened the new régime, as the Bonapartists and Monarchists won between them less than a hundred seats. Inevitably the Republicans now split up into a greater variety of groups. The moderates – men like Gambetta and Ferry – who called themselves 'républicains de gouvernement' while their enemies on the Left denounced them as 'opportunistes' were both divided amongst themselves and attacked from the left by the 'radicaux' who had a formidable spokesman in Georges Clemenceau (1841–1929), nicknamed 'Le Tigre', and by the Socialists and near-Socialists who gradually increased their strength in the 1880s.

During the last years of the Second Empire men like Gambetta and Ferry had been very radical in opposition, but they had gradually become more conservative. In 1872 in the midst of the struggle for the Republic Gambetta had used in a speech the famous phrase about the entry into politics of 'une nouvelle couche sociale'. What he had in mind was the replacement of the political influence of the 'notables' – the nobility and wealthy bourgeoisie – by that of self-made middle class people such as doctors, lawyers and tradesmen. This is clear from a speech which he made a couple of years later:

> Messieurs, j'ai dit les nouvelles couches, non pas les classes: c'est un mauvais mot que je n'emploie jamais. Oui, une nouvelle couche sociale s'est formée. On la trouve partout; elle se manifeste à tous les regards clairvoyants; elle se rencontre dans tous les milieux, à tous les étages de la société. C'est elle qui en arrivant à la fortune, à la notoriété, à la capacité, à la compétence, augmente la richesse, les ressources, l'intelligence et le nerf de la patrie. (*Discours*, IV. 155–156)

In another famous speech he even declared: 'Il n'y a pas une question sociale':

> Tenons-nous en garde contre les utopies de ceux qui, dupes de leur imagination ou attardés dans leur ignorance, croient à une panacée, à une formule qu'il s'agit de trouver pour faire le bonheur du monde. Croyez qu'il n'y a pas de remède social, parce qu'il n'y a pas une *question sociale*. Il y a une série de problèmes à résoudre, de difficultés

à vaincre, variant avec les lieux, les climats, les habitudes, l'état sanitaire, problèmes économiques, qui changent dans l'intérieur d'un même pays; eh bien! ces problèmes doivent être résolus un à un et non par une formule unique. (*Discours*, II. 263)

This was a clear rejection of Socialist theories.

A similarly negative attitude was taken up by Ferry in a remarkable speech, delivered in 1884 when he was prime minister. In it he stated the problem very clearly when he asked:

André Gill: cartoon of Jules Ferry in 1878.

> Le Gouvernement est-il chargé par sa mission même et par sa fonction de Gouvernement, de faire prévaloir un système déterminé d'extinction du paupérisme? En un mot, la solution du problème social ou des problèmes sociaux est-elle dans la main du Gouvernement, ou est-elle avant tout dans la main de l'individu? Voilà, je crois, la question qui s'est posée, formidable, devant nos pères de 1848 et qui a fait peser sur les destinées de la Seconde République un profond et funèbre malentendu. (*Discours*, VI. 226)

For him the answer was plain:

> Sans doute cette lutte pour la vie est âpre, . . . sans doute il est permis de rêver une société mieux organisée que cette société de bataille et de concurrence qui est la nôtre, une société plus fraternelle; mais aucun de nous, messieurs, ni aucun de ceux qui nous succèderont ne verra même le seuil de cette terre promise! (*Discours*, VI. 240)

The role of a republican government was limited to being 'le promoteur naturel de l'enseignement populaire, le surintendant de la prévoyance sociale et le tuteur des malheureux qui n'en ont pas.' In the previous year he had made the famous speech in which he denounced the more radical republicans – a speech which was summed up by contemporaries as 'Le péril est à gauche'. What he actually said was:

> Quelle conduite faut-il tenir en présence de ces tendances, qui constituent assurément pour la République un péril, et j'ose le dire, le plus grand, le seul péril du moment, car le péril monarchique n'existe plus. Le péril monarchique est enterré sous deux tombes,[1] sur lesquelles ne refleurira jamais un rameau d'avenir. Ce péril n'existe plus, mais un autre lui succède, et il nous faut le regarder en face, lui opposer le seul remède, la seule barrière: l'union, de plus en plus étroite, des forces républicaines capables de constituer un gouvernement. (*Discours*, VI. 171–172)

Such was the outlook of the 'républicains de gouvernement' in the early years after the triumph of the Republican party.

The radical answer to men like Gambetta and Ferry came from Clemenceau. In a speech delivered in 1884 he began by answering Gambetta:

> Je dis que cette question sociale existe. Je ne m'amuse pas à discuter le point de savoir s'il y a une ou des questions sociales. Il y a un ensemble de questions sociales qui viennent toutes se résumer en une question sociale, comme il y a un ensemble de questions politiques qui viennent toutes se résumer en une question politique.

---

[1] Those of the Prince Imperial (died 1879) and the Comte de Chambord (died 1883).

Clémenceau making a speech at an election meeting in 1885.

Oui, la question sociale ne peut être niée. Vous ne pouvez pas faire, à mesure que l'instruction se répand, que l'homme qui naît dans la misère, à qui la société ne fournit pas les moyens de prendre part, dans des conditions équitables, à cette lutte sociale dont on a parlé, ne se trouve, à un moment donné, dans un certain état d'esprit qui, dans un pays de suffrage universel, réagit sur ceux qui l'entourent et finit par créer un état d'opinion dont le gouvernement est obligé de tenir compte. (Chambre des Députes, 31 Jan. 1884)

For him the Republic meant 'l'égalité du droit à l'éducation, l'égalité du droit à la liberté, et l'égalité du droit à l'exercice le plus complet et le plus utile de chaque action humaine'. At moments in this speech he appears to speak in socialist terms, for instance, when he declares:

> Car, enfin, vous parlez de la liberté des contrats: est-ce qu'il y a liberté entre le capitaliste qui choisit ses ouvriers quand il veut, comme il veut, et le misérable qui est obligé de se soumettre aux obligations du contrat parce qu'il faut qu'il mange, parce qu'il faut qu'il soutienne sa famille, parce qu'il faut qu'il vive? (*Très bien! très bien! sur divers bancs à gauche.*) Cette liberté, Messieurs, c'est la liberté de l'oppression.

Yet even in his more radical earlier period Clemenceau would have nothing to do with revolutionary socialism and the class struggle. Both are clearly rejected in a speech delivered in a meeting later in the same year:

> Comment ne voyez-vous pas combien vous faites fausse route quand vous voulez instituer la lutte de classes et préparer la révolution?
>
> C'est sur ce point que je me sépare nettement d'avec vous . . . J'affirme que toute la politique d'une démocratie, c'est de faire émanciper le groupe le moins éclairé, dans le plus bref délai possible, par le groupe qui a l'avantage des lumières et de l'éducation. (Speech at the Cirque Fernando, pp. 42–43)

The early years of 'la République des Républicains' reveal all the divergences among the Republicans – conservative, radical and socialist – which were to persist down to 1914.

None the less their advent to power brought about a great many changes. First the President, then the two houses of Parliament returned from Versailles to Paris. The *Marseillaise*, treated as a seditious song under so many post-Revolutionary régimes, became in 1879 the national anthem, and in the following three the 14 July, the anniversary of the taking of the Bastille, was celebrated for the first time as a 'fête nationale'. A great many generals, ambassadors and high civil servants with strong anti-republican views were removed from office. The question of an amnesty for the *Communards* gave rise to protracted debates; however, a partial amnesty was voted in 1879 and in the following year it was made virtually complete.

The longstanding hostility of the Republicans to the Catholic Church – summed up in the famous formula of Gambetta, 'Le cléricalisme, voilà l'ennemi!' – was quickly translated into acts. Given the ultra-conservative line taken for generations by the overwhelming majority of Catholic priests and laymen it was hardly surprising that there should be a clash now that the

Republicans were in the saddle, as a liberal Catholic like the young Abbé Frémont had to admit in his diary:

> 19 juin 1880. – Le clergé, systématiquement, n'a jamais considéré les divers gouvernements qui se sont succédé en France, de 1789 à 1815, et de 1830 à 1880, que comme des gouvernements illégitimes, contre les principes politiques desquels il a toujours protesté secrètement ou publiquement. Cette manière d'agir nous a progressivement aliéné la sympathie des masses, et nous voilà de nouveau face à face avec la démocratie triomphante qui déclare que, puisque nous ne voulons pas d'elle, elle ne veut plus de nous. (Agnès Siegfried, *L'Abbé Georges Frémont*, I. 113)

It was in the field of education that the conflict took place; since the *Loi Falloux* of 1850 the influence of the clergy in the public sector had enormously increased, and under 'la République des Ducs' it had been further extended, in particular by the right to grant degrees being conferred on Catholic faculties. The government began by removing members of the clergy, along with other lay representatives, from the *Conseil supérieur de l'Instruction*, and confined its membership to teachers. The right to confer degrees was once again made a monopoly of the state institutions of higher education.

The biggest row, however, was over the fate of the unauthorized religious communities or congregations which had gradually established themselves since their dissolution in 1790. Nearly 2,000 of their members, including over 800 Jesuits, were engaged in teaching. The government brought forward a bill which contained the famous Article 7:

> Nul n'est admis à participer à l'enseignement public ou libre ni à diriger un établissement de quelque ordre que ce soit s'il appartient à une congrégation religieuse non autorisée.

When the clause was thrown out by the Senate, the government had recourse to decrees. These required that all unauthorized congregations should seek recognition from the State within three months and declared the dissolution of the Society of Jesus. The Jesuits were forcibly expelled from their buildings and, after attempts to negotiate a compromise had broken down, several thousand members of other unauthorized congregations were evicted. However, before long most of these monks came together again and the whole battle had to be fought once more twenty years later.

More positive measures were taken in these years to strengthen

'L'instruction, c'est la Lumière.'

and extend the State system of education. As Jules Ferry, now Minister of Education as well as prime minister, put it in a speech at the end of 1880:

Il importe à la République, à la société civile, il importe à tous ceux qui ont à coeur la tradition de 1789 que la direction des écoles, que l'inspection des écoles n'appartiennent pas à des ministres du culte qui ont, sur ces choses qui nous sont chères, et sur lesquelles repose

> la société, des opinions séparées des nôtres par un si profond abîme.
> (*Discours*, IV. 127)

Nearly all girls' primary schools, even those in the state system, were run by nuns, and few departments ran *écoles normales* for the training of women teachers. A law of 1879 made it compulsory for these to be set up in all departments within four years. Hitherto secondary education for girls had been available only in the home or in private schools, most of which were run by nuns. In 1880 a law was passed, against strong resistance from Catholics, setting up a state system of secondary education for girls.

The long struggle for the principles of 'gratuité, obligation, laïcité' in primary education was also brought to an end. In 1881 all fees in state primary schools were abolished, and in the following year attendance at school from the age of six to thirteen was made compulsory. What caused much more controversy was the secularization of primary education; this was denounced in furious terms as 'l'école sans Dieu'. Henceforth the clergy were to exercise no control over state primary schools, which were to remain completely neutral in matters of religion, though one day a week was to be left free for children to receive religious instruction outside the school if their parents should so desire.

This burst of reforms included new laws on public meetings and the press. Although the right of assembly continued to be restricted in somewhat odd ways, the law on public meetings did give a much greater freedom in this sphere than ever before. The new press law was also voted in 1881; as it covered posters, its existence is recalled to the visitor to France by the words painted in large letters on public buildings: 'Défense d'afficher. Loi du 29 juillet 1881'. The new law marked the end of the restrictions imposed by previous régimes such as government authorization, stamp-duty and caution-money to cover fines. The relatively few crimes left were to be tried by jury. In other words, by the standards of the time the law was extremely liberal. It was, however, fairly soon to be modified by various measures against pornography and by the laws passed in 1893 and 1894 as a result of the panic created by anarchist outrages. On the other hand the law gave practically no redress either to public figures or to private individuals who were the victims of gross libels; this accounts for the astonishing virulence of political controversy in France in the decades which followed.

In 1882 a new law was passed concerning local government; its most important provision concerned the appointment of the *maire* of the *commune*. Henceforth, instead of being appointed by the government, he was to be elected by the municipal council, the one exemption being Paris where the powers of the *maire* are in the hands of the *Préfet de la Seine*. The *maire* continued to represent the central government in his *commune*, but the fact that he was now elected strengthened local autonomy. Two years later the law on *syndicats* was passed and another law re-established divorce which had been introduced during the Revolution, but abolished under the Restoration.

In the same year a number of fairly minor modifications were made in the constitutional laws of 1875 by agreement between the Senate and the Chamber of Deputies. Characteristically the National Assembly struck out the part of one article in the 1875 constitutional law which read:

> Le dimanche qui suivra la rentrée, des prières publiques seront adressées à Dieu dans les églises et dans les temples pour appeler son secours sur les travaux de l'Assemblée.

In order to prevent a recurrence of the long delay between the dissolution of the Chamber and the holding of elections in 1877 it was laid down that these must take place within two months of a dissolution and that the new Chamber must meet within ten days of the end of the elections. A new paragraph was added which made monarchist propaganda anti-constitutional:

> La forme républicaine du gouvernement ne peut faire l'objet d'une proposition de révision. – Les membres des familles ayant régné sur la France sont inéligibles à la présidence de la République.

Finally the laws governing the election of members of the Senate ceased to be constitutional laws.

After long negotiations between the two chambers it was finally agreed that the 75 life members of the upper house should gradually be phased out, their seats being given to the more heavily populated departments, and that the number of the delegates which a *commune* sent to take part in elections to the Senate should vary according to its size. This reduced, but did not altogether remove the excessive weight given to the small rural *communes*. The elections which followed early in 1885 further reduced the number of Royalists in the Senate.

Before the elections to the Chamber of Deputies which took place later in the same year a law was passed to replace the *scrutin d'arrondissement* (one deputy for each constituency) by the *scrutin de liste* by which each department voted as a whole for a number of deputies which varied according to its population. This change was soon to lead the régime into serious trouble. The first ballot in the 1885 elections gave the Republicans a nasty shock, as the Right did extremely well in face of the divisions between moderates and Radicals on the Left; however, the Republican voters redressed the balance in the second ballot when they supported the candidate of the Left who had secured the highest number of votes in the first ballot. The result was that the Republicans obtained more seats than in 1877, but the Radicals were now greatly strengthened at the expense of the moderates.

As none of the three groups into which the Chamber was split was strong enough to form a ministry, there followed a period of governmental instability, which helped the meteoric rise of General Georges Boulanger (1837–1891) to fame and influence. He had a reputation as a thoroughly Republican general, and thanks to the influence of the Radical leader, Clemenceau, at the beginning of 1886 he was appointed Minister for War, a post then normally held by a general. He began by taking action against Royalist officers and by making improvements in the living conditions of other ranks, but his main appeal was to the latent nationalism of the masses. At the military review on the Longchamp race course on 14 July 1886 he received a great ovation from the spectators. Here was 'le général Revanche', the great military leader who would wipe out the defeat of 1870 and win back the lost provinces. A Paris *chansonnier* produced a song to suit the occasion; it proved tremendously popular:

> Gais et contents,
> Nous étions triomphants
> En allant à Longchamp,
> Le coeur à l'aise,
> Sans hésiter
> Car nous allions fêter,
> Voir et complimenter
> L'armée française . . .
> Moi j' faisais qu'admirer
> Not' brav' général Boulanger.

He kept his place in a new government formed at the end of the year, but suspicions about both his aspirations for personal power and his bellicose attitude meant that he was dropped from the new government which had to be formed in May 1887.

Then began a period of two years' agitation which placed the whole régime in serious danger. Boulanger became the idol of a great many people, including large numbers on the Left, as he grouped together all those discontented with the Republic. The disillusionment of many people with the whole régime is summed up in the famous saying of this period: 'Ah! que la République était belle sous l'Empire.' When the government, in order to get him away from Paris, sent him off to far-away Clermont-Ferrand to command an army corps there, an enormous crowd invaded the Gare de Lyon and tried to prevent him from leaving.

A vivid picture of the atmosphere of the time is to be found in *L'Appel au Soldat* (1900) of Maurice Barrès, a fervent *boulangiste*, who was to secure election as a deputy for Nancy in 1889 under the general's banner. The political situation in France in 1887 was further complicated by a presidential crisis; Grévy, who had been re-elected in 1885, was forced to resign at the end of the year as his son-in-law, Daniel Wilson, who lived in the Palais de l'Élysée, had engaged in various corrupt practices. In the meantime, although, as a serving officer, Boulanger was not eligible for election, he was put up by his supporters as a candidate at a number of by-elections. Various secret visits to Paris led in March 1888 to his being first dismissed from his post at Clermont and then retired from the army.

As he was now free to take part in politics, his party began to agitate, under the slogan 'Dissolution, Constituante, Révision', for a revision of the constitution of 1875 which would have installed an authoritarian régime in France. This gained a good deal of support (including large sums of money) from the Monarchists who hoped to see Boulanger play the same role as that of General Monk in the restoration of Charles II. The general now began putting up for one vacant seat after another in the Chamber; in April he was elected first in Dordogne and then in the Département du Nord. When he took his seat in the Chamber and expounded his programme, he was asked by the prime minister why he addressed the assembly as if he were General Bonaparte returning from a victorious campaign: 'A votre âge, Monsieur, Napoléon était mort.' A second clash between the two men led to a duel in which it was the civilian who wounded the general.

In August he put up in three departments simultaneously and was elected in all of them. As the climax of this campaign, in January 1889, Boulanger put up at a by-election in Paris itself. The result was declared on a Sunday evening: Boulanger had

Posters for the election of 27th January, 1889.

secured 244,000 votes against 162,000 for his main opponent, a
Radical. In a restaurant in the Place de la Madeleine, which was
surrounded by delirious crowds of his supporters, Boulanger was
urged by his entourage to carry out a *coup d'état* by marching on
the Palais de l'Élysée. The government was helpless as it could
rely neither on the police nor on the armed forces in the Paris
region. However, Boulanger refused to act, partly because he
remembered his father's horror at Louis Napoleon's *coup d'état*,

partly because it seemed a futile gesture since he was convinced that his party would sweep the country when the general election was held later in the year.

This was the high point of the movement; the rest of its history was a decided anti-climax. The Republicans in the Chamber quickly passed an electoral law abolishing *scrutin de liste*, which favoured the *boulangistes*, and restoring *scrutin d'arrondissement*. A new government (the sixth since the elections of 1885) was formed; it had a tough Minister of the Interior who was determined to defend the régime by any and every means. He dissolved the very right-wing *Ligue des Patriotes* and threatened Boulanger with trial by the Senate acting as a High Court of Justice for plotting against the security of the State. On 1 April the general fled to Brussels and then on to London. Proceedings were opened against him and two of his aides; on 14 August they were found guilty *in absentia* and sentenced to deportation. This made them ineligible for election to the Chamber.

The success of the 1889 exhibition which celebrated the hundredth anniversary of the French Revolution strengthened the Republic. Before the elections took place in September Parliament had taken further measures against Boulanger by passing a law which prevented any individual from being a candidate in more than one constituency and which laid down that votes cast in favour of a candidate who was ineligible would not be counted. Despite their divisions the Right, including the clergy, gave general support to Boulanger, but, although his supporters had some success in Paris and the provinces, they won only 38 seats. Once again the Republicans had a comfortable majority. Just over two years later the general committed suicide in Brussels on the grave of his mistress. *Boulangisme* gradually fizzled out, but while it was at its height in the years 1887–1889 it had placed the Republic in grave danger; it was also the forerunner of later mass movements exploiting all sorts of discontents.

Now that the Republic had survived for some twenty years it began to become obvious to an outside observer like Pope Leo XIII that it had come to stay and that the pro-monarchist attitude of French Catholics could only harm the Church in France. In 1890 Cardinal Lavigerie, the Archbishop of Algiers, endeavoured to put across the papal message in a speech proposing the toast of the French navy whose Mediterranean squadron was visiting North Africa:

Quand la volonté d'un peuple s'est nettement affirmée, que la forme
du gouvernement n'a rien en soi de contraire, comme le proclamait
dernièrement Léon XIII, aux principes qui seuls peuvent faire vivre
les nations chrétiennes et civilisées, lorsqu'il n'y a plus, pour arracher
son pays aux abîmes qui le menacent, que l'adhésion sans arrière-
pensée à la forme du gouvernement, le moment vient de déclarer
enfin l'épreuve faite . . . C'est ce que j'enseigne autour de moi, c'est
ce que je souhaite de voir imiter en France par tout notre clergé, et
en parlant ainsi je suis certain de n'être démenti par aucune voix
autorisée.

Most French Catholics, but especially the active royalists, received
this message with incredulity, though some politicians took up the
idea of accepting the Republic and forming a political party to
safeguard Catholic interests. Hostility to the régime continued,
however, and, in spite of a papal encylical of 1892 which urged
French Catholics to accept the Republican constitution but to
work for a revision of the laws which were unacceptable to the
Church, this view was not accepted by the majority of the faithful.

1892 also saw the passing of laws instituting high protective
tariffs on imported industrial and agricultural products. Then
came another threat to the Republic, despite continued successes
in Senatorial and local elections – this time the famous Panama
scandal. After the successful completion of the Suez Canal Ferdinand de Lesseps had formed a company to construct a canal in
Panama between the Atlantic and Pacific oceans. Work had
begun in 1879, but the project ran into all sorts of difficulties,
partly through mismanagement of its finances. In 1888, lotteries
being illegal, the Chamber had been prevailed upon to pass a law
to allow the company to float a lottery loan, but next year it went
bankrupt and proceedings were opened against the directors for
financial irregularities.

In November 1892 (the 1893 elections were approaching)
various opposition newspapers began a campaign to discredit the
Republican politicians, many of whom were accused of complicity in the financial scandal. Once again Barrès offers a vivid
account of the excitement caused by the affair, in the third part
of *Le Roman de l'énergie nationale – Leurs Figures* (1902). Three
governments fell between December 1892 and April 1893 as the
scandal was investigated by a parliamentary commission of
inquiry. Neither the newspapers nor the banks came well out of
the affair, but attention was concentrated on the politicians by
their opposition rivals. When the case came before the courts, a

former Minister for Public Works confessed to having received 300,000 francs in 1888 for his part in promoting a bill for the company and received a prison sentence. Although the other parliamentarians were acquitted, quite a number of prominent political figures, including Clemenceau, had to withdraw either temporarily or permanently from political life.

When the elections came in 1893, they attracted an exceptionally low number of voters. The new Catholic party, which followed the Pope's advice and accepted the Republic (its members were known as 'les ralliés'), had relatively little success, winning only 35 seats; its two most prominent leaders were both defeated. In general the conservatives lost pretty heavily, while on the extreme Left a motley collection of Socialists and near-Socialists won nearly fifty seats, and the Radicals also increased their numbers. On the other hand the moderate Republicans, who were tired of their allies on the Left and were anxious to govern with the support of the centre against both extremes, came out of the elections strong enough to do so down to 1898, except for a brief period of less than six months in 1895–1896, when the first purely Radical government to hold office was in power.

The development of a Socialist movement, if as yet torn by all sorts of dissensions, was causing increasing alarm among the parties in the centre and on the right. The period 1892–1894 was marked by a series of anarchist explosions in Paris. This 'propagande par le fait' had begun in 1892 with various dynamite explosions caused by a certain Ravachol who declared at his trial:

> La société est pourrie. Dans les ateliers, les mines et les champs, il y a des êtres humains qui travaillent et souffrent sans pouvoir espérer d'acquérir la millième partie du fruit de leur travail; ils ont des femmes qui meurent de faim et des enfants qu'ils ne peuvent nourrir faute de pain. A côté de cette misère terrible, nous voyons les bourgeois engraissés mener une vie de jouissances et répondre par un rire méprisant aux larmes des affamés.

The day before his trial began (he was executed later in the year for a murder committed earlier) an explosion which killed two people took place in the restaurant in which he had been arrested. Later in the year a bomb which had been left in a Paris office exploded when it had been removed to the police station and killed four policemen. In December an anarchist named Vaillant let off a bomb in the *Chambre des Députés*, injuring, though not seriously, a large number of people; he was executed. In February

1894 a young man named Émile Henry, the son of a *communard*, left a bomb in a café near the Gare Saint-Lazare; this killed several people as well as injuring a great many more. He too was executed. Four months later, while on a state visit to Lyons, the President of the Republic, Sadi Carnot, was stabbed to death by an Italian anarchist.

In December 1893 the government rushed through four bills, denounced by the extreme Left as 'les lois scélérates', as it was feared that these laws would be used to repress the Socialist movement. The most important of these greatly restricted the degree of freedom enjoyed by the press since 1881 as it imposed the penalty of up to five years' imprisonment for the crime of provocation, even if it was without result, to theft, murder, incendiarism or subversion. Such a penalty could also be applied to the apology for such crimes. However, the period of direct action soon died down.

Between the elections of 1893 and the latter part of 1895 no fewer than four different moderate Republican governments fell; and a Radical was then called upon to form a government. Having failed to secure any moderate support, he was compelled to form for the first time one consisting wholly of Radical ministers. Inevitably it was a highly unstable government which lasted only six months, but it was memorable for two other reasons: it brought in a bill to introduce an income tax (a subject which was to be debated for another twenty years before it was finally accepted by Parliament) and it found itself involved in the first of many clashes between a left-wing government and the Senate. The Senate, having defeated the government, maintained that constitutionally it must resign; the government took the view that only a defeat in the Chamber made this necessary.

This government was followed by another moderate Republican one under Méline, the apostle of high protective tariffs; by surviving for two years and two months this ministry set up what was at the time a record for the Third Republic. The 1898 elections did not produce very different results from those of 1893, but France now entered upon another phase, not only of government instability but of serious threats to the whole Republican régime. The origin of this period of crisis in 1898–1899 lay in 'l'affaire Dreyfus'.

Captain Dreyfus may have been a somewhat uninteresting person, but his fate and the agitation stirred up by the whole case brought France to the verge of civil war and, when that

Dreyfus hears the sentence of the court martial read out. (*L'Illustration*, 29th December, 1894)

danger had subsided, produced a marked swing to the Left in French politics. In 1894 this wealthy Alsatian Jew was arrested on a charge of handing over to Germany documents concerned with national defence. He was sentenced by court martial to be deported to a tiny tropical island with the sinister name of L'Ile du Diable, opposite Cayenne in French Guiana. He was alleged to have written the following covering letter (always referred to in the case as 'le bordereau') to the German military attaché in Paris:

> Sans nouvelles m'indiquant que vous désirez me voir, je vous adresse cependant monsieur quelques renseignements intéressants.

1° Une note sur le frein hydraulique du 120 et la manière dont s'est conduite cette pièce.

2° Une note sur les troupes de couverture (quelques modifications seront apportées par le nouveau plan).

3° Une note sur une modification aux formations de l'artillerie.

4° Une note relative à Madagascar.

5° Le projet de manuel de tir de l'artillerie de campagne (14 mars 1894).

Ce dernier document est extrêmement difficile à se procurer et je ne puis l'avoir à ma disposition que très peu de jours. Le ministère de la Guerre en a envoyé un nombre fixe dans les corps et ces corps en sont responsables, chaque officier détenteur doit remettre le sien après les manoeuvres. Si donc vous voulez y prendre ce qui vous intéresse et le tenir à ma disposition après, je le prendrai. A moins que vous ne vouliez que je le fasse copier in extenso et ne vous en adresse la copie.

Je vais partir en manoeuvres.

Dreyfus continued to protest his innocence, but a Jew was unlikely to meet with much sympathy in the higher ranks of the army, especially given the wave of anti-semitism which had been stirred up by Étienne Drumont (1844–1917) whose book, *La France juive*, had created a tremendous stir in 1886. Its tone may be judged by the following paragraphs from the introduction:

Le seul auquel la Révolution ait profité est le Juif. Tout vient du Juif; tout revient au Juif.

Il y a là une véritable conquête, une mise à la glèbe de toute une nation par une minorité infime mais cohésive, comparable à la mise à la glèbe des Saxons par les soixante mille Normands de Guillaume le Conquérant.

Les procédés sont différents, le résultat est le même. On retrouve ce qui caractérise la conquête: tout un peuple travaillant pour un autre qui s'approprie, par un vaste système d'exploitation financière, le bénéfice du travail d'autrui. Les immenses fortunes juives, les châteaux, les hôtels juifs ne sont le fruit d'aucun labeur effectif, d'aucune production, ils sont la prélibation d'une race dominante sur une race asservie. (I. vi)

In 1892 he had founded a very successful daily newspaper, *La Libre parole*; it gave the first news of the case to its readers with the characteristic headline: 'HAUTE TRAHISON! ARRESTATION D'UN OFFICIER JUIF, LE CAPITAINE DREYFUS.'

While Dreyfus was left to rot on the other side of the Atlantic, a staff colonel named Picquart discovered that the guilty man was an officer named Esterhazy; but when he communicated this discovery to his superiors, he was promptly dispatched to southern Tunisia. In July 1897 a senator, having vainly tried to convince his ministerial friends that a judicial error had been committed, raised the matter in the upper house, but the government refused to act. Finally Dreyfus's brother accused Esterhazy of being the author of the *bordereau*, but on 10 January 1898 he was acquitted by a court martial.

Three days later Zola published in *L'Aurore* the famous open

The front page of *L'Aurore* (13th January, 1898)

letter to the President of the Republic to which its editor, Clemenceau, gave the heading 'J'Accuse'. It ended:

J'accuse le lieutenant-colonel Du Paty de Clam d'avoir été l'ouvrier diabolique de l'erreur judiciaire, en inconscient, je veux le croire, et d'avoir ensuite défendu son oeuvre néfaste, depuis trois ans, par les machinations les plus saugrenues et les plus coupables.

J'accuse le général Mercier de s'être rendu complice, tout au moins par faiblesse d'esprit, d'une des plus grandes iniquités du siècle.

J'accuse le général Billot d'avoir eu entre les mains les preuves certaines de l'innocence de Dreyfus et de les avoir étouffées, de s'être rendu coupable de ce crime de lèse-humanité et de lèse-justice, dans un but politique et pour sauver l'état-major compromis.

J'accuse le général de Boisdeffre et le général Gonse de s'être rendus complices du même crime, l'un sans doute par passion cléricale, l'autre peut-être par cet esprit de corps qui fait des bureaux de la Guerre l'arche sainte, inattaquable.

J'accuse le général de Pellieux et le commandant Ravary d'avoir fait une enquête scélérate, j'entends par là une enquête de la plus monstrueuse partialité, dont nous avons, dans le rapport du second, un impérissable monument de naïve audace.

J'accuse les trois experts en écritures, les sieurs Belhomme, Varinard et Couard, d'avoir fait des rapports mensongers et frauduleux, à moins qu'un examen médical ne les déclare atteints d'une maladie de la vue et du jugement.

J'accuse les bureaux de la Guerre d'avoir mené dans la presse, particulièrement dans *L'Éclair* et dans *L'Écho de Paris*, une campagne abominable, pour égarer l'opinion et couvrir leur faute.

J'accuse enfin le premier conseil de guerre d'avoir violé le droit, en condamnant un accusé sur une pièce restée secrète, et j'accuse le second conseil de guerre d'avoir couvert cette illégalité, par ordre, en commettant à son tour le crime juridique d'acquitter sciemment un coupable.

En portant ces accusations, je n'ignore pas que je me mets sous le coup des articles 30 et 31 de la loi sur la presse du 29 juillet 1881, qui punit les délits de diffamation. Et c'est volontairement que je m'expose.

Quant aux gens que j'accuse, je ne les connais pas, je ne les ai jamais vus, je n'ai contre eux ni rancune ni haine. Ils ne sont pour moi que des entités, des esprits de malfaisance sociale. Et l'acte que j'accomplis ici n'est qu'un moyen révolutionnaire pour hâter l'explosion de la vérité et de la justice.

Je n'ai qu'une passion, celle de la lumière, au nom de l'humanité qui a tant souffert et qui a droit au bonheur. Ma protestation en-

flammée n'est que le cri de mon âme. Qu'on ose donc me traduire
en cour d'assises et que l'enquête ait lieu au grand jour !
  J'attends.
  Veuillez agréer, monsieur le Président, l'assurance de mon profond
respect. (*Oeuvres complètes*, XIV. 930–931)

By this time the controversy had become red-hot. Those who
were against a revision of the case (they were mainly on the Right)
did their best to whip up anti-semitism and nationalist sentiment;
for them the honour of the army was at stake. It was impossible
that the army could be wrong. Certain Catholic newspapers took
a prominent part in this campaign, with serious consequences for
their church. The Left, headed by men like Jaurès and Clemenceau, gradually came round to supporting the case for revision.
  Zola's bitter attack on the army leaders for aiding and abetting
this gross miscarriage of justice led to his being put on trial for
criminal libel. The trial was described by the Assumptionist
newspaper, *La Croix*, as 'un duel entre l'armée et le syndicat juif'.
Zola was denounced in furious terms:

Le très immonde Zola avait outragé notre Sauveur sous les formes
les plus horribles, donnant son Nom divin à d'immondes personnages; il avait écrit *Lourdes* contre la Vierge Immaculée, *Rome* contre
l'Église, et l'opinion publique l'avait acclamé, payant au poids de
l'or jusqu'aux expressions qu'on n'avait jamais imprimées qu'au
dictionnaire selon l'ordre alphabétique.

But now public opinion has changed:

Juifs et protestants sont enfin réputés dangereux par le peuple; celui-
ci n'écoute plus les politiques en vogue, pas même Zola le glorieux
ordurier; les événements tournent si singulierement, que ces infidèles
et hérétiques ont dû attaquer l'armée et que celle-ci, en se défendant
des soufflets les plus retentissants, entame ce soir le procès contre les
ennemis reconnus du Christ et de l'Église. Elle s'appuie sur la France
catholique.
  C'est donc la libre pensée, couronnée hier et avocate des juifs, des
protestants et de tous les ennemis de la France, qui est sur la sellette
de Zola et l'armée est obligée, malgré elle, d'ouvrir le feu.
  L'incendie ne va pas s'éteindre. (8 Feb. 1898)

Zola's life was threatened by the noisy mobs which assembled
outside the court. He was sentenced to the maximum penalty, a
year's imprisonment and a fine of 3,000 francs; he retired to exile
in England for a year. His condemnation had largely been secured
by the generals playing on the jury's fears about the effects of

revision on the army's prestige. One of them declared: 'C'est un crime d'ôter à l'armée la confiance qu'elle a dans ses chefs. Car si les soldats n'ont plus confiance, que feront les chefs, au jour du danger, qui est peut-être plus proche qu'on ne croit? . . . vos fils seront conduits à la boucherie.'

After the elections in May 1898 the Méline government resigned and power passed to a rather more left-inclined ministry. The Minister for War scored a great success with a speech in which he demonstrated beyond a doubt Dreyfus's guilt, his 'proofs' being a confession which he had not made and a letter of the German military attaché naming Dreyfus which was an obvious forgery. For a moment the hopes of the 'dreyfusards' for a revision of the case seemed utterly shattered. Then came a *coup de théâtre.* On 30 August the Agence Havas announced:

> Aujourd'hui, dans le cabinet du ministre de la Guerre, le lieutenant-colonel Henry a été reconnu et s'est reconnu l'auteur de la lettre, en date d'octobre 1896, où Dreyfus est nommé. Le ministre de la Guerre a ordonné immédiatement l'arrestation du lieutenant-colonel Henry, qui a été conduit à la forteresse du Mont-Valérien.

Next came the news that Henry had committed suicide, a clear confession of his guilt, though the right-wing press tried to maintain that this had been 'un faux patriotique' and the anti-semitic *Libre Parole* opened a subscription for his widow, to which large numbers of officers and members of the clergy contributed.

One Minister for War after another resigned and there were rumours of an army *coup* against the régime when the government decided that Dreyfus must have a new trial and referred the matter to the Court of Appeal. In the meantime the case had aroused the most furious passions; at the end of 1898, by which time another government had fallen, and at the beginning of 1899 it looked as if civil war was imminent and as if the whole régime might be brought down by the violent nationalist and anti-semitic demonstrations.

In the midst of all this agitation in February 1899, the President of the Republic, Félix Faure, who was notoriously hostile to revision, died suddenly and was succeeded by Émile Loubet (1838–1929). On returning to Paris from his election at Versailles he was insulted by a nationalist mob which, despite his pretty conservative views, saw in him the candidate supported by the Left. The funeral of his predecessor led to further nationalist demonstrations, and the leader of the *Ligue des Patriotes*, Paul Déroulède (1846–1914), tried to persuade a regiment which formed part of the Paris garrison to march on the Palais de l'Élysée. He was arrested, but when tried for inciting troops to disobey orders, he was acquitted. When the Court of Appeal declared itself in favour of a new trial for Dreyfus, the fury of the nationalists knew no bounds. The next day the President was insulted at the Auteuil races and a Monarchist knocked in his hat with a stick. Shortly after, the Chamber brought down the government and by a large majority declared itself 'résolue à ne soutenir qu'un ministère décidé à défendre avec énergie les institutions républicaines et à assurer l'ordre public'.

To form such a government was no easy task. Finally a fairly conservative Republican, René Waldeck-Rousseau (1846–1904), formed a 'gouvernement de défense républicaine' which drew its support in the Chamber all the way from the Socialists to the parties in the centre. He took care to keep most of the important ministries in the hands of moderate Republicans, but he made two surprising appointments. The first Socialist ever to hold office, Alexandre Millerand (1859–1943) (twenty-five years later he resigned as President of the Republic after a clash with the left-wing majority in the Chamber), became Minister for Trade and Industry, and introduced a series of reforms including a reduction in hours of work. A general who had distinguished himself in the brutal repression of the Commune, the Marquis de Galliffet (1830–1909), became Minister for War. On his appearance in the Chamber he was greeted with shouts of 'Vive la Commune!' from many Socialist deputies; but he had been chosen because he was in favour of a retrial for Dreyfus and had sufficient authority in the army to keep its leaders in order.

After a rather shaky start this government rapidly established itself and was to remain in power for almost three years, a long time for any government under the Third Republic. Gallifet carried out a purge of the higher ranks of the army, while twenty leaders of the nationalist and royalist agitation were brought before the Senate, sitting as a High Court of Justice; three of them, including Déroulède, were found guilty of plotting against the régime and sentenced to either banishment or imprisonment.

In the meantime Dreyfus had been brought back to France and faced a second court martial at Rennes. After a month's trial, by a majority of 5 votes to 2, this brought in the astonishing verdict: 'Coupable, mais avec des circonstances atténuantes'; Dreyfus was sentenced to ten years' imprisonment. The verdict pleased neither his enemies nor the *dreyfusards*. Finally Dreyfus was persuaded to accept a presidential pardon. It was only in 1906 that this verdict was finally quashed by the Court of Appeal; both houses of parliament then passed a law by which Dreyfus was reinstated as an officer and promoted to the rank of major.

Apart from the dramatic aspects of the whole case, 'l'Affaire' was important in modern French history because of its consequences. The violence of the clerical, nationalist and anti-semitic campaign pursued in these years by the Right led to a strong reaction from the Left. Its leaders were determined to smash the power, particularly the political power, of the Catholic Church. The final upshot was to be the denunciation of the Concordat signed a century earlier between Napoleon and the Papacy.

The government began its measures against the congregations by dissolving the Assumptionists, who had conducted a violent campaign against Jews, freemasons and the whole republican régime, particularly in their newspaper, *La Croix*. Waldeck-Rousseau declared that 'on voit véritablement dans ce pays trop de moines ligueurs et trop de moines d'affaires'. The congregations aroused particular resentment on the Left because of their growing wealth and the hold which they had over education. If at the primary level the number of girls in state schools had now outstripped that in Catholic schools, the latter still played a prominent part in the education of girls; and at the secondary level the Catholic schools, to which a high proportion of the children of the upper classes were sent, had more pupils than the *lycées*. Hence the famous words of Waldeck-Rousseau:

> Deux jeunesses . . . , moins séparées encore par leur condition que par l'éducation qu'elles reçoivent, grandissent sans se connaître, jusqu'au jour où elles se rencontreront, si dissemblables qu'elles risqueront de ne plus se comprendre.

Nevertheless he had no intention of putting an end to the Concordat or doing more than getting rid of such congregations as the Assumptionists and Jesuits who had played an active part in politics. His bill on associations which was brought forward in 1899 and finally became law two years later was merely intended to allow the State to keep an eye on other congregations. However, as finally amended by the Chamber and Senate, the law, besides regulating the legal status of associations in general, contained a separate section which dealt severely with congregations:

> ART. 13. Aucune congrégation religieuse ne peut se former sans une autorisation donnée par une loi qui déterminera les conditions de

son fonctionnement. Elle ne pourra fonder aucun nouvel établissement qu'en vertu d'un décret rendu en conseil d'État. La dissolution de la congrégation ou la fermeture de tout établissement pourront être prononcées par décret rendu en conseil des ministres.

ART. 14. Nul n'est admis à diriger, soit directement, soit par personne interposée, un établissement d'enseignement, de quelque ordre qu'il soit, ni à y donner l'enseignement, s'il appartient à une congrégation religieuse non autorisée. Les contrevenants seront punis des peines prévues par l'article 8, paragraphe 2. La fermeture de l'établissement pourra, en outre, être prononcée par le jugement de condamnation.

ART. 16. Toute congrégation formée sans autorisation sera déclarée illicite. Ceux qui en auront fait partie seront punis des peines édictées à l'article 8, paragraphe 2. La peine applicable aux fondateurs ou administrateurs sera portée au double.

ART. 18. Les congrégations existantes au moment de la promulgation de la présente loi, qui n'auraient pas été antérieurement autorisées ou reconnues, devront, dans le délai de trois mois, justifier qu'elles ont fait les diligences nécessaires pour se conformer à ces prescriptions. A défaut de cette justification, elles sont réputées dissoutes de plein droit. . . .

The application of the law proved a highly complicated matter, and in the last resort it depended on the results of the elections held in April–May 1902; these were mainly fought on the Church question. The Archbishop of Paris declared in a pastoral letter: 'Il s'agit de savoir si la société continuera à être régie par les enseignements de l'Évangile, ou si elle suivra les progrès des sectes antichrétiennes qui proclament l'indépendance absolue de la raison humaine.'

Although the election was hotly contested and produced a large turnout of voters, the Catholic, nationalist and conservative opposition failed in their attack on the government. The Socialist groups won nearly 50 seats, but the main victor was the *Parti Radical et Radical-Socialiste* with some 220. The party which had been on the extreme Left in the early days of the Third Republic had now become the governing party, a position it was to retain almost continuously until 1940. Partly for health reasons (he died in 1904), partly because the victory of the Left seemed to a very moderate Republican like himself to have gone too far, Waldeck-Rousseau handed in his resignation. A new government was formed by Émile Combes (1835–1921), a Senator who, after studying in a seminary and receiving a doctorate in theology, had abandoned the Church for medicine and was notorious for his strong anticlerical views.

By the standards of the Third Republic, his government was also long-lived, as it lasted for two and a half years, down to the beginning of 1905. It owed this long life to the fact that, until dissensions broke out among them, the parties in the coalition, brought together in regular meetings of their delegates in the so-called 'Délégation des Gauches', formed a solid majority. Although the Socialist groups were not represented in the government, they generally offered it their support, particularly in the carrying out of its anticlerical programme.

The law of 1901 on associations was now applied against the congregations. The 125 schools opened without permission since July 1901 (mainly primary schools run by nuns) were closed, while those schools opened before 1901 by the congregations were ordered to close since they had not applied for the necessary permission. This created a considerable hubbub in various parts of the country; not only the police, but the army had occasionally to be called in. Finally all the schools in question were closed except where there was not a State school to take in the pupils.

Next the Chamber voted *en bloc* to refuse authorization to all male congregations (these had some 20,000 members in some 1,500 houses scattered around the country); their closure again gave rise to scenes of disorder. There was a much smaller majority for refusing to authorize 81 female congregations (they had over 500 separate houses); they, however, dispersed quietly. Even those congregations which were authorized now came under attack; a law of 1904 laid it down that all schools run by teaching congregations must close within a period of ten years, but in practice means were generally found to evade it.

In the meantime a further conflict had developed with the Vatican over the appointment of bishops under the Concordat. Under its terms archbishops and bishops were appointed by the State and instituted by the Papacy. The practice of the Third Republic, as compared with that of earlier régimes, is thus described by a contemporary:

Si l'on appliquait le Concordat à la lettre, Rome apprendrait les nominations d'évêques par le *Journal officiel*. Au contraire, le Saint-Siège se trouve investi, par la pratique républicaine de l' 'entente préalable', d'attributions étendues dans un domaine où Charles X et Louis-Philippe ne souffraient point de partage. D'une manière générale, le Pape gouverne plus efficacement l'Église de France qu'il n'avait fait depuis mille ans; son autorité y est plus forte et s'étend sur plus de choses; elle est mieux obéie par le clergé et moins en-

travée par le pouvoir que sous le règne du 'Fils aîné de l'Église'.
(D'Avenel, *Les Français de mon temps*, p. 185)

Like many other French politicians, Combes was by no means in
favour of ending the Concordat since, so long as the members of
the clergy remained *fonctionnaires*, paid by the State, the secular
power could exercise some control over them. However, a quarrel
broke out in 1902 over the wording of the papal bull instituting a
new bishop, and Combes proceeded to make three new appointments without the customary consultations with Rome. The Pope
then declined to proceed with their institution. The death of Leo
XIII in 1903 and the election of a more intransigent successor
in Pius X led to the conflict becoming more bitter, especially as
the visit of the President of the Republic to the King of Italy in
Rome gave grave offence to the Vatican, which was not recon-
ciled to the loss of its temporal power. The dispatch of a note
of protest to the other Catholic states led to France breaking off
diplomatic relations with the Vatican.

Meanwhile the government majority in the Chamber was
gradually disintegrating and at the beginning of 1905 Combes
resigned; but, despite the change in government, by the end of the
year the law on the separation of Church and State had been
passed by both houses. It was based on principles which were set
forth in the first two articles:

ARTICLE PREMIER. – La République assure la liberté de conscience.
Elle garantit le libre exercice des cultes sous les seules restrictions
édictées ci-après dans l'intérêt de l'ordre public.
ART. 2. – La République ne reconnaît, ne salarie ni ne subventionne
aucun culte. En conséquence, à partir du 1er janvier qui suivra la
promulgation de la présente loi, seront supprimées du budget de
l'État, des départements et des communes, toutes dépenses relatives
à l'exercice des cultes . . .

The application of the law gave rise to much agitation and even
disorders, and it took several years for a working arrangement to
be reached with the Catholic Church, although Protestants and
Jews had no difficulty in complying with the requirements of the
law.

Inevitably the new law was condemned by the Pope, and a
series of conflicts arose between the government and French
Catholics. The law required that tax officials should make inventories of the contents of church buildings, including the sacred
vessels; the bishops protested and resistance was organized by the
Right to prevent the inventories being made. There were frequent

disorders in various parts of the country, and in one of these incidents a man was killed. Finally the government gave up the struggle. The law had also laid it down that 'associations cultuelles' of laymen should be formed to carry on the work of the churches, making use of buildings which belonged to the State, departments or *communes*:

> ART. 12. – Les édifices qui ont été mis à la disposition de la nation et qui, en vertu de la loi du 18 germinal an X, servent à l'exercice public des cultes ou au logement de leurs ministres (cathédrales, églises, chapelles, temples, synagogues, archevêchés, évêchés, presbytères, séminaires), ainsi que leurs dépendances immobilières et les objets mobiliers qui les garnissaient au moment où lesdits édifices ont été remis aux cultes, sont et demeurent propriétés de l'État, des départements et des communes . . .
>
> ART. 13. – Les édifices servant à l'exercice public du culte, ainsi que les objets mobiliers les garnissant, seront laissés gratuitement à la disposition des établissements publics du culte, puis des associations appelées à les remplacer, auxquels les biens de ces établissements auront été attribués . . .

While Calvinists, Lutherans and Jews made no difficulty about forming such associations, the Pope forbade Catholics to do so.

Since co-operation with the Catholic Church was now impossible, the government had to have recourse to a series of expedients. As the law of 1881 on public meetings required preliminary notification, in order to allow priests to hold church services a law had to be passed in 1907 which abolished this requirement: 'Les réunions publiques, quel qu'en soit l'objet, pourront être tenues sans déclaration préalable.' This incidentally further enlarged civil liberties for everyone. Various attempts were made to reach an agreement which would confer a legal status on the *curés* making use of places of worship, but these came to nothing and they simply remained in *de facto* occupation. From a long-term point of view this raised problems, as neither the State nor the *communes* were under any obligation to keep in repair the churches which they owned, and there were no associations to take them over. For the same reason a law of 1907 handed over seminaries, presbyteries and bishops' palaces to the State or the *communes*; most of the presbyteries were rented to the *curé* by the *commune*. Again, in the absence of associations to which the property of parochial and diocesan councils could be transferred, it was handed over to the State and the *communes* by a law passed in 1908 for public assistance purposes.

Though the Catholic Church ceased to have any official standing in the State and lost some of its material wealth, it can be argued that it gained rather than lost by the separation. The violent anticlerical passions of the early part of the present century have gradually subsided, although they are still kept alive to some extent by the controversy in the educational field between *l'école laïque* and *l'école libre*.

Despite the violent opposition which these changes encountered in Catholic and conservative circles, the elections held in May 1906 confirmed that the majority of Frenchmen approved of them. The parties of the Left gained some sixty seats and had a clear majority in the Chamber. It is true that the Socialist Party (S.F.I.O.), which had brought together in the previous year most members of the various Socialist movements and which had won over 50 seats, was now committed to a policy of non-co-operation with the bourgeois parties, but the *Parti Radical et Radical-Socialiste* had nearly 250 deputies and could count on the support of some independent Socialists. The Radical leader, Clemenceau, formed a government, the third of the long-lived governments of this period since it was to last until July 1909.

The programme announced by Clemenceau in 1906 included all manner of reforms such as retirement pensions, an income tax and the eight-hour day; but, despite the relatively long period during which this government remained in office, very little was accomplished. The years 1907–1909 were marked by a whole series of strikes which further divided Radicals and Socialists, especially as Clemenceau showed himself extremely authoritarian in his handling of them.

It is true that Clemenceau established for the first time a Ministry of Labour, which was occupied by René Viviani (1863–1925), an independent Socialist who had recently left the S.F.I.O. On his appointment he made the famous speech in which he declared:

> La Révolution française a déchaîné dans l'homme toutes les audaces de la conscience et toutes les ambitions de la pensée. Cela n'a pas suffi. La Révolution de 1848 a doté l'homme du suffrage universel, elle a relevé le travailleur courbé sur sa tâche, et elle a fait, du plus humble, l'égal politique du plus puissant. Cela n'a pas suffi. La IIIᵉ République a appelé autour d'elle les enfants des paysans, les enfants des ouvriers, et, dans ces cerveaux obscurs, dans ses consciences enténébrées, elle a versé peu à peu le germe révolutionnaire de l'instruction. Cela n'a pas suffi. Tous ensemble, par nos pères, par

nos aînés, par nous-mêmes, nous nous sommes attachés dans le passé à une oeuvre d'anticléricalisme, à une oeuvre d'irréligion. Nous avons arraché les consciences humaines à la croyance. Lorsqu'un misérable, fatigué du poids du jour, ployait les genoux, nous l'avons relevé, nous lui avons dit que derrière les nuages, il n'y avait que des chimères. Ensemble, et d'un geste magnifique, nous avons éteint dans le ciel des lumières qu'on ne rallumera plus.

However, such oratory did nothing to solve the conflicts which took place in this period of economic prosperity and social unrest.

Unlike the British trade unions, which were strongly represented in the Labour Party from its foundation in 1900, French trade unionists held themselves aloof from all political and especially parliamentary activity. At its fifteenth conference held at Amiens in 1906, the C.G.T. solemnly reaffirmed its independence of all political parties and laid down what it held to be the aims and methods of the trade union movement:

Dans l'oeuvre revendicatrice quotidienne, le syndicalisme poursuit la coordination des efforts ouvriers, l'accroissement du mieux-être des travailleurs par la réalisation d'améliorations immédiates, telles que la diminution des heures de travail, l'augmentation des salaires, etc.; mais cette besogne n'est qu'un côté de l'oeuvre du syndicalisme: il prépare l'émancipation intégrale qui ne peut se réaliser que par l'expropriation capitaliste; il préconise comme moyen d'action la grève générale et il considère que le syndicat, aujourd'hui groupement de résistance, sera dans l'avenir le groupement de production et de répartition, base de réorganisation sociale.

Partly under the influence of Georges Sorel (1847–1922), whose *Réflexions sur la violence* appeared in book form in 1908, many trade unionists were carried away by the theories of Syndicalism, according to which the lot of the workers must be changed, not by political means, but by the general strike, heralded by such direct action as sabotage and violence.

The use of strikes to back up trade union demands is familiar enough to us today, but at the beginning of the century it scandalized many people. In March 1907, for instance, the inhabitants of Paris had their lives disrupted by a two-day strike of electricity workers; this came to an end when Clemenceau threatened to replace them by army engineers. In the following month there was an attempt at a strike in the Paris food trades (this mainly affected bakeries), and then came a strike of seamen at Marseilles and other large ports. This coincided with tremendous turmoil in the wine-producing regions of the South, which led to monster meetings of protest, many acts of violence and even army mutinies. 1908 saw a strike in the Paris building trade, followed by a lockout. Then a strike of workers in the gravel-pits just outside Paris led to clashes between *gendarmes* and strikers in which two of the latter were killed; the C.G.T. promptly called a general strike of protest in Paris. This was a failure, but demonstrators set up barricades at Villeneuve–Saint–Georges; troops were called in; four people were killed and fifty injured in the fighting which followed. The government ordered the arrest of the leaders of the C.G.T., and this caused further strikes of protest.

In these years the government also had trouble with its civil servants who claimed the right to organize themselves in *syndicats*. The federation of primary school teachers (*instituteurs*) affiliated to the C.G.T. The right of civil servants to strike was rejected by the government and the Chamber when there was a series of strikes in the postal services in 1909. As a result considerable numbers of postal employees were dismissed.

During the Clemenceau ministry the Socialists found themselves more and more in opposition, partly because of the government's handling of the trade union movement and strikes, partly because of its failure to carry out its programme of reforms. In 1907 a bill to bring in an income tax was introduced by the government, but although it was passed by a large majority in the Chamber, it was buried by the Senate. Nothing came of the bill to bring in old age pensions. The nationalization of the *Chemin de Fer de l'Ouest* was all that emerged from the programme of reforms put forward by Clemenceau when his government took office. In July 1909 he resigned after being defeated in the Chamber.

After this period of ten years for most of which the three governments of Waldeck-Rousseau, Combes and Clemenceau had been in power, came a renewed period of government instability. Between July 1909 and August 1914 France had as many as ten different governments. It is true that the first two governments to follow that of Clemenceau and a short-lived one in 1913 were all headed by Aristide Briand (1862–1932), the former revolutionary Socialist who had come to the fore when he applied in a conciliatory fashion the law on the separation of Church and State. Early in 1910 the law on old age pensions was at last passed by both Chamber and Senate. A great deal of parliamentary time was taken up by arguments about the merits or otherwise of proportional representation, but in the end years of discussion got nowhere.

The elections of 1910 were chiefly marked by Socialist gains; the S.F.I.O. now held 74 seats, and the Independent Socialists another 30. There remained a large block of Radicals (over 250) but there was a widening gulf between the Socialists, led by Jaurès, and the Radicals who had long ceased to be a party demanding sweeping reforms. They now stood closer to more conservative parties, which also bore strangely misleading names – such as 'Républicains de gauche' and 'Progressistes'. The new Chamber saw no fewer than eight governments during its four-year term.

The breach between the Socialists and Radicals was widened by the railway strike which took place in October 1910 and created a considerable stir. The prime minister, Briand, who only a decade earlier had been a fervent apostle of the general strike, responded to this totally new situation by calling up railwaymen as reservists and thus broke the strike. A great many dismissals followed. When challenged in the Chamber, he replied:

> Je vais vous dire une chose, Messieurs, qui va peut-être vous faire bondir d'indignation: si, pour défendre l'existence de la Nation, le Gouvernement n'avait pas trouvé, dans la loi, de quoi rester maître de ses frontières, s'il n'avait pu disposer à cet effet de ses chemins de fer, c'est-à-dire d'un instrument essentiel de défense nationale, eh bien, aurait-il dû recourir à l'illégalité, il y serait allé!

This method of dealing with strikers has been used again more than once since 1910.

Shortly afterwards Briand resigned and formed a new government, but this lasted only three months. After two more governments had come and gone, Raymond Poincaré (1860–1934), a very moderate Republican, formed an administration which lasted for a year until he resigned on his election as President of the Republic, a post which he held throughout the war years, down to 1920. A great deal of parliamentary time continued to be spent arguing about proportional representation, but a bill on the subject came to nothing owing to disagreement between the Chamber and the Senate. Three new governments followed before the elections of 1914, but what dominated parliamentary debates until then was the bill to extend national service to three years.

After the Franco-Prussian war the principle of conscription had been laid down by a law of 1872, but in practice there were all sorts of exemptions, although men who were called up had to serve for five years. A law of 1889 had limited the period of service to three years and had also reduced the number of exemp-

Jean Jaurès (1859–1914)

tions, though these were still numerous. As recently as 1905 a new law had been passed which reduced the period of service to two years; this was made possible by abolishing virtually all exemptions. By 1913 the international situation had become so threatening that the new President insisted on a bill being brought forward to increase the period to three years. This split the Radical party and encountered violent opposition from the Socialists. However, the bill passed the Chamber and Senate by August 1913.

The elections of April–May 1914 were largely fought on this issue, Socialists and Radicals combining in their opposition to the new law. It is a paradox that these elections, held only a few months before the outbreak of war, produced a large left wing majority opposed to three-year military service. The S.F.I.O., led by Jaurès, made a striking advance; it gained 30 seats and increased the number of its deputies to 102. This was the Chamber which had to face all the problems of the bitter armed struggle which was to be fought out on French soil for the next four years.

It proved by no means an easy matter to form a new government. After one had been rejected on its very first appearance before the Chamber, the independent Socialist, René Viviani, formed a cabinet, ten of whose members had voted for the three-year period and five, including the prime minister, against. The new government was immediately attacked in the Chamber by Jaurès who declared: 'Cette majorité ardente et fidèle, vous ne l'obtiendrez pas, si notre parti socialiste n'en est pas. Et il n'en sera pas, si vous continuez à défendre cette loi de trois ans, qui n'est que l'organisation de l'inertie.' However, the new government secured a handsome majority.

On 13 July the budget for 1914 was finally approved by both chambers, the Senate having at last agreed to the principle of an income tax which had been voted by the Chamber before the elections. By this time France was on the very verge of war; it broke out finally on 3 August.

Events leading up to the 1914-1918 war

For the origins of the 1914–1918 war we must return to the Franco–Prussian war of 1870 which had left France both humiliated and isolated. It was now Germany, and no longer France, which was the dominant military power on the Continent. In contrast to the situation a generation later, in the early years of the

Third Republic nationalism was very strong on the left. This was not only a consequence of the disasters of 1870; it was also a survival of a tradition stretching back to the Revolution of 1789 which saw France as the centre of civilization and liberty, destined to bring these to the other peoples of Europe. The Nationalist leader, Paul Déroulède, was a fervent admirer of Gambetta when he published his enormously popular patriotic poems, *Les Chants du soldat* (1872) and his *Marches et Sonneries* (1881). Some idea of their tone is conveyed by the verse:

Je vis les yeux fixés sur la frontière
Et, front baissé, comme un boeuf au labour,
Je vais rêvant à notre France entière,
Des murs de Metz au clocher de Strasbourg.
Depuis dix ans j'ai commencé ce rêve,
Tout le traverse et rien ne l'interrompt,
Dieu veuille un jour qu'un grand Français l'achève,
Je ne suis, moi, qu'un sonneur de clairon.

The Republican founders of *l'école laïque* considered that patriotism was among the moral virtues which it should inculcate, and in 1881 they went so far as to foster the formation of *bataillons scolaires* in which small boys were given military training. It is true that before long these gradually faded out.

The isolation of France continued for over two decades after the end of the Franco-Prussian war. Germany's annexation of Alsace–Lorraine continued to rankle and to poison relations between the two countries. France's rapid recovery from the war and the rebuilding of her army caused a war scare in 1875 when there were rumours all round the capitals of Europe of a preventive German invasion of France. In 1887, at the height of General Boulanger's popularity, relations between the two countries were made extremely tense by a frontier incident. A French police official named Schnaebelé was arrested by the Germans on French territory on the frontier of Lorraine; however, the German government released him, and 'le général Revanche' whose Nationalist supporters gave cause for anxiety in Germany was pushed out of the government.

From 1880 onwards, after she had recovered from the effects of the Franco-Prussian war, France joined in the scramble for colonies. Indeed she had been urged to do so when she was represented at the Congress of Berlin which met in 1878 to deal with the Eastern Question. Colonial expansion gave rise to considerable controversy inside France. There were men like

Clemenceau who argued that, instead of wasting her strength in sending expeditions to faraway countries like Indo-China, France should conserve all her military resources to meet the threat of German aggression. In a speech delivered in 1885 he asked:

> Si des événements que nul ne peut prévoir et qu'il ne dépend pas de nous de prévenir nous obligeaient à défendre le sol de la République contre l'ennemi, que diriez-vous de l'homme qui aurait engagé follement le drapeau français dans l'Extrême-Orient et qui aurait envoyé périr à 3,000 lieues de la patrie des hommes que nous appellerions en vain dans le danger à la défense du territoire national? (*Discours prononcé à Draguignan*, 13 Sept. 1885, p. 31)

The motives behind the colonial expansion of the 1880s onwards are well expressed in a sentence in Gambetta's letter to Ferry congratulating him on the establishment of a protectorate over Tunisia in 1881: 'La France reprend son rang de grande puissance'; or in a famous speech delivered by Ferry in the *Chambre des Députés* shortly after his downfall in 1885 as a result of a French reverse in her conquest of Indo-China.

The first point in his defence of colonial expansion was that overseas territories provided an outlet for French capital and exports. His second point – the civilizing mission of France – soon involved him in a considerable interruptions:

> M. JULES FERRY. – . . . Il faut dire ouvertement qu'en effet les races supérieures ont un droit vis-à-vis des races inférieures . . . (*Rumeurs sur plusieurs bancs à l'extrême gauche.*)
>
> M. JULES MAIGNE. – Oh! Vous osez dire cela dans le pays où ont été proclamés les droits de l'homme!
>
> M. DE GUILLOUTET. – C'est la justification de l'esclavage et de la traite des nègres!
>
> M. JULES FERRY. – Si l'honorable M. Maigne a raison, si la déclaration des droits de l'homme a été écrite pour les noirs de l'Afrique équatoriale, alors, de quel droit allez-vous leur imposer les échanges, les trafics? Ils ne vous appellent pas . . . (*Interruptions à l'extrême gauche et à droite. Très bien! très bien! sur divers bancs à gauche.*)
>
> M. RAOUL DUVAL. – Nous ne voulons pas les leur imposer! C'est vous qui les leur imposez!
>
> M. JULES MAIGNE. – Proposer et imposer sont des choses fort différentes!
>
> M. GEORGES PERIN. – Vous ne pouvez pas cependant faire des échanges forcés!
>
> M. JULES FERRY. – Je répète qu'il y a pour les races supérieures un droit, parce qu'il y a un devoir pour elles. Elles ont le devoir de civiliser les races inférieures . . . (*Marques d'approbation sur les mêmes*

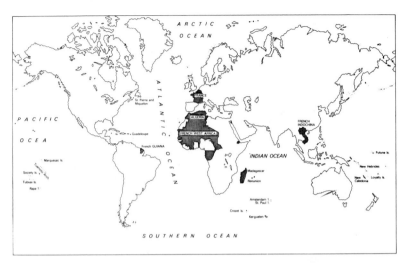

The French Colonial Empire in 1914.

bancs à gauche. Nouvelles interruptions à l'extrême gauche et à droite.)
(Chambre des Députés, 28 July 1885)

He then went on to argue that for France to sit back and do nothing after the disasters of 1870 would be a terrible mistake:

> Rayonner sans agir, sans se mêler aux affaires du monde, en se tenant à l'écart de toutes les combinaisons européennes, en regardant comme un piège, comme une aventure toute expansion vers l'Afrique ou vers l'Orient, vivre de cette sorte pour une grande nation, croyez-le bien, c'est abdiquer, et, dans un temps plus court que vous ne pouvez le croire, c'est descendre du premier rang au troisième et au quatrième.

It was this final argument which carried the day in favour of colonial expansion under the Third Republic.

This had begun in 1881 with the establishment of a protectorate over Tunisia, and by the end of the century France had also assumed control over an enormous area of Western and Central Africa. In 1895 a federation of her West African territories, administered by a governor-general in Dakar, was established under the title of *Afrique Occidentale Française*, and in 1908 *Afrique Équatoriale Française* was formed out of her colonies to the east and south. In addition, French Somaliland was annexed in 1885 and Madagascar in 1896. In the mid-1880s France extended her control from Cochin-China over the whole of Indo-China. Altogether between 1880 and 1900 she added 3 million square miles of territory to her colonial empire and increased its population by nearly 50 million. By 1900 her overseas possessions were second only to those of the British Empire.

In that year the foreign minister, Théophile Delcassé (1852–1923), in a speech to the Senate, could proudly declare:

> La France, messieurs, est avant tout une grande puissance européenne (*très bien, très bien! applaudissements*), qui est devenue, ou plutôt qui est redevenue une grande puissance coloniale. Un jour, on l'a crue abattue; le lendemain elle prouvait sa vitalité surabondante, en fondant au-delà des mers un empire plus magnifique encore que celui que, cent ans auparavant, elle avait perdu. Je ne sais pas si l'histoire coloniale fournit un exemple d'une expansion aussi prodigieuse à la fois, et aussi rapide. (3 April 1900)

The pride felt by many Frenchmen in their vastly enlarged colonial empire is well brought out in the words of an historian writing at the beginning of the century:

> Allez dans un de nos ports de commerce, au Havre, à Bordeaux, à Marseille; comptez les paquebots sous pression; informez-vous de leurs destinations diverses; combien de celles-ci étaient naguère, il y a vingt-cinq ans, presque ignorées, ne figuraient même pas sur les itinéraires de ces compagnies? Qui donc avait alors affaire au Sénégal, au Soudan, au Congo? Combien de voyageurs se sentaient appelés à Madagascar, dans l'Annam, au Tonkin? Combien vivait-il alors de Français dans cette Tunisie, où ils possèdent aujourd'hui plus de 300 000 hectares? Avions-nous des usines, des magasins, des écoles, des palais, des théâtres, des cercles, des champs de courses à Hué, à Phnum-Penh, à Tamatave, à Tananarive? Qu'étaient, à cette époque, ces villes aujourd'hui toutes françaises de Hanoï et Haïphong? Pouvait-on compter, comme aujourd'hui, autant de sujets de la France qu'il y a de Français dans la métropole? (A. Rambaud, *Jules Ferry*, p. xxxiv)

However, despite its rapid growth the French colonial empire was much less valuable than the British. What is more, its expansion involved France in a whole series of clashes with Britain.

Egypt, which since the time of Napoleon's expedition in 1798 had been a particular French sphere of influence, came under British control from 1882 onwards; France was simply pushed out. A clash over the Sudan in 1898 brought the two countries to the brink of war; a French expedition under Captain Marchand planted the French flag in the village of Fashoda, and war was only averted when it withdrew. It is true that these Franco-British conflicts were ended by the conclusion of the *Entente Cordiale* in 1904, but immediately afterwards France became involved in clashes with Germany over Morocco on which she had long had designs.

On the Continent France remained without allies until the 1890s. Her isolation stemmed partly from the fact that a Republic was a decided anomaly in a Europe in which monarchies, large and small, predominated. In 1879 Bismarck signed the Dual Alliance with Austria and three years later Italy joined in to form the Triple Alliance. What is more, pursuing a policy of keeping Russia and France apart, in 1884 Bismarck signed with Russia a secret treaty of reinsurance whereby the two countries agreed to maintain a policy of benevolent neutrality if one or the other were attacked. However, when Bismarck was dismissed from office in 1890, the way was left open for an alliance between France and Russia. Despite their very different political régimes the two countries were drawn together by fear of Germany under its new ruler, William II. Besides, Russia urgently needed French capital for both her economic development and the modernization of her army.

In 1891 negotiations began between the two countries and a secret understanding was reached; this was symbolized by the visit of a French naval squadron to the port of Kronstadt. In the following year a secret military agreement on simultaneous mobilization in the event of a threat from the Triple Alliance was concluded and this was confirmed by letters exchanged in 1893 and 1894. In the meantime a Russian naval squadron had visited Toulon; the Russian sailors received a tremendous welcome when they visited Paris. Though there was no formal treaty of alliance, the Franco-Russian *rapprochement* marked the end of French isolation in Europe. In 1896 the Tsar, Nicholas II, visited France and in the following year the French President returned his visit.

By this time France was also being wooed by Germany which was now involved in colonial and naval rivalry with England. In the 1890s anti-British feeling was strong in France and was fanned to white heat by the Fashoda incident in 1898. The outbreak of the Boer war (1899–1902) did not increase British popularity in France.

However, under Delcassé who held the post of Foreign Minister in successive governments for the exceptionally long period of seven years (1898–1905), French policy began to change direction, though still keeping the alliance with Russia as its foundation. Relations with Italy, the third partner in the Triple Alliance, were greatly improved; in 1902 a secret agreement was concluded which made it clear that, while remaining a member of the alliance, Italy would not take part in any aggression against France. The long-term result of this agreement was that when war broke out in 1914 Italy did not join Germany and Austria; in the following year she entered the war on the Allied side.

Of greater immediate consequence was the improvement of relations with England. At the turn of the century, on top of the sore caused by the loss of Alsace-Lorraine came colonial rivalry with Germany, particularly over the gradual economic and military penetration of Morocco by France. In 1903 the new king Edward VII, as Prince of Wales for long a familiar figure in Paris, came on an official visit, which the French President returned two months later. In the following year an agreement was signed between the two countries which put an end to the colonial rivalry which had strained relations for the past two centuries. Among other things the agreement gave England a free hand in Egypt which France had been urging her to evacuate since 1882, and in return France was given a free hand in Morocco.

If Delcassé's policies – a *rapprochement* with Italy and the *Entente Cordiale* with the traditional enemy, England – had so far met with success, the weakening of Russia as a result of her defeats in the Russo-Japanese war (1904–1905) and of the revolution which followed had raised serious doubts about the value of the Franco-Russian alliance. The German government, which was naturally displeased by the coming together of England and France, decided to intervene in Morocco to prevent France from establishing a protectorate there.

In March 1905 the Emperor William II made a theatrical landing at Tangiers and in a speech there described the Sultan of Morocco as an independent sovereign, deliberately ignoring French interests in the country. The German government then proceeded to demand the calling of an international conference to discuss the situation in Morocco. The French government finally agreed to this demand, whereupon Delcassé resigned. However, when the conference met in the following year at Algeciras, it was on the whole a success for France, as it did not seriously limit her penetration of Morocco.

In 1907 England and Russia, whose policies clashed in Persia, Afghanistan and Tibet and whose relations had been made worse by the conclusion of the Anglo-Japanese treaty of alliance of 1902, settled their differences, and the Triple Entente was formed. Europe was now divided into two heavily armed camps.

Morocco continued to be a bone of contention between France and Germany as France gradually extended her influence over the country by the use of military force. In 1911 came the so-called Agadir incident; the German government despatched a gunboat to this port in southern Morocco, allegedly to protect German interests there. This gesture gave rise to grave international complications, and matters were only temporarily patched up by Germany recognizing the French protectorate over Morocco in exchange for part of the French Congo.

These years of growing international tension saw changes in the attitude of the French people to relations with other countries. By now nationalism had become a right-wing force, while the Left had moved in the direction of internationalism. The C.G.T. had long stood for an aggressive type of anti-militarism which saw in the armed forces merely the defenders of the existing social order and which held that the general strike should be used to prevent national wars. In 1900 a young history master named Gustave Hervé created a tremendous stir when he published an article which, in denouncing Napoleon on the anniversary of the battle of Wagram, worked up to the famous climax:

> Tant qu'il y aura des casernes, pour l'édification et la moralisation des soldats de notre démocratie, pour déshonorer à leurs yeux le militarisme et la guerre de conquête, je voudrais qu'on rassemblât, dans la cour principale du quartier, toutes les ordures et tout le fumier de la caserne, et que, solennellement, en présence de toutes les troupes en tenue numéro un, au son de la musique militaire, le colonel, en grand plumet, vînt y planter le drapeau du régiment. (*Le Pioupiou de l'Yonne*, 1901)

At this stage in his career Hervé was an extremist (he was later to adopt ultra-nationalist and fascist views); but the Socialist party, under the active leadership of Jaurès, was critical of many aspects of French foreign policy, particularly of the military penetration of Morocco and the inevitable international friction which it caused. At party conferences in 1906 and 1907 anti-militarist motions were passed; emphasis was placed on the role of arbitration in international disputes, and a majority took the line that when a danger of war arose, it would be the duty of Socialists in the countries concerned to render it impossible by calling a general strike. At a special party conference held in Paris on 14–16 July 1914, when the international crisis was reaching its climax, the following motion was passed by a narrow majority:

Entre tous les moyens employés pour prévenir et empêcher la guerre et pour imposer aux gouvernements le recours à l'arbitrage, le Congrès considère comme particulièrement efficace la grève générale simultanément et internationalement organisée dans les pays intéressés, ainsi que l'agitation et l'action populaires sous les formes les plus actives.

It is scarcely necessary to point out that the events of the following weeks, in France and in the other belligerent countries, were to make nonsense of this resolution.

At the opposite extreme were Nationalists like Déroulède and Barrès, chairmen in succession of the *Ligue des Patriotes*, and Charles Maurras (1868–1952) who founded the *Action Française* movement in 1899. His blend of nationalism and monarchism which he propagated in various books and pamphlets and in the *Action Française* (a daily newspaper from 1908 onwards) had a considerable influence among sections of French youth. For Maurras Frenchmen had to choose between the Republic and national survival:

C'est une vérité générale que la politique extérieure est interdite à notre État républicain. C'en est une autre que la Nation francaise ne saurait se passer de manoeuvrer à l'extérieur. De ces deux principes, il résulte que la France républicaine, aussi longtemps qu'elle sera et républicaine et française, quels que puissent être les talents ou les intentions de son personnel dirigeant, demeurera condamnée à des manoeuvres gauches, énervantes et plus· que dangereuses pour l'intégrité du pays et l'indépendance des habitants. Le démembrement est au bout. (*Kiel et Tanger*, p. cxvii)

According to him France had ceased to be in the hands of Frenchmen; it had been 'colonized' by four alien groups – Jews, Protestants, freemasons and 'métèques' (a rude term for 'foreigners' living in France):

Le jeune médecin s'aperçoit que tout est pris, conquis par des étrangers. Le jeune ouvrier, le jeune employé prennent garde que l'Allemand, l'Italien, le Suisse, le Belge, le Polonais, le Juif leur font la guerre économique dans les rues de Paris, ou sur les chantiers de Marseille, dans les campagnes du Nord ou dans les usines de l'Est, tantôt en travaillant à des salaires de famine inabordables pour eux, et tantôt, au contraire, en occupant les sinécures les plus grassement rétribuées. Par en haut, par en bas, le Français est bloqué. Il ne perd plus beaucoup de temps à se plaindre, car si haut que puisse monter sa réclamation, il voit qu'elle est soumise, avant d'être écoutée, à quelques délégués des quatre États confédérés, – juif, protestant, maçon, métèque – avec qui s'identifie nécessairement le pouvoir réel. (*L'Action française*, 6 July 1912)

The influence of nationalist doctrines is well brought out in a book published in 1912, *Les Jeunes Gens d'aujourd'hui* which records the views of many young Frenchmen on the eve of the war, when international tension had already become very marked. One of those approached by the two writers concerned, declared:

Aujourd'hui pourquoi suis-je patriote? Pour deux ordres de raisons: premièrement, parce que depuis sept ans, l'Allemagne, – passez-moi l'expression, mais en ce moment je suis peuple, – parce que l'Allemagne m'embête; parce qu'elle me tient sous la menace d'une guerre, qui 'm'amuserait' (elle nous 'amuserait' tous), mais où je veux vaincre; c'est tout un ensemble de choses qui constituaient ma vision de la France; alors j'ai chéri celle-ci davantage, et haï, comme on hait l'homme qui veut vous retirer la vie, l'Allemagne. C'est là un patriotisme défensif. L'autre raison, c'est que, revenu de la griserie où me plongea aussi la première lecture des Slaves et des Germains, je m'aperçus que tout cela était très beau, mais que ce n'était pas moi . . . J'ai quitté Goethe pour Racine et Mallarmé, Tolstoï pour Balzac et Stendhal. J'ai senti que je me réalisais, que je me possédais, que je vivais dans la mesure même où ceux dont je faisais ma nourriture spirituelle étaient de ma chair et de mon sang. C'est avec mon amour pour eux que se confond mon amour le meilleur de la France; je veux les chérir sans entraves. Ceux qui s'opposent à leur influence sont les ennemis de ma patrie, de moi-même. ('Agathon', *Les Jeunes Gens d'aujourd'hui*, pp. 166–167)

The clash of two viewpoints was tragically illuminated by the murder of Jaurès by a Nationalist fanatic on 31 July 1914, three days before Germany declared war on France.

In 1914 events in the Balkans led to a European conflict a great part of which was to be fought out on French soil. The result was not only a vast amount of material destruction, but appalling losses in human lives (1,300,000 killed as well as 750,000 maimed). And a quarter of a century later France was to suffer yet another invasion.

4
The writer and his public

Of the various means of communication between the writer and public with which we are nowadays familiar, not only were radio and television lacking in our period, but even the cinema had not developed very far by 1914. The first public exhibition of films projected on a screen took place in 1895, both in America and in France, where two brothers, Louis (1864–1948) and Auguste (1862–1954) Lumière, were responsible for the invention. France, like England, played a leading part in the early development of the cinema. Georges Méliès (1861–1938) was the pioneer of story-telling on the screen with such films as *Cendrillon, Jeanne d'Arc, Barbe-Bleue* and *Le Petit Chaperon Rouge,* produced around 1900. The actor Max Linder (1882–1925), whom the young Charlie Chaplin openly acknowledged as his master, was the first French film star. By 1914 France already had over a thousand cinemas, roughly a quarter of the number which it was to have when the fashion for this form of entertainment reached its height, but although the cinema was already beginning to compete with the theatre, even by that date the silent film was still at a fairly primitive stage in its development.

For nearly the whole of our period the vehicles employed by the writer to communicate with the public were the theatre and the printed word in the shape of books, periodicals and newspapers. The printed book had emerged in the second half of the fifteenth century and a professional theatre some hundred years later, but the periodical press, which was to play an increasingly important part in assisting communication between the writer and his public, was still relatively little developed in 1814. France had had a weekly newspaper since 1631 in the shape of the *Gazette* founded by Théophraste Renaudot; in 1762 this became *La Gazette de France,* an official government organ and appeared henceforth twice weekly. It was not, however, until 1777 that Paris had its first daily newspaper, the *Journal de Paris ou la Poste du Soir*, an imitation of the *London Evening Post*, founded three-quarters of a century earlier. In 1665 France acquired its first learned periodical, the *Journal des Savants*, which appeared weekly; seven years later came *Le Mercure Galant*, a political and literary journal. Periodicals multiplied in number down to 1789, but while the Revolution brought to France for the first time freedom of the press and a proliferation of newspapers and periodicals, this sudden change was reversed by Napoleon who severely restricted their number and subjected them to a rigid censorship. While the newspapers and other periodicals of the Restoration period were less ruthlessly controlled, they were still technically extremely primitive and had a remarkably restricted circulation.

The situation was to be drastically altered by a revolution in the paper-making and printing industries which began in the early part of the nineteenth century and which has continued down to our time. This was primarily concerned with the special requirements of newspaper production, but these changes affected in turn both books and periodicals. These inventions, which very substantially lowered the costs of production, brought about the first real transformation of the printing industry since the time of Gutenberg. Paper, hitherto made by hand, could now be made more cheaply and more quickly by machine; the rags from which it had traditionally been made were now supplemented on a massive scale by such materials as esparto grass and particularly wood-pulp, from which the newsprint for the vastly expanded newspaper industry came. Printing was revolutionized by a whole series of technical inventions, starting with 'stereotyping', i.e. setting free the type once it was composed by moulding the pages and making a duplicate printing surface in the form of a cast metal plate. Hitherto the printing press had been made of wood; this was now replaced by iron. More important still was the application of steam-power to the printing press, which speeded up the process enormously, while the invention of the rotary press made possible the rapid production of large numbers of copies of newspapers. Letters, which had formerly been cast by hand, could also now be produced by machines. For a long time the 'copy' continued to be set up by hand, but in the course of the century various machines were invented to carry out the work more quickly; finally in the 1880s came the linotype machine, followed in the next decade by the monotype.

Education and literacy

This revolution in the printing industry coincided with a massive growth in the reading public. Seen from the viewpoint of the second half of the twentieth century and its 'education explosion' conditions in France a hundred or a hundred and fifty years ago seem extraordinarily primitive. Not only were considerable sections of the community still unable to read or write, but the layer of people at the top who received a university or even a secondary education was extremely thin.

Strictly speaking, down to 1896 there were no universities in France in our period. They had been abolished in the Revolution, and what Napoleon created by a decree of 1808 to take their place was one or more faculties of theology, law, medicine, arts and science in each of the regions (*académies*) into which the French Empire was divided for educational purposes. They acted mainly as examining boards, dealing with a few candidates for the *licence* (the equivalent of our bachelor's degree) and with considerably more for the *baccalauréat* which, while it is closely akin to the Advanced Level of the English General Certificate of Education, is in France a first degree and entitles the holder to enter a faculty to study for a *licence*. The faculties of arts (*Facultés des Lettres*) and science were new, but for decades they had virtually no students in the modern sense of the term; the professors gave public lectures when they felt so inclined, and while some of them, especially in Paris, drew large audiences, their lectures were often both ill-attended and at a very low level. Taine, for instance, made the following note at Poitiers in 1864:

> B . . . a vingt à soixante personnes à son cours, mais c'est le plus suivi. C . . . , professeur de philosophie, avait à peu près le même nombre d'auditeurs. La plupart sont des étudiants, ce qui empêche la bonne société d'y aller. En tout cas, selon B . . . , personne n'y prend intérêt, personne n'y travaille et n'est capable de suivre. Dans les villes comme Douai, Caen, c'est mieux: les gens du monde y amènent leurs filles; mais alors le cours devient anodin, agréable; une conversation de famille. (*Carnets de voyage*, p. 166)

It goes without saying that at this date there were no matriculated women students; in his famous dictionary, produced between 1863 and 1873, Littré defines *étudiante* as 'dans une espèce d'argot, grisette du quartier latin' and he goes on to give the example: 'Commis et grisettes, étudiants et étudiantes affluent dans ce bal.'

Constantin Guys: *La Grisette*.

A very high proportion of French students were, of course, in Paris, but when we read of their activities – political or otherwise – in the period down to about 1880, we have to remember that they were virtually all medical or law students together with the pupils of the famous *grandes écoles* founded during the Revolution, such as the *École Normale Supérieure* or the *École Polytechnique*.

The catastrophe of 1870 produced fresh thinking about higher education and with the gradual establishment of the Third Republic came considerable changes. Although it was not until

Gavarni: *Les Étudiants*.

1896 that a law was passed setting up afresh universities in France, the faculties had already been strengthened in the 1880s. However, when the new law at last came, it was a great disappointment to many reformers as they had hoped that a small number of large universities would be set up in Paris and a few provincial

centres; instead each of the sixteen *académies* was given its university. Many of these remained extremely small until after 1945.

In the closing years of the Second Empire France had some
5,000 students of law and 4,000 of medicine; by 1913 their
numbers had swollen to some 16,000 and 11,000 respectively, and
from the 1880s onwards the number of students in the faculties of
arts and science rose steadily to reach about 6,000 each by the eve
of the First World War. The students in these two faculties were
mainly absorbed into education. The total number of French
students in these years – some 40,000 – reads strangely in the 1970s
when it has reached almost twenty times that figure.

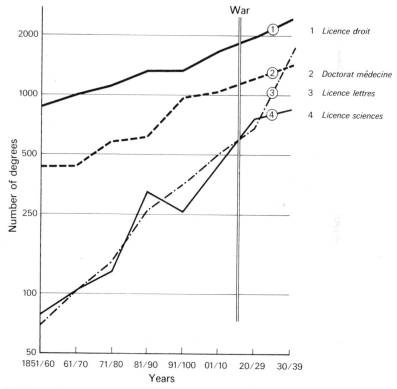

Number of university degrees conferred, 1850–1939.

If university graduates were a tiny proportion of the population even in 1914, the numbers receiving secondary education
were also extremely small by present day standards. The system of
state secondary schools goes back to Napoleon, who in 1802

established 45 *lycées*; the re-establishment of faculties in 1808 was
the result of a law setting up the so-called *Université* which also
embraced secondary education, that given in the *collèges* run by
local authorities as well as in the state *lycées*. On paper the *Université* had a monopoly of both higher and secondary education,
but in practice a great many Catholic schools existed outside the
system, though at this time these were mainly run by private
individuals.

   The number of boys receiving secondary education in the first
half of the century was extremely small – only some 50,000 in 1820
– and, if this figure had risen to 70,000 by 1842, it is probable
that secondary education was still making good the losses which
it had sustained through the Revolution.

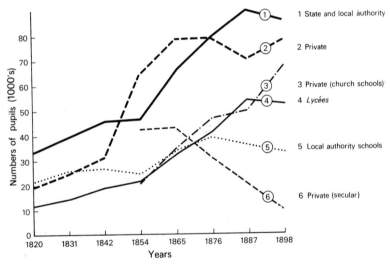

Secondary education, 1820–1898.

   From the 1840s onwards – the phenomenon was little more than
recognized by the famous *Loi Falloux* of 1850 – the Catholic hold
on secondary education steadily increased; the part played by the
religious orders was now predominant. In 1863 at Toulouse Taine
noted:

   A Toulouse il y a soixante-dix-sept maisons religieuses sur une
   population de cent mille âmes; entre autres, trois énormes collèges,
   l'un ayant cinq cents élèves. Quand le père Léotade a été condamné,[1]

---

[1] In 1847 Father Léotade, the bursar of a Catholic boarding school in Toulouse, was
sentenced to life imprisonment for the murder of a fourteen-year-old girl.

beaucoup de gens l'ont déclaré martyr; l'année suivante, son collège a eu quarante élèves de plus à la rentrée. – . . . A Poitiers, à Rennes, le lycée est tombé de moitié par la concurrence . . . – A Paris, les pensionnats religieux font entrer par an, à Saint-Cyr, soixante-dix à quatre-vingts jeunes gens, qui font bande à part. Jusqu'à des bicoques comme Rethel, ils prennent tout et font tomber le petit collège municipal; tout cela depuis 1852, principalement par les Jésuites. (*Carnets de voyage*, p. 86)

Student of the *École Normale* in 1848.

Between 1842 and 1898 there was a very considerable expansion of secondary education for boys: the total number of pupils in all types of secondary school rose from some 70,000 to over 160,000. Yet although the numbers in the *lycées* and to some extent those in the *collèges* run by local authorities expanded fairly rapidly, by 1898 there were as many pupils in schools outside the public system as there were in it. Indeed the Church secondary schools had substantially more pupils than the *lycées*. This development was one which did not please the Republican majority in Parliament. Hence the famous words of Waldeck-Rousseau on 'les deux jeunesses' being produced by the rival educational systems.

Secondary education for girls was no concern of the State until the establishment of the Third Republic. This did not mean that it did not exist, but it was given in private schools, run sometimes by lay teachers, but more often by nuns. Its scope was somewhat restricted, as the main stress was on preparing upper and middle class girls to run a household that was well provided with servants. Victor Duruy's first move towards offering a very modest and limited form of secondary education for girls – the establishment of public lectures given by masters from the *lycées* to which the girls could be brought by their mothers – aroused the furious hostility of the Catholic Church. However, when the Republicans were securely installed in power, they turned their attention to providing state secondary schools for girls. A law of 1880 set up at first only day schools, though local authorities were given power to make provision for boarders, and in the following year an *École Normale Supérieure* was set up at Sèvres to train teachers for these schools. Their number developed fairly rapidly: by 1883 there were 21 *lycées* and *collèges* for girls, and by 1913 this number had risen to 138.

While the gradual development of secondary and higher education slowly provided a better informed reading public, considerable progress was made, especially from the 1830s, in the field of primary education. However, even when this reached its maximum development under the Third Republic, it did not offer the great mass of French children much more than the bare rudiments since it did not lead on to secondary, let alone higher education.

Nowadays one takes it for granted that almost everybody one meets can read and write; and if apparently more than half of the present population of France never reads a book, this is seldom a matter of sheer inability to do so – it is simply that reading books is not yet an acquired taste. It would be a mistake to imagine that the masses in France in 1789 were utterly illiterate. It is not altogether easy to establish the degree of literacy under the *Ancien Régime*, but it is clear that in the course of the eighteenth century considerable progress was made. In 1877–1879 researches were carried out into the number of persons who at different dates were able to sign their names in the parish register when they were married. At the end of the seventeenth century the figures for men and women were 29 per cent and 14 per cent respectively; in the period 1786–1790 these percentages had risen to 47 and 27. By 1871–1875 these figures had reached 78 and 66 per cent. The proportion of literate conscripts showed a similar rise in the course of our period. It should be added that there were considerable variations in the degree of literacy between region and region,

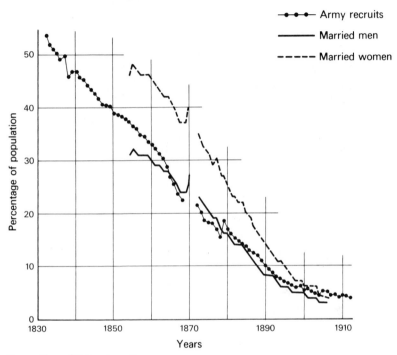

Proportion of illiterates, 1830–1914.

and between town and country as well as between men and women; the poor showing made by women was simply due to the slow progress in the education of girls.

Napoleon had not been interested in elementary education, and it is probable that it was in a worse state in 1814 than it had been in 1789. In the first half of the nineteenth century it continued, as in the past, to be dominated by the Church. Paid by the parish, the village schoolmaster was the *curé's* second in command, often acting as sexton, bell-ringer and precentor. During the Restoration the State left it largely to local initiative to found schools, and although a considerable number were set up in these years, it was only with the *Loi Guizot* (1833) that a state

Village schoolmaster (mid 19th century engraving).

system was established, though the education offered by it was
still neither compulsory nor free. However, provision was made
for the poorer children to pay no fees; in 1837 one in three was
receiving free education and by the 1870s this figure had risen to
over half. In these forty years considerable progress was undoubtedly made, though it varied very considerably from region
to region; it was much faster in the departments north of a line
drawn from Saint-Malo to Geneva than in those to the south of it.
Again, girls were much less favoured than boys. Often the village
began with a boys' school to which a few girls were admitted;
then when the school became too small, a separate one for girls –
often run by nuns – would be built. Again there were still very few
training colleges for women teachers. It was only in the period
1850–1880 that rapid progress was made in the education of girls,

whereas the big leap forward with boys had taken place by the middle of the century.

Especially in the country attendance at school was far from satisfactory even among the boys and girls who were nominally on the register. Many of them spent only a few years there, leaving

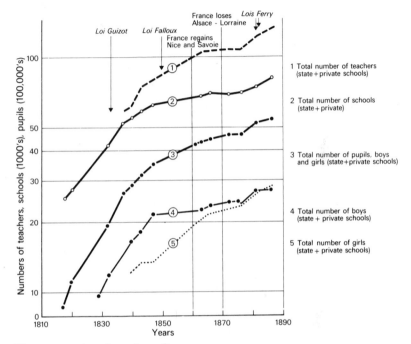

Elementary education, 1810–1890.

at 12 or even 10; again there were vast differences in attendance according to the season. Schools were most frequented in the depth of winter when there was nothing much to do on the land. Many peasants were unwilling or unable to see the advantages of education for their offspring. A gloomy account of the near-illiteracy of the average peasant is offered by an observer in 1871:

Lire, il ne sait pas lire, ou du moins il lit si obscurément et avec une telle peine que l'essayer lui cause beaucoup de répugnance et c'est ce qu'il fait rarement. Rien de plus simple. Il a fréquenté l'école depuis l'âge de six à sept ans jusqu'à douze, fort peu encouragé à ce faire par ses parents qui considéraient cela comme un temps perdu; les anciens du village, les hommes graves, les paysans riches, d'accord sur ce point, prononcent aujourd'hui, en 1871, qu'apprendre à lire

et à écrire aux enfants des villages est un véritable malheur; du reste,
pendant le temps consacré à des études si disputées, si contestées, il
va sans dire que les élèves ne paraissent jamais en classe lorsqu'il y a la
moisson à faire, de l'herbe à couper pour les lapins, des pommes de
terre à arracher, du bois mort à ramasser, etc. etc. etc. A la fin de
cinq à six années d'études aussi agitées, il n'y a rien d'extraordinaire
à ce que l'enfant, désormais réclamé absolument par les travaux des
champs et dont les études intellectuelles sont terminées pour jamais,
ne possède au bout de ses doigts qu'une écriture aux formes fantastiques appliquées à une orthographe des plus extravagantes et un
talent de lecture analogue . . . Le paysan ne sait donc en réalité ni
lire ni écrire. (Gobineau, *Ce qui est arrivé en France en 1870*, pp. 99–100)

While this passage would appear to contain an element of truth, it
does not reflect adequately the undoubted progress made in previous decades. One has to remember that non-attendance at
elementary schools continued to cause problems even after the
passing of the Ferry laws from 1881 onwards.

These laws made elementary education entirely free and compulsory for all children between the ages of 6 and 13. Increasingly
it was in the hands of the State, as more women teachers were
produced by the training colleges set up in every department by a
law of 1879. By a law of 1889 teachers in elementary schools became fully fledged civil servants (*fonctionnaires*), as the local
authorities were henceforth responsible only for providing the
buildings and equipment. A law of 1886 set up an *enseignement
primaire supérieur* which took pupils for several years beyond the
age of 13. Entrants to the training colleges were recruited from the
elementary sector of education, not from the secondary, and it was
extremely difficult for a pupil to pass from an elementary to a
secondary school. In other words, elementary and secondary
education were two different worlds; the pejorative sense of
'C'est un primaire' reflects the gap which existed between the two
systems.

Two things stand out in all this. On the one hand there is no
doubt that the progress made by elementary education and the
fairly rapid decline in illiteracy in the hundred years after 1814
gradually created a mass audience for the printed word, if only
for the popular newspapers which emerged from the 1860s onwards. On the other hand secondary education, even at the end of
our period, was offered to only a very small proportion of the
relevant age group, and university education only to a tiny
minority. Even in the period 1900–1914 the educational scene

was vastly different from what it is in the 1970s. Yet the changes
effected since 1789 undoubtedly produced a much larger reading
public than had existed in the days of Voltaire and Rousseau.

The writer's sources of income

In theory this should have greatly improved the lot of the writer,
and yet one finds repeated throughout our period the most gloomy
accounts of his poverty-stricken state. Vigny was a well-known
exponent of this view with his *Stello* (1831) and especially his
drame, *Chatterton* (1835), which represents the suicide by poison of
the youthful English poet as the inevitable product of a materialistic society which cares nothing for literature. It is true that in
the preface to his play Vigny declares that he is not concerned
either with the 'homme de lettres' or 'le grand écrivain' both of
whom, he considers, are able to look after themselves. 'Mais,' he
continues,

> il est une autre sorte de nature, nature plus passionnée, plus pure et
> plus rare. Celui qui vient d'elle est inhabile à tout ce qui n'est pas
> l'oeuvre divine, et vient au monde à de rares intervalles, heureuse-
> ment pour lui, malheureusement pour l'espèce humaine. Il y vient
> pour être à charge aux autres, quand il appartient complètement à
> cette race exquise et puissante qui fut celle des grands hommes
> inspirés . . . Il a besoin de *ne rien faire*, pour faire quelque chose en
> son art. Il faut qu'il ne fasse rien d'utile et de journalier pour avoir
> le temps d'écouter les accords qui se forment lentement dans son
> âme, et que le bruit grossier d'un travail positif et régulier inter-
> rompt et fait infailliblement évanouir. – C'est LE POÈTE. – Celui-
> là est retranché dès qu'il se montre: toutes vos larmes, toute votre
> pitié pour lui!

As Vigny will have nothing to do with what the French call 'un
second métier' for the writer, i.e. a job which will provide him
with the necessary money to live on and at least some leisure to
write, presumably what he is arguing for is some form of State
patronage for the writer or at any rate for an élite of writers.

In pre-Revolutionary France literary patronage had played an
extremely important role, although by the eighteenth century, as
in England, the growth in the reading public and increasing
returns from publishers and (for playwrights) from the theatre
were gradually making it possible for a certain number of writers
to make a living with their pen and thus to dispense with assistance
from either the State or private individuals. Patronage was not by

any means dead in the nineteenth century. Napoleon had continued the practice of the eighteenth-century monarchy of granting pensions to men of letters which were paid for by such periodicals as he allowed to appear. In 1805 he founded a large number of prizes to be distributed to men of letters for the best works produced in the course of the decade; however, when in 1810 the time came to award these prizes, it was decided because of the mediocrity of the works published in this period to postpone their award until 1819!

When the monarchy was restored five years before that date, Louis XVIII and Charles X continued the traditions of the *Ancien Régime* by rewarding various writers, among them the young Hugo. Louis Philippe does not appear to have followed their example, but, although his interest in literature was small, Louis Napoleon did occasionally act as a patron of men of letters. Yet there is no question that patronage was much less important than it had been in the eighteenth century, let alone in earlier periods when it was clearly impossible for a writer who lacked private means or some other form of paid employment to make a living with his pen.

Now the writer was for the most part left to wring a living out of publishers, theatre managers and the editors of periodicals and newspapers. Not all writers by any means were agreed that this was a good thing, even from the point of view of the dignity of the author. A characteristic expression of this attitude is to be found in a passage from the Goncourts' journal for 1859:

> Je lis dans la préface d'une étude sur Saint-Just le lieu commun d'usage sur la dignité apportée aux gens de lettres par la Révolution. Quoi? Parce que nous ne courtisons plus une Pompadour, un ministre? Mais nous courtisons Solar, Mirès; on brigue la poignée de mains de Lévy; chacun caresse l'éditeur. Dignité! (III. 130)

A very different view was put forward in 1880 by Zola in an article 'L'Argent et la littérature' published along with the more famous essay, *Le Roman expérimental*. After an impecunious early career by this date he had begun to make money with his novels and journalism. For him the present position of the writer was infinitely preferable to the bygone system of patronage:

> C'est l'argent, c'est le gain legitimement réalisé sur ses ouvrages qui l'a délivré de toute protection humiliante, qui a fait de l'ancien bateleur de cour, de l'ancien bouffon d'antichambre, un citoyen libre, un homme qui ne relève que de lui-même. Avec l'argent, il a osé tout

dire, il a porté son examen partout, jusqu'au roi, jusqu'à Dieu, sans craindre de perdre son pain. L'argent a émancipé l'écrivain, l'argent a créé les lettres modernes.

He has no patience with the laments for the good old days or complaints about the failure of the State to assist young writers:

Regretterez-vous le temps où l'on bâtonnait Voltaire, où Racine mourait d'une bouderie de Louis XIV, où toute la littérature était aux gages d'une noblesse brutale et imbécile? Comment! vous poussez l'ingratitude contre notre grande époque jusqu'à ne pas la comprendre, en l'accusant de mercantilisme, lorsqu'elle est avant tout le droit au travail et à la vie! Si vous ne pouvez vivre avec vos vers, avec vos premiers essais, faites autre chose, entrez dans une administration, attendez que le public vienne à vous. L'État ne vous doit rien. Il est peu honorable de rêver une littérature entretenue. Battez-vous, mangez des pommes de terre ou des truffes, cassez des pierres dans la journée et écrivez des chefs-d'oeuvre la nuit. Seulement, dites-vous bien ceci: c'est que, si vous avez un talent, une force, vous arriverez quand même à la gloire et à la fortune. (*Oeuvres complètes*, X. 1277–1278)

Not unnaturally such sentiments, expressed by a successful author, have not commanded universal approval among his fellow-writers in the last hundred years or so.

Many writers of the time did follow Zola's example of taking a job until they had begun to make a name for themselves. He had begun his career by working for the publisher, Hachette, eking out his meagre earnings with journalism. A considerable number of writers held quite minor routine posts in the various Paris ministries. Coppée, like his father before him, was a clerk in the Ministry for War; Huysmans served for thirty years in the Ministry of the Interior; Maupassant held a clerical post first in the Ministry for the Navy and then in the Ministry of Education. Although he had not drawn a salary for some years, it was only shortly before his death that he was persuaded to resign this post.

State and royal patronage

On the other hand literary patronage in one form or another continued throughout the whole of our period, although its importance grew progressively less. Victor Hugo's early career was undoubtedly assisted by the favours he received from Louis XVIII. The king had read to him poems from his volume of verse, *Odes et poésies diverses*, when it appeared in 1822 and gave the poet a pension of 1,000 francs from the privy purse. 'Avec mille francs par an, on pouvait se marier' wrote his wife in *Victor Hugo raconté par un témoin de sa vie* (II. p. 191). This was soon followed by a second pension of 2,000 francs which the king directed should be paid by the Ministry of the Interior; this meant that Hugo and his wife were now well enough off, with what he was managing to earn from his writings, to leave his father-in-law's and to set up house on their own. When Charles X came to the throne, he saw that both these pensions continued to be paid; indeed, when Hugo's play, *Marion de Lorme*, was banned by the censor in 1829, although the king upheld the ban, in compensation he offered Hugo an additional pension of 4,000 francs which he declined. Although the downfall of Charles X meant that Hugo lost the pension paid from.the privy purse, he continued to be on the books of the Ministry of the Interior for a pension of 2,000 francs, and when he renounced the pension in 1832, the minister replied that it would continue to be paid. Apparently Hugo never took the money, but his attempt to get it transferred to 'une pauvre jeune fille poète' was a failure.

Various ministries continued to pay out pensions or odd sums of money to a variety of writers during the reign of Louis Philippe even though the king himself does not appear to have taken a personal interest in contemporary literature. Louis Napoleon made some attempt to imitate his uncle's patronage of literature. The poet, Leconte de Lisle, for instance, drew a pension of 300 francs a month for a considerable number of years in return, his enemies later alleged, for spying in the literary salons of Paris. In 1858 the playwright Ponsard was given the substantial sum of 25,000 francs, and a certain Théophile Silvestre also managed to win the Imperial favour. As Maxime Du Camp amusingly put it:

> Ce Silvestre n'était pas bête; il avait persuadé à Napoléon III que sa misère seule l'empêchait d'être un grand écrivain. Par curiosité peut-être, et à coup sûr par bonté d'âme, l'empereur lui accorda une pension de six mille francs sur sa cassette. Silvestre empocha, ne fit rien et resta un grand écrivain à l'état latent. (*Souvenirs littéraires*, II. 345)

Again, Louis Napoleon made men of letters like Mérimée and Sainte-Beuve Senators, a post which carried with it not only prestige, but a very comfortable salary of 30,000 francs a year. Only the downfall of the whole régime prevented two other writers, Émile Augier and Maxime Du Camp, from being similarly favoured. Occasionally the Emperor's bounty was declined. In

1861 when the Academy failed to offer George Sand one of its
prizes for which her candidature had been put forward, Louis
Napoleon had soundings made to discover whether she would
accept an equivalent sum (20,000 francs), but she politely refused.
Since 1848 Lamartine had sunk deeper and deeper into debt
despite his large output of 'potboilers'; the Emperor offered to
come to the rescue with a 'don national' of 2 million francs but in
a public letter Lamartine declined the offer, saying that he wished
to remain 'l'homme qui a proclamé la République'. However, in
the end he had to accept an annuity of 25,000 francs which the
Corps Législatif voted for him.

The Emperor's cousin, Princess Mathilde, was much more
interested in literature and received in her salon in Paris and in her
country house many of the leading men of letters of the time, such
as Flaubert, the Goncourt brothers, Gautier and Sainte-Beuve.
Although Gautier received a modest pension from the government, the princess did not think it enough and appointed him her
librarian, a pure sinecure which gave him an additional 6,000
francs a year. The Goncourts noted the event in 1868 in somewhat
ironical terms:

> En descendant ce soir les escaliers de la Princesse, Gautier, nommé
> son bibliothécaire, nous demanda, en toute sincérité: 'Mais, au fait,
> dites-moi, est-ce que la Princesse a une bibliothèque? – Un conseil
> entre nous, Gautier; faites comme si elle n'en avait pas . . .' (*Journal*,
> VIII. 146)

Indeed they felt unable to share the accepted view of Gautier as
the poverty-stricken poet driven to earn a living through the
hackwork of dramatic criticism and other pieces of journalism. In
the following month they commented on the state of relative
affluence in which Gautier found himself towards the end of the
Second Empire:

> A voir le vrai et le fin fond des choses, ce bon Gautier est un de ces
> meurt-de-faim de la littérature les plus riches de ce temps-ci, avec sa
> place de bibliothèque, soit 6,000, – une pension sur la cassette de
> l'Empereur, soit 3,000, – à peu pres 20,000 francs au *Moniteur* par an
> et le revenant-bon de ses livres. Qui est-ce qui est aussi riche que
> cela dans les lettres à l'heure qu'il est? (VIII. 156)

Yet the frequent changes of political régime could have disastrous
effects on a writer's career, as Gautier explained to Edmond de
Goncourt in October 1870 after the collapse of Louis Napoleon's
empire:

Cette révolution, c'est ma fin, c'est mon *coup de lapin* . . . Du reste, je suis une victime des révolutions. Sans blague! Lors de la Révolution de Juillet, mon père était très légitimiste, il a joué à la hausse sur les Ordonnances de Juillet; vous pensez comme ça a réussi! Nous avons perdu toute notre fortune, quinze mille livres de rentes. J'étais destiné à entrer dans la vie en heureux, en homme de loisir; il a fallu gagner sa vie . . . Enfin, après des années, j'avais assez bien arrangé mon affaire, j'avais une petite maison, une petite voiture, deux petits chevaux. Février met tout ça à bas . . . Je retrouve l'équilibre, j'allais être nommé de l'Académie, . . . au Sénat: Sainte-Beuve mort, Mérimée prêt à mourir, il n'etait pas improbable que l'Empereur voulût y mettre un homme de lettres, n'est-ce pas? Je finissais par me caser . . . Tout fout le camp avec la République. (IX. 90)

Indeed Gautier did not long survive the disasters of 1870.

Under the Second Empire various ministries continued to assist men of letters. In 1855 Baudelaire reported to his mother a conversation with the notary who had been charged with the administration of the poet's estate because of his spendthrift habits:

Je disais ce matin même à Ancelle une chose que je trouve assez raisonnable. Je lui disais: préfériez-vous que je fisse ce que font tant d'hommes de lettres, qui ont moins d'orgueil que moi, et ce que je n'ai jamais fait sous aucun ministère, sous aucun gouvernement? Demander de l'argent à un ministre me fait horreur, et cependant cela est presque un usage; il y a des fonds pour cela. Quant à moi, j'ai un orgueil et une prudence qui m'ont toujours éloigné de ces moyens-là. Jamais mon nom ne paraîtra dans les ignobles paperasses d'un gouvernement. J'aime mieux devoir à tout le monde; j'aime mieux me disputer avec vous, et tourmenter ma mère, quelque pénible que cela soit. (*Correspondance générale*, I. 355–356)

Yet, two years later (on the very eve of the publication of *Les Fleurs du Mal*) despite these proud declarations of independence we find Baudelaire sending this humble letter to the Minister of Education:

Monsieur le Ministre,

Mon travail, sans suffire largement à mes besoins, m'avait permis jusqu'ici d'éviter des demandes qui m'ont toujours répugné; mais des besoins urgents me déterminent aujourd'hui à m'adresser à Votre Excellence pour solliciter un engagement sur les fonds des Sciences et des Lettres.

Si quelque considération pouvait atténuer le regret que j'éprouve de recourir à une pareille démarche, c'est la conscience que j'ai d'avoir fait tout ce qui était en moi pour l'éviter, et l'intérêt que je suis assuré de rencontrer chez Votre Excellence. Les témoignages récents de bienveillance qu'elle a donnés à la Société[1] dont je suis membre depuis douze ans me permettent d'espérer pour ma demande un accueil favorable. Je prends la liberté de joindre à ma demande la liste des principaux travaux que j'ai publiés, ainsi que l'annonce de ceux qui sont en ce moment sous presse.

Je prie Votre Excellence d'agréer l'hommage de mon profond respect. (ibid. II. 56–57)

The result of this appeal was an award of the paltry sum of 200 francs in recognition of the poet's translation of Poe. After addressing a petition to the Empress Eugénie which secured a reduction of the fine imposed upon him for publishing obscene poems in *Les Fleurs du Mal,* he received from the government other small sums, ranging from 100 to 500 francs.

Such modest subsidies to needy writers continued to be doled out by successive governments under the Third Republic. In 1895, for instance we find that notorious cadger, Léon Bloy, writing to an old acquaintance, Gabriel Hanotaux, who had become Minister for Foreign Affairs, asking for 500 francs to save his wife and small daughter from abject poverty. 'Ne suis-je pas éligible et, par conséquent, habile à participer aux fonds secrets dont un prévoyant Trésor inonde nos ministères?' he wrote in his diary. On this occasion his request was apparently successful as three days later we find the entry: 'Hanotaux s'est exécuté. Enfin son passage au ministère aura du moins servi à cela.' (*Journal,* I. 76) However, when in the following year he applied again, he was extremely grieved to receive only 20 francs.

It is clear that such assistance as the State continued to give was both on a very modest scale and offered only to necessitous writers. Zola makes this point when he compares the situation in the 1880s with that a century or two earlier:

D'ailleurs, les pensions ne sont plus données à titre honorifique et comme un témoignage de haute admiration; elles vont aux néces-siteux, aux écrivains dont la vieillesse n'est pas heureuse; et, le plus souvent, on les dissimule, en donnant une sinécure au pensionné, un emploi fictif qui met sa dignité à l'abri. En somme, les pensions se sont faites discrètes et comme honteuses; certes, elles n'entraînent aucune déchéance, mais elles sont l'indice certain d'un état de gêne qu'on aime mieux cacher. (*Oeuvres complètes,* X. 1274)

---

[1] The *Société des Gens de Lettres,* founded in 1838 (see below, p. 249).

This reference to the State disguising its financial assistance to a writer by giving him some sinecure particularly concerns appointments to posts in a variety of libraries.

Zola was perhaps thinking here of an illustrious example – that of Flaubert, who in his last years was extremely hard up because he had helped his niece's husband in his financial difficulties. Just over a year before he died his friends endeavoured to get some form of state assistance for him. In March 1879 he wrote to his niece: 'J'ai tout lieu de croire qu'on va *m'offrir* une pension; et je l'accepterai, bien que j'en sois *humilié* jusqu'à la moelle des os (aussi je désire là-dessus le secret le plus absolu).' (*Correspondance*, V. 508) Shortly afterwards Jules Ferry, who had recently become Minister of Education, had Flaubert appointed to a supernumerary post at the Bibliothèque Mazarine in Paris. This was a pure sinecure, but a modest salary of 3,000 francs was attached to it.

Librarianship

Throughout the whole of our period posts as librarians were offered to men of letters to enable them to keep the wolf from the door. Indeed a distinguished French librarian has recently attributed to this practice part of the blame for a certain backwardness in library provision in the France of our day. Most writers did not seem to take the job very seriously. A small library like the Mazarine offered, we are told, all sorts of advantages:

> On n'a affaire qu'à de rares travailleurs muets et bien élevés, et on est de service une fois par semaine, avec la faculté de se faire remplacer. Au bout de quelque temps écoulé, l'Institut[1] vous loge gratuitement dans un appartement spacieux, et souvent vous donne encore une clef de la bibliothèque pour y aller prendre des livres, et un cabinet isolé de l'appartement, des bruits du ménage. (Théodore de Banville, *Mes Souvenirs*, pp. 301–302)

How the writer Jules Sandeau, from whom George Sand had borrowed half his name when she became tired of being merely Mme Dudevant, carried out his modest duties is amusingly related by a contemporary:

> Il était bibliothécaire de la Bibliothèque Mazarine et comme on

---

[1] *L'Institut de France*, i.e. the body formed by the *Académie Française*, *Académie des Inscriptions et Belles-Lettres*, *Académie des Sciences*, *Académie des Beaux-Arts* and *Académie des Sciences morales et politiques*. It is housed in the Palais Mazarin where it has its own library.

n'arrivait pas à obtenir qu'il prît ses tours de service, on avait, pour sauver les apparences, fini par réduire sa tâche à une séance d'après-midi une fois par semaine. Il prenait place au fauteuil à l'heure voulue, et s'astreignait, au besoin, à la transmission des bulletins de demandes des lecteurs, mais lorsque l'un d'eux tentait d'obtenir de lui des renseignements ou un conseil comportant un effort ou un dérangement quelconque, alors il répondait, en souriant :

'Mon Dieu, Monsieur, je me permettrai de vous donner un avis utile : ne venez jamais le mercredi. C'est mon jour et je ne suis au courant de rien'. (M. Dreyfous, *Ce qu'il me reste à dire*, pp. 197–198)

On the other hand there is the sad case of Flaubert's friend, the poet and playwright Louis Bouilhet who, when he was appointed librarian at Rouen, unfortunately got so interested in the job that he tended to neglect his writing:

C'était un poste tranquille, fait pour lui. Tout en surveillant la besogne des employés et le prêt des livres, on peut rêver aux personnages du drame et chercher des rimes rares; mais la nouveauté de la fonction l'intéressa, du moins il le crut; il pensa à des classements, à des catalogues, à des installations logiques, et donna à la bibliothèque un temps que la poésie réclamait. Flaubert était furieux et ne lui épargnait pas les reproches: 'On t'a mis là pour faire des vers et non pour ranger des bouquins.' (Maxime du Camp, *Souvenirs littéraires*, II. 325)

No doubt Bouilhet was very much an exception among these writer-librarians.

Throughout the century all manner of writers derived from their appointments to library posts anything from a modest supplement to their income to a quite affluent position. The latter was the situation of Charles Nodier who in 1824 was appointed librarian of the Bibliothèque de l'Arsenal which was then the private property of the Comte d'Artois, soon to become Charles X. It was in his salon at the Arsenal that the first Romantic *cénacle* met. He held this post until his death in 1844, arousing Balzac's envy at the large income which he drew from this post, from his position as academician, from a state pension and in only a relatively minor way from his writings. In 1842 Balzac wrote to his future wife, Mme Hanska:

Nodier est logé dans les appartements de Sully,[1] Nodier a une place de 6,000 fr., 3,000 fr. comme académicien, 6,000 fr. comme chargé d'un travail pour le *Dictionnaire* et une pension de 2,000 fr. comme

---

[1] Henry IV's minister, the Duc de Sully.

homme de lettres; en tout 17,000 fr., et il gagne bien 3,000 fr. par an. (*Lettres à Madame Hanska*, II. 140)

The same post of librarian at the Arsenal was held for some years at the beginning of this century by the poet, José Maria de Heredia, who also held a literary salon there.

It would not seem altogether unnatural to see a scholar-critic like Sainte-Beuve in the role of librarian even though he did not apparently take his duties very seriously. In 1840, after thanking Thiers for his appointment, he wrote to a Swiss friend: 'Ma Mazarine, c'est quatre mille f. par an, plus un logement dans les bâtiments de l'Institut.' (*Correspondance générale*, III. 352) He did not resign this position until after the 1848 revolution. On the other hand Alfred de Musset, in the latter part of his life seldom sober, would seem a strange person to appoint to one of these posts except that they were mostly sinecures. Yet in 1838 he was appointed to the post of librarian in the Ministry of the Interior. After the 1848 revolution he lost it to a supporter of the new régime, but when the Second Empire came in, he was given a similar post in the Ministry of Education. Poets, who generally found it hard to make a living, were often assisted in this way. Despite his secret pension from Louis Napoleon, Leconte de Lisle was rewarded in 1872 for his firm Republican views and made a librarian at the Senate; as we have already seen, one of his disciples, Heredia, held a more exalted post at the Arsenal some thirty years later.

Profits from poetry

There were, of course, exceptions to the rule that poets were necessarily hard up in nineteenth-century France. In the first part of the period both Lamartine and Hugo succeeded in making money out of their poetry as well as from their other writings. Although Lamartine earned more from his prose writings (he got 250,000 francs for his eight-volumed *Histoire des Girondins* which appeared in 1847), he sold his volumes of poetry for fairly substantial sums. In 1823, after the earlier success of his first volume, *Les Méditations*, he was given 14,000 francs for his *Nouvelles méditations*, and in 1830 he received 27,000 for his *Harmonies poétiques*. The young Hugo made a very modest start with his first volume of poetry, which brought him only 750 francs, but he obtained 2,000 francs for his next collection, and in 1831 he received 6,000 francs for one year's sales of *Les Feuilles d'automne*. In 1835 and 1836 he pocketed 20,000 francs for reprints of his first three collections of poetry and for the first edition of a new one, *Les Voix intérieures*. In 1839 he signed an agreement for an edition of his collected works which brought him in 300,000 francs. With his tremendous output in poetry, prose and drama he could write in a letter of 1845:

> Vous me croyez riche, monsieur? Voici:
> Je travaille depuis vingt-huit ans, car j'ai commencé à quinze ans. Dans ces vingt-huit années j'ai gagné avec ma plume environ cinq cent cinquante mille francs. Je n'ai point hérité de mon père . . . (*Correspondance*, I. 625)

His later volumes of poetry brought substantial sums to the exiled poet. In 1856 he could write to a friend in Paris:

> La maison de Guernesey avec ses trois étages, son toit, son jardin, son perron, sa crypte, sa basse-cour, son *look-out* et sa plate-forme, sort tout entière des *Contemplations*. Depuis la première poutre jusqu'à la dernière tuile, les *Contemplations* paieront tout. Ce livre m'a donné un toit... (II. 257)

Some years later we find him signing a contract for another volume of poetry for which he was to receive 40,000 francs.

Lamartine and Hugo were obviously writers who managed to attract a large audience for their poetry; other poets of their time were much less prosperous. In 1852 Théophile Gautier – by no means a mere beginner, but a writer at the height of his powers – received the princely sum of 300 francs for his *Émaux et camées*. Later poets like Leconte de Lisle could not survive, as we have seen, without outside assistance. Things were particularly difficult for the young poet; then as now his verse was unlikely to appeal to publishers, and if it was published at all, it was in a very small edition and at his own expense. Coppée gives a frank account of what happened with his first two collections of poetry, published towards the end of the Second Empire:

> Des cinq cents exemplaires, imprimés, ai-je besoin d'en convenir? aux dépens de l'auteur, une centaine tout au plus s'écoula. Une autre centaine fut distribuée à des confrères illustres, à des critiques, à des amis, avec de flatteuses dédicaces . . . Enfin tout se passa dans l'ordre accoutumé; la majeure partie de l'édition du *Reliquaire* et des *Intimités* resta enfouie dans les arcanes de la librairie Lemerre, et l'on pouvait déjà prévoir le moment où, convertie en sacs et en cornets, elle envelopperait de rimes riches et de rythmes curieux le sucre de l'épicier ou le caporal du marchand de tabac. (*Souvenirs d'un Parisien*, pp. 148–149)

He too eked out a living by holding various librarians' posts, at the Senate and the Comédie Française, but he also did a good deal of journalism. Indeed in the same work he makes this confession: 'Comme la plupart de mes confrères contemporains, j'ai beaucoup écrit, beaucoup trop peut-être. Ce n'est pas de ma faute, c'est celle de mon temps, où la littérature est devenue une profession.' (p. 2)

If a poet like Coppée, who was extremely popular during his lifetime, could only make a living by journalism and posts in libraries, it can well be imagined that poets like Verlaine, Rimbaud and Mallarmé, most of whose work could only appeal to a very narrow section of the community, could not live by their pen. Verlaine and Rimbaud led, of course, extraordinarily unconventional lives, Verlaine starting out as a clerk in the Hôtel de Ville and ending up in a poverty-stricken bohemianism, and Rimbaud leading a wandering existence which took him as far as Abyssinia. In contrast Mallarmé led a much more conventional existence, teaching English in various *lycées*, at first in the provinces, then in Paris. When in 1870 just before the outbreak of the war, he suggested to another poet, Catulle Mendès, that he might move to Paris and earn a living with his pen, he received a very discouraging reply. Mendès explained that unless Mallarmé had a guaranteed income of 3,000 francs a year, it would be folly to make the move, and that, despite half killing himself with journalism, he had the utmost difficulty in making ends meet:

> 'Mais vous vivez', direz-vous. Mon ami, n'essayez pas d'endurer ce que j'endure! pour faire vivre ma femme, je meurs! C'est à peine si tous les trois mois, je puis arracher à la destinée trois heures pour faire un sonnet! Ah! cette misère, la misère! un poète qui assassinerait pour avoir de quoi travailler serait-il en effet criminel? Non, je n'ose pas vous dire: partagez cet enfer. J'ai eu des jours sans pain, avec des huissiers à la porte: j'en ai eu! (Mallarmé, *Correspondance, 1862–1871*, p. 328)

It should be added that this gloomy picture of the life of a poet is somewhat lightened by Mendès's remark that since he had obtained a pension of 1,500 francs from one of the ministries things were a little easier.

For a time Mallarmé toyed with the idea of supporting himself in Paris by translating and by running a course on French literature for a group of English girls, at the same time holding a post in one of the Paris libraries which would perhaps leave him his mornings free for writing. In the end he kept to school teaching, a career into which he had drifted, as he explained in a letter to Verlaine in 1885:

Il n'y avait pas, vous le savez, pour un poète à vivre de son art, même en l'abaissant de plusieurs crans, quand je suis entré dans la vie; et je ne l'ai jamais regretté. Ayant appris l'anglais simplement pour mieux lire Poe, je suis parti à vingt ans en Angleterre, afin de fuir, principalement; mais aussi pour parler la langue, et l'enseigner dans un coin, tranquille et sans autre gagne-pain obligé; je m'étais marié et cela pressait. (*Correspondance, 1871–1885*, p. 301)

In 1873 he had moved to Paris where the famous salon which he held in the Rue de Rome exercised a great influence on younger poets.

Among those who began to write around 1890, but reached the height of their fame only after 1914 were Claudel and Valéry, but neither of these could be said to have even attempted to live on their poetry and other writings, at any rate before the First World War. For over forty years Claudel was employed in the foreign service, travelling all over the world and ending his career in the 1930s as an ambassador, though even before 1914 he had made his name as a poet and dramatist. Valéry began publishing poetry in 1889 while he was a law student at Montpellier, but he gave this up in 1892, and secured a post in the Ministry of War which he left in 1900 to act as secretary to one of the directors of the Agence Havas. This post allowed him ample leisure, but it was only in 1912 that he returned to poetry, and down to 1922, when the death of his employer brought the relationship to an end, he continued to rely for a living on this post.

Right of property and copyright
Though writers were seldom able to earn much from their poetry, a considerable number, starting with Hugo and Lamartine, did succeed in making large sums of money with their pen. There is no doubt that writers as a whole 'had never had it so good'. The Revolution at last provided them with proper protection for their work inside France when in 1793 the Convention decreed:

Les auteurs d'écrits en tout genre, les compositeurs de musique, les peintres et dessinateurs qui feront graver des tableaux ou dessins, jouiront durant leur vie entière du droit exclusif de vendre, faire vendre, distribuer leurs ouvrages dans le territoire de la République, et d'en céder la propriété en tout ou en partie.

This law continued the author's right of property to his heirs for a period of ten years after his death at which time the copyright lapsed (or in French technical jargon the works 'tombaient dans le domaine public'), i.e. any publisher was free to reproduce them without payment. In 1810 this period was extended to twenty years. Round about 1840 there was considerable agitation among writers for a much longer period; some even went so far as to demand a perpetual right of property. Though this was a forlorn hope, a law of 1844 extended copyright to forty years after the author's death, and in 1866 this was raised to fifty years. This remains the present figure in France except that allowance is now made for the two world wars, which means that a work goes out of copyright only sixty-four years and 253 days after the author's death. It should be added that British legislation remained for a long time distinctly less favourable to an author's heirs; it was only in 1911 that the term was extended to fifty years after his death.

On the other hand for a great deal of our period French writers were undoubtedly deprived of a part of their legitimate earnings by the absence of an international copyright law. Given the fact that French continued to be an international language, their books both in the original and in translation could count on a wide sale in the rest of Europe as well as further afield, but it was obviously profitable for publishers abroad to reprint their works without paying the author a penny. The fact that English books were ruthlessly pirated in the United States for most of the century was no consolation; many were also reprinted in Germany . . . or even France! Until the matter was cleared up in 1886 by the Berne Convention and subsequent international agreements French writers undoubtedly lost part of their market abroad, and no doubt copies of the pirated editions found their way into France itself. Some strange things could happen; for instance, *Madame Bovary* first appeared in a review, the *Revue de Paris*, but in an incomplete text; before the French publisher could get out the work in book form, it had appeared, still incomplete, in Germany. The same had happened earlier with other works; Balzac's *Le Curé de Village* and Mérimée's *Colomba* made their first appearance in book form in Belgium.

Belgian piracy

In the early part of the century Belgian publishers made a particularly lucrative business out of reprinting new works published in France. They were not interested in publishing editions of older works which were now out of copyright; where they could easily undercut the original publishers was in producing cheap editions

of new books. Novels were particularly vulnerable as works which
nowadays easily go into one volume were then published in two
or even three volumes at 7.50 francs each. Belgian publishers
would print these in one volume at 3 francs or even less. The
Belgian output of pirated editions was at its height in the 1830s
and 1840s. In his letters to the Polish Madame Hanska Balzac is
continually moaning about the activities of Belgian publishers and
indulging in all sorts of pipe dreams as to how well off he would be
if only such pirated editions could be stopped. In 1840 he wrote
indignantly:

> La Belgique a ruiné la littérature française. Quelle ingénérosité chez
> ceux qui nous lisent! Si chacun avait refusé l'édition belge et voulu,
> comme vous le faites, l'édition française; s'il s'était rencontré deux
> mille personnes ainsi sur le continent, nous étions sauvés; et la
> Belgique nous vend à vingt ou trente mille! (*Lettres à Madame Hanska*,
> I. 680)

Three years later when it was rumoured that the Belgians were
about to agree to end this piracy, he dreamed of being rid of all his
mountain of debts: 'Si la contrefaçon belge est supprimée, oh, je
serai libéré en deux ans! Je gagnerai 100,000 fr. alors.' (II. 144)
This was, as so often with Balzac, a wild exaggeration. In any case
it was not until after his death that in 1852 an agreement was
reached between the two governments to put an end to these
pirated editions. Agreements were later negotiated with other
countries and finally, as we have seen, the Berne Convention
virtually disposed of the problem.

It would seem that French writers of the time tended to ex-
aggerate the ill-effects of the Belgian piracy. For one thing it was
fairly short-lived; it began in the Restoration period, reached its
peak in 1845, after which there was a rapid decline, several large
firms going bankrupt through excessive competition. Moreover in
1838 the Paris publisher, Gervais Charpentier, launched his
collection of 3.50 fr. reprints of recent works in one volume in a
small format, and his example was quickly followed by others, as
one of Balzac's numerous publishers noted in a work published
in 1860:

> Lorsque Charpentier s'avisa, en 1838, de coter à 3 fr. 50 c. d'élégants
> volumes, grand in-18 sur jésus, contenant la matière d'un livre
> in-8° ordinaire, qui s'était vendu ou pour mieux dire, s'était coté, de
> temps immémorial, de 7 fr. 50 c. à 9 fr., il opéra une véritable
> révolution en librairie.

Et alors les moutons de Panurge de se mettre en campagne! Et les Gosselin, les Delloye, une foule d'autres éditeurs, d'adopter, à l'envi, le type Charpentier! Et des milliers de volumes d'apparaître en très peu de temps, toujours à raison de 3 fr. 50 c.

. . . Depuis lors, le prix de ces volumes a continuellement baissé; il est descendu à 3 fr., à 2 fr.; il est maintenant à 1 fr., et il pourra fléchir encore. (Werdet, *La librairie française*, pp. 139–140)

This development no doubt contributed to the decline of the Belgian industry.

Circulating libraries and 'cabinets de lecture'

Another grievance of French writers, particularly in this part of the century, was the existence of circulating libraries which, they claimed, took away a considerable part of their potential sales. This reminds one of the recent agitation among some English authors for the Public Lending Right. In neither country would such a campaign have been conceivable in the first half of the nineteenth century; the first English Public Libraries Act dates from 1850 and, while it has led to a steady development of such libraries down to our own day, French librarians themselves admit

A *cabinet de lecture*, about 1830.

that, even though there has been a great development of public libraries in France since 1945, their impact on the public is still very much smaller than that of English public libraries.

Circulating libraries, in France as in England, go a long way back into the eighteenth century, but they greatly expanded their activities during the Revolution. Originally they had simply lent out copies of books, newspapers and periodicals in return for a small fee; now booksellers often provided a reading room where subscribers to the *cabinet de lecture* could both read and meet their friends. There is an amusing story of Hugo and his two brothers being sent as small boys by their mother to borrow books for her and using the opportunity to read works which might not have been considered suitable for their tender age. *Cabinets de lecture* increased in number during the Restoration and reached the peak of their popularity in the 1840s. In 1844 Paris alone had 177 *cabinets de lecture* as well as 38 bookshops which ran circulating libraries. Although some *cabinets de lecture* continued to flourish to the end of the century (the catalogue of the largest of them, published in 1888, lists some 160,000 volumes), the period of their greatest vogue was over by 1850. They suffered from the competition of cheap editions of books, from the publication of novels in newspapers and to some extent also from the still somewhat patchy public library system.

Cabinets de lecture must have bought a fair number of the copies of such works as novels published at the time; these novels were blown out into two or even three expensive volumes, full of blank spaces and blank pages, for each of which their owners could charge a separate fee. In the early decades of the century people naturally hesitated to pay 15 francs for a novel in two volumes when they could borrow it for a few *sous*. Balzac, for instance, wrote bitterly in his *Chronique de Paris* (1836) of the unwillingness of even well-to-do people actually to *buy* books:

> C'est à qui n'achètera pas un livre, on s'en défend comme d'un malheur. Les femmes les plus aimables prêtent à leurs amis les exemplaires dont l'auteur fait présent; les femmes les plus élégantes lisent un ouvrage après que Joseph Prudhomme y a déposé son tabac, que la dame d'un café y a imprimé la marque de ses doigts, et que l'étudiant y a crayonné ses notes drolatiques. (*Oeuvres diverses*, III. 308)

This, like the remarks of many observers of the time, makes clear the obvious point that the *cabinets de lecture* scattered over France undoubtedly made a considerable contribution to the enlarge-

ment of the reading public and so in the long run were of benefit
to writers.

Periodicals and newspapers

Another advantage which nineteenth-century writers had over
their predecessors was the opportunity for earning money, not
only from publishers, but also from an increasing number of
periodicals and, above all, from newspapers which grew in importance and wealth as well as in numbers. All this was again
obviously a reflection of the growing reading public; newspapers
in particular gradually came to appeal both to the educated and
wealthy classes, and to those who, with the development of
elementary education, had acquired the ability to read.

The ending of Napoleon's muzzling of the press brought with it
a great development of periodicals which devoted themselves
mainly to literature. From the Restoration onwards a considerable
number of *revues* were founded (this sense of the word was imported
from the English 'review'). Some of these were, of course, short-
lived (Balzac's *Revue parisienne* lasted for only three numbers in
1840); some were pretty impoverished. Yet for most of our period,
at any rate from 1830 onwards, there were in existence periodicals
which offered writers payment for novels, short stories, poems and
literary criticism. The rate of payment naturally varied according
to the prosperity of the review, but one periodical which in the
middle of our period, from 1831 onwards, did play a big part in
the literary life of the time, was the *Revue des Deux Mondes*; in its
pages appeared contributions from Hugo, Vigny, Musset, Balzac
and George Sand. Towards the end of our period one finds reviews like the *Mercure de France*, an old title revived in 1890 and at
first having close connections with Symbolism, or the *Nouvelle
Revue Française*, founded in 1908 by a group of writers which
included André Gide.

However, in the long run it was newspapers which in our period
provided much larger sources of income for writers, indeed did so
in a way which was not repeated to anything like the same extent
after 1914. This was a gradual development. The number of
newspapers had been severely restricted by Napoleon and those
which had been allowed to appear were subject to a strict censorship. The Restoration brought a greater degree of freedom, but
right down to the press law of 1881 the struggle for freedom of the
press had to be fought, with all manner of ups and downs. One
considerable brake on the expansion of newspapers was stamp

duty, which was only abolished in 1870. However, technological improvements in the printing of newspapers gradually made possible the production at high speed of large numbers of copies.

One tends to forget that throughout almost the whole of our period newspapers were much smaller than what we are accustomed to today; they had only four pages, the bottom part of which was separated off to form what was called a *feuilleton*. It was a great event when in 1901 the first popular newspaper could announce, with all the fanfares of publicity then available, that henceforth it would have six pages. What is more, at the beginning of our period newspapers were uniformly expensive and by present-day standards had an astonishingly small circulation.

Down to the mid-1830s a subscription to a Paris newspaper cost 80 francs a year; this undoubtedly restricted its circulation to the fairly well-to-do. During the Restoration a number of quite prominent daily newspapers had circulations of the order of some 5,000; anything above that figure was exceptional. Only two newspapers of the time had circulations which at times exceeded 20,000 – the *Journal des Débats* and the *Constitutionnel*. These small circulations continued in the reign of Louis Philippe. Indeed in 1836 these two newspapers had only 10,000 and 9,000 subscribers respectively, while the very prominent *National*, founded by Thiers amongst others in 1830, had barely 5,000.

1836 is an important date in the history of the French press as it was then that there appeared simultaneously two new papers, *La Presse* and *Le Siècle*, which cost 40 francs, half the price of the existing journals. Although a paper like the *Journal des Débats* had for some time derived a fair income from advertising, the new papers counted on being able to sell at half the price because of the revenue obtained from this source. Advertising revenue was, of course, to be attracted by a large circulation. In other words the modern newspaper was born. In order to attract custom the editors hit upon the idea of publishing novels in serial form; this meant that novelists could derive a double income from their works by publishing them first in a newspaper and then in book form. Indeed the rivalry between these two newspapers and between them and established papers like the *Journal des Débats* led to fierce competition to secure the collaboration of the leading novelists of the time. In 1844 Eugène Sue, after the success of *Les Mystères de Paris* in the *Journal des Débats*, received the record sum

Le Petit Journal

Bureaux : rue de La Fayette, 61 — Librairie du Petit Journal — QUOTIDIEN — UN NUMÉRO : 5 CENTIMES — Septième Année : n° 2,458 — Vendredi 24 Septembre 1869

Front page of *Le Petit Journal*, 24th September, 1869.

of 100,000 francs for his *roman-feuilleton*, *Le Juif errant*, from the *Constitutionnel* which under new management had reduced its price to 40 francs.

Significant for the future as was the appearance of these cheaper newspapers seeking the largest possible circulation in order to attract advertisements, their circulation still remained very small by our standards. In 1846 the *Journal des Débats* had only 9,000 subscribers; even *Le Siècle* had no more than 33,000 and the other two eight to ten thousand fewer.

Despite its repressive policies towards the press, the Second Empire saw considerable developments which no doubt reflected the economic prosperity of the period. The quality press continued to hold its own with papers like the *Journal des Débats* and, a newcomer, *Le Temps* (founded in 1861) even though in 1869 they had no more than some 10,000 subscribers. There were now a number of newspapers with circulations of somewhere between 15,000 and 65,000, but what was really striking was the appearance on the scene of the cheap newspaper aiming at a mass audience in the shape of *Le Petit Journal*. Launched in 1863, it had achieved six years later a circulation of 287,000, a staggering figure at that time for a newspaper anywhere in the world; its success was due to both its low price (5 sous) and its non-political nature. It specialized in crime reporting and in low grade *romans-feuilletons*.

The period between 1870 and 1914 was to see a vast expansion of both the Paris and the provincial press thanks to the introduction of such innovations as the rotary press and the linotype machine. Communications were speeded up by railways which were penetrating into quite remote corners of France; at the same time illiteracy was gradually being reduced to very small proportions. It is estimated that in the period between 1870 and 1910 the printing of Paris newspapers rose from some 1 million copies to 5 million. Even though the provincial press was not yet as important as it has become in recent decades, it was also growing very fast, partly because of the rise of low-priced newspapers in the larger cities; by the eve of the First World War it had probably reached a circulation of some 4 millions.

A great deal of the increase in the circulation of the Paris newspapers came from the development of the popular press. In the period down to 1890 the *Petit Journal* continued to hold the lead in circulation, reaching one million around that date. However, it encountered growing competition from more recently founded newspapers and its circulation was somewhat reduced by the success of *Le Matin* and *Le Journal* which reached a million by 1913 and above all by *Le Petit Parisien* which outstripped all its rivals with nearly $1\frac{1}{2}$ millions by that date.

One striking feature of the pre-1914 Paris press was its great diversity. In addition to these four large mass-circulation newspapers it offered a wide range of choice. There was, for instance, the Catholic *La Croix* founded in 1883, and the Socialist *L'Humanité*, founded by Jaurès in 1904; of the two *La Croix* had much the bigger circulation, as *L'Humanité* was often in considerable financial difficulties though its fortunes improved towards 1914 with the growth of the Socialist Party. The old established quality newspapers, the *Journal des Débats* and *Le Temps*, continued to prosper; their circulation was still relatively small, indeed tiny compared with that of the giants, but their influence remained considerable. In addition to a host of small papers some of which led a more or less nominal existence there were others with a fairly considerable readership such as *Le Figaro*, a daily since the Second Empire, and especially the *Écho de Paris* which, founded in 1884, had reached a circulation of 150,000 by 1913.

The rapid development of newspapers in the thirty or forty years before 1914 was something with which writers were particularly closely associated, indeed much more closely than either before or since. Yet from the Restoration onwards newspapers had been providing both a vehicle for their writings and a certain amount of payment for them. Throughout the whole period writers contributed literary and dramatic criticism to the *feuilletons* of newspapers. Many authors – Théophile Gautier is an outstanding example – derived most of their income from writing for the press.

The appearance of *La Presse* and *Le Siècle* in 1836 and the competition with the older papers which this involved provided writers with a new source of income in the *roman-feuilleton* which was used as a bait to attract subscribers. In the 1840s writers could obtain substantial sums of money for their novels on top of what they received from publishers.

However, although writers like Dumas *père* and Eugène Sue received very handsome payment for their novels at the height of the boom (Sue as much as 100,000 francs for one of them), other writers such as Balzac or George Sand did not reach these dizzy heights. 'E. Sue vient de vendre 100,000 fr. les *Mémoires du Juif Errant* à un journal!' wrote Balzac in 1844. 'C'est ce qui ne m'arrivera jamais.' (*Lettres à Madame Hanska*, II. 342) What is more, for a while the extreme popularity of the *roman-feuilleton*, especially when the newspaper bound up copies to use as a bait to draw in new subscribers, meant that publishers tended to reduce what they were willing to pay novelists because they claimed that sales of their works in book form were inevitably reduced.

During the reaction which followed the 1848 revolution *romans-feuilletons* were attacked as subversive; the vaguely socialistic novels of Eugène Sue were particularly criticized. A law of 1850 imposed an extra stamp duty on newspapers which published novels with the clear intention of putting an end to the practice. However, this clause was not repeated in the decree on the press issued in 1852 after the establishment of the Second Empire. Henceforth the *roman-feuilleton* was exploited by a succession of low-grade writers who filled out the space allotted to them with the most extraordinary and improbable adventures. The great name during the Second Empire was that of Ponson du Terrail whose stock character, Rocambole, endowed the French language with a new adjective, *rocambolesque*, used in such phrases as 'des aventures rocambolesques'. The Goncourt brothers penned the following portrait of the author in 1861, when he was at the height of his fame and affluence:

> On aperçoit, passant modestement, le profil de Ponson du Terrail, avec, à l'horizon, sur le boulevard, son dog-cart et son cocher, la seule voiture d'homme de lettres roulant sur le pavé de Paris. Le pauvre garçon, au reste, la gagne assez et par le travail et par l'humilité de la modestie. C'est lui qui dit aux directeurs de journaux où il a un immense roman en train: 'Prévenez-moi trois feuilletons d'avance, si ça ennuie le public; et en un feuilleton je finirai.' On vend des pruneaux avec plus de fierté. (*Journal*, IV. 213)

Although such writings gave the *roman-feuilleton* a bad name, it must not be forgotten that down to 1914 the most reputable novelists continued to sell their works to newspapers before publishing them in book form.

It was never, of course, a universal practice. Some novelists preferred publication in a review (this was the case with *Madame Bovary*, though Flaubert's *Trois Contes* were later published in newspapers), but the daily press paid much better, especially when a writer had made a name for himself. Novels of writers like Edmond de Goncourt, Daudet, Zola, Anatole France and Bourget made their first appearance in a wide variety of newspapers. Since a certain number of newspapers were willing for reasons of

prestige to publish their novels, the opportunity of receiving payment twice over was one of which many availed themselves. As
late as 1909 we find even Proust, when first contemplating the
writing of *A la Recherche du Temps Perdu*, receiving an offer from
the editor of the *Figaro* to publish his novel; he wrote in a letter to
a friend:

> Calmette, que j'ai vu ici, m'a demandé très gentiment et avec beau-
> coup d'insistance de publier en feuilleton dans *Le Figaro* un roman
> que je suis en train de faire. Je t'ajoute entre nous que, pour beau-
> coup de raisons, je ne crois pas que je donnerai ce roman au *Figaro* ni
> à aucun autre journal ou revue, et qu'il paraîtra seulement en
> volume. (*Contre Sainte-Beuve*, p. 826)

First publication in reviews continued far beyond 1914, but after
that date novels with literary pretentions no longer appeared in
newspapers.

The daily press came increasingly to offer more and more
openings for writers. Short stories, even poems, as well as novels,
appeared there and a considerable amount of space was given up
to both literature and the theatre; this was mainly filled by writers
though it is at times hard to draw the line between writers and
journalists. Many authors served their apprenticeship by writing
for newspapers – Zola is only one of many examples – and continued to write for them after they had acquired standing as men
of letters. Particularly with the expansion of the industry in the
opening decades of the Third Republic newspapers came to
represent a very important source of income for writers.

This point is made very clearly by Zola in his essay, 'L'Argent
dans la littérature':

> Le journalisme surtout a apporté des ressources considérables. Un
> journal est une grosse affaire qui donne du pain à un grand nombre
> de personnes. Les jeunes écrivains, à leurs débuts, peuvent y trouver
> immédiatement un travail chèrement payé. De grands critiques, des
> romanciers célèbres, sans compter les journalistes proprement dits,
> dont quelques-uns ont joué des rôles importants, gagnent dans les
> journaux des sommes considérables.

Zola goes on to stress that this had not always been the case:

> Ces hauts prix n'ont pas été donnés dès l'origine de la presse; très
> minimes d'abord, ils ont grandi peu à peu, et ils grandissent tou-
> jours. Il y a vingt ans, les hommes de lettres qui touchaient deux
> cents francs par mois dans un journal, devaient s'estimer très
> heureux; aujourd'hui les mêmes hommes de lettres touchent mille

francs et davantage. La littérature tend à devenir une marchandise extraordinairement chère, dès qu'elle est signée d'un nom en vogue. Sans doute, les journaux ne peuvent s'ouvrir à tous les débutants débarqués de province, mais ils nourrissent réellement beaucoup de jeunes gens; et la faute est à ceux-ci, s'ils ne se dégagent pas un jour, pour écrire de beaux livres. (*Oeuvres complètes*, X. 1270)

Certainly Zola was only one of the many writers of the time who made their way to literature with the help of journalism.

Book publishing
Their main income, however, continued to come from books. In 1837 Vigny penned these bitter paragraphs in his journal:

LA TRAITE DES AUTEURS. – Les éditeurs sont des négriers. – Rien de difficile à un auteur qui n'a que sa plume pour vivre, comme de se dérober à eux.

L'éditeur cherche des ouvriers qui rapportent et tâche d'abord de les réduire à la plus profonde misère.

Si un ami donne secours à l'écrivain, ils critiquent l'ami jusqu'à ce qu'il l'abandonne. Alors il travaille, on l'exploite, avec un traité on le lie pour un autre; on l'engage pour sa vie enfin, à tant par mois.

Un de ces exploiteurs est à mettre dans un roman – ou en comédie. (*Oeuvres complètes*, II. 1060–1061)

It would not be difficult to match this diatribe with similar outbursts from contemporaries of Vigny (Balzac,˙for instance) or later writers such as Flaubert; yet it is clear that writers of the seventeenth or even the eighteenth century would have been astounded at the wealth which was available to writers of our period whose books sold in the large quantities which a greatly expanded reading public made possible.

As book publishing gradually became a specialized occupation, the old term *libraire* which could also cover retail bookselling and even printing gradually gave way in our period to the modern, though somewhat ambiguous *éditeur*. However, down to our own day publishing firms have continued to use the term *librairie* as in 'Librairie Hachette' and 'Librairie Armand Colin' .By a decree of 1810 Napoleon had not only severely restricted the number of printers in Paris and the provinces; all *libraires* were henceforth required to possess a warrant (*brevet*) and to swear an oath of allegiance. As the *brevet* could be withdrawn by the government, this was a way of exercising pressure on the profession and was so used until it was abolished with the advent of the Third Republic.

Under the Restoration and even the July Monarchy publishers

were often small men with little capital behind them and they were liable to go bankrupt, particularly in periods of economic crisis. It cannot be said that they grew rich at their authors' expense. Some of the most solid flourished by publishing not new novels, plays or poetry, but new editions of standard authors. However, some names familiar to us today go back to this period – Hachette (1826), Garnier (1833) and Calmann-Lévy (1836); during the Second Empire other famous names emerged such as Larousse (1852) and Armand Colin (1870). Most of the successful firms of the period devoted a good deal of attention to educational publishing in the broad sense; for instance, Louis Hachette was responsible for publishing Littré's *Dictionnaire de la langue française* which appeared between 1863 and 1873, while Pierre Larousse edited and partly compiled his *Grand dictionnaire universel du XIXe siècle*, published between 1865 and 1876, a vast work which was the first of a long series of dictionaries and encyclopedias to be published by this firm.

No doubt there were many acrimonious arguments between writers and publishers in our period; quarrels were frequent and writers would often change publishers. Thus as a result of a row with Michel Lévy Flaubert changed to Georges Charpentier, the son and successor of the founder of the *Bibliothèque Charpentier*. On the other hand relations could be very friendly and writers often owed a great deal to the advice and even assistance which they received from publishers. For instance Georges Charpentier and his partner came to the rescue of Zola after the 1870 war; his original publisher for the *Rougon-Macquart* series had gone bankrupt and he was unable to find another to take on the rest of the mighty work he had planned. What he was looking for, far from hopefully, was a publisher who would provide him with a small, but steady income to keep himself, wife and mother while he got on with writing his novels. He offered Charpentier and his partner two novels a year in return for 500 francs a month, and to his surprise the offer was accepted. Zola never wrote more than one novel a year, but, although his publishers took a long time to get their money back, the success of *L'Assommoir* in 1877 transformed the whole relationship and Zola was offered a new and decidedly more favourable contract.

Writers in our period did not remain entirely isolated in their confrontation with publishers. It is true that long before writers in general formed their association playwrights had acquired a very tough organization – the *Société des Auteurs et Compositeurs drama-*

tiques. Beaumarchais had started to organize playwrights well
before the Revolution,[1] but it was not until 1838 that a group of
writers, among whom Balzac was especially prominent though he
soon quarrelled with the society, set up the *Société des Gens de
Lettres*, which remains extremely active to the present day. The
aim of its founders was to protect the interests of writers particularly in the matter of literary property. Unlike the playwrights'
association which collects on behalf of its members large sums of
money for the performance of their works, originally the only
collecting done by the *Société des Gens de Lettres* concerned fees
arising out of the reproduction in newspapers and periodicals of
works of its members which had already been published, though
nowadays it also handles such things as radio and television fees.

Some writers in our period were not altogether happy about the
way in which members of their profession were becoming more
and more concerned with vulgar questions of money. There was,
for instance, the famous article, 'De la littérature industrielle',
which Sainte-Beuve published in the year after the foundation of
the society. In it he makes fun of a letter which Balzac, the
president of the society, had recently published in *La Presse*. After
lamenting the poverty of many writers Balzac had argued that it
was up to the French government to put an end to Belgian piracy
of French books by subsidizing those authors whose works
suffered from it:

> Pourquoi l'État ne désintéresse-t-il pas les auteurs qui sont sujets à
> contrefaçon et ne fait-il point passer ainsi leurs oeuvres du domaine
> privé dans le domaine public? Aussitôt la Belgique succombe et la
> France a pour elle le marché européen. Après tout, que contrefait la
> Belgique? Les dix ou douze maréchaux de France littéraires, selon
> la belle expression de M. Victor Hugo, ceux qui font oeuvre,
> collection, et qui offrent à l'exploitation une certaine surface
> commerciale. (*Correspondance*, III. 676)

Sainte-Beuve pours ridicule on this proposal:

> Sa lettre sur la propriété littéraire . . . ne tend à rien moins qu'à
> proposer au Gouvernement d'acheter les oeuvres des *dix ou douze
> maréchaux de France*, à commencer par celles de l'auteur lui-même qui
> s'évalue à *deux millions*, si j'ai bien compris. Vouz imaginez-vous le
> Gouvernement désintéressant l'auteur de la *Physiologie du Mariage*,
> afin de la mieux répandre, et débitant les *Contes drolatiques* comme on
> vend du papier timbré? (*Portraits contemporains*, II. 468–469)

[1] See below pp. 267-9.

Similar lamentations about the commercial outlook of many men
of letters are to be found in the Goncourts' journal. In 1874, for
instance, Edmond wrote:

> Les jeunes de la littérature actuelle, et les plus distingués et les plus
> vaillants, savent au mieux les moyens d'action sur tel ou tel éditeur,
> les besoins de copie de tel ou tel journal, le *dada* momentané de tel ou
> tel directeur de revue, enfin les chances de placement de la prose
> dans telle ou telle boutique, dans telle maison, dans tel papier
> imprimé. Ils sont à l'affût de tous les bruits, de toutes les indiscrétions,
> de toutes les confidences qui se murmurent à l'oreille; ils possèdent,
> en vrais courtiers des lettres, tous les secrets financiers de l'industrie
> des lettres. C'est une connaissance de la place de Paris, qui manquait
> absolument à notre génération. Au fond, je crois bien que c'est le
> commencement de la fin de la pure littérature. (X. 177–178)

None the less the same writer was distinctly grieved when his books
failed to sell and bring in any money.

Earnings from books

Financial dealings between writer and publisher gradually settled
down to the sort of relationship with which we are familiar today;
the outright sale of a work for a lump sum, often small, was
gradually replaced by the royalty system under which the author
receives a stated percentage of the published price of each copy of
his work which is sold. None the less the operation of a royalty
system as we know it today came in only slowly in France down to
1914. Nowadays, although an author may obtain an advance
payment from his publisher in anticipation of future royalties,
these are paid only gradually according to the sales of his book,
and, of course, the author receives no further payment until his
advance has been covered by sales. In nineteenth-century France
it was apparently common practice for an author to receive a
fixed sum on publication, but under two rather different systems.

On the one hand a publisher would agree to pay an author a
stated sum in return for the right to publish a stated number of
copies of his work. This was in effect a kind of royalty system in the
sense that in practice for each copy the author received 50 centimes
or 1 franc or 2 francs. In 1833, for instance, George Sand signed
an agreement under which she was to receive 5,000 francs from a
publisher in return for the right to publish 1,600 copies of one of
her novels. In effect she was getting a royalty of some 3 francs a
copy, though it was specified that the whole sum of 5,000 francs
was to be paid within a fortnight of publication. Seen from the

standpoint of today a more striking feature of contracts of this type is that an author did not sell his copyright to the publisher; he merely gave him a licence to print a stated number of copies for a limited period of time. This period could be quite short – eighteen months or twelve or even less. After that the author was quite free to negotiate fresh terms for a second or subsequent editions either with the original publisher (some contracts laid it down that he should be given preference) or with another publisher or publishers. For this particular novel George Sand prescribed a period of nine months from the date of publication.

Alternatively an author could limit the period during which a publisher was allowed to sell his work, but in return for a lump sum would leave him free to print as many copies as he liked and in whatever sort of format he chose. This type of agreement seems to have become commoner in the second half of the century. Though the author retained his copyright, the period for which he licensed the publisher was now a matter of years, and the sum received on publication could be quite large. A famous example is that of *Les Misérables*. Hugo signed a contract, to run for eight years, which secured him the sum of 240,000 francs (on some interpretations 300,000), leaving the publisher entirely free to print as many copies as he liked in that period.

There were inevitably enormous differences between what the authors of famous novels of the time received for their works. By comparison with Hugo, Flaubert seems to have been extremely unfortunate over *Madame Bovary*, though clearly *Les Misérables* had a much wider appeal as it has distinct affinities with the *romans-feuilletons* of Eugène Sue. Hugo even claimed that a Paris newspaper had offered him 500,000 francs for the right to publish his work as a *roman-feuilleton*, but that this was impossible owing to the lack of freedom of the press under the Empire.

Flaubert had to content himself with publishing *Madame Bovary* in a review before it appeared in book form. In 1856 he excitedly announced to a cousin:

> Sache, ô cousin, que hier j'ai vendu un livre (terme ambitieux) moyennant la somme de deux mille francs . . . Je paraîtrai dans la *Revue de Paris*, pendant six numéros de suite à partir de juillet. – Après quoi, je revendrai mon affaire à un éditeur qui le mettra en volume. (*Lettres à son éditeur*, pp. 22–23)

If this was a fair sum to receive for publication in a review, the contract which he signed with Michel Lévy for the publication of the novel in book form seems decidedly odd. The agreement was concluded for five years but the sum offered – 800 francs – seems a derisory amount for a first printing of 6,750 copies. Moreover, two more impressions followed in the year of publication, 1857, and then came two more in 1858 and 1862, together with a cheap edition in one volume. Altogether in this five year period granted him by Flaubert Michel Lévy printed over 32,000 copies of *Madame Bovary* for which, as we have seen, he paid him . . . 800 francs. He gave him an extra 500 francs in August 1857, but this meant that altogether Flaubert received from this masterpiece only 3,300 francs, at any rate down to 1862. What he subsequently earned from the novel is by no means clear because its fate was linked up with that of his later works.

Thus in 1862 when he sold *Salammbô* to Michel Lévy for a period of ten years, *Madame Bovary* was included in the deal. This time the sum he received was vastly different – 10,000 francs; but it is obviously impossible to say how much of this was for *Madame Bovary*. When *L'Éducation sentimentale* appeared in 1869, Flaubert received not only the 10,000 francs stipulated in his contract, but an additional 6,000 francs as the novel was in two volumes. When he quarrelled with Michel Lévy in 1872, he went over to a new publisher, Georges Charpentier, and as his agreement of 1862 expired on 1 January 1873, he was now free to have *Madame Bovary* reprinted by him as well as by Alphonse Lemerre, the publisher one associates with the Parnassian poets. It seems doubtful whether Flaubert got much money out of these later reprints. In 1879, when he was distinctly hard up, we find him writing to Georges Charpentier in typically violent fashion, though one is struck by the timid tone of the closing sentences:

> La *Bovary* m'embête. On me *scie* avec ce livre-là. Car tout ce que j'ai fait depuis n'existe pas. Je vous assure que si je n'étais besoigneux, je m'arrangerais pour qu'on n'en fît plus de tirage. – Mais la nécessité me contraint. Donc, *tirez*, mon bon! Quant à l'argent, pas besoin de me l'envoyer ici. Vous me le donnerez quand je viendrai à Paris. Une observation: vous dites mille francs pour deux mille exemplaires, ce qui remet l'exemplaire à dix sols. Il me semble que vous me donniez douze, ou même treize sols par exemplaire; mais je peux me tromper (*Correspondance*, VIII. 207–208)

It is somewhat of a paradox that the only one of Flaubert's works which achieved popularity during his lifetime should have brought such a small financial reward.

It was scarcely surprising if Flaubert with his dedication to Art and his contempt for the bourgeois did not make money, though paradoxically he was very grieved when his later works had only a modest sale. In her old age George Sand, who during her long career had made a good deal of money with her pen, pointed this out to him very bluntly à propos of his *Éducation sentimentale*:

> J'ai déjà combattu ton hérésie favorite, qui est que l'on écrit pour vingt personnes intelligentes et qu'on se fiche du reste. Ce n'est pas vrai, puisque l'absence de succès t'irrite et t'affecte. D'ailleurs, il n'y a pas eu vingt critiques favorables à ce livre si bien fait et si considérable. Donc, il ne faut pas plus écrire pour vingt personnes que pour trois ou pour cent mille. (*Correspondance 1812–1876*, VI. 378)

A few years earlier she had written to another friend:

> Si vous voulez savoir ma position matérielle, elle est facile à établir. Mes comptes ne sont pas embrouillés. J'ai bien gagné un million avec mon travail; je n'ai pas mis un sou de côté: j'ai tout donné, sauf vingt mille francs, que j'ai placés, il y a deux ans, pour ne pas coûter trop de tisane à mes enfants, si je tombe malade. (ibid., V. 331)

'Un million' sounds impressive, but one has to remember that it was the equivalent of roughly £40,000 *in English money of the time.* Given the amount of inflation which has taken place since George Sand's time, it is impossible to say what her 'million' would be worth at the moment when these lines are being written, let alone when they are read.

According to Zola, by about 1880 this practice of selling a publisher the right to reproduce a book for a fairly long period of years was falling into disuse:

> Il n'y a pas longtemps encore, la librairie était un véritable jeu. Un éditeur achetait pour une certaine somme la propriété d'un manuscrit, pendant dix années; puis, il tâchait de rattraper son argent et de gagner le plus possible, en mettant l'oeuvre à toutes les sauces. Forcément, il y avait presque toujours une dupe; ou l'ouvrage obtenait un grand succès, et l'auteur criait sur les toits qu'il était volé; ou l'ouvrage ne se vendait pas, et l'éditeur se disait ruiné par les élucubrations d'un sot.

The old system was being replaced by a royalty system, i.e. the payment of a fixed sum for each copy sold by the publisher:

> Si quelques éditeurs continuent à suivre l'ancienne mode, le plus grand nombre paye un droit fixe par exemplaire tiré; si ce droit est, par exemple, de cinquante centimes, une édition de mille exemplaires rapportera cinq cents francs à l'auteur; et il touchera autant de fois

cinq cents francs, que l'éditeur tirera d'éditions. (*Oeuvres complètes*, X. 1270–1271)

While the new system related the author's earnings to the sales of his book, it was not quite the same as the royalty system which is practised nowadays. A French writer expected not to be paid at the end of each year for the number of copies sold during that year, but to receive a lump sum as soon as the work was printed or reprinted, without waiting for the copies to be sold. In 1909 when the present system was coming in, we find an author writing indignantly to a publisher complaining about the time he would have to wait before receiving any payment for his book:

> L'article 2 de notre contrat que j'ai été forcé de signer et sur lequel il n'y a pas à revenir, est une clause infiniment dure en ce qu'elle me prive, *même en cas de succès*, de tout salaire pendant six mois et que, même encore, ces six mois écoulés, je ne serai payé que sur les exemplaires *vendus*. Depuis bientôt trente ans que je m'efforce de vivre de ma plume, jamais cela ne m'était arrivé. Au *Mercure de France*, par exemple, un livre tiré à deux mille et mis en vente le 1er novembre, me vaudrait la somme de mille francs payés fort exactement à cette époque sur le chiffre du tirage. (Léon Bloy, *Journal*, III. 117)

Such protests naturally availed nothing.

As in the previous century French writers certainly considered that in Britain writing paid much better. From Balzac to Gide we meet the same song. In 1847 Balzac, struggling with his mountain of debt, looked with envy on the prosperity of a writer like Dickens. He wrote to his future wife:

> Je crois avoir le placement de 3 nouvelles, à 2 ou 3 mille fr. chaque, et je vais essayer d'en brocher une en deux jours. Trois fois cet effort me sauveraient. C'est Laurent-Jan qui m'a donné cette idée, avec *le Cricri du foyer* de Dickens. Ce petit livre est un chef-d'oeuvre sans aucun défaut. On paye cela 40,000 fr. à Dickens. On paye mieux en Angleterre qu'ici. (*Lettres à Madame Hanska*, IV. 90–91)

According to the Goncourts Gautier was similarly impressed with the comparative opulence of English men of letters when he visited London in the 1860s:

> Gautier revient de Londres avec l'idée que, décidément, sa copie ne lui est pas payée trop cher en France! Il a vu la fortune d'un homme de lettres anglais, de Thackeray, qui a un hôtel et un parc à Londres. Il a dîné chez lui et il a été servi par des domestiques à bas de soie. Thackeray lui a dit qu'en faisant des lectures de ses livres, il gagnait, par chaque lecture, trois ou quatre mille francs; mais que Dickens,

qui était meilleur déclamateur que lui, gagnait beaucoup plus. – Est-ce qu'il n'y aurait que les aristocraties pour rétribuer les lettres? (*Journal*, V. 126–127)

This source of income was, of course, unknown to French writers of the time, but quite apart from their readings the amount of money which English writers earned from their publishers was greater than that earned in France. Fifty years later Gide was to record in his journal with some awe his meeting at Cannes with Arnold Bennett,

> installé au Californie, gagne dans les mille francs par jour; on le paie à raison d'un schilling le mot; il écrit sans s'arrêter chaque jour de six heures du matin à neuf heures, puis passe dans le cabinet de toilette, s'ablutionne et ne pense plus au travail jusqu'au lendemain matin. (*Journal, 1889–1939*, p. 378)

No doubt one obtains from such passages an exaggerated view of the affluence of English men of letters of the time; they were certainly not all rolling in money. Yet the level of financial rewards for the successful writer does appear to have been higher than in France.

It is clear that the earnings of writers in the 1820s and 1830s, before the development of periodicals and newspapers, were much lower than in the 1880s and 1890s. Looking back on the situation in his youth round about 1830, Arsène Houssaye wrote in the 1880s:

> Les journaux politiques octroyaient à peine l'hospitalité à la critique de livres et à la critique théâtrale. On n'y publiait ni romans, ni études de moeurs, ni portraits littéraires; aussi tous les jeunes esprits dévorés de l'amour des lettres se résignaient-ils à vivre de rien. Je crois que la misère n'a jamais été plus aiguë que dans ces années si fécondes. Le théâtre donnait de quoi mal vivre, le roman de quoi ne pas mourir de faim. (*Les Confessions*, I. 191)

If Sainte-Beuve got only 400 francs for his first volume of poetry and if Gautier had to publish his at his own expense, writers of successful plays such as Dumas *père* and Hugo obtained quite substantial sums for their publication. *Henri III et sa cour* brought in 6,000 francs in 1829 and *Christine* 12,000 in the following year, while Hugo obtained 15,000 for *Hernani*, but these were very exceptional sums.

In contrast, when Zola scored his first really big success in 1877 with *L'Assommoir*, his publisher tore up his agreement, by which the writer was to receive merely a modest monthly salary, and paid him according to the sales of the novel which meant 18,500 francs. From then onwards Zola could obtain 20–30,000 francs for the publication of his novels in a newspaper before they appeared in book form, and the books sold like hot cakes. In 1880, 55,000 copies of *Nana* were sold by the date of publication. Such success did not necessarily make Zola a happy man as Edmond de Goncourt noted after he had listened to his sorrows:

> Voici un homme qui remplit le monde de son nom, dont les livres se vendent à cent mille, qui a peut-être, de tous les auteurs, fait le plus de bruit de son vivant: eh bien, par cet état maladif, par la tendance hypocondriaque de son esprit, il est plus désolé, il est plus noir que le plus déshérité des fruits secs! (*Journal*, XII. 94)

Zola was apparently not long in thinking of even higher sales. In 1894 Goncourt made the following note about him:

> Il parle de *Lourdes*, se plaignant que la campagne catholique faite contre son livre, qui serait une bonne chose pour un volume tiré à 30,000 est très préjudiciable à un livre tiré à 120,000 parce qu'elle lui enlève les 80,000 acheteurs qui pouvaient faire monter le tirage de son livre à 200,000 exemplaires. (ibid., XX. 137)

Though his own novels were now selling much better than those which he had written down to 1870 in collaboration with his brother, Jules, Edmond de Goncourt was unable to hide his envy of another younger writer with whom he was on intimate terms, Alphonse Daudet. After the success of his novels, *Fromont jeune et Risler aîné* (1874) and *Jack* (1876), he speaks of him as 'bombardé d'articles dans toute la presse, couronné et·renté par l'Académie, *polyglotté* dans toutes les langues, gorgé d'argent par les éditions, les traductions, les reproductions, mis à l'enchère par tous les rez-de-chaussée des journaux'. (ibid. XI. 85) In 1884 Goncourt records a confession made to him by Daudet when he was writing *Tartarin sur les Alpes*:

> Il fait, sans l'avouer à personne, il fait pour une société internationale, une sorte de *Tartarin en Suisse*, une machine qu'on lui paye *deux cent soixante-quinze mille francs*! Entendez-vous mânes de Gautier, Flaubert, Murger, etc., payées par Lévy 400 francs pour un volume et en toute propriété? (ibid., XIII. 166)

Five years later the same source records that Daudet was to receive 100,000 francs for the third volume of the Tartarin trilogy and that his earnings for the year would come to 200,000.

Whether such large earnings (tax-free as France had no income tax) continued, at any rate for a favoured few, into 'la belle époque' is not clear. In 1908 Paul Léautaud recorded the following conversation with Remy de Gourmont in the office of the Mercure:

> Nous avons parlé du changement des conditions de publication et de vente des romans, l'époque des vraies piles aux étalages des libraires, les Zola étagés en cubes, les 120,000 francs que gagnait par an Daudet, la publication des romans en feuilleton d'abord payés souvent 30 ou 40,000 francs. Tout cela a-t-il assez changé. Aujourd'hui, un livre qui va à 25,000, 30,000, est une rareté. Gourmont pense qu'on lit moins, ou que le public est devenu plus intelligent (cela à propos des succès de Daudet, surprenants quand on songe à ses livres, Daudet dont on ne parle plus du tout), et surtout qu'il est tourné vers des choses plus sérieuses, plus scientifiques. Que l'une ou l'autre de ces raisons soit exacte, le fait certain, je le dis à Gourmont, c'est que nous ne voyons plus aujourd'hui de succès de librairie comme les Zola ou les Daudet, pas plus que je ne crois que nous ayons des écrivains ayant aux yeux du public l'importance d'un Zola, ou d'un Daudet. (*Journal littéraire*, II. 78)

However that may be, there is no question that the average earnings of writers had risen very considerably in the course of the last hundred years.

Writing for the theatre

There seems no doubt that in nineteenth-century France the biggest financial rewards came from writing for the theatre. In the provinces theatres were more numerous than ever before, while in Paris since the upheaval of the Revolution they had also proliferated and, especially when from the middle of the century onwards the development of railways and steamships brought large numbers of tourists from the provinces and from much farther afield, they were on the whole extremely prosperous.

The Revolution and Napoleon had applied contradictory policies in this field. A decree of 1791 had laid the theatrical world open to free and unrestricted competition; it was no longer necessary to have government permission to open a theatre, nor was the choice of plays to be performed in any way restricted. The result was that a great many new theatres were opened. This policy was completely reversed by Napoleon. In 1807 he cut down the number of Paris theatres to eight; the four outside the official, subsidized theatres (Comédie Française, Odéon, Opéra and

Opéra-Comique) were restricted to such minor dramatic genres as melodrama and farce.

That was the situation which the Restoration inherited from the Empire. For the next fifty years a new theatre continued to require a government licence (*privilège*) which normally restricted

Poster by Chéret for the Folies-Bergères, 1879.

it to a particular type or types of dramatic performances. A fair number of such *privilèges* were granted over the years until finally in 1864 a decree swept away all these restrictions. Henceforth anyone could build and operate a theatre simply by declaring his intention to the authorities, and the choice of plays to be performed was entirely free except for the necessity of obtaining the author's permission for works which were still copyright.

The Comédie Française and the Odéon

There were thus available a large number of theatres to suit different tastes and different purses. There were the two subsidized theatres, the Comédie Française, installed since 1799 in its present quarters in the Rue de Richelieu, and the Odéon which occupied the site opposite the Luxembourg gardens to which the Comédie Française had moved in 1782. The Comédie Française was regulated by a decree issued by Naploeon from Moscow in 1812 and remained under fairly close government control. Its main task was to keep alive as many as possible of the plays in its rich repertoire going back to Corneille, Molière and Racine; but, with varying degrees of zeal, it also performed the task of encouraging new writers. A considerable number of new plays were given there in our period, from the neo-classical tragedies of the Restoration to the works of writers like Maurice Donnay and Henri Lavedan in 'la belle époque'.

Down to the 1850s it was far from prosperous; indeed without the government subsidy it could scarcely have remained open. Looking back from the 1880s, the dramatic critic, Francisque Sarcey, describes the poor audiences of his youth:

> J'ai vu, de mes yeux vu, du temps que j'étais au collège, entre 1840 et 1848, des représentations d'oeuvres classiques, jouées par un ensemble de comédiens éminents, et tels que nous ne possédons pas leurs pareils à cette heure; nous nous trouvions une cinquantaine au parterre, où les places ne coûtaient pourtant que quarante-quatre sous; les loges vides n'offraient aux yeux que de vastes trous noirs; l'orchestre seul était à peu près garni; c'était là que se rendaient les *habitués*, ces fameux *habitués*, qui avaient presque tous leurs entrées,[1] j'imagine. (*Quarante Ans de Théâtre*, I. 231–232)

The director who took over in 1849 at a time when the theatre still had a great attraction in the person of the famous tragic actress Rachel, explains the difficulty he had in drawing large audiences:

---

[1] i.e. were admitted free.

Paris n'était pas alors la capitale des étrangers; les chemins de fer,
qui n'étaient encore que des tronçons, ne jetaient pas tous les jours
ces milliers de provinciaux, qui aujourd'hui veulent avoir leur part
de la vie parisienne; la bourgeoisie n'aimait que les théâtres à bon
marché; le peuple agité ne songeait plus aux fêtes de l'intelligence.
Il fallait un vrai succès pour qu'une pièce fût jouée trente fois, avec
des recettes moyennes. Mlle Rachel remplissait la salle; mais dès
qu'elle jouait plus de trois fois par semaine, le public manquait.
Arsène Houssaye, *Les Confessions*, III. 37)

There is, of course, some exaggeration here. There were quite a
number of first runs of new plays well beyond 30 performances in
the first half of the century. Yet the greatest successes were not
those of the Romantic *drames* – Dumas's *Henri III et sa cour*, Hugo's
Hernani and Vigny's *Chatterton* – with their 43, 39 and 37 performances; these were far eclipsed by the most successful plays of the
period (most of them comedies) which enjoyed a first run of 80
or 90.

Gustave Doré: *La Comédie Française*.

However, from the Second Empire onwards the Comédie
Française shared in the general prosperity of the Paris theatres.
In 1859 for the first time a successful new play scored a run of over
100 performances, and a fair number of successes of this order

were achieved by writers like Augier and Dumas *fils*. In 1881 Pailleron's comedy, *Le Monde où l'on s'ennuie*, had a first run of 123 performances, followed by another 80 in the next year. Even this could not, of course, compare with some of the successes scored in other Paris theatres by such plays as Sardou's comedy, *Madame Sans-Gêne* (1893), which had over 300 performances at the Vaudeville or Rostand's *Cyrano de Bergerac*, (1897), the most successful play of the century, which ran for a year and a half at the Porte-Saint-Martin.

The Odéon had a decidedly chequered career, especially in the first part of the century. In 1818 its second fire shut it down completely for over a year. It did not always have a subsidy; at times it was operated by the Comédie Française, and at various periods it was simply closed. It had a succession of managers some of whom quickly went bankrupt. However, it did take some part in the Romantic revolution in drama with such plays as Vigny's *La Maréchale d'Ancre* and Dumas's *Christine*, and later it put on successful new plays by writers like Ponsard, Augier and George Sand. It undoubtedly played its part as the 'second Théâtre Français' and in certain periods gave their chance to young playwrights. The famous theatre manager, Antoine, who was in charge there from 1906 to 1912 after the experiment of the Théâtre Libre, did a great deal in this direction.

As it was situated on the Left Bank in the Latin Quarter the Odéon mostly drew much less fashionable audiences than the Comédie Française. Students – from the faculties of law and medicine for most of the period – formed an important part of the audience. In 1843 we find Sainte-Beuve writing of the success of Ponsard's neo-classical tragedy, *Lucrèce*:

> *Lucrèce* jouée samedi dernier a eu un vrai succès; la foule était accourue à cet Odéon désert. Les loges étaient des mieux occupées; le parterre d'étudiants intelligents et tapageurs faisait diversion et ajoutait à l'intérêt du drame. C'était évidemment un parterre instruit, car aux moindres velléités de s'étonner ou de se scandaliser, la masse semblait répondre: *mais c'est ainsi dans l'histoire, mais il faut que cela soit ainsi.* Le bachelier ès lettres était là en majorité, il était chez soi. (*Correspondance générale*, V. 109)

On occasion the Odéon did, of course, attract socially more elevated spectators as we see here; Louis Napoleon sometimes put in an appearance there as well as at the Comédie Française. This could give rise to hostile student demonstrations, as with their applause for Ponsard's satirical comedy, *L'Honneur et l'argent*, which in 1853 had attacked those who were battening on the successful establishment of the new régime. The Goncourts record a conversation with some students who had supported them in the battle over a play of theirs which was performed at the Comédie Française a decade or so later:

> En dînant ce soir avec des étudiants qui nous ont soutenus, l'un nous révélait comment les Écoles font le succès ou la chute d'une pièce. Il nous racontait comment de très bonne foi, ils avaient applaudi à tout rompre *L'Honneur et l'argent* de Ponsard, à cause d'une tirade de 'Vauriens, pieds plats. . . .' que Laferrière avait jeté, à la première, à la loge impériale. (*Journal*, VII. 149–150)

In 1864 when George Sand's adaptation of her novel, *Le Marquis de Villemer*, was put on at the Odéon, the first performance gave the Republican students an opportunity to salute her as the author of a violently anticlerical novel, *Mademoiselle La Quintinie*. At two o'clock the following morning she wrote to her son:

> Je reviens escortée par les étudiants aux cris de 'Vive George Sand! Vive *Mademoiselle La Quintinie*! A bas les cléricaux!' C'est une manifestation enragée en même temps qu'un succès comme on n'en a jamais vu, dit-on, au théâtre.
>
> Depuis dix heures du matin, les étudiants étaient sur la place de l'Odéon, et, tout le temps de la pièce, une masse compacte qui n'avait pu entrer occupait les rues environnantes et la rue Racine jusqu'à ma porte. (*Correspondance 1812–1876*, V. 16)

If the Emperor and other members of his family were present on this occasion, the normal audiences of the Odéon appear to have consisted of students and even of manual workers. In 1889 Edmond de Goncourt noted a conversation with an ex-student on the subject of his adaptation of *Germinie Lacerteux* which had recently been performed there.

> Il a assisté à six ou sept représentations, a étudié le public et me donne quelques renseignements curieux. J'ai pour moi tous les étudiants de l'École de Médecine, et pour moi encore les étudiants de l'École de Droit, qui ne sont pas des assidus au théâtre, les étudiants pas fortunés, pas *chic*. Le monde des petites places est également très impressionné par la pièce, et M. Marillier me disait que les ouvriers avec lesquels il avait causé étaient enthousiasmés de l'oeuvre. (*Journal*, XVI. 7–8)

In other words the Odéon, like some of the other Paris theatres, did draw in a certain number of working-class spectators.

Other Theatres

In addition to these two theatres there were a considerable number
of private ventures, some of them with roots in the *Ancien Régime*.
They did not always have a long life; some were a financial failure,
others vanished to make room for Louis Napoleon's rebuilding of
Paris. Under different management they might change the type
of performance which they offered, especially after the decree of
1864 made this possible. Down to about 1850 the Gymnase,
founded in 1820, specialized in the somewhat light *comédies-
vaudevilles* of Scribe and then turned to rather more serious
comedy and *drames*, performing plays by writers like Dumas *fils*,
Sardou and Labiche, and later those of Daudet among others. By
the end of the century it had become a very distinguished theatre,
regarded by many as the rival of the Comédie Française. The
Vaudeville, founded in 1792, had two moves (one due to a fire) in
the course of the century; despite its name (a *vaudeville* being a
very light form of comedy interspersed with songs) it gradually
came to perform more serious plays such as Dumas *fils*'s *La Dame
aux Camélias* and rivalled theatres like the Comédie Française and
the Gymnase.

Some theatres whose names have a familiar ring because well-
known plays were given their first performance there had only a
short life. Hugo's *Ruy Blas* had a highly successful first run when it
was put on for the opening performances of the Théâtre de la
Renaissance in 1838; Dumas *père* and Hugo had backed the new
theatre, but it had to close down after three years. Six years later
Dumas obtained a *privilège* for another theatre, his Théâtre
Historique, which mainly performed dramatized versions of his
novels though it also put on one of Balzac's plays. However, the
theatre went bankrupt in 1851.

One of the most successful theatres in our period was the
Théâtre des Variétés which mainly specialized in *vaudevilles* including some by Scribe. During the Second Empire it enjoyed a
tremendous success with the operettas of Meilhac and Halévy set
to the music of Offenbach. Towards the end of the century it put
on a considerable number of comedies by well-known playwrights
of the time. The Porte-Saint-Martin was particularly prominent
in the period down to the middle of the century. To begin with it
specialized in spectacular melodrama and *féeries*, but it also put on
some of the plays of Hugo and Dumas *père*. Two of the most
famous actors of the time, Frédérick Lemaître and Marie Dorval,
frequently performed there and drew large crowds.

Théâtre des Variétés in 1830.

The Porte-Saint-Martin was one of the Boulevard theatres. Close by in the Boulevard du Temple were two theatres whose history went back to the 1760s, the Ambigu-Comique and the Gaîté. In the opening decades of the nineteenth century both theatres specialized in melodrama; indeed for a period the Gaîté was managed by Pixerécourt, the leading practitioner of this genre. These melodramas portrayed all sorts of dastardly crimes. As a satirist of the time put it:

L. L. Boilly: *Entrée gratis à l'Ambigu.*

Parricides, infanticides, vols sur les grands chemins, effractions, assassinats, rapts, faux en écriture publique et privée, séquestration de personnes, fabrication de fausse monnaie, tous les délits, tous les crimes ont été exploités par la muse du boulevard. Le Code pénal, voilà son art poétique, c'est aux annales de la Morgue, aux deux premières colonnes de l'ancien *Journal de Paris* qu'elle emprunte ses dénouements, le fer, le feu, le poison, l'échafaud, presque toutes les variantes de la mort ont été jusqu'ici présentées aux amateurs de cauchemars et d'émotions fortes. (*Le Figaro*, 27 June, 1828)

This earned for the boulevard on which these two theatres stood the nickname of 'le Boulevard du Crime'.

In the last decades of our period Paris had its *théâtres d'avant-garde* experimenting with new types of plays and new methods of production and acting. In 1887 Antoine founded his Théâtre Libre, a subscription theatre (this kept out the censor) and proceeded to perform a mixture of naturalist plays and very different types of drama including Ibsen's *Ghosts*. Owing to financial difficulties Antoine had to abandon this enterprise, but in 1897 he started again with the Théâtre Antoine before moving to the Odéon in 1906. In 1890 another *avant-garde* theatre was founded to produce Symbolist plays; this was the Théâtre de l'Oeuvre, known at first as the Théâtre d'Art. Its manager and chief actor down to 1929 was Lugné-Poë, who in 1912 was responsible for the staging of *L'Annonce faite à Marie*, the first of Claudel's plays to be performed. Such experimental theatres as these obviously appealed only to a very limited audience.

Quite a number of the theatres of the time went through bad patches, with financial difficulties caused by lack of public support or quite frequently because of fires (the Comédie Française went up in flames in 1900 and it took most of the year to repair the damage). None the less theatre-going was extremely popular in nineteenth-century Paris before competition had arrived from the cinema, radio and television. It was not confined to members of the middle classes; theatres like the Ambigu-Comique, the Gaîté and the Porte-Saint-Martin attracted a wide range of spectators as many of their seats were extremely cheap. Some amusing glimpses of these more plebeian spectators are to be found in a work published in the 1840s where one learns, for instance, that one of the main amusements of spectators in the gods was to 'lancer sur le parterre ou dans les loges des coquilles de noix, des noyaux de cerise dans la saison, mais surtout des trognons de pomme, car il paraît que ce fruit doit toujours donner de mauvaises pensées aux habitants du paradis'. (*La Grande Ville. Nouveau Tableau de Paris*, I. 345–346). In describing the *grisettes* who frequented such theatres, the writer tells us:

> Quelquefois un ouvrier en casquette, un homme du peuple assis près d'elles, leur adresse la parole et semble avoir envie de faire leur connaissance; mais elles le reçoivent fort mal, et souvent ne lui répondent pas; pour faire la conquête de ces demoiselles, il faut être artiste, ou tout au moins porter un chapeau rond et un pantalon à sous-pieds. (p. 354)

The same work stresses the popular nature of the audiences in such theatres:

> Après tout, il faut bien en convenir, le véritable public des théâtres de mélodrames est le public en manches de chemise et en blouse. Celui-là seul, n'en déplaise aux avant-scènes et aux loges, prend au sérieux les fictions dramatiques: témoin ces deux hommes qui se placèrent un soir en embuscade à la sortie des acteurs, attendant le traître qui, pendant cinq actes, avait excité leur colère, et se promettant de l'assommer au passage. (II. 270)

There were also theatres which drew their audiences from a particular *quartier*, such as the Théâtre Montparnasse which the

Goncourts visited in 1866 out of sheer curiosity as they had heard that a recent play of theirs was being put on there. They found the massacre of their own play sheer torture, but they were fascinated by the audience and its reaction to a thirty-year-old *drame* from the Porte-Saint-Martin:

> Un théâtre d'où sortent des hommes en blouse et des femmes qui remettent leurs sabots sur leurs chaussons à la porte. Dans la salle, un public mi-ouvriers, mi-portiers retirés du cordon. Nous avons d'abord vu jouer *La Chambre ardente*, où quand la Brinvilliers empoisonne, j'entends des femmes dire derrière moi: 'La garce!' Un enfant était fort curieux de savoir si on verrait Henri IV dans la pièce et le demandait à sa mère. Un public sincère, de bonne foi, mais sur lequel la pièce historique exerce une fascination. (*Journal*, VII. 160)

Seen from Paris, the provincial theatres did not seem so very different from the lower grade theatres of the capital. At the beginning of the present century we find an observer writing: 'Remarquons d'ailleurs que la province s'alimente surtout d'oeuvres un peu grosses, vaudevilles ou mélodrames composés à son intention; joués à Paris sur une scène de troisième ordre, ces ouvrages d'exportation partent aussitôt pour les départements.' (J. Bayet, *La Société des Auteurs et Compositeurs Dramatiques*, p. 347). This is undoubtedly an exaggeration as throughout our period the stars of the Paris stage would from time to time go on tour in the provinces, performing there in the same plays as in the theatres of the capital.

Performing rights

As the profession could bring large financial rewards, there was inevitably fierce competition among playwrights and aspiring playwrights, but there was a wider range of theatres than ever before to which plays could be offered. Moreover the position of playwrights had been immensely strengthened since the days when Beaumarchais had taken up the cudgels for them. No longer was the product of a very successful play confined to the receipts from 20 or 30 performances at the Comédie Française after which any company, including the original theatre, was free to perform it without payment once it had been printed. Now, if an author wrote a successful play he could count on a long run – up to 100 performances or even 200 or 300. Copyright in their printed texts had been secured to playwrights by the Convention in 1793, and their rights in the performance of their plays had been guaranteed

two years earlier by the same law as had laid the theatrical world
open to unrestricted competition. The relevant section of the law
passed by the Constituent Assembly ran as follows:

> Les ouvrages des auteurs vivants ne pourront être représentés sur
> aucun théâtre public, dans toute l'étendue de la France, sans le
> consentement formel et par écrit des auteurs, sous peine de con-
> fiscation du produit total des représentations au profit des auteurs.

Needless to say, in the disorder of the Revolutionary period it took
some time to establish the principle, now accepted in all civilized
countries, that a playwright and his heirs are entitled to a share in
the proceeds of his works whenever and wherever they are
performed.

The organization set up by Beaumarchais took on the task of
securing the rights of its authors both in Paris and in the rest of
France. In the 1790s two agencies with correspondents in the
provinces were established to collect the money due to them for
performances of their plays. However, it was not until 1829 that
the present society – the *Société des Auteurs et Compositeurs Dramatiques* – was formally set up; indeed it was only in 1837, in the year
before the founding of the *Société des Gens de Lettres*, that it acquired
legal status as a 'société civile'.

The society formed in 1829 proved an extremely tough trade
union. In the interests of its members it exercised an iron control
over them as well as over the managements of theatres. Once
admitted to membership, a playwright was unable to withdraw
from the society; he was not free to make what arrangements he
liked with a theatre concerning payment for his plays. He had to
adhere to the terms negotiated between the society and that
particular theatre. The society collected for him the proceeds
from performances of his plays in Paris, the provinces, the colonies,
French-speaking countries such as Belgium and Switzerland, and
such other countries as it could make arrangements for. Exactly
the same percentage of the proceeds of the performance went to
the beginner as to the veteran playwright with a long series of
successes behind him. The society even went so far as to extract
money from all the Paris theatres except the Comédie Française
for the performances of plays which were no longer copyright, the
proceeds going either to the direct heirs of the author or to the
society's relief fund. The Comédie Française was in a special
position owing to its obligation to keep alive the masterpieces of
the past, and in any case it paid a generous proportion of its

receipts (15 per cent) to authors of new plays. The other leading Paris theatres paid 12 per cent plus a large number of tickets which the author was free to sell; tickets were exacted even for plays which were no longer copyright.

From time to time there were dissensions inside the society, particularly as it swelled enormously in size after the decree of 1864 abolishing restrictions on the running of theatres. Younger playwrights, for instance, complained that the society's rigorous enforcement of the rule that all plays performed at a given theatre should receive the same proportion of the receipts made it difficult for young writers to get their first plays accepted. Managers naturally tended to take fewer risks and to put on plays by established writers. In practice members of the society seem to have got round the rule surreptitiously, for instance, by giving part of the proceeds back to the theatre to pay for special scenery or costumes. Again the collection of performing fees in the provinces and abroad did not always work perfectly as there were ample opportunities for fraud.

However, thanks to the society playwrights were in an extremely strong position. Theatre managers, as might be expected, were not so pleased but, though from time to time a theatre might revolt against its yoke, the society always won as it simply prevented any of its members' plays being put on by the offender. There is no doubt that the successful playwrights of our period could earn large sums of money. Scribe, who had been mainly responsible for the foundation of the society in 1829, produced a vast number of plays, either alone or in collaboration, and made a considerable fortune, estimated by one contemporary at 3 million francs. Later in the century writers such as Dumas *fils*, Augier, Sardou and Labiche grew rich on the theatre, although others like Henri Becque, the author of *Les Corbeaux*, never shared their good fortune and died poor. With a bigger theatre-going public the first run of a new play could reach large figures, while, once it had been abandoned by one theatre, it could in due course be revived at another and continue to bring in money to the author.

Financial attractions of the theatre

There is no doubt that, as in the past, the quickest way for a writer to make a name for himself was to score a success at the Comédie Française or the Odéon or one of the other leading theatres. What is more, success could also bring in a lot of money. Once again Zola makes this point very clearly when he compares the modest returns from a novel with what could be earned from writing for the theatre. In the case of a novel, sales of 3–4,000, he declares, 'c'est déjà une belle vente', bringing in at the most 2,000 francs, whereas earnings from a successful play are of an altogether different order:

> Une pièce a cent représentations, le chiffre courant aujourd'hui pour les succès; la moyenne des recettes a été de 4,000 francs, ce qui a donc mis dans la caisse du théâtre 400,000 francs, et ce qui rapporte à l'auteur une somme de 40,000 francs, si les droits sont de 10 pour 100. Or, pour gagner la même somme avec un roman, il faudrait, en touchant cinquante centimes par exemplaire, que ce roman fût tiré à quatre-vingt mille exemplaires, tirage tellement exceptionnel, qu'on peut en citer quatre ou cinq exemples au plus, pendant ces cinquante dernières années. Et je ne parle pas des représentations en province, des traités à l'étranger, des reprises de la pièce. (*Oeuvres complètes*, X. 1271)

Hence the attraction which the theatre exercised on writers who had already made a name for themselves as poets or novelists. It has been argued that Romantic writers like Hugo, Musset or Vigny were really poets and that their failure as dramatists, despite all the hubbub created by their ventures on to the stage, proved that they were not born playwrights. However that may be, it is interesting to see how again and again the great novelists of the period ended up by seeking success on the stage.

This could be done in a variety of ways. After receiving money for his novel from, first, a newspaper and then a publisher, a writer could obtain some extra remuneration by allowing a professional to adapt his work for the stage, or he could collaborate with such a writer in producing a stage version. It was also possible to take one's own novel and adapt it oneself; George Sand, for instance, did this with *François le Champi*, which had a run of well over 100 performances at the Odéon in the winter of 1849–1850. Finally a considerable number of novelists wrote directly for the theatre.

From 1840 onwards Balzac had several plays performed in a variety of theatres. He had long dreamed great dreams of wiping out all his debts with successful plays which would bring in large sums of money. In 1835 he had written to Mme Hanska: 'Pour me liquider, cette effroyable production de livres, qui a entraîné des masses d'épreuves, ne suffit pas. Il faut en venir au *théâtre*, dont les revenus sont énormes comparés à ceux que nous font les livres.' (*Lettres à Madame Hanska*, I. 354) Three years later he reverted to the same theme: 'Cependant mon salut est au théâtre. Un succès y donne près de cent mille francs. Deux succès m'acquittent, et, deux succès, c'est une affaire d'intelligence et de travail, voilà tout.' (ibid. I. 615) Unfortunately his hopes were repeatedly dashed. At the end of the first performance of *Vautrin* in 1840 at the Porte-Saint-Martin with Frédérick Lemaître in the leading role, everything seemed set for a most successful run when the play was banned by the government; Louis Philippe is said to have seen a caricature of himself in the wig worn by Lemaître in the fourth act. Three other attempts at three different theatres never produced more than what was politely termed a 'succès d'estime', and Balzac's dreams of wealth came to nothing. Ironically in the year after his death his comedy *Mercadet*, otherwise known as *Le Faiseur*, had a most successful first run when adapted by an experienced playwright, and it has frequently been revived since.

It was also in 1840, this time at the Comédie Française, that George Sand made her first attempt to augment her income by writing for the stage. However, her *drame*, *Cosima*, was a failure, and it was not until 1848 that she returned to the theatre, first with a prologue performed in the heady days after the February Revolution at the Théâtre de la République (as the Comédie Française was temporarily called) and then in the following year with her very successful adaptation of *François le Champi* at the Odéon. Thus encouraged, she produced over the next twenty years roughly that number of plays, sometimes in collaboration, sometimes merely adapting her own novels, but mostly writing directly for the stage. All this activity led to only a very small number of successes.

The Goncourt brothers met with a bitter disappointment when their play *Henriette Maréchal* was put on at the Comédie Française in 1865. The performances were turned into a demonstration against the Impérial régime by a mob of students led by a young gentleman nicknamed *Pipe-en-bois*. The brothers noted bitterly in their journal:

> Ce gouvernement, si fort à ce qu'il croit et à ce qu'il fait dire, est le plus lâche des pouvoirs. Entre nous, qui ne sommes pour lui que deux hommes de lettres, et un ou plusieurs *Pipe-en-bois*, c'est-à-dire une espèce d'émeute qui a une espèce de popularité d'École il n'a pas hésité un instant. Il nous fait à peu près promettre la croix[1] pour le 1er janvier: il ne nous la donnera pas, de peur de paraître faire une

---

[1] Of the Legion of Honour.

protestation contre *Pipe-en-bois*. Il a laissé *Pipe-en-bois* nous prendre à peu près un gain assuré de 50,000 francs. Il est heureux pour nous que *Pipe-en-bois* ne lui demande pas plus. (VII. 154)

The play had only six stormy performances. In 1885 it was revived with some success at the Odéon, and when Édouard produced an adaptation of their novel, *Germinie Lacerteux*, despite the hostility of the critics it had a fair run at the same theatre when it was put on at the end of 1888; but this was scarcely the success of which the two brothers had dreamed.

Flaubert too had to try his hand at writing plays. He devoted a great deal of time and energy to re-working a play, *Le Sexe faible*, left behind by his friend, Louis Bouilhet, but in the end he could not get any of the Paris theatres to put it on. He had great hopes of his political comedy, *Le Candidat*, when it was performed at the Vaudeville in 1874, but it was a failure. Although in one letter to George Sand he made light of this, in the next he confessed his disappointment: 'Mais j'avoue que je regrette les '*milles*' francs que j'aurais pu gagner. Mon petit pot au lait est brisé. Je voulais renouveler le mobilier de Croiset, bernique!' (*Correspondance*, VII. 128)

Zola was also keen on securing a theatrical success. His adaptation of his novel, *Thérèse Raquin*, met with a cool reception when it was first put on in 1873, and an original play, a comedy entitled *Les Héritiers Rabourdin*, fared little better in the following year. A little farce, *Le Bouton de rose*, did not reach the end of its first performance and his *Madeleine Férat*, which had begun as a play and was then made into a novel, had to wait until Antoine put it on at the Théâtre Libre. His only theatrical successes were at second-hand when another writer adapted his novels; *L'Assommoir* had a triumphant success (300 performances) at the Théâtre de l'Ambigu in 1879.

Alphonse Daudet stands rather apart from the other novelists of the time in the sense that, quite early on in his career, in the 1860s, before he had made a name with his novels, he began writing for the stage, partly in collaboration, though for the most part without any real success. In 1872 he expanded one of the stories in his *Lettres de mon moulin*, 'L'Arlésienne', into a play with incidental music by Bizet; this was a failure at the time, though it was well received when it was revived in 1885. In the next twenty years he adapted several of his novels for the stage and also wrote two plays directly for it; but despite all his efforts success in the theatre always eluded him. As with Zola, it was only when his novels were adapted by other writers that they went down well in the theatre.

Censorship and press laws

The failure of a play was, of course, a hazard which novelists who ventured to write for the stage shared with those who concentrated their efforts mainly or wholly on the various forms of drama. Among the other hazards of the theatrical profession, particularly in the decades before the Third Republic was finally installed, was the censorship. It was naturally fairly rigorous during the Restoration period; any references to Napoleon were cut out. We have seen how in 1829 Charles X upheld the censor's ban on Hugo's *Marion de Lorme* because of the unfavourable light in which his ancestor, Louis XIII, appeared in it. This was all done very politely by the old king who, as we have seen, made Hugo through his minister an offer of an additional pension in compensation. Three years later Hugo was filled with rage when, after the first performance of *Le Roi s'amuse*, the government banned his play on the grounds that in numerous passages 'les moeurs sont outragées'. In the preface to his play Hugo invokes the words of the revised *Charte* of 1830: 'La censure ne pourra jamais être rétablie,' and continues: 'Or le texte ne dit pas *la censure des journaux, la censure des livres*, il dit *la censure*, la censure en général, toute censure, celle du théâtre comme celle des écrits.' However, all his protests were in vain and the play did not have its second performance at the Comédie Française until fifty years later. Numerous plays which gave offence on political or moral grounds were banned.

It can well be imagined that under such a repressive regime as the Second Empire the theatre censorship was extremely vigilant and pernickety. When after the fall of the régime some of the censors' reports were published, they showed how rigorous it had been, both in insisting on all sorts of alterations to plays which were eventually performed and in banning certain others completely. In 1864, for instance, a proposal to put on Musset's *drame*, *Lorenzaccio*, at the Odéon came to nothing, presumably because the censors considered the hero's murder of the tyrant duke 'un spectacle dangereux à présenter au public'. Even supporters of the régime like Augier had their difficulties over allegedly immoral characters and situations in their plays.

The theatre censorship was abolished by the Third Republic in 1870, but it was brought back in 1874 under the Mac-Mahon régime and, despite many attacks on it, continued to operate throughout the period. Difficulties have chiefly arisen over political and social questions. Thus an adaptation of Zola's *Germinal* with its portrayal of a clash between striking miners and the forces of order was banned for a time. Plays which had passed the censor could also run into difficulties. In 1891 there was the famous row at the Comédie Française over Sardou's *Thermidor*; this play aroused such furious passions among spectators with opposing views on the French Revolution that after two performances it was banned from the State theatres.

For most of our period writers were far from being free to print what they wanted to say as they wanted to say it; they were hindered by the rigid press laws which, with varying degrees of severity, were in force from the Restoration through the July Monarchy and Second Empire down to the early years of the Third Republic, until the law was revised in 1881. It has been pointed out that the Belgian manufacture of pirated versions of French books was assisted under the Restoration by the severity of the French press laws; as in the seventeenth and eighteenth centuries a fair number of French books which were banned or likely to be banned received their first printing in Belgium. The publication of works which gave offence to the authorities could well land a writer in prison; that was the fate of the pamphleteer, Paul Louis Courier in 1821, and later in the same year Béranger's *chansons* earned him a spell of imprisonment. In 1828 he received a second and longer sentence with a fine of 10,000 francs. If under the July Monarchy no such prominent figures suffered for their writings, that does not mean that the new régime was particularly liberal in such matters; the laws passed in September 1835 were peculiarly restrictive for all branches of the press.

The Second Empire, especially in its earlier years, is notorious for its stringent press laws and its stringent application of them. To existing legislation it added, for instance, laws severely restricting *colportage*; these covered not only the pedlars who hawked books round the countryside, but also *cabinets de lecture* and bookstalls, including those in railway stations. All copies of books sold in a particular department had to bear the stamp of the *préfet*; and a commission which was established to draw up a list of approved works, rejected a great number. The realist writer Champfleury relates how under this régime two of his novels were banned from station bookstalls and how, after he paid a visit to the Ministry of the Interior, the ban was finally lifted when he pointed out that one of them had appeared as a *roman-feuilleton* in the official government newspaper, *Le Moniteur.* 'Pouvez-vous admettre, monsieur,' he asked, 'que le journal officiel imprime des oeuvres contraires à la morale?' (*Souvenirs*, pp. 316–317)

Such clashes did not always end so happily. In 1853, for instance, the Goncourt brothers found themselves in the dock for having quoted in a newspaper article five lines of a sixteenth-century poet; they were acquitted but the court censured them for reproducing 'des images évidemment licencieuses'. Four years later first Flaubert, then Baudelaire appeared in court on charges of 'outrage à la morale publique et religieuse et aux bonnes moeurs'. The court acquitted Flaubert although it made some criticisms of the morality of *Madame Bovary*, but Baudelaire was less fortunate; he was found guilty, fined and ordered to remove six poems from subsequent editions of the *Fleurs du Mal*.

Such prosecutions continued in the opening years of the Third Republic, but they did not concern such famous writers. Even the new press laws of 1881 passed after the triumph of the Republicans did not by any means bring them completely to an end, though writers who were prosecuted were quite often acquitted by the jury. There was, however, the lamentable case of a young writer, part author of a novel of country life, *Autour d'un clocher*, published in Brussels; he was hauled before a court in 1884 and despite his obvious ill-health sentenced to a month's imprisonment. This broke him and he died shortly afterwards.

Social status of the writer

Despite these drawbacks the career of man of letters came in our period to offer at least opportunities of wealth and, perhaps more important, a status in society which raised him far above the writer of the *Ancien Régime* who in varying degrees had depended on patronage and had clearly been seen as socially inferior. The changes of the previous hundred years are clearly summed up by Zola:

L'instruction se répand, des milliers de lecteurs sont créés. Le journal pénètre partout, les campagnes elles-mêmes achètent des livres. En un demi-siècle, le livre, qui était un objet de luxe, devient un objet de consommation courante. Autrefois, il coûtait très cher; aujourd'hui, les bourses les plus humbles peuvent se faire une petite bibliothèque. Ce sont là des faits décisifs: dès que le peuple sait lire, et dès qu'il peut lire à bon marché, le commerce de la librairie décuple ses affaires, l'écrivain trouve largement le moyen de vivre de sa plume. Donc la protection des grands n'est plus nécessaire, le parasitisme disparaît des moeurs, un auteur est un ouvrier comme un autre, qui gagne sa vie par son travail. (*Oeuvres complètes*, X. 1269)

Zola was not the only person to note this change in the status of the writer. At the beginning of the present century an observer remarked:

> Il eût eté ébahi, le grand Racine qu'il était, d'entendre un de nos dramaturges contemporains traiter de haut un ministre d'aujour-d'hui, dont le procédé lui avait déplu et ajouter sérieusement: 'J'ai fait sentir à cet homme toute la distance qu'il y a d'un simple ministre à un auteur dramatique comme moi!' (D'Avenel, *Les Français de mon temps*, p. 308)

The same writer notes, as Zola had done, the decline in the literary influence of the salons compared with their importance under the *Ancien Régime*:

> . . . Les seuls salons dont on se souvient sont justement ceux où se rencontraient les lettrés. Si la majorité de ces derniers n'attache plus autant de prix à fusionner avec les mondains, c'est que les mondains ont perdu de leur prestige et que les lettrés en ont acquis assez pour se suffire à eux-mêmes; ils constituent un clan distinct où ils se plaisent davantage.

Members of the aristocracy, he goes on, tend for the most part still to consider themselves superior to writers:

> Cette opinion, bien que soigneusement voilée, révolte, au vingtième siècle, ceux qui, au dix-huitième, ne s'en fussent point choqués. Ils entendent être conviés pour leur personne, non pour leur réputation et comme objets de parade. Un poète renommé, invité pour la première fois chez une grande dame qui lui faisait demander, en même temps, s'il ne consentirait pas à dire quelques pièces de vers, après dîner, répondit narquoisement: 'Il m'arrive de réciter mes vers chez des intimes; ailleurs, c'est mille francs la strophe et je n'en dis jamais moins de trente'. (ibid., pp. 309–310)

The writer had certainly come a long way since the days of Boileau's 'poète crotté'.

One striking feature of French life from the Restoration down to the present day is the influence exercised by the political views of writers. A number of them – and some of the very greatest – have played a prominent role as politicians, but even if they did not enter directly into politics, their views have continued to have their importance.

During the Restoration Chateaubriand was an outstanding figure in political life, serving three times as ambassador and holding for a period the post of Foreign Minister. When summarily dismissed from this post in 1824, he formed around him a right-wing opposition which contributed to the downfall of the Bourbons. After that he withdrew from political life. Lamartine played an important part as a critic of the July Monarchy, not only as a deputy, but also as a powerful orator at public meetings and as the author of the *Histoire des Girondins*, the revolutionary fervour of which made a deep impression when it appeared in 1847. When the February Revolution followed, he became Foreign Minister and virtual head of the provisional government. From this height he was precipitated by the *Journées de Juin*, and his hopes of becoming the first President of the new republic came to nothing.

Hugo's political career was less impressive in the sense that he never took part in a government, but none the less he gradually came to exercise a considerable influence. His seat in the *Chambre des Pairs* under Louis Philippe was not of any great political importance, nor even his role as a deputy during the Second Republic from 1849 to 1851. But his resistance to Louis Napoleon's *coup d'état*, his long years of exile, his fiery attacks on the Second Empire in *Napoléon le Petit* and *Les Châtiments* made him into a legendary figure for Republicans when he returned to Paris after the collapse of the Second Empire. He was elected to the National Assembly in 1871 and later became a senator; the veneration in which he was held in his last years was apparent from the enormous crowds present at the lying in state at the Arc de Triomphe and the burial in the Panthéon which followed his death in 1885.

It is difficult to imagine that the uproar created in 1898 by the intervention of a mere writer like Zola in the Dreyfus affair could have been paralleled in Britain in the career of a novelist, however successful. Other writers of that period were also sucked into politics by 'l'Affaire'; Anatole France, for instance, who, improbable as it may seem to the present-day readers of his works, was soon to be seen addressing Socialist meetings. Naturally other writers were to be found on the opposite side, and both groups were busily engaged in composing and signing manifestos of the kind which are still produced in France today by their successors.

There is no doubt that in our period the lot of the great mass of French writers was a very much happier one than that of their predecessors before 1789. If starving poets were not entirely unknown, writers enjoyed in increasing measure the benefits to be derived from a more affluent society and from a greatly expanded reading public. To say this is not to imply that in twentieth-century France the writer has no problems; far from it. It can well be argued that, as in Britain, the period before 1914 was the golden age of the professional writer and that in the 1970s the average author is worse off than his predecessor two or three generations ago.

5
Language and Literature

One fact about the French language in our period stands out starkly: its position in Europe suffered an undoubted decline. By 1914 French was less important among the languages of the world, despite the enduring prestige of French culture, than it had been a hundred years earlier.

From the reign of Louis XIV to the Napoleonic era French had played the role of an international language, spoken and written by the cultured classes of most of Europe. Throughout the nineteenth century it still remained the language of diplomacy; the negotiations for the Treaty of Frankfort which sealed the victory of Germany over France in 1870 were conducted in French and the treaty was drawn up in French. Yet in the world at large it was already giving way to English, a language which was spoken by vastly more people, and which served as the vehicle of a great deal of technological progress coming from both sides of the Atlantic, from Britain and the United States. By 1914 these two countries alone had a population roughly three times the size of the French-speaking populations of France, Belgium, Switzerland and Canada together. Although France's overseas possessions had doubled her total population, in practice this had not greatly increased the number of French-speaking people by 1914. Writing at the end of the nineteenth century, Ferdinand Brunot stated emphatically:

> Dans les pays de protectorat et les colonies, qui comprennent de neuf à dix millions de kilomètres carrés et de 30 à 40 millions d'habitants, nous eussions dû trouver quelques compensations aux échecs subis ailleurs. L'incurie des gouvernements en a décidé autrement. Sauf dans les anciennes colonies Saint-Pierre et Miquelon (6,000 habitants), la Guadeloupe (167,000), la Martinique (190,000), la Réunion (168,000), où du reste le français s'est transformé dans la bouche de

279

mulâtres en un patois créole, les fonctionnaires, marins, militaires, sont à peu près seuls avec quelques rares colons à parler français. La masse indigène n'est vraiment entamée nulle part. Même en Algérie pacifiée depuis cinquante ans, le nombre des enfants qui connaissent notre langue est dérisoire. Les statistiques ne sont pas fournies – on n'oserait point – mais nous savons par ailleurs où en est la question. (*La langue française au XIXe siècle*, p. 862)

Clearly the decline of French as an international language was slow and gradual; the position in, say, 1900 was very different from what it had been in the Restoration period. By that date the place of the French language in Europe and in the world at large was not at all what it had been in the 1780s when Rivarol had won the prize offered by the Berlin Academy with his essay, *De l'Universalité de la langue française.*

On the other hand, inside the frontiers of France the language continued its advance against dialects and against the other tongues spoken in the outlying regions – Italian in Corsica, Breton in Brittany, Basque in the extreme south-west and a form of German in Alsace. Improvements in communications, the gradual establishment of conscription and the spread of education meant that if the dialects of French and the other languages spoken within her frontiers were far from being wiped out, they felt the impact of standard French and even many country-dwellers who retained their native speech became more or less bilingual and could understand and possibly speak French if the need arose. The situation in Alsace was, of course, complicated by the pre-dominance of German from 1871 down to its return to France in 1918.

Changes in language

The vocabulary of French was enormously expanded in the course of our period by the changes which took place in so many different spheres of French life. The Revolution and Napoleonic era had brought a tremendous change in the language of politics and institutions. The abolition of so many features of French life as it had developed through the ages killed off a great many terms, but these were replaced by a whole set of new ones – sometimes entirely new words, sometimes new senses given to existing words. The 1798 edition of the *Dictionnaire de l'Académie Française* contains an interesting appendix – 'Supplément contenant les mots nou-veaux en usage depuis la Révolution'. Some of these words, such as *jacobin* and *sans-culotte*, are of purely historical interest, but others persist in common usage down to this day, starting with the words brought in by the adoption of the metric system – *mètre, gramme, litre, are* and their derivatives – as well as *franc* and *centime*. New words like *centralisation* and *bureaucratie* made their appearance, but what is perhaps equally interesting is the way in which old words acquired new meanings. This was the case with *département, canton, arrondissement* and *commune* to designate the new units of local government. The sudden emergence of parliamentary institutions in 1789 added new meanings to old-established words as the appropriate vocabulary was forged in terms like *ajournement, amendement, constitutionnel, décret, législature, majorité, minorité, motion* and *session*. Under the very different régime set up by Napoleon we find old words being given a meaning which goes back to Roman times with *consul, empereur* and *préfet*.

The increased amount of political activity which began with the Restoration naturally gave rise to a further expansion of the vocabulary of politics and social questions. *Parlement* and *parlementaire* acquired a totally different meaning from what they had had before 1789, while the new word *parlementarisme* was created. The different political movements which emerged during the century added fresh words or fresh meaning to existing words – *légitimiste* during the Restoration, *socialisme* and *communisme* during the July Monarchy, *opportunistes* during the Third Republic. A whole host of terms emerged in these hundred years which one takes for granted today – *capitalisme, collectivisme, industrialisme, prolétariat* and so on. The term *sociologie* was introduced into the French language as early as 1830.

The ever more rapid advance of science undoubtedly enriched the language. Though the use of many of its technical terms was confined to specialists, their impact on a much wider public was none the less considerable, partly through schools and newspapers which made them familiar. *Aquarium, benzine, chlore, créosote, dynamite, galvaniser, insecticide* and *phylloxéra*, were all new words which came into current use. New medical terms likewise secured a wide currency – *antisepsie, ausculter, bronchite, chloroforme, cocaïne, diagnostiquer, entérite, laryngite, microbe, névralgie* and *péritonite*.

The development of trade, industry, banking and communications in our period inevitably introduced a whole series of new words and expressions. *Timbre-poste, télégramme* and *téléphone* were all new words as were *bicyclette, pneu, automobile* and *garage*. The Stock Exchange produced new words or new meanings of words

such as *boursier, boursicoter, coulissier* and *obligation,* while the
increasing demand for energy is reflected in *charbonnage, cheval-
vapeur, turbine, dynamo, électrode, électrocuter* and *électrification.* The
list of new words and new meanings in this field could be extended
almost indefinitely.

These changes in vocabulary were no doubt spread all over the
country by the rapid development of the newspaper industry. In
our period it was impossible to blame their diffusion, like that of
slipshod, ungrammatical uses of language, on the as yet non-
existent radio and television; newspapers still had a virtual monopoly of information and entertainment both in the cities and in
the countryside.

Other languages continued to offer new words which were
adopted in French; sometimes these survived only for a short
time, but often they have remained in common use down to our
day. German and Italian furnished a variety of new words, but
the chief source by far in our period was undoubtedly English –
by which must be understood the transatlantic version as well as
the original brand. Our period saw another wave of English
words and expressions, larger than that produced by what was
derisively called *anglomanie* in the eighteenth century and smaller
than that denounced as creating a new language called *franglais*
in our day.

One area in which the process was particularly noticeable in our
period was that of technology; for a good part of it England, as we
have seen, held the lead in industrial progress, and later America
became an important source of technological change. The classic
case of English influence is in the field of railways, where down to
this day a great many of the commonest terms – *rail, locomotive,
tender, wagon, tunnel, terminus* and *viaduc* – were clearly derived
from English. *Tramway, trolley, ticket* and *cargo* come from the
same source along with *macadam, pipe-line,* and the verbs *puddler*
and *prospecter. Film* and *celluloïd* were also imported together with
dumping, lock-out, trust and *chèque.*

Medical and scientific terms – *appendicite, électron* and *watt,* for
instance – were also taken over, while a great number of abstract
terms too were absorbed – for example, *agnostique, bluff, folklore,
respectabilité* and *standing.* Political terms (*leader, meeting, speech*)
were imported as well as words connected with journalism such
as *interview* and *reporter* and with crime (*détective, lyncher*). Outdoor
pursuits were heavily represented; *sport* and *sportsman* came in early
on and were eventually accompanied by *match, handicap, football,*

rugby, tennis, knock-out, record and *camping.* All manner of other English words penetrated into French – *dandy* and *snob, water-closet* and *week-end, cold-cream* and *shampooing, bar* and *cocktail, bridge* and *flirt, music-hall* and *récital, confortable* and *pyjama . . .* and so the list might go on for several pages.

The development of the literary language reflected in many ways this enormous expansion of the vocabulary; it gradually came to absorb not only deliberately archaic words and expressions going as far back into the past as the Middle Ages, but also the varied forms of slang (*argot*) from all sections of society, including the underworld. This was indeed a major revolution when one considers that at the beginning of our period the official purist view, backed by the Academy, was that the French language had now reached a state of perfection, any departure from which could only mean a decline; at all costs the French language must be kept in the state in which it had been inherited from the great writers of the seventeenth and eighteenth centuries.

The *style noble* – a style noble and elevated, purged of all realistic and everyday words and expressions – still held sway in all the higher forms of poetry, including, of course, tragedy. Words and expressions which were realistic, bourgeois, plebeian or technical must be banished from works of this kind. In other words the language of poetry was clearly differentiated from the language of prose. This view was totally rejected by the Romantic poets. It is true that in the 1820s, despite the new content of their poetry, these young writers continued to accept in large measure the traditional language of poetry. Indeed even in their later writings poets like Lamartine and Vigny never moved really far beyond it.

Nevertheless in the 1829 edition of his adaptation of *Othello* Vigny makes fun of the devices used by the neo-classical writers in order to observe the conventions of the *style noble* – the periphrasis which turned *mon père* into the more elegant *l'auteur de mes jours.* In this preface which takes the form of a letter addressed to 'Lord ***' Vigny writes:

> Je ne crois pas qu'un étranger puisse facilement arriver à comprendre à quel degré de faux étaient parvenus quelques *versificateurs pour la scène,* je ne veux pas dire poètes. Pour vous en donner quelques exemples entre cent mille, quand on voulait dire des espions, on disait:
> Ces mortels dont l'État gage la vigilance.
> Vous sentez qu'une extrême politesse . envers la corporation des

espions a pu seule donner naissance à une périphrase aussi élégante,
et que ceux de ces *mortels* qui, d'aventure, se trouvaient alors dans la
salle en étaient assurément reconnaissants.

He then goes on to offer an ironical defence of the writer who had
perpetrated this line:

Je pense qu'il lui était impossible de dire un mot rude et vrai, avec le
style qu'il avait employé; ce mot eût fait l'effet d'un jurement dans
la bouche d'une jeune fille qui chante une romance plaintive. Il ne
l'aurait pu dire qu'en commençant à faire entendre *l'expression simple*
dès le premier vers. Mais lorsqu'on a dit pendant cinq actes: *reine* au
lieu de *Votre Majesté, hymen* pour *mariage, immoler* en place d'*assassiner*,
et mille autres gentillesses pareilles, comment proférer un mot tel
qu'*espion*? (*Oeuvres complètes*, I. 287–289)

However, there is no question that the great revolutionary in
matters of language was Victor Hugo.

In a famous poem, 'Réponse à un acte d'accusation', he was
later to describe in vivid terms how the French language at the
beginning of our period had kept the hierarchy of words established in the seventeenth century:

... l'idiome,
Peuple et noblesse, était l'image du royaume;
La poésie était la monarchie; un mot
Était un duc et pair, ou n'était qu'un grimaud;
Les syllabes pas plus que Paris et que Londre
Ne se mêlaient; ainsi marchaient sans se confondre
Piétons et cavaliers traversant le pont Neuf;
La langue était l'État avant quatre-vingt-neuf;
Les mots, bien ou mal nés, vivaient parqués en castes;
Les uns, nobles, hantant les Phèdres, les Jocastes,
Les Méropes, ayant le décorum pour loi,
Et montant à Versaille aux carrosses du roi;
Les autres, tas de gueux, drôles patibulaires,
Habitant les patois; quelques-uns aux galères
Dans l'argot; dévoués à tous les genres bas,
Déchirés, en haillons, dans les halles; sans bas,
Sans perruque; créés pour la prose et la farce;
Populace du style au fond de l'ombre éparse;
Vilains, rustres, croquants, que Vaugelas leur chef
Dans le bagne Lexique avait marqués d'une F;[1]
N'exprimant que la vie abjecte et familière,
Vils, dégradés, flétris, bourgeois, bons pour Molière.

[1] For 'familier'.

All these distinctions between words Hugo had swept away:

Alors, brigand, je vins; je m'écriai: Pourquoi
Ceux-ci toujours devant, ceux-là toujours derrière?
Et sur l'Académie, aïeule et douairière,
Cachant sous ses jupons les tropes effarés,
Et sur les bataillons d'alexandrins carrés,
Je fis souffler un vent révolutionnaire.
Je mis un bonnet rouge au vieux dictionnaire.
Plus de mot sénateur! plus de mot roturier!
Je fis une tempête au fond de l'encrier,
Et je mêlai, parmi les ombres débordées,
Au peuple noir des mots l'essaim blanc des idées;
Et je dis: Pas de mot où l'idée au vol pur
Ne puisse se poser, toute humide d'azur!

These lines offer an excellent example not only of the way in which Hugo broke up the rigid pattern of the classical alexandrine, but also of his enlargement of the vocabulary of poetry. In his abnormally long career as a poet he uses an increasingly rich vocabulary, ranging from the elevated words of the *style noble* to archaic, exotic, familiar, even vulgar expressions.

It was in the verse dramas of the Romantics that their innovations in language naturally caused the greatest scandal. Although Vigny could scarcely be considered a radical in such matters, his use of the word *mouchoir* in his adaptation of *Othello* created a rumpus when the play was put on in 1829 at the Comédie Française. Othello's words to Desdemona – 'Ce mouchoir qui te fut si cher et que j'aimais . . .' – were said on the stage, Vigny declares in his preface,

à l'épouvante et évanouissement des faibles qui jetèrent ce jour-là des cris longs et douloureux, mais à la satisfaction du public qui, en grande majorité, a coutume de nommer un mouchoir *mouchoir*. Le mot a fait son entrée; ridicule triomphe! Nous faudra-t-il toujours un siècle par mot vrai introduit sur la scène? (*Oeuvres complètes*, I. 291)

Looking back some forty years later on the *Bataille d'Hernani* in which he had played a leading part in 1830, Théophile Gautier attributes part of the hostility which Hugo's play encountered to its innovations in language. 'A cette époque, en France,' he writes, 'dans la poésie et même dans la prose, l'horreur du mot propre était poussée à un degré inimaginable.' He goes on:

Quand on assiste aujourd'hui à une représentation d'*Hernani*, . . . on éprouve une surprise indicible que les générations actuelles, dé-

barrassées de ces niaiseries par nos vaillants efforts, ne comprendront jamais tout à fait. Comment s'imaginer qu'un vers comme celui-ci :
> Est-il minuit ? – Minuit bientôt

ait soulevé des tempêtes et qu'on se soit battu trois jours autour de cet hémistiche ? On le trouvait trivial, familier, inconvenant; un roi demande l'heure comme un bourgeois et on lui répond comme à un rustre : Minuit. C'est bien fait. S'il s'était servi d'une belle périphrase, on aurait été poli; par exemple :

> L'heure
> Atteindra bientôt sa dernière demeure.
> (*Histoire du Romantisme*, pp. 110-111)

This gives some measure of the tenacity with which the notion of a special language for poetry was held in 1830.

The enormously rich and varied vocabulary made available to poets by the breaking down of the barriers between the language of poetry and the language of prose was made use of not only by Hugo, but also by his successors throughout the rest of the nineteenth century. Gautier, Baudelaire, Leconte de Lisle and the so-called Parnassian poets all profited from this new-found freedom to use the language of everyday life, including technical terms, archaisms and rare and exotic words. Indeed the *Symbolistes* and *Décadents* of the 1880s and 1890s (particularly the latter) indulged in a positive orgy of neologisms, archaisms and technical terms.

Paradoxically one finds in poets like Mallarmé and Rimbaud a return to the notion of a separate language for poetry. In the famous words of 'Le Tombeau d'Edgar Poe' Mallarmé sought deliberately to 'donner un sens plus pur aux mots de la tribu', to strip away from words as much as possible of their ordinary everyday meanings. If the obscurity of much of his poetry derives from his highly eccentric grammar and syntax, it is also due in part to the way he gives his own special meanings to words. In his very different way Rimbaud too sought to create a language of his own for his poetry and his poems in prose: 'Avec des rythmes instinctifs,' he wrote in the section 'Alchimie du Verbe' of *Une Saison en enfer*, 'je me flattai d'inventer un verbe poétique accessible, un jour ou l'autre, à tous les sens. Je réservais la traduction.' (*Oeuvres complètes*, p. 106) Although this attitude to language has been adopted by many French poets of the last hundred years, a very different view has continued to be held by others, a view summed up by Anatole France when he wrote in *Le Temps* in 1888, at the high point of Symbolism :

La langue n'appartient pas en propre aux lettrés. Ce n'est pas un bien dont ils puissent user à leur guise. La langue est à tout le monde. L'artiste le plus savant est tenu de lui garder son caractère national et populaire; il doit parler le langage public. S'il veut se tailler un idiome particulier dans l'idiome de ses concitoyens, s'il croit qu'il peut changer à son gré le sens et les rapports des mots, il sera puni de son orgueil et de son impiété: comme les ouvriers de Babel, ce mauvais artisan du parler maternel ne sera entendu de personne, et il ne sortira de ses lèvres qu'un inintelligible murmure. (*Oeuvres complètes*, VI. 524)

The controversy between the upholders of 'la clarté française' and the poets who claim the right to create a language of their own has continued down to the present day.

The prose writers of our period, in particular the novelists, naturally made full use of the extremely rich and varied vocabulary which was now at their disposal. Constant's *Adolphe*, published at the beginning of our period in 1816, employs a vocabulary which, it has been pointed out, was not noticeably larger than that employed by Madame de Lafayette in *La Princesse de Clèves* nearly a century and a half earlier. Only a few years later a novelist like Balzac makes use of an enormously rich vocabulary into which enter all manner of technical terms and, in the speech of his characters, the language appropriate to all the different classes of society from which they are drawn. Various kinds of *argot*, including that of the underworld, appear in his novels, along with neologisms; though these are not always happy inventions, some of them such as *exclusivité* have lived on. A writer like Flaubert, with much greater skill and artistry, avails himself of all the riches of the language. Yet there continued to be limits to what was considered suitable in a novel; in 1877 Zola's portrayal in *L'Assommoir* of 'la déchéance fatale d'une famille ouvrière dans le milieu empesté de nos faubourgs', scandalized many readers by its language when it appeared in a newspaper. 'On s'est fâché contre les mots,' he wrote in the preface. 'Mon crime est d'avoir eu la curiosité littéraire de ramasser et de couler dans un moule très travaillé la langue du peuple.' As in the course of our period the great majority of novels aimed to reproduce the everyday world familiar to the writer, they inevitably reflect the enormous expansion of the vocabulary of French which took place between the downfall of Napoleon and the outbreak of the 1914–1918 war.

Emergence of different publics

The decline in illiteracy and the expansion of the public for
literature which took place in these years naturally meant the
emergence of a variety of different publics to absorb the increasing
number of books which were published and the larger and more
numerous editions of these works which met with some degree of
popularity. Not that this situation was something entirely new.
Before the Revolution there had been a variety of publics, and
how many readers a work attracted depended on its nature. It is
fairly certain that Voltaire's *Candide* was read by many times more
people than his *Poème sur le désastre de Lisbonne*, and that Rousseau's
best-selling novel, *La Nouvelle Héloïse*, was devoured by people who
had never even heard of his *Contrat social*. The growing popularity
of the novel had led to the production of substantial numbers of
mediocre and ephemeral works; they none the less found readers
who were not particularly demanding. Again at the opposite
extreme from the Paris-dominated works of literature appealing
in the first instance to a small upper class audience in the capital
were the crude little volumes of the chapbooks of the *Bibliothèque bleue* which, along with almanachs, works of devotion and
all manner of other writings, offered crude versions of fairy tales,
legends and romances to readers who had obviously not emerged
very far from illiteracy. In Paris the *Théâtres de la Foire* and
later the *Théâtres des Boulevards* put on plays which, while they
never failed to attract a certain number of spectators from higher
up the social scale, were mainly designed to suit the tastes of the
lower orders in the capital.

However, all the changes which took place in nineteenth-
century France did create an even wider range of publics, though
here again it was possible for individual works to embrace, if not
all of them from the sophisticated to the semi-illiterate, at least a
considerable area of the spectrum. At one extreme came the
livres de colportage, the chapbooks sold at fairs and markets and
hawked over the countryside by pedlars. Down to about the
middle of the century these were more popular than ever before
because of the gradual increase in literacy; they also changed in
character. Alongside the traditional works in the *Bibliothèque bleue*
came a flood of third-rate novels, often reprinted for the purpose
or else publishers' remainders. Many of the works sold in this
fashion also contributed to the formation of the 'légende napoléonienne' with their glorification of the Emperor's exploits. In the

closing decades of the century, however, *livres de colportage* gradually declined in importance as their market was taken away by the cheap popular newspapers which provided a variety of reading matter, including *romans-feuilletons*.

Again, there were large numbers of works of a fairly low-brow character appealing mainly to a somewhat unsophisticated audience. These things are naturally always complicated; the tremendously popular *romans-feuilletons* of writers like Eugène Sue and Dumas *père* in the 1840s seem to have appealed to a large public; even though they were published in relatively expensive newspapers, they appear to have been widely read. A satirical work of the period makes this clear when an editor tells a budding author:

> Aujourd'hui, pour réussir, il faut faire un feuilleton de ménage, passez-moi l'expression. Dégusté par le père et par la mère, le feuilleton va de droit aux enfants, qui le prêtent à la domesticité, d'où il descend chez le portier, si celui-ci n'en a pas eu la primeur. Comprenez-vous quelles racines un feuilleton ainsi consommé a dans un intérieur, et quelle situation cela assure sur-le-champ à un journal? Désormais ce journal fait partie intégrante de la famille.
> (L. Reybaud, *Jérôme Paturot à la recherche d'une position sociale*, p. 59)

Though, as we have seen, it was in a newspaper that many reputable novels continued to make their first appearance in print down to the end of our period, *romans-feuilletons*, specially written for serial publication and carefully ending each day at some most exciting point in the story, followed by the words 'La suite au prochain numéro', became more and more the speciality of the cheap popular newspaper appealing to a mass readership. Again, among the increasing flood of books turned out by the speeded up printing presses low-brow novels and stories became increasingly prominent and found a ready market. Similarly in the theatres of Paris and the provinces large numbers of melo-dramatic plays (not always bearing the title of *mélodrame*) as well as ephemeral comedies and farces found audiences ready to applaud them.

Needless to say this mass of popular, ephemeral literature is scarcely touched today except by specialists in search of material on the taste of the masses or insights into the social history of the age. The works which are at all widely read and enjoyed in the twentieth century are only a tiny fraction of the poetry, plays, novels and short stories which were written in the course of the century. Naturally nineteenth-century works which are still in print today in all manner of cheap editions, often with an extremely wide readership, were not necessarily the most popular publications of their day. Even if we leave aside for the moment the special case of those poets whose works could obviously not appeal to any but the most limited audience, it remains a fact that several of the great novelists of the age were not in their own day authors who commanded a wide following. The case of Stendhal is notorious; neither *Le Rouge et le Noir* nor *La Chartreuse de Parme* found much of a following during Henri Beyle's lifetime. Nor did he expect one; he ended *La Chartreuse de Parme* in his somewhat bizarre English with the words 'To the Happy Few' and in a letter to Balzac thanking him for his review of the work he declared: 'Je pensais n'etre pas lu avant 1880.' (*Correspondance*, III. 393) Balzac was certainly better known during his lifetime; for one thing he published an enormous amount, but while his financial difficulties were mainly due to extravagance and foolish speculations, he never secured a really striking success with his books and the famous collected edition of his novels under the title of *La Comédie humaine* did not sell at all well during his lifetime. A writer of the time who had begun his career in the book trade bears eloquent witness to this fact:

> Je vis publier divers romans nouveaux de Balzac pendant mon séjour sur le quai des Augustins; l'accueil qu'ils recevaient du public n'était pas encourageant.
> Balzac se vendait médiocrement, Stendhal pas du tout.
> Les sinistres ballots qui revenaient de province contenaient toujours des quantités de volumes de Balzac . . . En 1838, personne dans le Paris lettré ne prononçait le nom de l'auteur de *la Chartreuse de Parme*. (Champfleury, *Souvenirs et portraits de jeunesse*, p. 78)

Flaubert undoubtedly scored an immediate success with *Madame Bovary*, perhaps partly because of the publicity given to the book by the prosecution brought against him for obscenity; but, much to his grief, none of his later novels had anything like the same sales. *L'Éducation sentimentale* which many people today regard as his finest work did not sell particularly well.

As the example of *Madame Bovary* shows, it was possible for a great work to have an immediate success; it could undoubtedly happen that works which at once won the applause of the critics and those who regarded themselves as connoisseurs of literature made an immediate appeal to a very wide public. Moreover, works which were scorned by the critics, but are today regarded as great literature, could also win immediate favour with a wide spectrum of the reading public.

Poets like Lamartine and Hugo undoubtedly made an immediate appeal to a large audience, and to one which increased as their career went on and they published more and more collections of verse. It is clear that they and other Romantic poets like Vigny and Musset addressed themselves to quite a wide readership since a century and more later their poetry can be understood without any great difficulty by sixth-formers in English schools. If the somewhat difficult poetry of Nerval had to wait a century before it came into its own, a poet like Baudelaire, even though he does not appear to have found many readers during his relatively brief lifetime, certainly wrote poetry which is accessible to a fairly wide audience.

In France as in Britain the novel achieved in the nineteenth century a popularity which had been foreshadowed by its growing vogue in the previous age; it has been calculated that some ten thousand novels were published in France in the course of the nineteenth century. If some of the popular novelists of the age are nowadays mere names to all except specialists, some of those whose works are still read today made an obvious appeal at the time to a very wide readership. George Sand's enormous output of novels spread over a forty-year period was deliberately designed to appeal to a wide audience, more especially in her socialistic period in the 1840s. Hugo the novelist was clearly not writing for a minority group when he composed *Notre-Dame de Paris* and especially a work like *Les Misérables* which had at once an enormous audience both in France and in many other countries. Daudet had similarly a wide appeal, not only in the *Tartarin* series, but in his more realistic novels. Zola gradually overcame the hostility of the critics and reached the mass audience to which his novels were obviously directed, and although his success was exceptional, other novelists towards the end of our period both sought and obtained a following among a wide variety of publics.

The situation in the theatre was rather different because, as we have seen, the large number of theatres in Paris tended to attract different types of public. Theatre-going embraced a wide social spectrum, from the 'best people' through the middle classes down to spectators with more modest purses, including quite a number of manual workers. George Sand had a disappointing experience when in 1851 she tried to attract these more modest spectators to the Théâtre de la Gaîté with her *drame, Molière*. After its brief first run she wrote to one of her *protégés*, a 'poète ouvrier' in Toulon:

> Le public des premières représentations a très bien accueilli ce *Molière*. Mais je dois dire, *entre nous*, que le public des boulevards, ce public à dix sous qui doit être le peuple, et à qui j'ai sacrifié le public bien payant du Théâtre Français, ne m'a pas tenu compte de mon dévouement. Le peuple est encore ingrat ou ignorant. Il aime mieux les meurtres, les empoisonnements, que la littérature de style et du coeur. Enfin, c'est encore le peuple du *boulevard du crime*, et on aura de la peine à l'améliorer comme goût et comme morale. La pièce, délaissée par ce public-là, n'a eu que douze représentations, peu suivies par lui, et soutenues seulement par les lettrés et les bourgeois. (*Correspondance 1812–1876*, III. 254–255)

An extremely high proportion of French people could never have had an opportunity of going near a theatre, let alone going into one; to begin with the population was still predominantly rural, and though there were theatres in the provinces, inevitably these were only to be found in towns of some size. In Paris itself, despite the popularity of theatre-going, only a minority among the adult and near-adult population can ever have seen a play actually performed, even though for a good part of our period theatres continued the *Ancien Régime* custom of offering free performances (*gratis*) to celebrate notable events. Though there was naturally a certain amount of movement from one type of theatre to another, many of the spectators who were accustomed to the modest prices of the cheaper seats in the more popular theatres could not afford the higher prices of the more expensive and select ones or else never had the idea of going to them.

None the less there were considerable differences in the breadth of the appeal which playwrights sought to give to their works. Only the *avant-garde* theatres which emerged towards the end of the century were able and willing to put on plays which were clearly directed at a small public; neither the subsidized nor the commercial theatres would look at plays of that kind at any period, though, of course, they often put their money on works which they thought would be popular and which proved a complete flop. It is obvious on the other hand that a great many of the ephemeral comedies and farces of the period were written to attract a wide range of spectators and quite a number succeeded in doing so. The successful *drames* and social comedies of the period were clearly written for a fairly wide audience as any play must be if it is to be accepted by a commercial or even a subsidized theatre.

Given the French society of the day, it was inevitable that Paris theatre audiences should be predominantly middle-class in composition. In 1892 Edmond de Goncourt noted in his journal:

> Pour être connu en littérature, être universellement connu, on ne sait pas combien il importe d'être homme de théâtre. Car le théâtre, pensez-y bien, c'est toute la littérature de bien des gens, et de gens supérieurs, mais si occupés qu'ils n'ouvrent jamais un volume n'ayant pas trait à leur profession, – l'unique littérature en un mot des savants, des avocats, des médecins. (XVIII. 122)

It was precisely against what he regarded as the predominance of middle-class standards in the theatre that Théophile Gautier protested again and again in his dramatic criticism. Writing some twenty years after the first performance (in 1835) of Vigny's *Chatterton*, he speaks of the hatred for everything bourgeois felt by the young writers and artists who applauded its first performance:

> Le parterre devant lequel déclamait Chatterton était plein de pâles adolescents aux longs cheveux, croyant fermement qu'il n'y avait d'autre occupation acceptable sur ce globe que de faire des vers ou de la peinture, – de l'art comme on disait, – et regardant les *bourgeois* avec un mépris dont celui des *renards* de Heidelberg ou d'Iéna pour les *philistins* approche à peine. Les bourgeois! c'était à peu près tout le monde; les banquiers, les agents de change, les notaires, les négociants, les gens de boutique et autres, quiconque ne faisait pas partie du mystérieux cénacle et gagnait prosaïquement sa vie. (*Histoire du Romantisme*, pp. 153–154)

Gautier attacks again and again the comedies of Scribe for the bourgeois values which contributed to their enormous popularity with audiences of the time. In discussing his *Oscar ou le Mari qui trompe sa femme*, performed at the Comédie Française in 1842, he lets himself go on the subject of this extraordinary success:

> M. Scribe est bourgeois (qu'on nous permette de nous servir ici de ce terme emprunté à l'*argot* des ateliers et qui rend notre pensée mieux que tout autre), c'est-à-dire qu'il n'entend rien à aucun art, n'a le sentiment ni de la forme ni du style, est dénué d'enthousiasme, de passion, et n'admire pas la nature. – Son mobile dramatique est l'argent; sa philosophie consiste à démontrer qu'il vaut mieux épouser un portefeuille de billets de banque qu'une femme qu'on aime, et que les intrigues d'amour offrent beaucoup d'inconvénients tels que chutes, coryzas, sauts périlleux, surprises et duels. La raison suprême, suivant M. Scribe, est un égoïsme douillet que rien ne doit faire sortir de sa chambre matelassée et de ses pantoufles de fourrure. (*Histoire de l'Art dramatique*, II. 234)

One could go on quoting for pages from Gautier's denunciations of Scribe.

He has similar remarks to make about other authors and the way in which they reflect the materialistic, money-grubbing society of the age. For instance, a propos of a *vaudeville* performed at the Palais Royal theatre in 1846, he writes scornfully:

> Les amours de M. Alfred et de mademoiselle Henriette ont perdu le pouvoir d'exciter la sympathie de la génération présente. Pauvre Alfred! pauvre Henriette! l'un si tendre, si délicat, si romanesque, l'autre si naïve, si chaste et si désintéressée! Une page de chiffres contenant le total d'une somme et la capitalisation des intérêts, fait plus rêver les jeunes imaginations de ce siècle que la description de regards d'azur, de joues de rose et de seins de neige. Chacun vérifie le calcul, et, le trouvant juste, s'écrie: 'O grand auteur!'
>
> Si l'on veut aujourd'hui rendre un personnage intéressant, on ne le fait plus fatal, mystérieux, byronien, ravagé par les passions, on lui constitue un ou deux millions de rentes, on décrit son hôtel et son écurie, et aussitôt don Juan, Lovelace, Oswald, Grandison, Des Grieux sont oubliés.
>
> Les plus jeunes filles sont incapables de se prendre d'amourette pour un Roméo sans inscriptions de rentes, fût-il frais comme l'aurore et beau comme le jour. On serait mal reçu à enjamber la balustrade des balcons, si l'on n'avait pas ses poches bourrées d'actions du Nord.[1] (ibid., IV. 239–240).

In penning such lines Gautier gives clear expression to the divorce which grew up in our period between the artist and the philistine, middle-class-dominated society in which he lived.

That divorce goes back to the Romantics of the 1820s and continues right through our period. The exaggerations of the Romantic writers, their eccentricities, their contempt for conventional moral standards were a challenge to the whole outlook of the bourgeois whom they deliberately sought to provoke and scandalize. This tradition was carried to extremes by the younger generation of Romantics in the 1830s, the so-called *Jeunes-France* or *bousingots* among whom Gautier was a leading figure; these young men, some of whom were later to become famous, led a bohemian existence and indulged in all manner of eccentricities to 'épater le bourgeois'.

This same equation of 'bourgeois' and 'philistine' was made by a much greater writer, Flaubert. 'J'appelle bourgeois,' he told his disciple, Maupassant, 'quiconque pense bassement.' His worship

---

[1] Shares in the *Compagnie des Chemins de Fer du Nord*.

of Art made it impossible for him to seek to win the favour of the
multitude though he was in practice extremely grieved at the
failure of his works after *Madame Bovary* to achieve a popular
success. In 1872 he wrote to George Sand:

> J'écris (je parle d'un auteur qui se respecte) non pour le lecteur
> d'aujourd'hui, mais pour tous les lecteurs qui pourraient se présenter,
> tant que la langue vivra. Ma marchandise ne peut donc être con-
> sommée maintenant, car elle n'est pas faite exclusivement pour mes
> contemporains. Mon service reste donc indéfini et, par conséquent,
> impayable. (*Correspondance*, VI. 456)

In his next letter to George Sand he explains his position more
clearly:

> N'allez pas croire que je compte 'sur la postérité pour me venger de
> l'indifférence de mes contemporains'. J'ai voulu dire seulement ceci:
> quand on ne s'adresse pas à la foule, il est juste que la foule ne vous
> paye pas. C'est de l'économie politique. Or je maintiens qu'une
> oeuvre d'art (digne de ce nom et faite avec conscience) est in-
> appréciable, n'a pas de valeur commerciale, ne peut pas se payer.
> Conclusion: si l'artiste n'a pas de rentes, il doit crever de faim! On
> trouve que l'écrivain, parce qu'il ne reçoit plus de pension des
> grands, est bien plus libre, plus noble. Toute sa noblesse sociale
> maintenant consiste à être l'égal d'un épicier. Quel progrès! (VI.
> 458)

For a writer like Flaubert, who despised the society of his day and
in particular the base, utilitarian outlook of the middle class to
which he himself belonged, the only salvation lay in his art, in his
pursuit of the perfect form.

Yet, as the success of *Madame Bovary* proved, Flaubert could
produce work which was capable of being understood and appre-
ciated by a fairly considerable number of his contemporaries. If
he and Baudelaire could never appeal to as wide a circle of readers
as Hugo or Zola, they did not, as many later writers were to do,
turn their back on contemporary society and write only for a tiny
group of readers. Rimbaud, for instance, may have exercised a
tremendous influence on later poets, including Claudel, but the
kind of poetry which he produced could only have an extremely
limited appeal. Mallarmé again was extraordinarily influential;
during his lifetime he was almost idolized by the narrow group
who frequented his salon in the Rue de Rome and Valéry was
only one of the younger poets on whom he left his mark. Yet
though during his lifetime he met with recognition in a small

circle, clearly he never sought to reach anything but a tiny group among the vast reading public of his day.

In varying degrees later writers of prose as well as poetry deliberately chose to offer their works to a similarly limited public. Claudel, for instance, cannot have expected his *Cinq Grandes Odes* to sell like hot cakes when they were published in 1910, while the verse dramas which he produced from 1890 onwards often appeared only in limited editions; it was not until 1912 that one of them was at last staged, and then in an *avant-garde* theatre.

Thus a good deal of French literature in our period has only a very tenuous connection with the society of the day, since it refused to concern itself with contemporary problems and controversies and devoted itself to aesthetic ends in the spirit of 'l'Art pour l'Art'. Yet it is also true that a great many works produced in these hundred years reflect very closely the political and social history of the age. This is obviously true of the *chansons* of Béranger whose enormous popularity contributed both to the downfall of the Bourbons and to the formation of the Napoleonic legend; and it would be impossible to make much of a work like Stendhal's *Le Rouge et le Noir* without some acquaintance both with Napoleon and the Restoration period, as the novel is given the sub-title of 'Chronique du XIXe siècle'.

Political and social involvement

More important is the way in which the whole Romantic movement was embedded in the political and social history of these years. The young writers who emerged in the 1820s were to begin as fervent supporters of the traditional Catholic and monarchist outlook. Hugo, for instance, produced in his *Odes et Ballades* poems with such thoroughly royalist titles as 'La Mort du Duc de Berry', 'La Naissance du Duc de Bordeaux', 'Les Funérailles de Louis XVIII' and 'Le Sacre de Charles X'. In 1853, while in exile in Jersey, he penned a new preface to these youthful poems, contrasting 'ces odes royalistes d'enfant et d'adolescent' with the democratic poems and books of his middle age. In it he declares: 'De toutes les échelles qui vont de l'ombre à la lumière, la plus méritoire et la plus difficile à gravir certes, c'est celle-ci: être né aristocrate et royaliste, et devenir démocrate.' Lamartine who came from a very royalist background and served the Bourbons as a diplomat in Italy, also wrote an ode on the coronation of

Charles X and, like Hugo, was rewarded with the Legion of Honour. Vigny grew up in an ultra-royalist atmosphere and held a commission in the royal bodyguard until he left the army in 1827.

Paradoxically under the Restoration those who sought great changes in literature were the upholders of the traditional attitude to politics and religion, while a great deal of the hostility to the new movement came from the liberal opposition who upheld the values of the eighteenth century and consequently Classicism in literature. There were, of course, exceptions; although hostile to the monarchist-clerical reaction which marked the Restoration, Stendhal in his *Racine et Shakespeare* (1823, 1825) fought for the new form of literature, but in general the conflict between Classicism and Romanticism in the 1820s found the exponents of these literary doctrines on the opposite side of the political fence from the one which one might have expected.

It was indeed not until after the July Revolution that the Romantics saw clearly the connection between the literary revolution which they were seeking to bring about and the long political revolution which had taken place in France between 1789 and 1830. Writing in 1847, a contemporary denounced this new trend:

> Dans les années qui précédèrent la révolution de juillet, la mélancolie et le doute convulsif de Byron étaient à l'ordre du jour. Après 1830, la mélancolie fut remplacée par l'ambition. Les poètes, devenus humanitaires, affichèrent la prétention de gouverner le monde. Ils avaient, disaient-ils, une mission d'en haut et se comparaient avec une fatuité naïve à la colonne lumineuse qui guidait les Israélites à travers le désert. Après avoir prêché leur siècle, ils l'insultèrent et le maudirent sous prétexte qu'il était rebelle à leurs avis et sourd à leur voix. (Louandre, *Statistique littéraire*, p. 680)

Lamartine soon embarked on the political career which was to lead him into the role of severe critic of the July Monarchy and to a prominent part in the events of 1848. Hugo's political position was long to remain ambiguous; he had by now broken with what he calls in the preface to *Les Feuilles d'Automne*, written towards the end of 1831, 'les opinions, les crédulités, et même les erreurs de ma première jeunesse'. Indeed, even before 1830, as the son of one of Napoleon's generals, he had made an outstanding contribution to the legend by his 'Ode à la Colonne de la Place Vendôme'. One thing he was by now sure of was that the poet had a mission, to act as the guide and prophet of humanity.

In the preface to his *drame, Lucrèce Borgia*, published in 1833 he speaks of the playwright's mission:

> A ses yeux, il y a beaucoup de questions sociales dans les questions littéraires, et toute oeuvre est une action . . . Le théâtre est une tribune. Le théâtre est une chaire . . . L'auteur de ce drame sait combien c'est une grande et sérieuse chose que le théâtre. Il sait que le drame, sans sortir des limites impartiales de l'art, a une mission nationale, une mission sociale, une mission humaine . . . Le poète aussi a charge d'âmes. Il ne faut pas que la multitude sorte du théâtre sans emporter avec elle quelque moralité austère et profonde.

Six years later, in a poem entitled 'La Fonction du Poète', he begins by setting forth at some length the view that the poet should stand aside from the conflicts of his age and sing his songs in solitude:

> La nature est la grande lyre,
> Le poète est l'archet divin!

This view is quickly rejected:

> Le poète en des jours impies
> Vient préparer des jours meilleurs.
> Il est l'homme des utopies,
> Les pieds ici, les yeux ailleurs.
> C'est lui qui sur toutes les têtes,
> En tout temps, pareil aux prophètes,
> Dans sa main où tout peut tenir
> Doit, qu'on l'insulte ou qu'on le loue,
> Comme une torche qu'il secoue,
> Faire flamboyer l'avenir!

The poem concludes:

> Peuples! écoutez le poète!
> Écoutez le rêveur sacré!
> Dans votre nuit, sans lui complète,
> Lui seul a le front éclairé.
> Des temps futurs perçant les ombres,
> Lui seul distingue en leurs flancs sombres
> Le germe qui n'est pas éclos.
> Homme, il est doux comme une femme.
> Dieu parle à voix basse à son âme
> Comme aux forêts et comme aux flots. (*Les Rayons et les Ombres*, I)

Even writers like Vigny whose detachment from contemporary events was later emphasized by Sainte-Beuve's much abused reference to 'sa tour d'ivoire', were attracted for a brief period by the political and social doctrines of the followers of Saint-Simon, who made a great splash at the beginning of the reign of Louis Philippe. However, Vigny was soon to speak with scorn of poets like Lamartine who embarked on a political career. In 'La Maison du Berger' he addresses the muse in sorrowful terms:

> Vestale aux feux éteints! les hommes les plus graves
> Ne posent qu'à demi ta couronne à leur front;
> Ils se croient arrêtés, marchant dans tes entraves,
> Et n'être que poète est pour eux un affront.
> Ils jettent leurs pensées aux vents de la tribune,
> Et ces vents, aveuglés comme l'est la Fortune,
> Les rouleront comme elle et les emporteront.

Musset likewise rejected the notion of mixing poetry and politics when he wrote in his 'Sonnet au lecteur':

> La politique, hélas! voilà notre misère.
> Mes meilleurs ennemis me conseillent d'en faire.
> Etre rouge ce soir, blanc demain; ma foi, non.
>
> Je veux, quand on m'a lu, qu'on puisse me relire.
> Si deux noms, par hasard, s'embrouillent sur ma lyre,
> Ce ne sera jamais que Ninette ou Ninon.

The most violent attack on the involvement of poetry in contemporary political and social questions came in 1834 from the pen of the young Théophile Gautier in the preface to his long forgotten novel, *Mademoiselle de Maupin*.

Gautier denounces with youthful ferocity what he calls 'les critiques utilitaires' into whose mouth he puts the views which he detested:

> A quoi sert ce livre? Comment peut-on l'appliquer à la moralisation et au bien-être de la classe la plus nombreuse et la plus pauvre? Quoi? pas un mot des besoins de la société, rien de civilisant et de progressif? Comment, au lieu de faire la grande synthèse de l'humanité et de suivre, à travers les événements de l'histoire, les phases de l'idée régénératrice et providentielle, peut-on faire des poésies et des romans qui ne mènent à rien, et qui ne font pas avancer la génération dans le chemin de l'avenir? Comment peut-on s'occuper de la forme, du style, de la rime en présence de si graves intérêts? (p. 27)

To this attitude Gautier makes the truculent retort:

> Il n'y a de vraiment beau que ce qui ne peut servir à rien; tout ce qui est utile est laid; car c'est l'expression de quelque besoin; et ceux de l'homme sont ignobles et dégoûtants, comme sa pauvre et infirme

nature. – L'endroit le plus utile d'une maison, ce sont les latrines. (pp. 31–32)

Here, put somewhat crudely, is the famous doctrine of 'l'Art pour l'Art' which assigns no other purpose to art beyond the creation of beauty. Some twenty years later Gautier put the idea in the following terms: 'Nous croyons à l'autonomie de l'art; l'art pour nous n'est pas le moyen, mais le but; tout artiste qui se propose autre chose que le beau n'est pas un artiste à nos yeux.' (*L'Artiste*, 14 Dec. 1856) His ideal was put into poetic form in the famous lines of 'L'Art':

> Oui, l'oeuvre sort plus belle
> D'une forme au travail
>   Rebelle,
> Vers, marbre, onyx, émail.

This stress on perfection of form exercised an enormous influence. Baudelaire dedicated *Les Fleurs du Mal* 'Au Poète impeccable, au parfait magicien ès lettres françaises, à mon très cher et très vénéré maître et ami, Théophile Gautier', and Gautier was also regarded as a master by Leconte de Lisle and the Parnassian poets grouped around him.

Despite Gautier's resounding protest a good deal of the literature of the reign of Louis Philippe was concerned with the political and social questions of the age. Balzac is generally praised, particularly by some historians, for his magnificently vivid portrayal of French society under the Restoration and July Monarchy. In his novels and short stories he certainly offers an extremely broad picture of that society, from the aristocratic salons of the capital to scenes from provincial life, which bring in the peasants as well as the inhabitants of the towns. This picture is, however, somewhat distorted by the rather confused political and social theories which he puts into his novels. Two of them, *Le Médecin de campagne* and *Le Curé de village*, are filled with long digressions on such topics and at times read more like tracts than novels. He was converted to Legitimism by the events of 1830. Two years later he wrote: 'Ainsi, le parti royaliste est philosophiquement rationnel dans ses deux dogmes fondamentaux: Dieu et le Roi. Ces deux principes sont les seuls qui puissent maintenir la partie ignorante de la nation dans les bornes de sa vie patiente et résignée.' (*Oeuvres diverses*, III. 179) Yet many of his ideas on the economic, social and political problems of the age were repudiated by the Legitimists. His fear of the masses reached its height in 1848, but long before that he had come to paint many of the plebeian characters in the *Comédie humaine* in a most unfavourable light; it should be added that neither aristocracy nor middle classes are painted very flatteringly either. Remarkable as his insight was into the day to day workings of the society of his age, at times it none the less reflects that society in somewhat bizarre and prejudiced ways.

The 1840s saw the entry of quite radical ideas into the novel. The glaring inequalities of the society of the day are denounced from a more or less socialistic angle in such works as Eugène Sue's *Les Mystères de Paris* and *Le Juif errant*. The conclusion of the latter novel contains such characteristic sentences as these:

> Nous avons dit et nous répétons qu'il y a d'affreuses et innombrables misères, que les masses, de plus en plus éclairées sur leurs droits, mais encore calmes, patientes, résignées, demandent que ceux qui gouvernent s'occupent enfin de l'amélioration de leur déplorable position, chaque jour aggravée par l'anarchie et l'impitoyable concurrence qui règne dans l'industrie.
>
> Oui, nous avons dit et nous répétons que l'homme laborieux et probe *a droit* à un travail qui lui donne un salaire suffisant. (X. 233)

Such sentiments already have the ring of 1848 about them, and in 1850 Sue was to scare the right-wing majority in the Legislative Assembly by securing election as one of the deputies for Paris.

In the 1840s George Sand was strongly influenced by the socialistic doctrines which were then proliferating. As early as 1835 she had written to a correspondent lines which reflect her profound disgust with the July monarchy:

> Certainement si vous raisonnez comme Thiers et Guizot, si la liberté est pour vous compatible avec la monarchie, si la dignité humaine sans l'égalité vous paraît admissible, si vous appelez *abolition des distinctions sociales* le principe qui serre comme un cadenas dans le coeur de l'homme l'amour de la propriété, l'égoïsme, l'oubli complet du pauvre, qui érige en vertu dite *ordre public*, le droit de tuer quiconque demande du pain d'une voix forte et avec l'autorité de la justice naturelle *de la faim*, certes si vous acceptez tout cela, vous raisonnez *bien* et je n'ai pas le plus petit mot à dire. Mais s'il vous reste du saint-simonisme, au moins la religion du principe fondamental, *la loi de partage et de l'égalité*, comment pouvez-vous faire ces concessions, même avec de bonnes intentions, à un état de choses odieux! (*Correspondance*, III. 71–72)

Three novels published between 1840 and 1847 illustrate her

emotional involvement in the cause of the under-privileged and
the moral basis of her appeal for better conditions for them.

Even in *Le péché de M. Antoine*, where George Sand makes her
most coherent criticism of the capitalist system and her one
attempt to approach the problems of workers engaged in large-
scale industry, her message consists in a plea for a personal and
self-sacrificing initiative on the part of individual capitalists. The
factory-owner in the story, a hard master and a stern exponent of
economic liberalism, is addressed by his conscience-stricken son
in these terms:

> O mon père, au lieu de lutter avec les forts contre les faibles, luttons
> avec les faibles contre les forts . . . Renonçons au gain personnel en
> embrassant le travail. Puisque nous ne pouvons à nous seuls créer une
> société où tous seraient solidaires les uns des autres, soyons comme
> ouvriers de l'avenir, dévoués aux faibles et aux incapables d'à présent
> . . . Associons tous nos travailleurs à tous nos bénéfices, que notre
> grande fortune ne soit pas votre propriété et mon héritage, mais la
> richesse de quiconque nous aura aidés suivant ses moyens et ses
> forces à la fonder, que le manoeuvre qui apporte sa pierre soit mis à
> même de connaître autant de jouissances matérielles que vous qui
> apportez votre génie; qu'il puisse, lui aussi, habiter une belle maison,
> respirer un air pur, se nourrir d'aliments sains, se reposer après la
> fatigue, et donner de l'éducation à ses enfants; que notre récompense
> ne soit pas dans le vain luxe dont nous pouvons nous entourer, vous
> et moi, mais dans la joie d'avoir fait des heureux. (Chap. XIII)

The tone, as in her other social novels, is that of one proclaiming a
gospel rather than offering detailed policies or specific remedies.

It is to this period that belongs the conception of Hugo's famous
novel, *Les Misérables*, though it was not completed until much
later and not finally published until 1862. From his exile in
Guernsey Hugo introduced this vast novel with the following
words on the social evils of the age:

> Tant qu'il existera, par le fait des lois et des moeurs, une damnation
> sociale créant artificiellement, en pleine civilisation, des enfers, et
> compliquant d'une fatalité humaine la destinée qui est divine; tant
> que les trois problèmes du siècle, la dégradation de l'homme par le
> prolétariat, la déchéance de la femme par la faim, l'atrophie de
> l'enfant par la nuit, ne seront pas résolus; tant que, dans de certaines
> régions, l'asphyxie sociale sera possible; en d'autres termes, et à un
> point de vue plus étendu encore, tant qu'il y aura sur la terre
> ignorance et misère, des livres de la nature de celui-ci pourront ne
> pas être inutiles.

Though this aim is sometimes rather lost sight of as the reader makes the long journey through the innumerable adventures of the ex-convict, Jean Valjean, and all the persons with whom he comes into contact, the novel is none the less intended by Hugo to carry a clear message deploring the poverty and ignorance to which so many were condemned. His bishop Myriel, of candlestick fame, declares: 'La société est coupable de ne pas donner l'instruction gratis; elle répond de la nuit qu'elle produit. Cette âme est pleine d'ombre, le péché s'y commet. Le coupable n'est pas celui qui fait le péché, mais celui qui fait l'ombre.' (I. 22). That society is responsible for degradation through poverty is also brought out in the case of Fantine, who stands for 'la déchéance de la femme' of which Hugo speaks: 'Qu'est-ce que cette histoire de Fantine? C'est la société achetant une esclave. A qui? A la misère.' (I. 232)

Hugo's ideas about specific reforms were even more nebulous than those of George Sand, who did subscribe to some current doctrines, utopian though many of them were. His novel convicts the age of unbridled materialism: 'Nous vivons dans une société sombre. Réussir, voilà l'enseignement qui tombe goute à goutte de la corruption en surplomb.' (I. 68) And yet, having prescribed 'veiller et espérer' as the twin duties of mankind, he easily falls victim to his own optimism and has visions of the human race rising higher and higher on the supporting wings of progress, so that the submerged classes are automatically lifted out of their miserable state: 'L'effacement de la misère se fera par une simple élévation de niveau.' (II. 210)

Many of these writers played a prominent part in the events which followed on the collapse of the hated régime in February 1848. Lamartine stood for several months at the pinnacle of power, only to be precipitated from it. As soon as she heard the news of the events in Paris, George Sand rushed there from her home at Nohant, took a prominent part in the secret councils of the left-wing leaders and inserted inflammatory passages in the *Bulletin de la République*. Even Vigny stood, unsuccessfully, for election as a deputy to the Constituent Assembly in April 1848. Hugo who had been made a peer by Louis Philippe, failed to secure election as a deputy for Paris on this occasion, but was successful, along with Louis Bonaparte, when by-elections were held at the beginning of June. At this point Hugo publicly supported Bonaparte in his electoral campaign for the presidency, but gradually their paths diverged and in December 1851, after a vain attempt to organize resistance to the *coup d'état*, Hugo went into exile.

From there he was able to lead a violent campaign against the usurper with his pamphlet, *Napoléon le Petit*, and the verse satires of *Les Châtiments* and gradually to become in exile the venerable figurehead of republicanism, internationalism and a vague socialism. More significant in many ways was the reaction of writers who remained in France; the events of 1848 and the following years had brought a vast disillusionment to those who had dreamed of a thorough-going reconstruction of society. George Sand returned to Nohant before the *Journées de Juin* and lay low for a long time, fearing that she might well be arrested in the re-action which followed; she naturally disapproved of the *coup d'état*, but incurred some odium in left-wing circles when she used her contacts with Louis Napoleon and his cousin to secure the release of imprisoned or deported Republicans. Her writings, both novels and plays, now became entirely non-political.

The most improbable people had taken part in the 1848 Revolution and had for a time placed great hopes on it. The role of Baudelaire in the events of 1848 is somewhat mysterious. The only absolutely certain piece of evidence we have to go on is contained in a passage in *Mon coeur mis à nu*: 'Mon ivresse de 1848. De quelle nature était cette ivresse? Goût de la vengeance. Plaisir naturel de la démolition. Ivresse littéraire; souvenir des lectures.' (*Oeuvres complètes*, II. 644) Exactly what Baudelaire meant by these cryptic lines is far from clear, but there is some evidence that he appeared on the revolutionary side of the barri-cades not only in February, but even in June. Yet before long we find him with characteristic instability editing for a very brief period a conservative newspaper at Châteauroux. Thereafter politics, in so far as they played any part in his preoccupations, meant for him hostility to all ideas of democracy.

The case of another poet, Leconte de Lisle, was rather different. In the years before 1848 he had been strongly attracted by the socialist ideas which were in the air. Indeed, from 1845 onwards he had been a regular contributor to *La Démocratie pacifique*, a daily newspaper, and *La Phalange*, a monthly review, which were the organs of the followers of Charles Fourier. Though there is no evidence to show that he shared the more bizarre notions of the founder of the movement, he was undoubtedly among the many writers of his generation who set their hopes on a regeneration of society. After the February Revolution he was despatched to Brittany to help to ensure that the elections to the Constituent Assembly turned out favourably for the republicans. This province was, however, stony ground for advanced ideas and his mission ended in complete failure. He later claimed that he had taken part in the *Journées de Juin* on the side of the insurgents and had even been held under arrest for two days. However, 1848 made him completely disillusioned with politics.

In 1849 he wrote to another poet who had been compelled to seek refuge in Belgium after being sentenced to imprisonment for publishing an account of the events of 1848 in which he had criticized severely the repression which followed the *Journées de Juin*:

> Les grandes oeuvres d'art pèsent dans la balance d'un autre poids que cinq cent millions d'almanachs démocratiques et sociaux. J'aime à croire, – et puisse le rapprochement monstrueux m'être pardonné, – que l'oeuvre d'Homère comptera un peu plus dans la somme des efforts moraux de l'humanité que celle de Blanqui . . .[1] Ne t'enfonce pas dans cette atmosphère où tu ne sauras respirer. Je te le dis sincèrement, la plus grande peine que je pourrais éprouver serait de te voir, toi que j'aime et que j'estime entre tous, comme homme et comme poète, descendre pour toujours dans ces bas fonds de notre malheureuse époque de décadence, pour y consumer en efforts stériles, en déviations déplorables, ta jeunesse et ton intelligence . . .
>
> Donnons notre vie pour les idées politiques et sociales, soit, mais ne leur sacrifions pas notre intelligence, qui est d'un prix bien autre que la vie et la mort, car c'est grâce à elle que nous secouerons sur cette sale terre passionnée la poussière de nos pieds pour monter à jamais dans les magnificences de la vie stellaire. Ainsi soit-il! (Estève, *Leconte de Lisle*, p. 70)

In his subsequent poetry Leconte de Lisle turned his back entirely on contemporary society and sought inspiration in remote civilizations and exotic climates.

Flaubert was by no means indifferent to the political events of his day; the events of 1848 play an important part in his novel, *L'Éducation sentimentale*, but he was utterly opposed from the beginning to the whole idea of using literature for propaganda purposes. As early as 1846 he denounced this fashion in a letter:

> Il est facile, avec un jargon convenu, avec deux ou trois idées qui sont de cours, de se faire passer pour un écrivain socialiste, humanitaire, rénovateur et précurseur de cet avenir évangélique rêvé par les pauvres et par les fous. C'est là la manie actuelle; on rougit de

---

[1] Louis Auguste Blanqui (1805–1881) had a long career as revolutionary agitator from the 1830s to the Commune.

son métier. Faire tout bonnement des vers, écrire un roman, creuser du marbre, ah! fi donc! C'était bon autrefois, quand on n'avait pas la _mission sociale_ du poète. Il faut que chaque oeuvre maintenant ait sa signification morale, son enseignement gradué; il faut donner une portée philosophique à un sonnet, qu'un drame tape sur les doigts aux monarques et qu'une aquarelle adoucisse les moeurs . . . Il est plus beau, ce me semble, d'aller à plusieurs siècles de distance faire battre le coeur des générations et l'emplir de joies pures. (_Correspondance_, I. 322–323)

Flaubert's attitude to politics as revealed in his correspondence was one of cynical detachment. After the February Revolution he wrote characteristically:

Vous me demandez mon avis sur tout ce qui vient de s'accomplir. Eh bien! tout cela est fort drôle. Il y a des mines de déconfits bien réjouissantes à voir. Je me délecte profondément dans la contemplation de toutes les ambitions aplaties. Je ne sais si la forme nouvelle du gouvernement et l'état social qui en résultera sera favorable à l'Art. C'est une question. On ne pourra pas être plus bourgeois ni plus nul. Quant à plus bête, est-ce possible? (_Correspondance_, II. 80)

His reaction to the _coup d'état_ was one of similar detachment:

Je me suis trouvé, comme vous savez, à Paris, lors du coup d'état. J'ai manqué d'être assommé plusieurs fois, sans préjudice des autres où j'ai manqué d'être sabré, fusillé ou canonné, car il y en avait pour tous les goûts et de toutes les manières. Mais aussi j'ai parfaitement vu: c'était le prix de la contremarque.[1] La Providence, qui me sait amateur de pittoresque, a toujours soin de m'envoyer aux premières représentations quand elles en valent la peine. Cette fois-ci je n'ai pas été volé; c'était coquet. (ibid., II. 338)

For Flaubert all that counted was his art, the pursuit of beauty and perfection of form; politics was simply beneath contempt, an absurd conflict of base passions which led France from one disaster to another. The same attitude was shown by the Goncourts. In 1863 Jules denounced in their Journal the sordid motives of self-interest which underlay all political activity:

Cela amène à la longue une désillusion énorme, une lassitude de toute croyance, une patience de tout pouvoir, une tolérance des canailles aimables, – que je vois dans toute la génération de mon âge. dans tous mes compagnons d'art, dans Flaubert comme chez moi. On voit qu'il ne faut mourir pour rien et qu'il faut vivre avec tout, rester honnête homme, parce que cela est dans votre sang, mais ne

---

[1] A ticket allowing a spectator to leave the theatre temporarily during a performance.

croire à rien qu'à l'art, ne respecter que cela et ne confesser que la littérature. Tout le reste est mensonge et attrape-nigaud. (*Journal*, VI. 19)

The two brothers concentrated on documenting their novels of contemporary life and polishing their mannered style, the so-called 'écriture artiste'.

During the Second Empire there were, of course, writers who were quite happy with the régime. One thinks, for instance, of playwrights like Dumas *fils* and Augier, though at times they had their difficulties with the censorship. But for the collapse of 1870 Augier would have been made a senator. Mérimée who had been on friendly terms with the Empress and her mother before she married Louis Napoleon, was welcomed at the imperial court and was made a senator early in the reign. Sainte-Beuve received various favours as a supporter of the régime, though his appointment to a chair at the Collège de France had to be cancelled as noisy hostile demonstrations made it impossible for him to lecture. He too ended up in the Senate; in a famous speech delivered there he had the courage to oppose the attempt by the clerical party to censor the books placed in public libraries.

On the other hand the repressive régime set up by Louis Napoleon aroused increasing hostility among the younger generation of writers who began to emerge during the Second Empire, though in most cases their opposition to the régime found open expression in literary form only after its collapse. One thinks, for instance, of Jules Vallès and his famous autobiographical novel, *Jacques Vingtras*. *L'Enfant*, the first volume, relates his childhood down to 1849 by which date he had come to Paris where he quickly became involved in revolutionary activities during the Second Republic. The second volume, *Le Bachelier*, covers the period down to 1857 and relates the story of how, like many other impecunious provincials, he led a life of desperate poverty as he struggled to make a living by teaching and journalism; the work is dedicated to 'ceux qui, nourris de grec et de latin, sont morts de faim'. The final volume, *L'Insurgé*, offers a vivid picture of the journalism and politics of the later years of the Second Empire and ends with an unforgettable account of the confusion of the Commune in which Vallès played a prominent part. However, all three volumes were written only after 1871, the first two during Vallès's exile in England to which he had managed to escape after the collapse of the Commune, the last (never completed) after the amnesty and his return to Paris in 1880. *L'Enfant* and *Le Bachelier* did not appear

until 1879 and 1881, while *L'Insurgé* was published only after
Vallès's death in 1885.

A famous work which is set in the Second Empire is the twenty-
volumed *Les Rougon-Macquart* of Zola who described this collection
of novels as 'l'histoire naturelle et sociale d'une famille sous le
Second Empire'. Although the series was begun under the Second
Empire and was originally intended to have a setting in contemporary history, very little of it had been written before the
collapse of the régime in 1870. As its publication was spread over
a long period, from 1871 to 1893, which takes one well into the
Third Republic, despite its setting it continually reflects the
economic, social, political and ideological conflicts of the opening
decades of the new régime. This is, of course, also true of his later
novels – the trilogy, *Les Trois Villes* (*Lourdes, Rome, Paris*), published between 1894 and 1898, and the unfinished *Les Quatre
Évangiles* (*Fécondité, Travail, Vérité*), which appeared between 1899
and 1903 (the last volume posthumously).

After the collapse of the Second Empire, Zola could claim that
he had not simply jumped on to the republican bandwagon in
1870, but that he had been 'un républicain de la veille'. However,
his republicanism before 1870 had been fairly mild and it was only
gradually that he came to adopt a more radical attitude to political questions. While the opening volumes of the *Rougon-Macquart*
offer a critical picture of the origins and workings of the authoritarian régime set up by Louis Napoleon, they are not by any
means an out-and-out attack on it as Zola endeavours to preserve
an artistic impartiality.

The first novel of the series to deal with a social problem (and
also the first to be a best-seller) was *L'Assommoir*, published in
1877. Yet Zola could maintain that this was not a political novel,
but 'le roman des moeurs du peuple'; he does not seek to make
anyone responsible for the gradual degradation of his working
class characters. In choosing such characters for this and for
certain of his later novels Zola was not entirely original. Thirteen
years earlier the Goncourt brothers had published *Germinie
Lacerteux* in which they depicted the gradual degradation of a
domestic servant who ends her days in the workhouse. In the
preface to their novel they had defended their choice of subject-
matter in the following terms:

Vivant au dix-neuvième siècle, dans un temps de suffrage universel,
de démocratie, de libéralisme, nous nous sommes demandé si ce
qu'on appelle les 'basses classes' n'avait pas droit au roman; si ce

monde sous un monde, le peuple, devait rester sous le coup de l'interdit littéraire et des dédains d'auteurs qui ont fait jusqu'ici le silence sur l'âme et le coeur qu'il peut avoir, nous nous sommes demandé s'il y avait encore pour l'écrivain et pour le lecteur, en ces années d'égalité où nous sommes, des classes indignes, des malheurs trop bas, des drames trop mal embouchés, des catastrophes d'une terreur trop peu noble.

Their attempt to portray the life of the 'basses classes' was not well received by the critics; one spoke of the novel as 'un attentat littéraire' and another as 'une prodigieuse erreur de goût'.

L'Assommoir caused an even greater scandal than *Germinie Lacerteux*. In writing such a novel, Zola explains elsewhere, he held that characters drawn from the lower classes of town and country offered a clearer picture of human nature than those taken from the middle classes or the aristocracy:

Nos ouvriers et nos paysans seuls ont la carrure simple et forte des héros d'Homère. Dès qu'on s'adresse aux classes élevées, bourgeoisie et noblesse, on n'a plus que la créature humaine modifiée et déviée par la civilisation. On doit dès lors observer des nuances infinies, tenir compte des conventions sociales, avoir un langage fabriqué, tout falsifier et tout adoucir. Avec les classes d'en bas, au contraire, on touche à la terre, on trouve l'être humain tel qu'il est sorti du sol, on se rapproche du berceau du monde.

   . . . On ne sait point encore quel cadre vaste et puissant peuvent être les moeurs de nos faubourgs; les drames y ont une force et une largeur incomparables; toutes les émotions humaines y sont, les douces et les violentes, mais prises à leurs sources, toutes neuves. Il y a là des éléments qu'on ne soupçonne pas et qui réunissent ces deux qualités demandées pour les chefs-d'oeuvre, la puissance et la simplicité. C'est une mine dans laquelle les romanciers de demain puiseront à coup sûr. (*Oeuvres complètes*, XI. 777–778)

Zola's portrayal of working-class life in Paris and of the ravages of alcohol is completely objective in its sordid brutality, so much so that various left-wing critics accused him of despising the common people and thus of being hostile to democracy and universal suffrage. Zola replied to his critics in the preface of the novel which had first appeared in serial form:

J'ai voulu peindre la déchéance fatale d'une famille ouvrière, dans le milieu empesté de nos faubourgs. Au bout de l'ivrognerie et de la fainéantise, il y a le relâchement des liens de la famille, les ordures de la promiscuité, l'oubli progressif des sentiments honnêtes, puis comme dénoûment, la honte et la mort. C'est de la morale en action, simplement.

. . . Mon oeuvre me défendra. C'est une oeuvre de vérité, le premier roman sur le peuple, qui ne mente pas et qui ait l'odeur du peuple. Et il ne faut point conclure que le peuple tout entier est mauvais, car mes personnages ne sont pas mauvais. Ils ne sont qu'ignorants et gâtés par le milieu de rude besogne et de misère où ils vivent.

It was indeed only in the *Rougon-Macquart* novels published after 1880 that Zola began to offer some sort of a solution to the variety of contemporary problems with which they deal.

Perhaps the most famous of these later novels is *Germinal*, published in 1885, with its vivid description of life in a mining village in north-eastern France in a time of bitter social conflict. Although the action of the novel is supposed to take place during the Second Empire, Zola's picture of a miners' strike was to some extent coloured by more recent events of this kind in the Pas-de-Calais coalfield which he had visited during a two-month conflict, just before he began to write the novel. Although a deputation of miners from the Pas-de-Calais shouting 'Germinal! Germinal!' formed part of the procession at Zola's funeral in 1902, the novel is by no means a socialist tract. It is true that when socialist newspapers including Vallès's *Cri du Peuple* asked permission to reproduce it as a *roman-feuilleton*, he replied: 'Prenez *Germinal* et reproduisez-le. Je ne vous demande rien, puisque votre journal est pauvre et que vous défendez les misérables'; but despite the terrible picture which he paints of the grinding poverty, atrocious housing conditions and sordid lives of the miners and their families, in depicting what in his notes for the novel he described as 'la lutte du capital et du travail' Zola carefully avoids blaming this blatant example of social injustice on the characters who represent capitalism. They are not as individuals responsible for the suffer-ings of the miners and their families; it is the social system which tramples them underfoot. Moreover, the novel reflects what in a letter to a friend Zola called 'mon tempérament lyrique, mon agrandissement de la vérité'. 'Vous n'êtes pas stupéfait, comme les autres,' he went on, 'de trouver en moi un poète.' The novel is more than a mere social document; it is a work of literature.

GERMINAL
PAR ÉMILE ZOLA

An illustration for Zola's *Germinal*, published in the *Cri du Peuple*, 15th July, 1885.

La Terre, published two years after *Germinal*, takes the reader to the land and to the peasants of the Beauce. 'La Terre,' wrote Zola in his notes for the novel, 'c'est l'héroïne de mon livre, la terre nourricière, la terre qui donne la vie et qui la reprend impassible. Un personnage énorme, toujours présent, emplissant le livre.' But he also wrote in these same notes:

> *La Terre* est l'histoire du paysan français, son amour du sol, sa longue lutte pour le posséder, ses travaux écrasants, ses courtes joies et ses grandes misères, le paysan s'y trouve étudié dans ses rapports avec la religion et la politique, et sa condition présente y est expliquée par son histoire passée; même l'avenir y est indiqué, le rôle possible du paysan dans une révolution socialiste . . . En somme, j'ai voulu faire pour le paysan, dans *La Terre*, ce que j'ai fait dans *L'Assommoir*, pour le peuple des faubourgs de Paris: écrire son histoire, ses moeurs, ses passions, ses souffrances, sous la fatalité du milieu et des circonstances historiques.

At the time this attempt of Zola to depict the lot of the peasants (mostly small and impoverished) was severely criticized. Anatole France declared in a review of Zola's novel: 'Certes, je ne lui nierai point sa détestable gloire. Personne avant lui n'avait élevé un si haut tas d'immondices. C'est là son monument, dont on ne peut contester la grandeur.' (*Oeuvres complètes*, VI. 213) Yet although Zola's picture of the brutal passions and sordid lives of his peasants was bitterly attacked at the time, recent research has shown that it was true in all its essentials.

Once he had completed the enormous task of producing the twenty novels of *Les Rougon-Macquart*, Zola turned his attention to his trilogy, *Les Trois Villes*, the three volumes of which – *Lourdes*, *Rome* and *Paris* – appeared between 1894 and 1898. These novels reflect very clearly the controversies of the 1890s – the clash between religion and science, the attempt by Pope Leo XIII to effect a reconciliation with the French Republic through the *Ralliement*, and the emergence of socialism as a political force in France. Before the last of them appeared Zola had found himself involved in the Dreyfus affair. During his exile in England he began to write the first novel in the next series, *Les Quatre Évangiles*, which his sudden death prevented him from completing. The first novel in the series, *Fécondité*, deals with the pressing problem of France's declining birthrate and advocates the obvious remedy; his hero marries at twenty a girl of seventeen; they retire to the provinces and produce twelve children . . . *Travail*, which depicts a town which has grown up around a steel-works and all its social tensions, preaches socialism, but a very odd socialism, one derived from the writings of Fourier whose wildly utopian ideas were almost a hundred years old when Zola's novel appeared in 1901. The last novel which he lived to complete, *Vérité*, a transposition of the events of the Dreyfus Affair, contains a fierce attack on Catholic obscurantism which, he argues, will be overcome by an improved system of primary education. The novel ends with an enthusiastic eulogy of 'l'école laïque' and looks forward to a happy future in which Catholicism will have been vanquished:

> La France n'était plus menacée d'être ensevelie sous la cendre d'une religion morte, elle était redevenue maîtresse d'elle-même, elle pouvait marcher à ses destinées de libératrice et de justicière. Et elle n'avait vaincu que par cet enseignement primaire, tirant les humbles, les petits des campagnes, de leur ignorance d'esclaves, de l'imbécillité meurtrière où le catholicisme les maintenait depuis des siècles. (*Oeuvres complètes*, VIII. 1489)

So deeply are Zola's novels embedded in the events and controversies of the second half of the nineteenth century that it is difficult to see how today a reader can make much of them without some knowledge of French history of this period.

A figure very different from Zola was his contemporary, Anatole France, and yet they ended up on the same side of the barricades. 'L'Affaire Dreyfus,' said France, 'm'a conduit au socialisme.' The critic who had earlier denounced Zola's novels in scathing terms appeared, along with Jaurès, as one of the witnesses for the defence at Zola's trial, and it was he who pronounced the oration at his funeral which ended: 'Envions-le, sa destinée et son coeur lui firent le sort le plus grand: Il fut un moment de la conscience humaine.' Although he had early broken with the Catholicism of his teachers and had even dabbled for a time in opposition to the Second Empire, France was horrified by the Commune which he had seen at first hand. As late as 1896 in his *discours de réception* at the Academy (he was soon to be cold-shouldered there because of his support for Dreyfus) he had drawn comparisons between the Second Empire and the Third Republic unfavourable to the latter.

The four volumes of his *Histoire contemporaine*, which were first published in newspapers between 1895 and 1900, are extremely interesting from this point of view. The opening novels – *L'Orme du Mail* and *Le Mannequin d'osier* – which appeared in print by the summer of 1897 before France found himself involved in the Dreyfus Affair, are fiercely anticlerical in the author's best ironical manner. France entirely rejects the sincerity of the Catholic Church's acceptance of the Republic in the so-called *Ralliement*: clergymen who profess republican sentiments to obtain promotion to a bishopric from the Republican government are shown to proclaim their monarchist views once safely installed in their new diocese. But the Republic itself is the butt of France's irony. In *L'Orme du mail* into the mouth of the hero of the four novels, M. Bergeret, he puts the following contemptuous observations on the republic of the *opportunistes*:

> Nos ministres se moquent de nous en parlant de péril clérical ou de péril socialiste. Il n'y a qu'un péril, le péril financier. La République commence à s'en apercevoir. Je la plains, je la regretterai. J'ai été nourri sous l'Empire, dans l'amour de la République. 'Elle est la justice,' me disait mon père, professeur de rhétorique au lycée de Saint-Omer. Il ne la connaissait pas. Elle n'est pas la justice. Mais elle est la facilité. Monsieur l'abbé, si vous aviez l'âme moins haute, moins grave et plus accessible aux riantes pensées, je vous confierais que la République actuelle, la République de 1897, me plaît et me touche par sa modestie. Elle consent à n'être point admirée. Elle n'exige que peu de respect et renonce même à l'estime. Il lui suffit de vivre. C'est là tout son désir: il est légitime. Les êtres les plus humbles tiennent à la vie. (*Oeuvres complètes*, XI. 154–155)

'Mais elle est la facilité' covers not only scandals such as the Panama affair, but, behind the façade of republican institutions, the reign of high finance and big business in the midst of the general political apathy. Socialism as a possible remedy for this depressing state of affairs only makes its appearance incidentally towards the end of *Le Mannequin d'osier* when M. Bergeret tells a free-thinker that he can see no difference between his outlook and that of Catholics in the affairs of everyday life:

> N'avez-vous point la même morale relativement à l'organisation du travail, à la propriété privée, au capital, à toute l'économie de la société actuelle, dont vous supportez les uns et les autres avec une égale patience les injustices, quand vous n'en souffrez point? Il faudrait que vous fussiez socialiste pour qu'il en allât autrement. (*Oeuvres complètes*, XI. 436)

However, these few lines are very far from summing up any sort of message; the first two novels of the series are essentially negative in their all-embracing irony.

Gradually in the course of 1898 as he continued the third novel in the series, *L'Anneau d'améthyste*, and more openly still in *M. Bergeret à Paris* which was written in 1899 and 1900, France's intervention in the Dreyfus affair led him to pen the severest satire of the nationalists and their clerical allies. M. Panneton de La Barge, a fanatical defender of the army in the Dreyfus Affair, receives a devastating reply from M. Bergeret when he angrily declares:

> – Cette campagne en faveur du traître, cette campagne si obstinée et si ardente, quelles que soient les intentions de ceux qui la mènent, l'effet en est certain, visible, indéniable. L'armée en est affaiblie, ses chefs en sont atteints.
> – Je vais maintenant vous dire des choses extrêmement simples, répondit M. Bergeret. Si l'armée est atteinte dans la personne de quelques-uns de ses chefs, ce n'est point la faute de ceux qui ont demandé la justice; c'est la faute de ceux qui l'ont si longtemps refusée; ce n'est pas la faute de ceux qui ont exigé la lumière, c'est la faute de ceux qui l'ont dérobée obstinément avec une imbécillité démesurée et une scélératesse atroce. (*Oeuvres complètes*, XII. 327)

But the novel has its positive side too – the proclamation of faith in a socialist solution to the problems facing France. M. Bergeret explains to his daughter the virtues of collectivism and seeks to show her how it already exists in some degree:

> Après les travaux séculaires de l'égoïsme et de l'avarice, en dépit des efforts violents des individus pour saisir et garder des trésors, les biens individuels dont jouissent les plus riches d'entre nous sont encore peu de chose en comparaison de ceux qui appartiennent indistinctement à tous les hommes. Et dans notre société même ne vois-tu pas que les biens les plus doux ou les plus splendides, routes, fleuves, forêts autrefois royales, bibliothèques, musées, appartiennent à tous? Aucun riche ne possède plus que moi ce vieux chêne de Fontainebleau ou ce tableau du Louvre. Et ils sont plus à moi qu'au riche si je sais mieux en jouir. La propriété collective, qu'on redoute comme un monstre lointain, nous entoure déjà sous mille formes familières. Elle effraye quand on l'annonce et l'on use déjà des avantages qu'elle procure. (*Oeuvres complètes*, XII. 448)

France's socialism is, however, decidedly gradualist; as M. Bergeret explains, 'tous les changements dans l'ordre social comme dans l'ordre naturel sont lents et presque insensibles'. (p. 451)

Partly under the influence of Jaurès, France became much sought after as an orator in Socialist meetings; he played a prominent part in the founding of *L'Humanité* and was a frequent contributor to it. Yet, so far as his literary works were concerned, he kept his independence. *L'Ile des Pinguoins*, published in 1908, is another satire, partly inspired by the reactionary policies pursued by Clemenceau when he at last attained power and by the dissensions within the Socialist party; its bitter irony scarcely reveals much optimism about the future. *Les Dieux ont soif* which followed four years later treats the Revolution and in particular the period of the Terror in a manner which could not satisfy a Socialist like Jaurès.

If writers like Zola and Anatole France reflect in their works the ideas of the Left in the heyday of the Third Republic – their hostility both to the Catholic Church and to the conservative forces which wielded immense power in the economic and social life of the country – the other side was by no means under-represented in the literature of these decades. Royalism continued to be powerfully entrenched among influential people; nationalism, which gradually became a right-wing phenomenon as internationalist ideas became stronger on the Left, found wide support among both Royalists and the more conservative Republicans; Catholicism, often linked with right-wing movements, experienced a considerable revival in intellectual and literary circles. This revival was inevitably closely linked with politics since the Catholic Church was almost continuously under attack from the Republicans from the moment they at last assumed power in 1879 right down to 1914.

From the 1880s there emerged a succession of outstanding Catholic writers such as Huysmans, Bourget, Claudel and Péguy who reacted with all the fervour of the newly converted against the dominant scientific philosophy of writers like Taine and Renan and against what they regarded as the materialistic values of contemporary society. Their revolt was often expressed in the most violent terms, as for instance in the astonishing outburst in the middle of 'Magnificat', one of Claudel's *Cinq Grandes Odes*, published in 1910:

> Restez avec moi, Seigneur, parce que le soir approche, et ne m'abandonnez pas!
> Ne me perdez point avec les Voltaire et les Renan, et les Michelet, et les Hugo, et tous les autres infâmes!
> Leur âme est avec les chiens morts, leurs livres sont joints

au fumier.
Ils sont morts, et leur nom même après leur mort est un poison
et une pourriture.

Or one finds Huysmans making the principal character in his
novel, *L'Oblat*, published in 1903, declare that the Dreyfus
Affair 'n'a été, en somme, qu'un prétexte pour sauter à la gorge
de l'Église; c'est la sortie en armes des juifs et des protestants.'
(*Oeuvres complètes*, XVII. 75)

However, writers like Huysmans and Claudel do not normally
concern themselves with politics in their writings, though it is a
curious fact – and one which was later a source of embarrassment to the very right-wing ambassador that Claudel later
became – that some of his early plays of the 1890s were strongly
influenced by the wave of anarchism which swept over France
in these years. Bourget and Péguy were much more involved in
the political and ideological struggles between the 1880s and 1914.
With them one may associate Barrès, a writer who was even more
deeply concerned with the politics of the period. Though he never
accepted Catholicism, he was one of the main right-wing spokesmen of these years and was certainly sympathetic towards the
Church.

While it was not until 1901 that Bourget was received into the
Catholic Church, he had been evolving in that direction for a
considerable period. In later life he attributed his passion for
order to the experience of the Commune which he had witnessed
as an eighteen-year-old schoolboy in Paris. It has been pointed
out that, as he gradually won fame as a novelist, the society which
he studied in his works changed from that of the wealthy middle
classes to the aristocracy in which he saw certain traditional
virtues scorned in the egalitarian society of his day. In 1894 he had
come back from a visit to the United States a convinced Royalist,
determined to undo the work of the Revolution and Napoleon:

Nous devrions chercher ce qui reste de la vieille France et nous y
rattacher par toutes nos fibres, retrouver la province d'unité naturelle et héréditaire sous le département artificiel et morcelé, l'autonomie municipale sous la centralisation administrative, les univer-
sités locales et fécondes sous notre Université officielle et morte,
reconstituer la famille terrienne par la liberté de tester, protéger le
travail par le rétablissement des corporations, rendre à la vie religieuse sa vigueur et sa dignité par la suppression du budget des
cultes et par le droit de posséder librement assuré aux associations
religieuses, – en un mot, sur ce point comme sur l'autre, défaire

systématiquement l'oeuvre meurtrière de la Révolution française. (*Outre-Mer*, II. 319–320)

It need hardly be added that he was entirely opposed to the revision of the Dreyfus case.

One of the most striking of the many novels which he produced in his long career is *Le Disciple* (1889), chiefly famous as an indictment of positivist philosophy, represented by the person of Adrien Sixte. The young man who becomes his disciple accepts his master's determinist view of human behaviour and seduces the daughter of an aristocratic family in which he is acting as tutor to a younger brother. She consents to spend one night with him on condition that they both proceed to swallow a dose of poison; when the time has come, he refuses to take the poison or to allow her to do so. However, she later commits suicide after sending a letter to her brother to tell him the whole story. When the seducer is on the point of being sentenced to death for poisoning, her brother intervenes to secure his acquittal, but then proceeds to shoot him. The philosopher is horrified at being held responsible for his disciple's acts: in the last lines of the novel it is half hinted that he abandons his philosophy in favour of religious beliefs.

The novel contains a lengthy preface in which, in speaking of the recovery of France since the disasters of 1870, the author offers a eulogy of the middle classes combined with a blistering attack on the republican politicians:

> Ah! la brave classe moyenne, la solide et vaillante Bourgeoisie, que possède encore la France! Qu'elle a fourni, depuis ces vingt ans, d'officiers laborieux, cette bourgeoisie, d'agents diplomatiques habiles et tenaces, de professeurs excellents, d'artistes intègres! J'entends dire parfois: 'Quelle vitalité dans ce pays! Il continue d'aller, là où un autre mourrait . . .' Hé bien! s'il va, en effet, depuis vingt ans, c'est d'abord par la bonne volonté de cette jeune bourgeoisie qui a tout accepté pour servir le pays. Elle a vu d'ignobles maîtres d'un jour proscrire au nom de la liberté ses plus chères croyances, des politiciens abominables jouer du suffrage universel comme d'un instrument de règne, et installer leur médiocrité menteuse dans les plus hautes places. Elle l'a subi, ce suffrage universel, la plus monstrueuse et la plus inique des tyrannies, – car la force du nombre est la plus brutale des forces, n'ayant même pas pour elle l'audace et le talent. (*Oeuvres*, III. 5)

His later novels express even more clearly his conservatism, his hatred of the secular republic, which was the precise opposite of his Catholic, royalist ideal.

L'Étape, for instance, published in 1902 at the height of the conflict between the Republicans and their opponents which arose out of the Dreyfus Affair, is directed against both anticlericalism and the egalitarian tendencies of contemporary France. The chief character is a Paris *lycée* master of radical anticlerical views. His wife is a vulgar, useless woman; his youngest son is an ill-mannered schoolboy, his eldest forges cheques and steals from the bank where he is employed, his daughter is seduced by a young nobleman of socialist views whom she tries to shoot before turning the revolver on herself. The greatest blow to the father is that his second son, passionately in love with the daughter of a colleague of conservative and Catholic views and of independent means, rejects the negative attitude to religion on which he has been brought up and moves towards Catholicism. The whole régime is indicted by Bourget. The father is blind to the fact 'que le nombre ne crée ni ne connaît la compétence, et que faire gouverner un pays par les élus du suffrage universel, autant dire par une majorité de charlatans issus d'une majorité d'ignorants, c'est le dégrader!' (VII. 331–332) Socialism is also denounced for trying to make out that a gulf separates the unfortunate worker from the bourgeois:

> Il n'y a lieu ni de le plaindre, car sa destinée est très douce, par rapport à celle de tant de petits commerçants; ni de le mépriser, car il est intelligent, et son niveau moral n'est pas plus bas que celui du reste de l'époque; ni de le magnifier, car ce niveau n'est pas haut, et il ne peut guère monter, vu l'âge de la race. Il y a lieu, en revanche, de le redouter, car trop de gens pratiquent, à son égard, l'abominable programme de l'agitateur allemand qui disait: 'Il faut apprendre au peuple qu'il est malheureux,' et, en lui donnant le droit de conduire seul les affaires de l'État, puisqu'il constitue les majorités – prodigieuse erreur qui fera de la France, dans les siècles à venir, l'ilote de l'histoire – on lui a mis en main de quoi porter à la civilisation dans notre pays des coups irréparables. (VII. 76)

However, the chief message of the novel, as its title indicates, is that this family (the father is a peasant's son) has risen too rapidly in the social scale; hence all the calamities which befall it. This message is hammered home from beginning to end of the novel. In the early pages the schoolmaster of conservative and Catholic views explains the situation to his daughter:

> Cette famille Monneron a commis une première faute, dans le grandpère, qui était un simple cultivateur. Il avait un fils très intelligent. Il a voulu en faire un bourgeois. Pourquoi? Par orgueil. Il a méprisé sa

caste, ce jour-là, et il a trouvé un complice dans l'État, tel que la Révolution nous l'a fait. Nous vivons, depuis cent ans, sur des lois dont l'esprit est de niveler les classes, d'égaliser pour tous le point de départ, de faciliter à l'individu les ascensions immédiates, en dehors de la famille. Ce ne sont pas non plus des lois saines et généreuses. Ce sont des lois d'orgueil. A quel sentiment s'est-on adressé chez Monneron, au collège? A l'orgueil. Dans ses examens? A l'orgueil. Quand je l'ai rencontré à l'École normale, tout son développement n'était qu'un développement d'orgueil. Voilà pourquoi il n'a pas cru. Il a pensé à l'encontre de notre tradition religieuse. Ce faisant, il a estimé qu'il obéissait à sa raison. En réalité, il s'est fourni des prétextes pour justifier une attitude qui n'était que l'instinct déposé en lui par toutes ces données. Il est un vrai représentant d'une époque dont l'aberration consiste à vouloir que chaque génération recommence la société. Son irréligion est comme son radicalisme, la preuve qu'il ne vit pas avec ses morts, lui, pour prendre ton mot de tout à l'heure. On l'en a séparé et il s'en est séparé. Sa pensée et sa volonté vont contre sa race, au lieu d'en être la continuation, le prolongement. (VII. 21)

And on the last page of the novel he repeats the same message to his future son-in-law: 'Votre grand-père et votre père ont cru, avec tout notre pays depuis cent ans, que l'on peut brûler l'étape. On ne le peut pas.'

Although Barrès rejected the monarchist views of writers like Bourget and Maurras, he came gradually to be regarded as one of the leading spokesmen of the authoritarian and nationalist right in the period down to 1914. Soon after he began his literary career he was drawn into the Boulangist movement and in 1889, at the age of twenty-seven, he found himself elected a deputy for Nancy on that ticket. He lost his seat in 1893, but in 1901 he was elected a deputy for Paris and retained his seat there until his death in 1923. He alone among the writers we are discussing had a practical experience of politics though, of course, always in helpless opposition. In 1897 he began the publication of his three novels to which he gave the general title of *Le Roman de l'Énergie nationale* with *Les Déracinés*, dedicated to Bourget. This was followed by two novels full of anti-parliamentary passion; they deal with, first, General Boulanger (*L'Appel au Soldat*, 1900) and then with the Panama scandal (*Leurs Figures*, 1902). The whole series forms a strange contrast with Anatole France's *Histoire contemporaine* which appeared in almost exactly the same years.

Although it makes much less exciting reading than the two later novels, which offer a gripping account of these two recent crises in French history, *Les Déracinés* is more important as an exposition of Barrès's ideas. The novel begins at the *lycée* of Nancy where the class in philosophy, the final school year for his pupils, is taken by a rootless teacher who ends up as a Republican deputy (he is a real person under a different name):

> Fils d'un ouvrier de Lille, remarqué à huit ans pour son intelligence précoce et studieuse, il avait obtenu une bourse jusqu'à l'École normale d'où il sortit le premier. Enlevé si jeune à son milieu naturel et passant ses vacances mêmes au lycée, orphelin et réduit pour toute satisfaction sentimentale à l'estime de ses maîtres, il est un produit pédagogique, un fils de la raison, étranger à nos habitudes traditionnelles, locales ou de famille, tout abstrait, et vraiment suspendu dans le vide. (*Oeuvres*, III. 24)

Seven of his pupils, much influenced by his Kantian philosophy, leave their native Lorraine where they have roots and rush to Paris to make their way in the world. The novel describes how in their rootless state they are in various ways demoralized by life in the capital, two of them going so far as to commit a murder for which one is guillotined. After recounting the trial Barrès interrupts his narrative to point the moral:

> Hélas! la Lorraine a fait une grande tentative: elle a expédié un certain nombre de ses fils, pour que de Neufchâteau, de Nomeny, de Custines, de Varennes, ils s'élevassent à un idéal supérieur. En haussant les sept jeunes Lorrains de leur petite patrie à la France, et même à l'humanité, on pensait les approcher de la Raison. Voici déjà deux cruelles déceptions; pour Racadot et Mouchefrin [the two murderers], l'effort a complètement échoué. Ceux qui avaient dirigé cette émigration avaient-ils senti qu'ils avaient charge d'âmes? Avaient-ils vu la périlleuse gravité de leur acte? A ces déracinés, ils ne surent pas offrir un bon terrain de 'replantement'. Ne sachant s'ils voulaient en faire des citoyens de l'humanité, ou des Français de France, ils les tirèrent de leurs maisons séculaires bien conditionnées, et ne s'en occupèrent pas davantage, ayant ainsi travaillé pour faire de jeunes bêtes sans tanières. De leur ordre naturel, peut-être humble, mais enfin social, ils sont passés à l'anarchie, à un désordre mortel. (III. 345)

At the end of the third novel of the trilogy one of the young men reaches the obvious conclusion;

> Ma tâche est nette: c'est de me faire de plus en plus Lorrain, d'être la Lorraine pour qu'elle traverse intacte cette période où la France décérébrée et dissociée semble faire de la paralysie générale. Un petit monde posé à l'Est comme un bastion du classicisme reçut son

.rôle d'une antiquité reculée; qu'il garde conscience de lui-même, au moins par ses meilleurs fils, et qu'en dépit de maladies de l'ensemble cette partie demeure capable de fournir des fruits austrasiens.[1] (IV. 446–447)

The term 'bastion' was shortly to be used by Barrès as the general title for two nationalist novels dealing with the eastern provinces of Alsace and Lorraine – *Les Bastions de l'Est.*

The first of these, *Au service de l'Allemagne*, published in 1905, is devoted to the problems of those inhabitants of Alsace who, despite thirty years' of German pressure, remained devoted to France, and particularly those of the young men called up for military service. A recent novel, *Les Oberlé*, by René Bazin, had solved this dilemma by making the hero, Jean Oberlé, desert from the German army and cross the frontier into France. Barrès argues that this is the wrong policy to adopt since if more and more Alsatians leave their native soil, the province will become increasingly Germanized. In an appendix to *Au Service de l'Allemagne* he writes:

> Jean Oberlé, généreux garçon que je salue avec respect, voulez-vous être un héros? Ne quittez point l'Alsace! – 'Eh! dit-il, qu'y puis-je faire d'utile, humble suspect en face d'un empire colossal?' – Je ne vous demande point d'agir, mais seulement de vivre. Je ne vous demande même point de protester, mais naturellement, chacune de vos respirations sera une respiration rythmée par deux siècles d'accord avec le coeur français. Demeurez un caillou de France sous la botte de l'envahisseur. Subissez l'inévitable et maintenez ce qui ne meurt pas. (*L'Oeuvre*, VI. 132)

The young medical student whom Barrès depicts in this work has been brought up by his father, a factory owner in Colmar, to reject the idea of leaving Alsace for France:

> Depuis que je suis au monde, j'entends dire et redire: 'Il faut rester au pays; ne soyons pas, comme en 70, des soldats pleins de coeur avec une mauvaise idée directrice. Ce n'est pas une conception juste d'aller en France, nous n'avons rien à y faire d'indispensable. Notre devoir d'Alsacien est en Alsace.' (VI. 74)

So the son, despite his hatred of everything German, does his military service in the Kaiser's army.

In *Colette Baudoche*, published in 1909, Barrès turns to the problems facing the inhabitants of the severed portion of his

---

[1] Austrasia (meaning 'East Kingdom') was the name for the eastern possessions of the Franks, embracing Lorraine, Belgium and the right bank of the Rhine, with their centre at Metz.

native province of Lorraine, in particular in Metz. A young German schoolmaster from Königsberg takes lodgings in the house of an elderly woman with a grand-daughter. Under the civilizing influence of the two women he gradually comes to some degree of understanding of the attitude of these people separated from France in 1871. Finally he proposes to the girl, who is torn between her love and her attachment to France. The story ends with all three of them attending the annual service for the French soldiers who died in the battles around Metz in 1870:

> Au bas de l'église, Colette à genoux, entre son Allemand et sa grand-mère, subit en pleurant toutes les puissances de cette solennité. Elle ne leur oppose aucun raisonnement. Elle repose, elle baigne dans les grandes idées qui mettent en émoi tout le fond religieux de notre race. Durant un mois, elle s'est demandé: 'Après trente-cinq ans, est-il excusable d'épouser un Allemand?' Mais aujourd'hui, trêve de dialectique: elle voit bien que le temps écoulé ne fait pas une excuse et que les trente-cinq années ne sont que le trop long délai depuis lequel les héros attendent une réparation. Leurs ombres l'effleurent, la surveillent. Osera-t-elle les décevoir, leur faire injure, les renier? Cette cathédrale, ces chants, ces notables, tout ce vaste appareil ébranle la pauvre fille, mais par-dessus tout la présence des tré-passés. Colette reconnaît l'impossibilité de transiger avec ces morts qui sont là présents. (VI. 247)

And so, outside the cathedral, she gives her answer: 'Monsieur le docteur, je ne peux pas vous épouser.'

An interesting figure of the period before 1914 is Charles Péguy, whose life was to be cut short at the very beginning of the war, like that of Alain-Fournier, the author of *Le Grand Meaulnes*. Péguy began his career as an ardent *dreyfusard*. 'Ce crime,' he later wrote, 'a inauguré notre vie publique, notre vie civique.' (*Oeuvres en prose* 1909–1914, p. 44) Yet the one-time *dreyfusard* was gradually to become a fervent nationalist, though he rejected the embrace of the Royalist, Maurras, and insisted that he remained a Republi-can. In the same years he gradually moved from anticlericalism to a fervent Catholicism expressed in *Le Mystère de la Charité de Jeanne d'Arc*. The publication of this work in 1910 was hailed in an enthusiastic review by Barrès; the *Action Française* joined in the chorus of praise.

Péguy's early socialism gave way to a feeling of betrayal by politicians like Jaurès. In 1913, in *L'Argent suite*, published in his review, *Les Cahiers de la Quinzaine*, he wrote bitterly of his disillusionment:

> Trente ans nous avons été trahis. De notre socialisme, qui était un système de justice économique et sociale, de vérité économique et sociale, de santé économique et sociale, en un mot de justice et de vérité et de santé temporelles et un système de la bonne et de la vraie et de la juste et de la saine organisation du travail économique et social, du travail temporel ils ont fait un reniement de tout, une basse politique, un sabotage ignoble, proprement une trahison militaire contre le peuple français. (p. 1241)

The nationalist Péguy was affronted by the internationalism of a Socialist like Jaurès and by the anti-militarist activities of the syndicalist movement. By this date, not much more than a year before the outbreak of the 1914 war, Péguy's nationalism was preached in the shrillest of tones. Jaurès is denounced in the most violent terms: 'Il est pangermaniste. (Il faudrait l'en féliciter, s'il était né sujet allemand.) Il est un agent du parti allemand. Il travaille pour la plus grande Allemagne.' (p. 1192) According to Péguy, Jaurès's efforts to save the peace, pursued down to the moment of his assassination, deserve the guillotine:

> Je suis un bon républicain. Je suis un vieux révolutionnaire. En temps de guerre il n'y a plus qu'une politique, et c'est la politique de la Convention Nationale. Mais il ne faut pas se dissimuler que la politique de la Convention Nationale c'est Jaurès dans une charrette et un roulement de tambour pour couvrir cette grande voix. (p. 1184)

Such inflammatory language was at least partly responsible for the murder of the Socialist leader on the eve of the outbreak of war.

His volumes of poetry, from *Le Mystère de la Charité de Jeanne d'Arc* (1910) down to his *Ève*, published at the end of 1913, are filled with a blend of mystical Catholicism and strong nationalist feeling. Joan of Arc (Péguy came from Orleans) is a prominent figure in his poetry; the first of these poems was written in preparation for 'le cinq centième anniversaire de la naissance de Jeanne d'Arc, qui tombera pour le jour des Rois de l'an 1912'. The movement for her canonization was then well under way and already she had become the focus of patriotic, not to say nationalist sentiment in France. Péguy's blend of Catholicism and nationalism comes out clearly in such lines as these from *Ève*:

> – Heureux ceux qui sont morts pour la terre charnelle,
> Mais pourvu que ce fût dans une juste guerre.
> Heureux ceux qui sont morts pour quatre coins de terre.
> Heureux ceux qui sont morts d'une mort solennelle.

Heureux ceux qui sont morts dans les grandes batailles,
Couchés dessus le sol à la face de Dieu.
Heureux ceux qui sont morts sur un dernier haut lieu,
Parmi tout l'appareil des grandes funérailles.

Heureux ceux qui sont morts pour des cités charnelles.
Car elles sont le corps de la cité de Dieu.
Heureux ceux qui sont morts pour leur âtre et leur feu,
Et les pauvres honneurs des maisons paternelles.

Car elles sont l'image et le commencement
Et le corps et l'essai de la maison de Dieu.
Heureux ceux qui sont morts dans cet embrassement,
Dans l'étreinte d'honneur et le terrestre aveu.

(Oeuvres poétiques, p. 664)

The poem appeared only some eight months before Péguy's tragic death in the battle of the Marne.

In the hundred years of French literature with which we are concerned there were many writers who did not concern themselves either in their private lives or in their works with contemporary social, political and ideological controversies. Again there were also men and women who, while in private deeply or superficially concerned with such issues, deliberately shut them out of their minds when they put pen to paper. Yet in a period when, in contrast to what had been the case in the seventeenth century and in the eighteenth too down to 1789, such problems had, despite various forms of censorship, become matters of public debate, inevitably many writers brought the problems confronting the society of the day into their novels, plays, poetry and other works. The examples given in this chapter show how this involvement stretches all the way from the young Hugo's *Odes et Ballades* in the 1820s to the poetry of Charles Péguy.

Conclusion

An account of French history which stops at 1914 is bound to end on a somewhat melancholy note. 'La belle époque', with its glaring inequalities and its social conflicts, ended in over four years of murderous warfare fought out on French soil. If in 1914, in contrast to what happened in 1870 and again in 1940, the German invasion was halted at the battle of the Marne, for over four years some of the richest industrial and agricultural regions of France were either in enemy hands or devastated by the fighting. It was not until November 1918 that the Allied armies were strong enough to break the long stalemate on the Western front and drive the invaders out of France.

Although the tremendous material damage in the regions which had been fought over for so long was fairly rapidly made good in the 1920s, French losses in the war had a disastrous effect on an already almost stationary population in which the proportion of old people to young people was exceptionally high. Even with the return of Alsace-Lorraine at the end of the war the population of France was slightly smaller than it had been in 1914. On top of the small number of births during the war years came a further decline in the birth-rate in the two decades which followed. Shortage of manpower led to more immigration, but while the economic depression of the 1930s drove away many of these new-comers, the number of marriages began to fall with the arrival at adult status of the small number of young people born during the war years. The birth-rate fell to a level below that of any large country, and from 1935 onwards the number of deaths regularly exceeded the number of births. Between 1921 and 1939 the population rose only to just under 42 millions.

If the 1939–1945 war further aggravated his situation, its effects were nothing like as serious as those of the First World War.

Though civilian deaths were much higher, those in the armed forces were less than a sixth of what they had been in 1914–1918. From 1942 onwards – partly as a result of the so-called *Code de la famille*, promulgated on the very eve of the war, which greatly extended family allowances, from the second child onwards – the population trend was reversed. Although at the end of the war the population of France had fallen to 41½ millions, by the 1968 census it had reached very nearly 50 millions and by 1972 was over 51 millions. One consequence of this change is that nowadays France is the western European country with the highest proportion of young people under twenty, a striking contrast with the situation earlier in the present century.

The period between the two wars was, as in Britain, a period of economic stagnation. After the stabilization of the franc in 1926 at one-fifth of its pre-war value there followed a period of relative prosperity (industrial production reached a peak which was not to be attained again until 1951); the world economic crisis which began in 1929 affected France more slowly than other large countries. However, her recovery in the 1930s was slower than elsewhere. Then came the Second World War and the German occupation with its ruthless exploitation of the resources of the country. When the war ended in 1945, France's economy was in a parlous state. It was difficult for anyone who saw the apparently insuperable economic difficulties which faced France in the immediate post-war period to imagine the progress which was to be made by the 1970s.

At the end of the war the *Commissariat Général du Plan* was set up to give priority to the basic industries of the country and to provide it with adequate supplies of energy and an up-to-date industrial equipment. The aim was to make good not only the destruction of the war years, but also the sluggish growth of the French economy in the inter-war period. The successive plans (the sixth covered the period 1971–1975) have also involved co-operation with other European countries. In 1950 the Coal and Steel Pool was set up, and seven years later France, along with the five other founder members, signed the Treaty of Rome setting up the European Economic Community.

While agriculture still remains a very important part of the French economy (France is the largest producer of corn, wine, meat and milk in the European Economic Community), the number of people engaged in it has fallen dramatically since the war. In 1945 the proportion of the active population engaged in agriculture was still 25 per cent; by 1970 the figure had fallen to 14 per cent. As recently as 1926 over half the population had been classified as rural; in the 1970s roughly two-thirds of the population reside in *communes* of over 2,000 inhabitants and are classified as urban. In other words the 'exode rural' of which so much was heard in the nineteenth century has become quite a flood and has had as its consequence the rapid expansion both of the Paris region and of many provincial cities from Marseilles to Rennes.

There has been a tremendous increase in industrial production since France began to recover from the effects of the war from about 1950 onwards. Between 1962 and 1971 the index of industrial production rose from 100 to 168. The total production of the various forms of energy increased dramatically in the 1950s and 1960s; if coal production declined, there was an enormous increase in the consumption of petroleum products, a steep rise in the use of electricity (a small amount of nuclear origin) and also of gas, a useful contribution being made by natural gas from S.W. France. Between 1950 and 1970 the production of iron ore very nearly doubled, while the output of iron and steel increased even more. Most striking of all has been the growth of the chemical industries; their output has expanded more rapidly still. Production of motor vehicles, needless to say, has also gone up, from half a million in 1952 to over 3 million in 1972. A check on this rapid economic growth has, of course, been imposed by the energy crisis which began at the end of 1973.

All this has been accomplished despite some political instability in recent decades. The long life of the Third Republic came to an end in the collapse of 1940. The short-lived *État Français* of Marshal Pétain vanished with the allied invasion of France in 1944, and two years later the Fourth Republic was installed. If the government instability of the Third Republic continued under its successor (France had over twenty different governments between 1946 and 1958), undoubtedly the foundations for the economic expansion of the 1960s and 1970s were laid under the Fourth Republic. The Fifth Republic, founded by General de Gaulle in 1958, led a somewhat shaky existence until the Algerian problem was solved in 1962; the new régime which has much in common with the Second Empire has continued to have its troubles, in particular the famous 'événements' of May and June 1968, but since 1958 France has certainly experienced unusually long periods of governmental stability.

France's position, both in Europe and the world at large, has altered radically since 1914. After the narrow victory of 1918 and the regaining of Alsace-Lorraine her search for security led her to form alliances with Poland, Czechoslovakia, Romania and Yugoslavia in the so-called Petite Entente. In the 1920s, in face of a weak Germany and Soviet Union, France appeared to be the strongest military power on the Continent; but the hollowness of her position was rapidly exposed in the 1930s after Hitler's rise to power. The overwhelming defeat which followed in 1940 left France in a very weak position when the Allied victory came in 1945.

Little remains today of the colonial empire which she had built up, mainly under the Third Republic. In 1954, after the military disaster of Dien-bien-phu, France had to clear out of Indo-China. Of her North African possessions Tunisia and Morocco had to be given their independence in 1956. In the meantime Algeria, a territory reckoned to be part of metropolitan France, was fighting a fierce struggle for her independence which had finally to be conceded in 1962. The rest of France's colonial empire, renamed 'L'Union Française' in the 1946 constitution and 'La Communauté' in that of 1958, can almost be said to have disintegrated. The status of *départements* of France has been retained by nine small overseas territories – Martinique, Guadeloupe, Réunion, Guiana, St. Pierre-et-Miquelon, the Comoro Archipelago, French Somaliland, Polynesia and New Caledonia; they elect deputies and senators to the French Parliament though they enjoy a certain degree of autonomy. The remaining overseas territories, twelve in number, mainly in black Africa, all finally chose independence. This does not mean the breaking of all ties with France; all receive technical and educational aid on a considerable scale and are associated through France with the European Economic Community. The future of France – 'l'Hexagone' as it has now become fashionable to call it – now appears to lie firmly in Europe.

The France of President Giscard d'Estaing is undoubtedly a very different country from the France which entered the 1914–1918 war, and her position in the world, like that of Britain, has altered radically. The nineteenth century, even 'la belle époque', seem to belong to another age of history; and yet, despite all the changes which have taken place both in France and the rest of the world, the hundred years down to 1914 are still close enough to us to be brought to life again without too great an effort of the imagination.

Main historical events

1814	First abdication of Napoleon
	First Restoration of Bourbon Monarchy
	Accession of Louis XVIII
	First Treaty of Paris
	Proclamation of Constitutional Charter
1814– 1815	Congress of Vienna
1815	Landing of Napoleon from Elba
	Flight of Louis XVIII to Ghent
	The 'Hundred Days'
	Battle of Waterloo (June 18) and defeat of Napoleon
	Second abdication of Napoleon
	Second Restoration of Bourbon Monarchy
	Second Treaty of Paris – harsher terms
	'La Chambre introuvable', i.e. Ultra-Royalist
	'White Terror'
1816	Ultra-Royalist Chamber dissolved by Louis XVIII
	Election of new Chamber with Constitutional majority
1818	Withdrawal of allied army of occupation
1820	Assassination of the Duc de Berry
1821	Ministry of Villèle – Ultras in power
	Posthumous birth of the Duc de Bordeaux, son of the Duc de Berry
	Death of Napoleon
1823	Successful French intervention in Spain on behalf of the reactionary Bourbon King of Spain
1824	New elections with overwhelming majority of Ultras
	Death of Louis XVIII
	Accession of his brother, Charles X
1825	Indemnity granted to émigrés
1828	Resignation of Villèle
	Ministry of Martignac (Right Centre)
1829	Ministry of Polignac (extreme Right)
1830	Conquest of Algiers and beginning of French colonial empire in Africa
	The Four Ordinances (July 26)
	Revolution in Paris
	Abdication of Charles X in favour of his grandson, the Duc de Bordeaux (later, the Comte de Chambord)

Louis-Philippe, the Duc d'Orléans, proclaimed 'King of the French' (August 7)

Revision of Charter in direction of greater liberty

1831 Ministries of Laffitte and Périer

Insurrection in Lyons

1832 Outbreak of cholera in Paris

Death of Périer from cholera

Republican riots in Paris (cloister of Saint-Merri)

1832– Succession of short-lived ministries

1836 Republican agitation

1834 Republican riots in Paris (Massacre of the Rue Transnonain)

1835 September laws

1839 Publication of *L'Organisation du travail* by Louis Blanc

1840 Publication of *Qu'est-ce que la propriété?* by Pierre Proudhon

Short lived Ministry of Thiers

Napoleon I buried in the Invalides

1840– Ministry of Guizot: 'Enrichissez-vous par le travail et par
1848 l'épargne...' (Guizot)

1846– Economic crisis
1847

1847 Conquest of greater part of Algeria

Reform Banquets

1848 February Revolution

Abdication of Louis-Philippe in favour of his grandson, the Comte de Paris (February 24)

Provisional Government: Proclamation of the Second Republic

National Workshops set up in Paris (February)

Constituent Assembly elected by universal male suffrage (April 29): defeat of extreme Radicals and Socialists

National Workshops abolished; uprising in Paris, sternly suppressed by Cavaignac (June)

Louis Napoleon elected President under the new constitution (December 10)

1849 Legislative Assembly elected (May)

Restoration of the Pope's temporal power by French expeditionary force

1850 Loi Falloux breaks monopoly of State education, giving Catholics the right to set up schools of their own

Universal suffrage abolished

1851 *Coup d'état* of Louis Napoleon (December 2)

1852 New French Constitution (January)

1852 Napoleon III proclaimed Emperor: ratification by plebiscite of November 21

1854– Crimean War: England and France allied against Russia
1856

1857 Conquest of Algeria completed

1858 Orsini attempts to assassinate Napoleon III

1859 Treaty between France and Piedmont

France and Piedmont declare war against Austria

French win battles of Magenta and Solferino against Austria

Peace of Villafranca

1860 Treaty of Turin cedes Nice and Savoy to France

Treaty of Commerce with England; freer trade between the two countries

1863– French intervention in Mexico
1867

1864 Legal recognition of right to strike

French protectorate established over Cambodia

1865 Napoleon III and Bismarck meet at Biarritz

1867 Right of interpellation granted to Legislative Body

Withdrawal of French troops from Mexico

Execution of Emperor Maximilian in Mexico

1868 Greater freedom of the press and legalisation of public meetings

1869 Opening of Suez Canal, the work of the French engineer de Lesseps

1870– Franco–Prussian War
1871

1870 Battle of Sedan (September 1): Napoleon III taken prisoner

Third Republic proclaimed (September 4): Government of National Defence

1871 Capitulation of Paris

National Assembly meets at Bordeaux

Elections (February) – massive Royalist majority

Thiers appointed 'Chief of the Executive Power of the French Republic'

The Paris Commune (March–May)

Treaty of Frankfort (May) – France cedes Alsace and part of Lorraine to Germany

1873 Death of Napoleon III

Thiers resigns – Mac-Mahon elected President to keep place warm for restoration of the monarchy

Evacuation of France by German troops

1875 Final establishment of the Constitutional laws of the French Republic

1876 Elections – Republican majority in Chamber

1877 Mac-Mahon with the consent of the conservative Senate, dissolves Chamber (the so-called *coup d'état* of May 16)

Republicans defeat Mac-Mahon at the polls

1879 Resignation of Mac-Mahon

Grévy, a Republican, elected President

The Prince Imperial, only son of Napoleon III, killed in Zulu wars

Limited amnesty granted to Communards

Founding of the Parti Ouvrier Français by Jules Guesde

1880 Jesuits' expelled from France; authorised congregations alone allowed to teach

1881 Liberty of assembly and freedom of the press established by law

1882 Free, compulsory and secular primary education

Death of Gambetta

1882– Stagnation of French economy
1895

1883 Death of the Comte de Chambord ('Henry V') without issue; the Comte de Paris acknowledged by legitimists as head of the House of France.

1884 French military intervention in Tonkin

1885 Re-election of Grévy as President

China recognises French protectorate over Annam

1886 Boulanger becomes Minister of War

1887 Boulanger excluded from new Ministry

Grévy resigns

Sadi Carnot elected President

1888 Growing popular enthusiasm for Boulanger, especially in Paris; governmental fear of *coup d'état*

1889 Boulanger, threatened with legal action, flees to Brussels – end of Boulangist crisis

1890 Anglo–French Treaty delimits spheres of interest in Niger Valley

1891 Franco–Russian entente

1892 Méline's Customs Tariff

Pope Leo XIII orders French Catholics to accept the Republic

The Panama Scandal

1894 Franco–Russian alliance

French occupation of Timbuctoo

Murder of President Carnot

Casimir-Périer elected President

Trial and condemnation of Dreyfus

1894– Dreyfus Affair
1906

1895 Founding of the Confédération Générale du Travail

Resignation of Casimir-Périer

Félix Faure elected President

1896 Annexation of Madagascar

1897 Indo-Chinese Union

1899 Death of Faure

Émile Loubet elected President

1901 Law of associations

1903 Entente Cordiale established with England

1904 Anglo–French agreement on Morocco and Egypt

1905 Separation of Church and State

Founding of French Socialist Party (S.F.I.O.)

William II at Tangiers

1906 Dreyfus finally declared innocent

Armand Fallières elected President

1907 Triple Entente of France, Russia and Great Britain

1911 The Agadir crisis

1912 French protectorate established over Morocco

1913 Raymond Poincaré elected President

Three years' military service becomes law

1914 Assassination of Jaurès, the Socialist leader

Outbreak of the First World War

Some dates

The French have the disconcerting habit of referring to historical events by omitting the year in which they occurred and giving only the month and occasionally the day of the month. The following is a list of some of the events of the period 1814–1914 which are frequently referred to in this way.

FEBRUARY

Février, Journées de [*1848*]: the collapse of the July Monarchy (q.v.) on 22–24 February.

le 24 février [*1848*]: the abdication of Louis Philippe and the proclamation of the Second Republic.

APRIL

Avril, Journées d' [*1834*]: insurrections in Paris, Lyons and other cities.

MAY

le 15 mai [*1848*]: invasion of the National Assembly, followed by an attempt to set up a new and more radical provisional government.

le 16 mai [*1877*]: President Mac-Mahon dismisses a Republican government with a parliamentary majority and appoints the Duc de Broglie as prime minister.

le 24 mai [*1873*]: defeat of Thiers in the National Assembly and election of Marshal Mac-Mahon as President of the Republic with the Duc de Broglie at the head of a 'gouvernement d'ordre moral'.

le 31 mai [1850]: law passed by Legislative Assembly reducing the number of electors from 9,600,000 to 6,800,000.

JUNE

Juin, Journées de [*1848*]: popular rising in Paris on 23–26 June.

JULY

Juillet, Journées de [1830] ('les trois glorieuses'): popular rising in Paris against Charles X on 27–29 July.

Juillet, Monarchie de: the reign of Louis Philippe (1830–1848).

SEPTEMBER

le 4 septembre [*1870*]: fall of the Second Empire and proclamation of the Third Republic.

Septembre, lois de [*1835*]: a series of laws designed to break the Republican opposition.

DECEMBER

le 2 décembre [*1851*]: the *coup d'état* carried out by Louis Napoleon on the anniversary of his uncle's victory at Austerlitz in 1805.

Some suggestions for further reading

1 Social and political background

G. de Bertier de Sauvigny, *La Restauration*, Paris (Flammarion), 1963.

G. Bourgin, *La Troisième République 1870–1914*, Paris (Armand Colin), 1967.

J. P. T. Bury, *France 1814–1940*, London (Metheun), 1969.

E. Cahm, *Politics and Society in Contemporary France (1789–1971). A Documentary History*, London (Harrap), 1972.

A. Daumard, *Les Bourgeois de Paris au XIXᵉ siècle*, Paris (Flammarion), 1970.

R. Giraudet, *Le Nationalisme Français 1871–1914*, Paris (Armand Colin), 1966.

T. Kemp, *Economic Forces in French History. An Essay on the Development of the French Economy 1760–1914*, London (Dobson), 1971.

J. McManners, *Church and State in France 1870–1914*, London (SPCK), 1972.

G. P. Palmade, *Capitalisme et Capitalistes français au XIXᵉ siècle*, Paris (Armand Colin), 1961.

G. Pradalié, *Le Second Empire*, Paris (Collection 'Que sais-je?'), 1969.

J. Vidalenc, *La Restauration (1814–1830)*, Paris (Collection 'Que sais-je?'), 1968.

J. Vigier, *La Monarchie de Juillet*, Paris (Collection 'Que sais-je?'), 1969. *La Second République*, Paris (Collection 'Que sais-je?'), 1970.

2 Literary background

J. Bertaut, *La Vie Littéraire. L'Époque romantique*, Paris (Tallandier), 1947.

A. Billy, *La Vie Littéraire. L'Époque 1900*, Paris (Tallandier), 1951.

C. Bruneau, *Petite Histoire de la Langue française*. Vol. II. *De la Révolution à nos jours*, Paris (Armand Colin), 1958.

R. Dumesnil, *La Vie Littéraire. L'Époque Réaliste et Naturaliste*, Paris, (Tallandier), 1945.

French Literature and its Background, ed. J. Cruickshank. Vol. IV. *The Early Nineteenth Century*. Vol. V. *The Late Nineteenth Century*, London (Oxford University Press), 1969.

P. Guiral, *La Société française 1815–1914 vue par les Romanciers*, London (Longman), 1974.

F. W. J. Hemmings, *Culture and Society in France 1848–1898*, London (Batsford), 1971.

A. Prost, *L'Enseignement en France 1800–1967*, Paris (Armand Colin), 1968.

A. W. Raitt, *Life and Letters in France. The Nineteenth Century*, London (Nelson), 1965.

A great many extracts from the memoirs and diaries of the period have been given in the text; full bibliographical details of these are available in the 'Index of Authors Quoted' for those interested in carrying their reading further. The peasant writer, E. Guillaumin, provides a wonderfully vivid picture of the life of the poorer classes in the countryside in the nineteenth century in *La Vie d'un simple*, first published in 1904 and frequently reprinted.

Index of Authors Quoted

The editions listed are not necessarily the earliest, but are those referred to in the text

Agathon [Massis, H. and Tarde, A.], *Les Jeunes Gens d'aujourd'hui*, Paris, 1913 209

Antonelli, E., *Trente-trois Ans de la sécurité sociale en France*, Montpellier, 1963 164

Avenel, Vicomte, G. d', *Les Français de mon temps*, Paris, n.d. 192–3, 276

Balzac, H. de, *Correspondance*, ed. R. Pierrot, Paris, 1960–9, 5 vols. 249

   Lettres à Madame Hanska, ed. R. Pierrot, Paris, 1967–71, 4 vols. 231–2, 237, 244, 254, 269, 270

   Oeuvres diverses, Paris, 1962–3, 4 vols. 239, 300

Banville, T. de, *Mes Souvenirs*, Paris, 1882 230

Barrès, M., *L'Oeuvre*, Paris, 1965–9, 20 vols. 321–3

Barrot, O., *Mémoires posthumes*, Paris, 1875–6, 4 vols. 64

Baudelaire, C., *Correspondance générale*, ed. J. Crépet and C. Pichois, Paris, 1947–53, 6 vols. 228–9

   Oeuvres, ed. Y. G. Le Dantec, Paris, 1932–5, 2 vols. 304

Bayet, J., *La Société des Auteurs et Compositeurs dramatiques*, Paris, 1908 267

Béranger, P. J., *Oeuvres complètes*, Paris, 1837, 3 vols. 41, 42–4, 55, 57

Bloy, L., *Journal*, Paris, 1963, 4 vols. 229, 254

Bourget, P., *Oeuvres complètes*, Paris, 1899–1911, 9 vols. 318–320

   Outre-Mer, Paris, 1895, 2 vols. 317–20

254–5, 256, 262, 267, 271–2, 293, 306–7
Germinie Lacerteux, Paris, 1864 308–9

Guizot, F., *Mémoires pour servir à l'histoire de mon temps*, Paris, 1858–67, 8 vols. 46–7, 73–5

Hervé, G., *Le Pioupiou de l'Yonne*, 1901 207

Houssaye, A., *Les Confessions, souvenirs d'un demi-siècle, 1830–1880*, Paris, 1885–91, 6 vols. 255, 260

Hugo, A., *Victor Hugo raconté par un témoin de sa vie*, Paris, n.d., 2 vols. 67–8, 225–6

Hugo, V., *Oeuvres complètes*, Paris, 1904–52, 48 vols. 36, 40–1, 54, 58–9, 119, 233, 273, 284–5, 296, 297, 298
Les Misérables, ed. M. F. Guyard, Paris, 1963, 2 vols. 302–3

Huret, J., *Enquête sur la question sociale en Europe*, Paris, 1897 160, 162–4

Huysmans, J. K., *Oeuvres complètes*, Paris, 1928–34, 23 vols. 317

Kock, P. de, et al., *La Grande Ville. Nouveau Tableau de Paris*, Paris, 1844, 2 vols. 266

La Croix, Paris, 8 Feb. 1898 187

Lamartine, A. de, *Correspondance générale de 1830 à 1848*, ed. M. Levaillant et al., Paris, 1943–49, 2 vols. 69

Lamennais, F. R. de, *Le Peuple constituant*, 11 July 1848 107

Lavisse, E., *Souvenirs*, Paris, 1912 110

Léautaud, P., *Journal littéraire*, Paris, 1955–66, 19 vols. 257

Louandre, C., 'Statistique littéraire. De la production intellectuelle en France depuis quinze ans', *Revue des Deux Mondes*, 1847, Vol. 20 297

Mallarmé, S., *Correspondance, 1862–1871*, ed. H. Mondor and J. P. Richard, Paris, 1959 234
Correspondance, 1871–1885, ed. H. Mondor and L. J. Austin, Paris, 1965 235
Oeuvres complètes, ed. H. Mondor and G. J. Aubry, Paris, 1945 286

Maurras, C., *Kiel et Tanger*, Paris, 1913, 2nd edition 208
L'Action Française, 6 July 1912 208–9

Ménière, P., *Mémoires anecdotiques sur les salons du Second Empire*, ed. E. Ménière, Paris, 1903 81

Musset, A. de, *Poésies complètes*, ed. M. Allem, Paris, 1957 78, 299

Paul-Boncour, J., *Entre deux guerres. Souvenirs sur la IIIe République*, Paris, 1945–46, 3 vols. 144, 165

Péguy, C., *Oeuvres en prose 1909–1914*, Paris, 1957 323–4
Oeuvres poétiques complètes, Paris, 1954 324–5

Prévost-Paradol, L. A., *La France nouvelle*, Paris, 1868 85

Villermé, A. C., *Tableau de l'état physique et moral des ouvriers employés dans les manufactures de coton, de laine et de soie*, Paris, 1840, 2 vols. 34–6

Werdet, E., *De la Librairie française*, Paris, 1860 237–8

Zola, E., *Oeuvres complètes*, ed. H. Mitterand, Paris, 1966–70, 15 vols. 97, 98, 186–7, 224–5, 229, 246–7, 253–4, 270, 275–6, 287, 309–10, 311, 312, 313

Index